VOICES OF
SILENCE

VOICES OF SILENCE

THE ALTERNATIVE BOOK OF FIRST WORLD WAR POETRY

VIVIEN NOAKES

SUTTON PUBLISHING

First published in the United Kingdom in 2006 by
Sutton Publishing Limited · Phoenix Mill
Thrupp · Stroud · Gloucestershire · GL5 2BU

Endpapers: Soldiers in profile. *(US National Archive)*

British Library Cataloguing in Publication Data
A catalogue record for this book is available from the British Library.

ISBN 0-7509-4521-4

Typeset in 10/13pt New Baskerville.
Typesetting and origination by
Sutton Publishing Limited.
Printed and bound in England by
J.H. Haynes & Co. Ltd, Sparkford.

In memory of my uncle
2nd Lt Richard Langley,
13th Bttn, Alexandra, Princess of Wales's Own Yorkshire Regiment,
The Green Howards.
Reported wounded and missing, 27 September 1916.
Reported missing believed killed, 25 October 1916.
His name appeared on a German list of prisoners of war,
8 December 1916.
He died as a consequence of his wounds, 16 July 1935.

Contents

Acknowledgements

For any anthologist, the first and greatest thanks must go to the writers whose work makes up the collection. The last survivor, Geoffrey Dearmer, died aged 103 in 1996; it was my great privilege to be at his hundredth birthday celebration at the Imperial War Museum in 1993. But for these men and women, there would be no *Voices of Silence*.

Catherine Riley's *Bibliography of First World War Poetry* is indispensable to anyone searching for poems of the Great War. For their generous help I am grateful to: Colin Badcock; Emily Bird of the Commonwealth War Graves Commission; Anthony Boden; Mark Brown; Adrian Gregory; Jill, Duchess of Hamilton; Sally Harrower of the National Library of Scotland; William Hetherington of the Peace Pledge Union; Dominic Hibberd; Nigel Jaques; Colin Johnston, Principal Archivist of the Bath and North East Somerset Council; Michael Meredith; Joe Mulholland; Allen Packwood of the Churchill Archive Centre, Cambridge; Andrew Partridge; Robert Pike; Ann Riker; Nigel Steel; Dr David Sutton, Director of Research Projects at Reading University Library; Bill Turner; and Kevin Tye.

The staff of the following libraries have been most courteous and helpful: the British Library; the Newspaper Library, Collindale; Friends' House; the Imperial War Museum Department of Documents and Library; the London Library; the Royal Air Force Museum.

For permission to use material that is still in copyright I would like to thank: Blackwell Publishing Ltd for 'A Song of the Air', 'Reconnaissance' and 'Two Pictures' by Gordon Alchin, 'From the Youth of all Nations' by Henry Cecil Harwood and 'The Draft' by A.P. Herbert; Mrs Anne Charlton for 'Noon' by Robert Nichols; Mrs Peregrine Spencer Churchill for 'Y Beach'; Jonathan Cutbill for 'Lieutenant Tattoon, M.C.' by Edward Carpenter; Lord Elton for 'The War Memorial' by Godfrey Elton; Samuel French Ltd on behalf of the estate of John Drinkwater for 'England to Belgium' by John Drinkwater; Michael Gibson and Pan Macmillan for 'Bacchanal', 'Between the Lines', 'Mad,' 'Ragtime' and 'The Messages' by Wilfrid Gibson; Duff Hart-Davis for 'The Song of the Mud' by Mary Borden; Patrick W.H. Harvey for 'A True Tale of the Listening Post', 'At Afternoon Tea', 'Back to the Trenches', 'Ballad of Army Pay', 'Gonnehem', 'Loneliness', 'Peace – The Dead Speak', 'Requiescat', 'The Route March', 'To Certain Persons' and 'To the Kaiser – Confidentially' by F.W. Harvey; David Higham for 'Tears' by Osbert Sitwell; Mrs John Hills for 'Valete' by William Box;

The Earl of Home for 'The School at War – 1914' by C.A. Alington; Jarrold & Sons Ltd for 'For a Horse Flag Day' by Jessie Anderson and 'Dumb Heroes' by T.A. Girling; the estate of Richard and Roger Lancelyn Green for 'All Souls, 1914' by Gordon Bottomley; Macmillan for 'A Flemish Village' by Herbert Asquith, 'Meditation in June, 1917', 'On Trek' and 'The Old Soldiers' by Edward Shanks and 'In the Third Year of the War' and 'Return' by E. Hilton Young; Mary Claire O'Donnell for 'After Loos', 'I oft go out at night-time', 'In the Morning' and 'The Dawn' by Patrick MacGill; *Punch* for 'Oxford Revisited' by Cyril Bretherton, 'Requisitional' by W. Hodgson Burnet, 'The Infantryman' by E.F. Clarke, 'On Christmas Leave' by W.W. Blair Fish, 'Missing' by Geraldine Robertson Glasgow, 'Beasts and Superbeasts', 'The Freedom of the Press', 'The Missing Leader' and 'Winston's Last Phase' by Charles Graves, 'Literary War Worker' by T. Hodgkinson, 'The Four Sea Lords' by Richard Keigwin, 'Mufti Once More' by Edmund Knox, 'The General' by George Menzies, 'From a Full Heart' and 'Gold Braid' by A.A. Milne, 'The Widow' by C.M. Mitchell, 'Verdun' by F.W. Platt, 'A Canadian to his Parents', 'My American Cousins', 'Raids', 'More Peace-Talk in Berlin', '"Punch" in the Enemy Trenches' and 'The Soul of a Nation' by C. Conway Plumbe, 'Deportment for Women' by Jessie Pope, 'Another "Scrap of Paper"' and 'Model Dialogues for Air-raids' by Owen Seamen, 'A Vision of Blighty' by J. Shirley, 'To a Bad Correspondent in Camp' by F.C. Walker; Stephen Rhys for 'Lost in France' by Ernest Rhys; John Shakespeare for 'The Refugees' and 'Ypres Cathedral' by William G. Shakespeare; Major James Cannan Slater for 'English Leave', 'For a Girl', ' Perfect Epilogue' and 'The Armistice' by May Cannan; Sir Roy Strong for 'Night Duty in the Station', 'The Menin Road', 'March 1919' and 'Unloading Ambulance Train' by Carola Oman; A.P. Watt Ltd on behalf of Timothy d'Arch Smith for 'Eyes in the Air', 'Gun-Teams', Headquarters', 'Only an Officer', 'Poison', 'The Other Side', 'The Reason', 'Unknown', 'Urgent or Ordinary' and 'Wails to the Mail' by Gilbert Frankau; Revd Juliet Woollcombe for 'Gommecourt' and 'Mudros, After the Evacuation' by Geoffrey Dearmer. 'A Halt on the March' by J.B. Priestley (Copyright © Estate of J.B. Priestly 1918) is reproduced by permission of PFD (www.pfd.co.uk) on behalf of the Estate of J.B. Priestley. I would also like to acknowledge the many anonymous authors whom it has been impossible to identify.

Every effort has been made to trace all the copyright holders, but if any has been inadvertently overlooked, the publisher will be pleased to make the necessary arrangements at the first opportunity.

It has been a joy to work with the staff at Sutton Publishing, particularly Christopher Feeney, Hilary Walford, Jane Entrican, Martin Latham, Mary Critchley, Yvette Cowles and Felicity Teague. Lastly, thank you to my husband, Michael Noakes, for his continued support.

Introduction

No war in history has produced as much poetry as did the First World War, and with no other war has poetry so much influenced popular perception and understanding of the conflict.

Most anthologies in which we find this poetry have based their selection primarily on literary quality, creating what is now an accepted canon of Great War poetry. This centres on the work of a few important writers whom we think of as the First World War Poets – such men as Wilfred Owen, Isaac Rosenberg, Siegfried Sassoon and Edward Thomas. Yet these represent only a small part of the nation's poetic response to the events of those years, and many survivors regretted that the emphasis placed on this work meant that other very different – less literary but, in their view, often more characteristic – responses to the war had been largely ignored. These were the work of less gifted writers who spoke for their own time but in a different way.

A number of excellent general anthologies in recent years have broadened our understanding by including work by these little-known writers – in particular Dominic Hibberd and John Onion's *Poetry of the Great War: An Anthology*, Martin Stephen's *Never Such Innocence: Poems of the First World War* and George Walter's *In Flanders Fields: Poetry of the First World War*. None, however, has concentrated almost exclusively on these poets. It was a wish to redress this imbalance that was the starting point for this book.

My first thought was that perhaps this poetry – much of which could more accurately be described as verse – had been passed over because it was not worth reviving. I soon discovered how wrong I was. Of course, it does not pretend to aspire in quality to the great poetry of the war – to 'Dead Man's Dump' or 'Strange Meeting' or 'At the Team's Head-Brass', for example – but what I discovered was a body of rich, exciting, often deeply moving work that complements the established literary canon; the two should be read side by side. Much of the poetry here is the work of men and women who would not normally have considered themselves poets at all, and it is precisely because it does not have to answer to high literary demands that it is often a more immediate, less poetically self-conscious, response to war. Indeed, many of these poems have an even greater immediacy than letters, for they express what was felt without caution or reserve, offering a true insight into the minds of the fighting men.

Typical of this is the characteristic, important and recurring feature that has been little represented in earlier anthologies, and that is humour. Hundreds of comic and comico-tragic poems were written by soldiers to raise the spirits of their comrades and make more bearable the shared tragedy of their suffering. This often juvenile jollity – which, incidentally, reminds us how young so many of these men were – has nothing to do with the much-derided 'smiling Tommy' of the newsreels. These verses were not composed to reassure the people at home. They were written by the men for the men. For an outsider, anyone who had not known the full horror of war, to attempt a humorous interpretation of its experience would have been a grotesque insult. For the men themselves, however, such humour was a lifeline, but one established on their own terms. In his poem 'Apologia pro poemate meo', Wilfred Owen examines the complexity of this dichotomy, and in its final lines he points to the exclusivity of the soldiers' brotherhood: 'These men are worth | Your tears. You are not worth their merriment.'

Sometimes the humour is deeply black, but more often it reflects a determination to make the best of appalling situations. 'One has to [. . .] hang on to one's humour like grim death,' wrote a young officer in August 1915, 'otherwise I think you are bound to crack.'[1] Often it is a defence against what Edmund Blunden described as 'socket-eyed despair'.[2] Those who refused to see what humour could be found, who dragged others down by looking only on the dark side of things, were despised and castigated for lowering morale. It was an approach that soldiers wished to extend beyond the front: 'the greatest thing you can do for me is to remain cheerful,' wrote a soldier to his mother.[3] Absurdities of military organisation, farcical situations that erupted even in the midst of battle, are picked up and mocked in a way that any soldier, even today, would immediately recognise. It is, perhaps, the poetical equivalent of Bairnsfather's Old Bill.

This response to often unspeakable hardship was both a broad characteristic of the British turn of mind of the time and also a particular product of the war itself. Edward de Stein, author of four poems included here, spoke in 1919 of 'that wonderful spirit of light-heartedness, that perpetual sense of the ridiculous which, even under the most appalling conditions, never seemed to desert the men with whom I was privileged to serve and which indeed seemed to flourish more freely in the mud and rain of the front-line trenches than in the comparative comfort of billets or "cushy jobs"'.[4] It is a tribute we find expressed over and over again in contemporary writings; many wondered if it would survive the break-up of the camaraderie that is such an important characteristic of any war.

It is tempting, in a more cynical age, to regard such humour as blind folly, a way of white-washing the truth, something akin to Karl Marx's opium of the people. But that is to misinterpret its nature. These men knew and understood the reality. They did not take the experience of war lightly. But those who employed humour – and many did not – found in it an almost instinctive mechanism for spiritual and emotional survival. Often it masked fear. Captain, later Lieutenant-Colonel, F.J. Roberts, MC, founding editor of the most famous trench newspaper, the *Wipers Times*, cautioned that the 'hilarity was more often hysterical than natural'.[5] For all its apparent absurdity, it reached into the deep tragedy of war, throwing powerful light on our understanding of how they were able to endure.

Beyond the humour, there are here many expressions of the suffering the men both witnessed and experienced, and of the deep anger many of them felt. By and large, the general disillusionment that we now associate with the First World War was a product of the peace rather than of the war, of broken promises and a sense of betrayal, of a growing realisation of incompetence and of the empty futility of so much of the sacrifice. Many people now find this difficult to understand, but most of those who have worked through contemporary documents – particularly personal documents such as letters and diaries – will endorse this view, as do many modern historians. As I searched through poems written during the war, I found much mockery of the Staff with their insensitive remoteness from the line, but little criticism of the actual military conduct of the war – even Sassoon was careful to exclude this from his protest.[6] And there is overwhelming evidence that most men, even as late as 1918, felt that they were fighting for something worthwhile, a cause in which they still believed.

But there was anger that war, with all its suffering, should be accepted as a means of settling international dispute, and against those whose follies and vanities had led to this particular war. And there was a sense of bitterness against those at home who were responsible for its prolongation, who profited from the rich business opportunities it offered and were so often unwilling even to try to understand what they were asking of the serving man and the price that the ordinary soldier was paying for these follies. There was much resentment, too, of conscientious objectors, the despised 'conshies' who refused to kill their fellow men and who were seen by many of the soldiers as contemptible shirkers who would live to enjoy freedoms that others had died to achieve. A group of poems in this book is the work of these pacifists, explaining their beliefs and their punishment.

In selecting the poems, I have searched through trench newspapers and hospital gazettes, private scrapbooks and autograph albums, old newspapers, magazines and journals, gift books and collections of poems published in aid of a particular cause, and many slim volumes of single poets' work that were published during or shortly after the war. I have looked at advertisements, at postcards that were sold on the streets by unemployed ex-servicemen, at In Memoriam notices in local newspapers and at the headstones of war graves. It was my privilege to handle an illicit, handwritten magazine literally sewn together before being passed from cell to cell by jailed conscientious objectors.

In the decades since the war, most of these works have been unavailable to the general reader, out of print and accessible only in specialist libraries, museums or newspaper archives.

With a handful of exceptions, I have not knowingly selected any work that describes an event not witnessed or experienced by the writer, give or take the considerations of fantasy and humour – I doubt if anyone ever actually saw a Sentry-pede, and I do not think that Harold met his maker because of the abundance of souvenirs he brought home with him. Gilbert Frankau's 'Eyes in the Air' is a first-person account of aerial combat over the line; Frankau was not in the Royal Flying Corps, but from the trenches he was able to watch dog-fights at first hand. Wilfrid Gibson served in the army in England but did not go overseas; despite this, his response to the accounts of front-line experience that he heard from his fellow-soldiers is so acute that he is thought to be one of the most significant poets of the war. A.A. Milne was not wounded at Loos but he saw active service with those who were – whether or not they were greengrocers from Fulham is open to speculation. C. Fox-Smith's 'The Call' is written by a woman, but accurately expresses the thoughts of many of the men as the end of the war approached. Readers must make up their own minds about the chapter entitled 'L'Envoi'.

There are poems by writers whom we do not usually associate with war poetry – Gordon Bottomley, John Drinkwater and J.B. Priestley, for example. Sometimes the poet may be well known, but the poem I have chosen is not: Alan Seeger's 'I have a Rendezvous with Death' is found in most anthologies but his 'On Returning to the Front after Leave' is not, nor is Geoffrey Dearmer's fine poem 'Gommecourt'. There is a single poem, 'Noon', by Robert Nichols, a poem I have not found in any other anthology.

The use of Robert Nichols's poem leads me on to an explanation of the general arrangement of the work. As I began to sort and order the poems I had chosen, it became clear that the most sensible way to assemble them would be to follow a broadly chronological pattern built round times and battles or particular themes: it is within the description of daily life in the trenches that 'Noon' finds its place. Gradually the material evolved into the story of the experience of the Great War told in verse by those who were there. Although, as an anthology, it lends itself to dipping, it has been designed as a whole. A few rather better-known poems, like 'Beaucourt Revisited' and 'The General', have been included for narrative reasons within this design, and a handful of works of a less obvious poetical standard than the rest, such as the text of postcards, are included because they speak powerfully of their time.

One of the richest, and certainly the most fascinating, sources was trench newspapers. We cannot now know how many of these ephemeral publications there were, but most units produced something that was written, sometimes illustrated, and then assembled by their men, often in the most impossible conditions. Fortunately, a number have survived, in the British Library, in regimental museums or in private ownership, but many more must have been lost.

One of the earliest of these was the remarkable *Fifth Gloucester Gazette*, published between 1915 and 1919. As with other notably successful trench publications, a single poet contributed work of remarkable quality – in this case, F.W. Harvey. But the most famous, and most lasting, of these publications was the *Wipers Times* and the newspapers – such as the *Somme-Times* and the *'Better Times'* – that were its sequels, published between February 1916 and December 1918. A facsimile edition first appeared in 1930 and has been followed by others since. Here, it is Gilbert Frankau who has made the most enduring contribution.

Compared to others, the *Wipers Times* was a relatively sophisticated production. In his Preface to the 1930 facsimile, written in the spring of 1918, the editor tells us that the first number was produced in a wrecked printing house near to the Cloth Hall in Ypres – pronounced Wipers by the British soldiers – which had been discovered by a sergeant who had been a printer in civilian life. 'There were parts of the building remaining, the rest was on top of the press. The type was all over the country-side. [. . .] Paper was there, ink in plenty, everything in fact except "copy" ', which the men then set about providing. The editorial 'den' was in a rat-infested, water-logged cellar in the old Ypres ramparts. The twelve pages had to be printed one by one, as there were not enough 'y's' and 'e's' to do more than a page at a time. When this original press was shattered by a 5.9 shell, a replacement, 'a lovely little hand-jigger and a lot more type', were found near Hell-fire Corner (of all places) and brought back into Ypres so that production could continue. This new, lighter press moved with them wherever they went, the newspaper changing its name as they moved. All but the final number were printed close to the front, on one occasion above ground within 700 yards of the line. 'Have you ever sat in a trench in the middle of a battle and corrected proofs?' asked Roberts. 'Try it.'[7] Only the edition that was in production at the opening of the March offensive of 1918 had to be abandoned, because of thoughtless enemy activity.

Other trench newspapers were more primitive – often no more than a single folded sheet. *The Spud* was typed and then duplicated, as was *Depot Review*, which was entirely the work of private soldiers. The altogether more ambitious compilation, *The Anzac Book*, was written and drawn, again largely by private soldiers, during the closing weeks of the Gallipoli campaign of 1915. Unusually, the idea for this publication had come from a member of the Staff who set up a production committee on the peninsular and then asked for contributions. It was also unusual in being intended for a broader readership – not only the men in the trenches but also those at home. The editor was Australia's official war correspondent, the noted C.E.W. Bean of the *Sydney Morning Herald*. What was grandly described as his editorial office was situated in a dug-out overlooking Anzac cove.

The very nature of this war means that most of the poems are written by men, but there were also women at the front, notably the remarkable Mary Borden, who served in French military hospitals, often close to the line. Both in England and abroad, women worked as VAD nurses, in the auxiliary forces or in factories. Others – the wives, and the mothers of small children or of men at the front – waited and all too often mourned. Their writings are vivid testimony to the tragedy of anxiety and loss.

Given their variety and richness, and their importance as social and historical testaments, it is inevitable that the poems in this book would have been rediscovered sooner or later. Some may surprise and others discomfort. Together they broaden and enrich our understanding of an event that has had such a profound effect on our national history and consciousness.

A few words about editorial decisions are necessary. In this collection we have followed, wherever possible, the conventions of presentation of the original poems. All poems are complete – a group of dots in the text is a group of dots in the original poem and does not indicate excision. Asterisks indicate a break in a sequence of sonnets. Editorial intrusion has been restricted to the tacit correction of obvious mistakes – generally the result of the makeshift conditions of publication – and to the occasional removal of such incidental things as unnecessary inverted commas round titles. Where a poem appeared for the first time during the war and was later tidied up and reissued in a post-war edition of the poet's work, the earlier version has been chosen. Within the text of poems, the early twentieth-century convention of full stops within acronyms has been retained; in editorial comment the modern convention of dropping these has been followed.

Notes

1. Captain Eric Gore-Booth, quoted in Malcolm Brown, *The Imperial War Museum Book of the Western Front*, p. 104.
2. *Undertones of War*, Penguin edn (1937), p. 168.
3. Quoted in Malcolm Brown, *Tommy Goes to War*, p. 40.
4. Preface to *The Poets in Picardy, and Other Poems*, p. 11.
5. Preface, 'How it Happened', to the collected edition of the *Wipers Times*, ed. F.J. Roberts, Eveleigh Nash and Grayson, 1930, p. vii.
6. For a contemporary poem about Siegfried Sassoon and his protest, see 'Lieutenant Tattoon, M.C.', p. 143.
7. Preface, 'How it Happened', pp. v–vii.

How it Began

In 1815 the armies of France, Britain and Prussia came face to face on Belgian soil at the battle of Waterloo. In the aftermath of the Napoleon wars, a treaty was drawn up at the London Conference of 1838–9 which guaranteed that this small country, so often the cockpit of Europe, would henceforth be a perpetually neutral state. The treaty was signed by Britain, France, Prussia, Austria and Russia.

On the other side of Europe, the Ottoman Empire was breaking up. The Greeks had launched their war for independence in 1821, and as the century progressed more countries struggled to be free. But Turkish domination was replaced by rival bids for territorial rights, and the opening years of the twentieth century found the Balkans in turmoil. In 1908 the Austro-Hungarian Empire annexed the Balkan state of Bosnia-Hercegovina, a land populated by Slavs. In the years that followed, its neighbour Serbia emerged as the leader of the Slavic people, determined to oust the Austro-Hungarian overlords. It was a cause that Russia championed. Austria, angered by the threat this posed, awaited an opportunity to overthrow Serbia.

Meanwhile, a growing rivalry between France and Prussia for European mastery was reaching a climax. In 1870 the Prussians nominated a Hohenzollern prince as a candidate for the Spanish throne. Bismark's wilful distortion of the facts of diplomatic intervention led on both sides to cries for war. In July 1870 France declared war on Germany. But France was ill prepared. Early in 1871, after a siege of four-and-a-half months, Paris fell and France surrendered. By the terms of the peace, it relinquished to Germany its eastern state of Alsace and much of Lorraine. An indemnity was demanded and a German army of occupation installed until the payment was complete. In a France determined to make good its inglorious defeat, *la revanche* was born.

In the summer of 1914, against a background of territorial ambition, increasing armaments and growing tension and fear, there existed in Europe two opposing camps. The Triple Alliance, pledging military support under certain circumstances, was made up of Germany, Austria and Italy; the Triple Entente, a collaboration that grew from the settlement of long-standing differences rather than from promises of military alliance, comprised Russia, France and Britain. Between Russia and France there existed also a military alliance in which Britain had no part. The newly united state of Germany, ruled by Prussians with expansionist, imperialist dreams, felt itself encircled by enemies. In particular it feared Russia's rapidly increasing industrial and military strength.

On Sunday 28 June 1914, a young Slavic nationalist, Gavrilo Princep, assassinated the Austrian Archduke Franz Ferdinand and his wife, who were visiting the Bosnian town of Sarajevo. Austria, realising that this was the opportunity it needed to confront and crush Serbia, accused it of complicity in the murder. On 5 July the Kaiser assured his Austrian ally that Germany would stand by Austria, even if an Austrian march into Serbia should unleash a great war. Indeed, Germany had long been preparing for such a war that would sweep away its rivals and secure European domination. Its plans were well laid and its preparations complete.

On 23 July the Austro-Hungarian government issued an ultimatum to Serbia, demanding that it put an end to intrigues whose purpose was to take from Austro-Hungary territories that it claimed were rightfully its own. The ultimatum included a number of impossible demands.

On 25 July the Serbian government conceded most of the points and suggested that the others should be subject to international arbitration. Austria would agree to no such compromise and on 28 July declared war on Serbia. As a precaution against possible Russian support of Serbia, Austria mobilised its forces along its Russian border.

The next day Russia responded by ordering partial mobilisation; two days later this mobilisation was complete. On that day, Friday 31 July, Germany sent a note to Russia demanding that it should halt all military preparations within twelve hours. Its own troops were already mobilised. France, meanwhile, waited anxiously to see what happened next.

On 1 August, Germany declared war on Russia. The next day German troops entered Poland and Luxembourg, and patrols crossed the borders into France. On the same day it declared war on France, and delivered an ultimatum to Belgium demanding free passage across its country. No agreement was given, and on 3 August, following its plan to invade France from the north rather than across the heavily defended land of Alsace-Lorraine, Germany crossed into neutral Belgium. On Tuesday 4 August Britain delivered an ultimatum to Germany stating that, unless it withdrew its forces from Belgium, a state of war would be declared. No reply was received, and at midnight German time – 11 p.m. in London – Britain declared war on Germany.

ONE

The Outbreak of War

Belgium and the Kaiser, 'Call to Arms', early training,
the BEF leaves for France

Unlike other countries that came into the war in the summer of 1914, Britain had no compulsory military service. Her regular army was small and much of it was posted overseas, particularly in India. There were reservists, who were immediately recalled to the colours, and Territorials whose purpose was to protect their homeland rather than to serve overseas, though this was soon to change. It would take time to create an army large enough to fight a major European war.

Despite the situation, conscription was not introduced. Instead, an immediate appeal was made for 100,000 volunteers – fit, unmarried men between the ages of 19 and 35. Lord Kitchener was put in charge of recruitment, and posters which showed him proclaiming 'YOUR KING AND COUNTRY NEED YOU' were displayed countrywide. Moral blackmail was also used. 'What did you do in the Great War Daddy?' was a question and a poster designed to shame those who held back from enlisting, as was the practice of handing out white feathers to young men not in uniform. Those who failed to 'take the King's shilling' were despised as shirkers. In fact, the response was so immediate and so overwhelming that many recruits had to begin training without uniforms or weapons.

There was much local pride in the number of volunteers that came forward, and in some towns friends from the same streets and workplaces were encouraged to join up together, forming what were known as Pals' Brigades. One such town was Accrington in Lancashire, where 1,100 men enlisted inside ten days, with a further 400 being turned away. In theory such mutual support and comradeship was an excellent idea, but later in the war – particularly during the Battle of the Somme in 1916, when single units suffered appalling casualties – it meant that whole communities of young men were almost wiped out. At the beginning, though, many people thought that Kitchener's New Armies, as they were called, would never be called upon to fight, for the war would be over by Christmas.

Meanwhile, the battles of 1914 were fought by regular soldiers. The first members of the British Expeditionary Force – the BEF – under the command of Sir John French, crossed to France on 9 August.

The Kaiser and Belgium

He said: 'Thou petty people, let me pass!
    What canst thou do but bow to me and kneel?'
But sudden a dry land caught fire like grass,
    And answer hurtled but from shell and steel.
He looked for silence, but a thunder came;
    Upon him from Liège a leaden hail.
All Belgium flew up at his throat in flame,
    Till at her gates amazed his legions quail!

Take heed, for now on haunted ground thy tread;
    There bowed a mightier War-Lord to his fall;
Fear! Lest that very grass again grow red
    With blood of German now, as then of Gaul!
If him whom God destroys He maddens first,
    Then thy destruction slake thy madman's thirst!

Stephen Phillips

England to Belgium

Not lusting for a brief renown
    Nor apt in any vain dispute
You throw the scythes of autumn down,
    And leave your dues of autumn fruit
Unharvested, and dare the wrong
    Of death's immitigable wing,
And on your banners burn a song
    That gods unrisen yet shall sing.

Because your Belgian fields are dear,
    And now they suffer black despite,
Because your womanhood can hear
    The menace on the lips of night,
Because you are a little clan
    Of brothers, and because there comes
The thief among you, to a man
    You take the challenge of your drums.

Not all our tears and wrath shall weigh
    The utter bitterness that falls,
O Belgian hearts, on you this day,
    The sorrow of your broken walls,
And desolated hearths, the crime
    Of Prussian sword and Prussian flame,
But, brothers, with the world we chime
    The story of your Belgian name.

We will be comrades at your side,
    Your battle and our battle one
To turn again this monstrous pride
    That veils but does not know the sun;
Our blood and thews with yours are set
    Against this creed of bar and goad,
The Ironside is in us yet
    As when the ranks of Cromwell rode.

For all things clean, for all things brave,
    For peace, for spiritual light,
To keep love's body whole, to save
    The hills of intellectual sight,
Girt at your Belgian gate we stand,
    Our trampled faith undaunted still,
With heart unseared and iron hand
    And old indomitable will.

                  John Drinkwater

The Old Soldiers

We come from dock and shipyard, we come from car and train,
We come from foreign countries to slope our arms again
And, forming fours by numbers or turning to the right,
We're learning all our drills again and 'tis a pretty sight.

Our names are all unspoken, our regiments forgotten,
For some of us were pretty bad and some of us were rotten,
And some will misremember what once they learnt with pain
And hit a bloody serjeant and go to clink again.

                  Edward Shanks

March up to the Colours

Come on, come in, and like a river flowing,
In volume irresistible toward the raging sea;
Let all the nations see that Britons now are willing
To fight for right and justice in 'The War of Liberty'.

Let there be no laggards of our able bodied youth,
In silken dalliance toying, as in piping times of peace;
When 'home land' is in danger it is a time forsooth,
To show you are true metal and to take a gun apiece.

The war may be a short one, or it may last for years,
You are ready to endure it, to prove your country right;
If Belgium now is burning amid a rain of tears,
It might have been 'Our England!' so strike with all your might.

Kitchener has called for you to take a Briton's share,
Your country has need of you, so do not hesitate
To march up to the colours, with many a mother's prayer,
For England, home and beauty – remember Belgium's fate.

W.J. Wilkinson

The Skunk

The Skunk is quite a nasty beast,
Unsavoury, to say the least.
A football match he likes to watch,
Smoke cigarettes, and call for 'Scotch',

The daily papers he enjoys
That tell about the other boys;
But when the War is done, the Skunk
Will wish he hadn't been a funk!

St John Hamund

The Sloth

The Sloth is of another kind;
He doesn't *want* to stop behind;
He means to fight. 'Some day' perhaps
He'll go and join the other chaps.
And when at last he's at the Front
He's just the sort to bear the brunt.
Let's stick a pin in him to show
That NOW'S the proper time to go!

St John Hamund

Cricket Field or Battle Field?
('This is not the time to play games.' – Lord Roberts)

Battles are won in the playing fields –
    But won when the world's at rest:
Not when the heart of the world is sore
    And the soul of the world distressed.
Not when the score is a thousand score,
    And a thousand score of the best!
Battles are won in the playing fields –
    But won when the world's at rest:

Battles are won in the playing fields –
    But not in the time of strife:
Not when the eye of the world is stern,
    And it's war, my sons, to the knife!
Not when the call is for each and all,
    And the Cause is your country's life!
Battles are won in the playing fields –
    But not in the time of strife.

Battles are won in the playing fields –
    But not when your King's umpire:
Not when the breath of your batsmen faints
    And the arms of your bowlers tire;
Not when the runs are acclaimed by guns,
    And the ball is a ball of fire!
Battles are won in the playing fields –
    But not when your King's umpire!

Battles are won in the playing fields –
    But what of another place?
Throw off your white for the khaki cloth,
    And a worthier wicket face!
And then if you win, by the grace of God,
    Return to the God of Grace!
Battles are won in the playing fields –
    But what of that other place?

Battles are won in the playing fields –
    But won when the world's at rest:
Not when the score is a thousand score,
    And a thousand score of the best;
Not when the heart of the world is sore
    And the soul of the world distressed.
Battles are won in the playing fields –
    But won when the world's at rest!

                      L. Godfrey-Turner

First Week in the Army
(As interpreted by some of the 'Derby' Jocks)

On Saturday I listed in the tartan boys brigade,
And said good-bye to all my pals, long hair, and lemonade.

'Twas Sunday night I kissed the girls I had to leave behind,
I only wept a pint or so – some more I'd sure to find.

On Monday I reported quite punctual at eight,
Got fitted out in khaki, and in kilts I felt first rate.

On Tuesday I encountered Sergeant Major's fearsome glare,
And my knees they knocked like ninepins, they weren't used to being bare.

On Wednesday I did squad drill and doubling by the hour,
Until everything inside me had turned completely sour.

On Thursday came a route march which I voted quite a treat,
Until the Friday morning when I had to dress my feet.

On Friday morn I stood in line to get my first week's pay,
With Ripon Town so near at hand, it soon had gone astray.

On Saturday I had the time to dream of things I'd miss,
And cursed the blooming Kaiser who brought me into this.

Pro Patria

In bowler hats, top coats,
With woollen mufflers round their throats,
    They played at war,
These man I watched to-day.
Weary with office work, pinched-faced, depressed,
About the field they marched and counter-marched,
Halting and marking time and all the rest –
Meanwhile the world went on its way
To see the football heroes play.

No music, no applause,
No splendour for them but a Cause
   Hid deep at heart.
They drilled there soberly,
Their one half-holiday – the various show
Of theatres all resisted, home renounced;
The Picture Palace with its kindly glow
Forgotten now, that they may be
Worthy of England's chivalry.

Winifred M. Letts

The Volunteers

Time: 7.30 p.m. *Scene: A large disused barn, where forty members of the local Volunteer Training Corps are assembled for drill. They are mostly men well over thirty-eight years of age, but there is a sprinkling of lads of under nineteen, while a few are men of 'military age' who for some good and sufficient reason have been unable to join the army. They are all full of enthusiasm, but at present they possess neither uniform nor arms. Please note that in the following dialogue the Sergeant alone speaks aloud; the other person* thinks, *but gives no utterance to his words.*

The Sergeant. Fall in! Fall in! Come smartly there, fall in
   And recollect that when you've fallen in
   You stand at ease, a ten-inch space between
   Your feet – like this; your hands behind your back –
   Your weight well poised on both feet, not on one.
   Dress by the right, and let each rear rank man
   Quick cover off his special front rank man.
   That's it; that's good. Now when I say, 'Squad, 'shun',
   Let every left heel swiftly join the right
   Without a shuffling or a scraping sound
   And let the angle of your two feet be
   Just forty-five, the while you smartly drop
   Hands to your sides, the fingers lightly bent,
   Thumbs to the front, but every careful thumb
   Kept well behind your trouser-seams. Squad, 'shun!
The Volunteer. Ha! Though I cannot find my trouser-seams,
   I rather think I did that pretty well.
   Thomas, my footman, who is on my left,
   And Batts, the draper, drilling on my right,
   And e'en the very Sergeant must have seen

The lithe precision of my rapid spring.
The Sergeant. When next I call you to attention, note
    You need not slap your hands against your thighs.
    It is not right to slap your thighs at all.
The Volunteer. He's looking at me; I am half afraid
    I used unnecessary violence
    And slapped my thighs unduly. It is bad
    That Thomas should have cause to grin at me
    And lose his proper feeling of respect,
    Being a flighty fellow at the best;
    And Batts the draper must not ——
The Sergeant.   Stand at ease!
The Volunteer. Aha! He wants to catch me, but he ——
The Sergeant.   'Shun!
The Volunteer. Bravo, myself! I did not slap them then.
    I am indubitably getting on.
    I wonder if the Germans do these things,
    And what they sound like in the German tongue.
    The Germans are a ——
The Sergeant.   Sharply number off
    From right to left, and do not jerk your heads.
                        [*They number off.*
The Volunteer. I'm six, an even number, and must do
    The lion's share in forming fours. What luck
    For Batts, who's five, and Thomas, who is seven.
    They also serve, but only stand and wait,
    While I behind the portly form of Batts
    Insert myself and then slip out again
    Clear to the front, observing at the word
    The ordered sequence of my moving feet.
    Come let me brace myself and dare ——
The Sergeant.   Form fours!
The Volunteer. I cannot see the Sergeant; I'm obscured
    Behind the acreage of Batts's back.
    Indeed it is a very noble back
    And would protect me if we charged in fours
    Against the Germans, but I rather think
    We charge two deep, and therefore ——
The Sergeant.   Form two deep!
The Volunteer. Thank Heaven I'm there, although I mixed my feet!

I am oblivious of the little things
That mark the due observance of a drill;
And Thomas sees my faults and grins again.
Let him grin on; my time will come once more
At dinner, when he hands the Brussels sprouts.
                              [*The drill proceeds.*
Now we're in fours and marching like the wind.
This is more like it; this is what we need
To make us quit ourselves like regulars.
Left, right, left, right! The Sergeant gives it out
As if he meant it. Stepping out like this
We should breed terror in the German hordes
And drive them off. The Sergeant has a gleam
In either eye; I think he's proud of us.
Or does he meditate some stratagem
To spoil our marching?

The Sergeant.   On the left form squad!
The Volunteer. There! He has done it! He has ruined us!
    I'm lost past hope, and Thomas, too, is lost;
    And in a press of lost and tangled men
    The great broad back of Batts heaves miles away.
                              [*The Sergeant explains and the drill proceeds.*
The Volunteer. No matter; we shall some day learn it all,
    The standing difference 'twixt our left and right,
    The bayonet exercise, the musketry,
    And all the things a soldier does with ease.
    I must remember it's a long, long way
    To Tipperary, but my heart's ——

The Sergeant.   Dismiss!

[A subaltern known as Colquhoun]

A subaltern known as Colquhoun,
Was considered, at home, a buffoquhoun,
        He would not have been
        If his parents had seen
Him drilling his Scottish Platolquhoun.

The Barrack Room

'Lights out' has sounded long ago, and midnight must be near;
The wind without roars winterly, the moon shines cold and clear;
Each window on the ceiling casts a phantom window white,
Which o'er the long, bare, narrow room reflects an eerie light.

It shines on thirty wooden beds, six inches from the floor,
Where thirty fellows for a while the officers ignore;
The silent bugle gives them peace, and now, until the day,
Their bodies rest; their dreams may fly who knows how far away?

For scarcely two were of one trade, whom war's demands unite,
Who left the office, study, plough, for one great cause to fight;
The veteran hard beside the boy who never drilled before,
Each with what little soldiers need ranged near him on the floor.

There's cheeky Jimmy, the recruit, who does the shuffle dance,
He left his fifteen bob a week to capture Huns in France;
There's Algy Somebody, Esquire, neglecting an estate,
And all the pheasant shooting, too, to learn 'deliberate'.

There's 'Whistlefield', the farmer chiel – find soldiering hard? Not he!
Who'd dance sometimes till two A.M., and yoke his cart at three;
There's poor old Bill, the banker's clerk, who started work at ten,
And thought he'd learn to ride a horse instead of drive a pen!

For each the work, the grub, the luck, the hope and fear the same,
Who comes for motives all diverse to learn the grimmest game;
And surely when, or soon or late, the weary war is done,
He'll be more quick to see a pal in every mother's son!

W. Kersley Holmes

[Have you seen the Pals, sir?]

Have you seen the Pals, sir?
As they swing out through the town,
There's Tom and Dick and Harry,
Smith, Robinson and Brown.

A credit to their Colonel, sir,
    In their uniforms so neat,
I'm sure we all are proud of them,
    As they march along the street.

    And don't they look so smart,
When they're out upon parade,
    Men from every rank of life,
    And every kind of trade.
Married men and single men,
    All ready to face the foe.
God guard the Pals of Accrington,
    Wherever they may go.

    Their officers are proud of them,
These lads in navy blue,
    All workers not shirkers,
    [   ]
All volunteers, not conscripts,
    Beloved by all the girls,
Give them a cheer when they appear,
    They're worth it are the Pals.

C. Wolstencroft

The Call to Arms

There's a woman sobs her heart out,
With her head against the door,
For the man that's called to leave her,
– God have pity on the poor!
    But it's beat, drums, beat,
    While the lads march down the street,
    And it's blow, trumpets, blow,
    Keep your tears until they go.

There's a crowd of little children
That march along and shout,
For it's fine to play at soldiers
Now their fathers are called out.
    So it's beat, drums, beat;
    But who'll find them food to eat?

And it's blow, trumpets, blow,
Ah! the children little know.

There's a mother who stands watching
For the last look of her son,
A worn poor widow woman,
And he her only one.
    But it's beat, drums, beat,
    Though God knows when we shall meet;
    And it's blow, trumpets, blow,
    We must smile and cheer them so.

There's a young girl who stands laughing,
For she thinks a war is grand,
And it's fine to see the lads pass,
And it's fine to hear the band.
    So it's beat, drums, beat,
    To the fall of many feet;
    And it's blow, trumpets, blow,
    God go with you where you go.

Winifred M. Letts

On Trek

Under a grey dawn, timidly breaking,
Through the little village the men are waking,
Easing their stiff limbs and rubbing their eyes;
From my misted window I watch the sun rise.
In the middle of the village a fountain stands,
Round it the men sit, washing their red hands.
Slowly the light grows, we call the roll over,
Bring the laggards stumbling from their warm cover,
Slowly the company gathers all together
And the men and the officer look shyly at the weather.
By the left, quick march! Off the column goes.
All through the village all the windows unclose:
At every window stands a child, early waking,
To see what road the company is taking.

Edward Shanks

The House by the Highway

All night, from the quiet street
    Comes the sound, without pause or break,
Of the marching legions' feet
    To listeners lying awake.

Their faces may none descry;
    Night folds them close like a pall;
But the feet of them passing by
    Tramp on the hearts of all.

What comforting makes them strong?
    What trust and what fears have they
That march without music or song
    To death at the end of the way?

What faith in our victory?
    What hopes that beguile and bless?
What heaven-sent hilarity?
    What mirth and what weariness?

What valour from vanished years
    In the heart of youth confined?
What wellsprings of unshed tears
    For the loves they leave behind?

No sleep, my soul to befriend;
    No voice, neither answering light!
But darkness that knows no end
    And feet going by in the night.

Elinor Jenkins

The Last Evening

Round a bright isle, set in a sea of gloom,
We sat together, dining,
And spoke and laughed even as in better times
Though each one knew no other might misdoubt
The doom that marched moment by moment nigher,

Whose couriers knocked on every heart like death,
And changed all things familiar to our sight
Into strange shapes and grieving ghosts that wept.
The crimson-shaded light
Shed in the garden roses of red fire
That burned and bloomed on the decorous limes.
The hungry night that lay in wait without
Made blind, blue eyes against the silver's shining
And waked the affrighted candles with its breath
Out of their steady sleep, while round the room
The shadows crouched and crept.
Among the legions of beleaguering fears,
Still we sat on and kept them still at bay,
A little while, a little longer yet,
And wooed the hurrying moments to forget
What we remembered well,
– Till the hour struck – then desperately we sought
And found no further respite – only tears
We would not shed, and words we might not say.
We needs must know that now the time was come
Yet still against the strangling foe we fought,
And some of us were brave and some
Borrowed a bubble courage nigh to breaking,
And he that went, perforce went speedily
And stayed not for leave-taking.
But even in going, as he would dispel
The bitterness of incomplete good-byes,
He paused within the circle of dim light,
And turned to us a face, lit seemingly
Less by the lamp than by his shining eyes.
So, in the radiance of his mastered fate,
A moment stood our soldier by the gate
And laughed his long farewell –
Then passed into the silence and the night.

                                                    Elinor Jenkins

TWO

Early Months

Retreat from Mons, Kaiser's 'Scrap of Paper', spy mania,
Kaiser's ambition to invade Britain, the First Battle of Ypres,
the Christmas truce

After landing in France, the British Expeditionary Force (or BEF), under the command of Sir John French, moved north to take up positions beside the French army to halt the German advance through Belgium. On Sunday 23 August they came face to face with the attacking forces in the small mining town of Mons. After a fierce battle down the streets and among the slag heaps, they were forced to withdraw. The Retreat from Mons, covering 250 miles in fierce summer heat, continued until 5 September. As rearguards turned to fight, the main body of troops marched until their feet were bloody and they moved almost in their sleep. They sang as they marched, and there were stories that ghosts of the English killed at Agincourt appeared to support them – 'The Angels of Mons.'

The German advance seemed unstoppable as they implemented the Schlieffen Plan, a long-planned strategy that would lead to the fall of Paris and would bring France to its knees inside six weeks, before the Russian armies had had time to mobilise effectively. But the plan depended upon a swift, undefended passage through Belgium. Instead, faced with unexpectedly strong resistance, Von Kluck, the German commander, altered the thrust of his attack. Suddenly he found himself threatened with being outflanked, and his armies were forced to withdraw first to the River Marne and then to the Aisne; his plans for a swift victory were gone. Now, his men began to move towards the Channel ports; if these fell, the British Army would be cut off and the British Isles isolated from the Continent.

In what became known as 'The Race for the Sea', the BEF moved rapidly north once more. The decisive confrontation came at the end of October near the medieval Flemish wool town of Ypres. The British were heavily outnumbered and the German Crown Prince, certain of victory, arrived to watch the defeat of what the Kaiser had called a 'contemptible little Army'. The British held on by a whisker, but by the end of the battle on 21 November the BEF had almost ceased to exist. Ypres became a symbol of the invincibility of the British Army that, though a vulnerable salient, was now to be held at all costs. Open warfare was over; with the coming of winter a line of trenches was drawn from the North Sea to the Swiss border – the Western Front. On Christmas Day, exhausted men on both sides of the line called an unofficial truce.

Meanwhile, in a fraught atmosphere at home, the terrible news of the retreat and the near encirclement of the BEF was replaced by reports of the successful defence of Ypres. Spy mania and rumour flourished. Everything German was suspect – from waiters and governesses to dachshunds and hock – and there were stories that Russian soldiers, with snow still on their boots, had been seen in England on their way from Archangel to support the Allies in France.

[There was a strange Man of Coblenz]

There was a strange Man of Coblenz, the length of whose legs was immense;
He went with one prance from Russia to France,
That excitable man of Coblenz.

Retreat

It was a nightmare week of thirst and dust –
With fairly heavy scraps at the beginning –
And disappointment, mixed with a queer trust
That we were winning.

They say one German rush stopped strangely short –
        The Boches fell back; their horses couldn't face
Something! when we were in a tightish place –
        Somewhere near Agincourt!

I wasn't there – and of that whole crammed week
        Only two little things stick in my mind;
Our battery – we were rearmost, so to speak –
        Had left me miles behind

In a great field of roots – there crouching tight
        Across those turnips casting backwards glances –
Less than a mile behind on a low height
        I caught a gleam of lances!

(I'd felt that thrill in my small boy existence
        When Porsena of Clusium in his pride
Marched upon Rome – and the 'wan burghers spied'
        His vanguard in the distance!)

Behind that hill was hid a host too vast
        To count – much too tremendous to alarm me!
These were *their* first – and I the very last
        Of French's little army!

– Oh yes, we'd lots of shelling, heaps of scraps –
        They all but had us once – and shot my stallion
From Fez – but funked a dozen Highland chaps
        Who tricked a whole Battalion!

One other thing – I'd halted fairly beat –
        A baking road – some poplars over-arching –
Men simply tumbling down with thirst and heat,
        And crumpled up with marching.

There was a weedy 'Sub', who used to shy
        At work and drill and such-like useless trifles!
Just then he passed me, limping, *whistling*, by
        Hung stiff with Tommies' rifles!

*   *   *

Though of that week I never want to talk –
  I'll think of Mons, whenever I remember
The valse tune that he whistled – or I walk
  Through turnips in September!

Charles T. Foxcroft

The Mouth-Organ

When drum and fife are silent,
  When the pipes are packed away,
    And the soldiers go
    Too near the foe
  For the bugle's noisy bray;
When our haversacks are heavy,
  And our packs like Christian's load,
    Then Jimmy Morgan
    Plays his old mouth-organ,
  To cheer us on our road.
    'It's a long, long way to Tipperary –'

When by the shrunken river
  Reclined the great god Pan,
    And to his needs,
    Cut down the reeds –
  And music first began;
Then all mankind did marvel
  At a melody so sweet;
    But when Jimmy Morgan
    Plays his old mouth-organ,
  Even Pan takes second seat!

When Orpheus, of old time,
  Did strike his magic lute,
    He lorded it,
    As he thought fit,
  O'er boulder, bird and brute;
And great trees were uprooted,
  And *root*-marched, so to say,
    But when Jimmy Morgan
    Plays his old mouth-organ,
  You should see us march away.

When the Piper Pied of Hamlin,
　　In the legend of renown,
　　　　His pipe did play,
　　　　He charmed away
　　The children from the town:
But behold our whole Battalion –
　　To the joy of wife and wench –
　　　　Led by Jimmy Morgan,
　　　　And his old mouth-organ
　　March forward to the trench.
　　　　'Here we are, here we are, here we are again!'

O, an overture by Wagner
　　Strikes sweetly on mine ear,
　　　　And the noble three,
　　　　Brahms, Bach, and Bee-
　　thoven, I love to hear;
But when the rains are falling,
　　And when the roads are long,
　　　　Give me Jimmy Morgan
　　　　And his old mouth-organ
　　To lead our little song.
　　　　'A-roving, a-roving; we'll gang nae mair a-roving!'

Sometimes he pipes us grave notes,
　　Sometimes he pipes up gay;
　　　　Till broken feet
　　　　Take up the beat
　　Of quick-step or Strathspey:
But he plays upon our heart-strings
　　When he plays a Scottish tune –
　　　　Hear Jimmy Morgan
　　　　And his old mouth-organ
　　At 'The Banks o' Bonnie Doon'!

He has a twist upon his mouth,
　　A twinkle in his e'e;
　　　　A roguish air,
　　　　A deil-ma-care,
　　Like the Piper o' Dundee:

Faith! we would dance thro' half o' France,
    And a' the trenches carry,
        If Jimmy Morgan
        On his old mouth-organ,
    Did but give us 'Annie Laurie'!

And when the war is over –
    The war we mean to win –
        And Kaiser Bill
        Has had his pill,
    And we boys march thro' Berlin;
'Unter den Linden' going,
    We'll need no pipes to blow –
        Just Jimmy Morgan
        And his old mouth-organ,
    Leading us as we go!
'Highland laddie, Highland laddie; whar hae you been a' the day?'

And when this life is ended,
    And Morgan gone aloft,
        He will not carp
        Tho' he get no harp,
    Nor trumpet sweet and soft;
But if there be a place for him
    In the Angelic choir,
        Give Jimmy Morgan
        His old mouth-organ,
    And he'll play and never tire.

                                Joseph Lee

Singing 'Tipperary'

We've each our Tipperary, who shout that haunting song,
And all the more worth reaching because the way is long;
You'll hear the hackneyed chorus until it tires your brain
Unless you feel the thousand hopes disguised in that refrain.

We've each our Tipperary – some hamlet, village, town,
To which our ghosts would hasten though we laid our bodies down,
Some spot of little showing our spirits still would seek,
And strive, unseen, to utter what now we fear to speak.

We've each our Tipperary, our labour to inspire,
Some mountain-top or haven, some goal of far desire –
Some old forlorn ambition, or humble, happy hope
That shines beyond the doubting with which our spirits cope.

We've each our Tipperary – near by or wildly far;
For some it means a fireside, for some it means a star;
For some it's but a journey by homely roads they know,
For some a spirit's venture where none but theirs may go.

We've each our Tipperary, where rest and love and peace
Mean just a mortal maiden, or Dante's Beatrice:
We growl a song together, to keep the marching swing,
But who shall dare interpret the chorus that we sing?

W. Kersley Holmes

Another 'Scrap of Paper'

(*The Times* of October 1st vouches for the following Army Order issued by the German Kaiser on August 19th. 'It is my Royal and Imperial Command that you concentrate your energies, for the immediate present, upon one single purpose, and that is that you address all your skill and all the valour of my soldiers to exterminate first the treacherous English and walk over General French's contemptible little Army.')

Wilhelm, I do not know your whereabouts.
　　The gods elude us. When we would detect your
Earthly address, 'tis veiled in misty doubts
　　　　Of devious conjecture.

At Nancy, in a moist trench, I am told
　　That you performed an unrehearsed lustration;
That there you linger, having caught a cold,
　　　　Followed by inflammation.

Others assert that your asbestos hut,
　　Conveyed (with you inside) to Polish regions,
Promises to afford a likely butt
　　　　To Russia's wingèd legions.

But, whether this or that (or both) be true,
　　Or merely tales of which we have the air full,

In any case I say, 'O Wilhelm, do,
    Do, if you can, be careful!'

For if, by evil chance, upon your head,
    Your precious head, some impious shell alighted,
I should regard my dearest hopes as dead,
    My occupation blighted.

I want to save you for another scene,
    Having perused a certain Manifesto
That stimulates an itching, very keen,
    In every Briton's best toe –

An Order issued to your Army's flower,
    Giving instructions most precise and stringent
For the immediate wiping out of our
    'Contemptible' contingent.

Well, that's a reason why I'd see you spared;
    So take no risks, but rather heed my warning,
Because I have a little plan prepared
    For Potsdam, one fine morning.

I see you ringed about with conquering foes –
    See you, in penitential robe (with taper),
Invited to assume a bending pose
    And eat that scrap of paper!

                    Owen Seaman

The Freedom of the Press

Waking at six, I lie and wait
Until the papers come at eight.
I skim them with an anxious eye
Ere duly to my bath I hie,
Postponing till I'm fully dressed
My study of the daily pest.
Then, seated at my frugal board,
My rasher served, my tea outpoured,
I disentangle news official
From reams of comment unjudicial,

Until at half-past nine I rise
Bemused by all this 'wild surmise',
And for my daily treadmill bound
Fare eastward on the underground.
But, whether in the train or when
I reach my dim official den,
Placards designed to thrill and scare
Affront my vision everywhere,
And double windows can't keep out
The newsboy's penetrating shout.
For when the morning papers fail
The evening press takes up the tale,
And, fired by curious competition,
Edition following on edition,
The headline demons strain and strive
Without a check from ten till five,
Extracting from stale news some phrase
To shock, to startle or amaze,
Or finding a daring innuendo –
All swelling in one long crescendo,
Till, shortly after five o'clock,
When business people homeward flock,
From all superfluous verbiage freed
Comes Joffre's calm laconic screed,
And all the bellowings of the town
Quelled by the voice of Truth die down,
Enabling you and me to win
Twelve hours' release from Rumour's din.

C.L. Graves

News from the Front
(With apologies to the Censor)

The Army has suffered an awful rout
In the terrible battle of (*place left out*),
But the enemy's hordes have been defeated
On the banks of the River (*name deleted*).
The Austrians, under General Dank,
Attacked the Russians at (*name left blank*).
On the road near (*cut*) they fled in fear,
But they turned and fought at (*blue-pencilled here*).

Our men have had but little rest
Since the fighting began at (*name suppressed*).
But a funny thing happened – we had to laugh –
When (*word gone*) we (*missing paragraph*).
If the Censor destroys this letter, well –
I wish the Censor would go to ——
(*Deletion by Censor*).

[There once was a Man, Kaiser Will]

There once was a Man, Kaiser Will, who seldom, if ever, stood still;
He ran up and down with a horrible frown,
And his ideas of culture were *nil.*

Where are the Russians?
A Plea to the Censor

Oh! where are those Russians,
Those hairy-faced Russians,
That sailed from Archangel and landed in Leith;
Who came o'er in millions,
Some say, sir, in trillions,
With big furry caps on and armed to the teeth?

Explain, Mister Censor,
And end our suspense, sir,
And don't keep us all in this horrible stew,
Pray say where you've trained them,
Or where you've detained them,
We know for a fact that these Russians passed through.

For uncles, aunts, cousins,
   In scores and in dozens,
From all over England have written to say,
   They gave them hot coffee,
   'Chocks', fruit and mint toffee,
And bade them God-speed as their train steamed away.

   Besides, and moreover,
   From Leith down to Dover,
Guards, drivers, and pointsmen could tell us all but,
   They'd quickly get sacked, sir,
   And so with great tact, sir,
They wink at our questions and keep their mouths shut.

   And in 'Dispatch' daily,
   And news 'Daily Maily',
We've heard of these Russians, but much news we lack,
   For somehow or other,
   We cannot discover,
Where Kitchener's put them, and we're on the rack.

   And it's really most horrid,
   The way we are worried,
And humbugged and bothered and kept in a stew,
   So drop, sir, this mystery,
   For you know 'tis history,
These hairy-faced Russians stopped two hours at Crewe.

   Pray say where you've put them,
   Or shipped them or shut them,
In England, France, Belgium, or in Timbuctoo,
   For 'tis tantalizing,
   Thus daily surmising,
Come, dear Mr Censor, pray tell us, NOW DO.

                                     T. Clayton

The German Herr

This is the round-eyed German Herr,
Still found in England here and there.
His ears are long, and I'll be bound
That they can catch the slightest sound.
He's timid and elusive too;
But mischief he contrives to do,
And so of him we should beware,
And first must catch – then cook our Herr!

St John Hamund

The Traitor

'Down with the Teutons!' rose the people's cry;
    'Who said that England's honour was for sale?'
Myself, I hunted out the local spy,
    Tore down his pole and cast him into jail.
'An English barber now,' said I, 'or none!
This thatch shall never fall before a Hun!'

And all was well until that fateful morn
    When, truss'd for shearing in a stranger's shop,
'Be careful, please,' I said, 'I want it shorn
    Close round the ears, but leave it long on top';
And, thrilling with a pleasant pride of race,
I watched the fellow's homely British face.

An optimist he was. 'Those German brutes,
    They'll get wot for. You mark my words,' he said,
And dragged great chunks of hair out by the roots,
    Forgetting mine was not a German head.

'Oh, yes, they'll get it in the neck,' said he,
And gaily emphasized his prophecy.

Ah me, that ruthless Britisher! He scored
   His parallel entrenchments round and round
My quivering scalp. 'Invade us 'ere?' he roared;
   'Not bloomin' likely! Not on British ground!'
His nimble scissors left a row of scars
To point the prowess of our gallant Tars.

I bore it without movement, save a start
   Induc'd by one shrewd gash behind the ear.
With silent fortitude I watch'd him part
   The ruin on my skull. And then a tear,
A fat, round tear, well'd up from either eye –
O traitorous tribute to the local spy!

R.A. Thorold

Ten Little Germans

Ten little Germans marching in a line,
Thought they'd march thro' Belgium – then there were nine;

Nine little Germans gave vent to their hate,
Tommy A. got on their track – then there were eight;

Eight little Germans, generalled from Heaven,
Chased the Allies to the Marne – then there were seven;

Seven little Germans, in a nasty fix
Had to fight a battle there – then there were six;

Six little Germans, only just alive,
Made a dash for Calais – then there were five;

Five little Germans thro' the French line tore,
Ran against the British – then there were four;

Four little Germans, sniping in a tree,
One was soon located – then there were three;

Three little Germans, in a fearful stew,
Thought they'd have a right bust up – then there were two;

Two little Germans, tired of all the fun,
Desperately tried again – then were was one;

One little German, whose little game is done,
Send him to the hangman – then there will be none;

No little Germans to make our lives a pest,
Peace will once more reign supreme – then *we* can have a rest.

[There once was a Ruler enraged]

There once was a Ruler enraged, when his troops in retreat were engaged;
He tore off his boots, and subsisted on roots,
That irascible Ruler enraged.

Kaiser Bill
Tune: Jack and Jill

Kaiser Bill once climbed a hill
And saw the cliffs of Dover.
Said he: 'What fun
To get a gun
And send some big shells over.
It will be grand with my German Band
To occupy these islands'.

He forgot for a second,
Or never had reckoned,
He'd meet with some men from the Highlands.

So with his son and a great big gun
He started off for Calais.
He smiled a smile,
He thought by guile
He'd keep the Belgians pally;

But King Albert swore by the crown he wore
To fight his people's cause.
So the Kaiser found
He'd to go to ground,
And there he's had to pause.

Old Von Kluck, who was sent to chuck
    The French all out of Paris,
        Met General French,
        With some men in a trench,
And got stuck up at Arras.
Von Hinderman said, 'I'll not rest in my bed,
    Till at Warsaw I call a halt';
        But he's not there yet,
        Nor likely to get,
But he says it's the Russians' fault.

Von Tirpitz, they say, is an Admiral gay,
    And commands the German Navy.
        But somehow they feel,
        When they come out from Kiel,
    They will go down to Jones – first name Davy.
A ship or two came into view,
    In the seas off Falkland Island;
        But Sturdee was there
        And took good care
To blow them up to Skyland.

The Kaiser's dream, so it would seem,
    To be Lord of all creation,
        Was stopped quite short
        By a loud report
When he got to Ypres Station.
For there he found his men half drowned,
    And it nearly made him balmy,
        To find that the trenches
        That stopped him held French's
Contemptible little army.

The Kaiser thought that if he fought,
    We would stand by – and watch him.
        But now he knows,
        And our Army shows,
    We're British, and we'll Scotch him.
And when we're done there'll be no Hun
    To kill our Allies' babies.
        Our flag will fly
        'Neath every sky,
And there'll be no German Navies.

Ypres Cathedral

Hope and mirth are gone. Beauty is departed.
Heaven's hid in smoke, if there's Heaven still.
Silent the city, friendless, broken-hearted,
Crying in quiet as a widow will.
Oh for the sound here of a good man's laughter,
Of one blind beggar singing in the street,
Where there's no sound, except a blazing rafter
Falls, or the patter of a starved dog's feet.

I have seen Death, and comrades' crumbled faces,
Yea, I have closed dear eyes with half a smile,
But horror's in this havoc of old places
Where driven men once rested from their hurry,
And girls were happy for a little while
Forgiving, praying, singing, feeling sorry.

William G. Shakespeare

Ypres

City of stark desolation,
Infinite voices of silence,
Crying aloud in the daytime,
Whispering shrill in the moonlight,
Ask of the world, appealing,
'What are you now but a name?'

Hushed are your streets, and the rumble
Of lorries and wagons and limbers

And low, dull tread of battalions,
Moving stubbornly cheerful
Back of invisible fighters
Muddily bedded in Flanders –
These alone for your roadways,
And these for the hours of darkness.
Wide to inscrutable heaven
Lie, in their ruin all equal,
Houses and hovels abandoned,
Windowless yawnings and pillars,
Chasms and doorways and gables,
Tottering spectres of brickwork
Strewn through the naked chambers –
Never a home for the seeking,
Not through the whole of the city,
Save for the spirit-fled body.
And over the breakage and rubble,
Furious wastage of warfare,
Rise in their piteous grandeur,
Oaks, still battling the tempest,
Riven and broken Cathedral,
Shattered, half-pinnacled Cloth-Hall,
Towers of solemn, grey greatness
Calling on heaven to witness,
Listening, steadfastly watchful
For boom that will herald disaster
Down on their remnants of glory,
Asking the world, appealing,
'What are we now but a name?'

City of wanton destruction
Standing nakedly awful,
Token of agonized country,
When was an answer demanded
In so relentless a silence?
How can the asking be empty?
Name and nought else in your ruins,
Crowned in the hearts as an emblem,
Child of the ravenous booming,
Page of heroical story
Greatest in still desolation,

Never in all your peace-slumber
Garnered you fame as in fury.
Silent mother of splendour,
Stand when your ruins have crumbled
And, sinking to soul of Flanders,
Merged with the valiant sleepers;
And after that and for always,
As long as the breath of men's honour
Is to the earth as the springtime,
Speak with your voices undying; –
How in the anguish and glory
Belgium and Britain you stood for,
World of men's honour undaunted
Just in the lines round your city,
Where the fierce waves of ambition,
Ruthlessly seeking their purpose,
Sank with the dead into Flanders.
Desolate spirit unconquered,
Here where the fury lingered,
Here where the graves of the honoured
Around your ruins are clustered,
Rise in your triumph eternal,
Built in the heart of man.

R. Gorell Barnes

The Refugees

Past the marching men, where the great road runs,
    Out of burning Ypres, three pale women came.
One was a widow (listen to the guns!) –
    She wheeled a heaped-up barrow. One walked lame
And dragged two tired children at her side,
    Frightened and coughing with the dust. The third
Nestled a dead child on her breast, and tried
    To suckle him. They never spoke a word . . .

So they came down along the great Ypres road.
    A soldier stayed his mirth to watch them pass,
Turned, and in silence helped them with their load,
    And led them to a field and gave them bread . . .

I saw them hide their faces in the grass
    And cry, as women cried when Christ was dead.

                            William G. Shakespeare

To the Kaiser – Confidentially

I met a man – a refugee,
    And he was blind in both his eyes, Sir,
And in his pate
    A silver plate
('Twas rather comical to see!)
    Shone where the bone skull used to be
Before your shrapnel struck him, Kaiser,
    Shattering in the self same blast
(Blind as a tyrant in his dotage)
    The foolish wife
Who risked her life,
    As peasants will do to the last,
Clinging to one small Belgian cottage.

That was their home. The whining child
    Beside him in the railway carriage
Was born there, and
    The little land
Around it (now untilled and wild)
    Was brought him by his wife on marriage.
The child was whining for its mother,
    And interrupting half he said, Sir.
I'll never see the pair again . . .
    Nor they the mother that lies dead, Sir.

That's all – a foolish tale, not worth
    The ear of noble lord or Kaiser,
A man un-named,
    By shrapnel maimed,
Wife slain, home levelled to the earth –
    That's all. You see no point? Nor I, Sir.
Yet on the day you come to die, Sir,
    When all your war dreams cease to be,
Perchance will rise
    Before your eyes

(Piercing your hollow heart, Sir Kaiser!)
  The picture that I chanced to see
Riding (we'll say) from A to B.

F.W. Harvey

All Souls, 1914

On All Souls' night a year ago
The gentle, ghostly dead
Beat at my thoughts as moths beat low,
Near to my quiet bed,
Upon the pane; I did not know
What words they would have said.

They were remote within my mind
Remote beyond the pane;
Whether with evil wills or kind,
They could not come again –
They had but swerved, as things resigned
To learn return was vain.

To-night the young uneasy dead
Obscure the moonless night;
Their energies of hope and dread,
Of passion and delight,
Are still unspent; their hearts unread
Surge mutinous in flight.

The life of earth beats in them yet,
Their pulses are not done;
They suffer by their nerves that fret
To feel no wind nor sun;
They fade, but cannot yet forget
Their conflicts are not won.

Gordon Bottomley

The School at War – 1914

We don't forget – while in this dark December
  We sit in schoolrooms that you know so well,

And hear the sounds that you so well remember –
    The clock, the hurrying feet, the chapel bell:
Others are sitting in the seats you sat in:
    There's nothing else seems altered here – and yet
Through all of it, the same old Greek and Latin,
      You know we don't forget.

We don't forget you – in the wintry weather
    You man the trench or tramp the frozen snow;
We play the games we used to play together
    In days of peace that seem so long ago;
But through it all, the shouting and the cheering,
    Those other hosts in graver conflict met,
Those other sadder sounds your ears are hearing,
      Be sure we don't forget.

And you, our brothers, who, for all our praying,
    To this dear school of ours come back no more;
Who lie, our country's debt of honour paying –
    And not in vain – upon the Belgian shore;
Till that great day when at the Throne of Heaven
    The Books are opened and the Judgment set,
Your lives for honour and for England given
      The School will not forget.

                    C.A. Alington

'Punch' in the Enemy's Trenches

(To the officer whose letter, reproduced in *The Daily Telegraph*, after reporting the irregular exchange of Christmas gifts between our men and the enemy, goes on to say: – 'In order to put a stop to a situation which was proving impossible, I went out myself after a time with a copy of *Punch*, which I presented to a dingy Saxon in exchange for a small packet of excellent cigars and cigarettes.')

    A scent of truce was in the air,
      And mutual compliments were paid –
    A sausage here, a mince-pie there,
      In lieu of bomb and hand-grenade;
    And foes forgot, that Christmastide,
    Their business was to kill the other side.

Then, greatly shocked, you rose and said,
    'This is not my idea of War;
On milk of human kindness fed,
    Our men will lose their taste for gore;
All this unauthorized good-will
Must be corrected by a bitter pill.

And forth you strode with stiffened spine
    And met a Saxon in the mud
(Not Anglo-) and with fell design
    To blast his joyaunce in the bud,
And knock his rising spirits flat,
You handed him a *Punch* and said, 'Take that!'

A smile upon his visage gleamed.
    Little suspecting your intent,
He proffered what he truly deemed
    To be a fair equivalent –
A bunch of fags of local brand
And Deutschodoros from the Vaterland.

You found them excellent, I hear;
    Let's hope your gift had equal worth,
Though meant to curb his Christmas cheer
    And check the interchange of mirth;
I should be very glad to feel
It operated for his inner weal.

For there he found, our dingy friend,
    Amid the trench's sobering slosh,
What must have left him, by the end,
    A wiser, if a sadder, Bosch,
Seeing himself with chastened mien
In that pellucid well of Truth serene.

Owen Seaman

THREE

Autumn 1914 in England

The role of women, flag days, Zeppelin raids

Many women in England immediately began to do what they could to support the war effort, although the attempts of some at emulating their military relatives in dress and demeanour were seen by others – including other women – as slightly absurd.

For some, particularly young mothers with children, the coming of war brought real hardship, as the breadwinner was either called back into the army or volunteered. Separation allowances were paid, but they were often slow in coming. As the men were called away, their jobs, and the new production tasks demanded by war, were filled by women. For many who became munition workers, drivers or bus conductresses, it was their first opportunity of working outside the home and earning reasonable money. Others joined the Voluntary Aid Detachment as trainee nurses, or took on voluntary work. Everywhere women were knitting, making socks and gloves and comforters for the men at the front. But motherhood was not forgotten; the war, after all, was being fought to protect the freedom of future generations.

The fear of invasion was joined by the reality of naval bombardment. In the middle of December 1914, Scarborough, Hartlepool and Whitby on the east coast were attacked by naval guns; there were 500 civilian casualties. A month later there were zeppelin raids over Yarmouth, Cromer and King's Lynn in East Anglia, and London suffered its first air attack at the end of May 1915.

>—·‹•›·—◦—·‹•›·—‹

The Women

Theirs not to go where martial strains are sounding,
Guarding grim fortress-walls or city gate;
Theirs not to breast the battle-tide surrounding,
But 'mid life's broken calm to watch and wait.

Theirs not to feel the passion of o'ercoming,
　　The pulsing beat of hearts that strive for right;
Theirs but to live while fears, like wild birds homing,
　　Come thro' the shadows of each sleepless night.

Theirs not to know where lov'd ones' feet are marching,
　　Where darling heads are pillow'd far away;
Theirs but to look towards Heav'n's great spaces arching,
　　To breathe in loneliness dear names and pray.

Theirs to stand fast, a mighty trust safe keeping,
　　Theirs to flinch never, tho' hard paths be trod,
Theirs to hold high Hope's lamp o'er woe and weeping,
　　Theirs – Duty nobly done – the rest with God.

Augusta Hancock

Deportment for Women
By One of Them

Sisters, when fashion first decreed
　　To our devoted sex
That beauty must be broken-kneed
　　And spinal cords convex;
When sheathlike skirts without a crease
　　Were potent to attract,
Those were the piping times of peace
　　When everybody slacked.

But, since the menace of 'The Day'
　　Has commandeered the Nut,
Since *demi-saison* modes display
　　A military cut,
It's up to us to do our bit
　　Each time we take the road,
For, if we wear a warlike kit,
　　The mien must match the *mode*.

What! would you set a 'forage cap'
　　Upon a drooping brow?
The feet that used to mince and tap
　　Must stride with vigour now;

No longer must a plastic crouch
    Debilitate the knees;
We've finished with the 'Slinker Slouch';
    Heads up, girls, if you please!

Jessie Pope

Khaki

Say, girls, I've just been round the town,
    It took my breath away
To find that we have sisters still
    Who bow to fashion's sway.
For nice Spring hats and nice Spring gowns
    Are everywhere displayed,
And purple seems to be just now
    The latest leading shade.

These purple hats are not for us,
    Nor purple frocks and hose;
Till times have changed, we're proud to wear
    Our Country's choice of clothes.
No envy do we feel for those
    In purple hue arrayed.
For surely khaki is, just now,
    A more becoming shade.

I. Grindlay

Leave your Change

When you go down town a-shopping, for let's say a blouse or hat,
    Or the hundred things a pretty woman wears,
Will you kindly think a moment as you look on this or that,
    How many folk just now have family cares?
Think of husbands, wives and widows who are now in deep distress,
    And who daily sit in sorrow, sad, and brood,
How hard it is to manage, and how painful to confess
    That they haven't got the wherewithal for food.

When you've made your pretty purchase, be it pipe or cigarettes,
    Caps, collars, cuffs, umbrellas, boots or shoes,
Will you ponder just a moment whilst your goods the shopman gets,
    Of the many poor about you and their woes?

Think a moment of the trouble that the war has brought about,
    And of all the many blessings you have got;
Think of rents and coals and foodstuffs that the poor are nigh without,
    And be thankful that yours ain't the poor man's lot.

Though your country hasn't called you to go fighting 'Kaiser Bill';
    Though you haven't perhaps been prompted to enlist,
Still your country expects something, each has got some niche to fill,
    And it's up to all and sundry to assist.
So don't pass this 'Leave Your Change' box, do not count it coppers lost,
    Simply say you'll bank in Heaven for a while,
Where Lloyd Georgie cannot tax it, where you know it won't be lost,
    And the angels sweet will bless you with a smile.

T. Clayton

Britain's Daughters

They talk about the Tommy and the brave things he has done,
    The brave things he is just about to do.
'Tis mountains high the homage and the praise that he has won;
    The world acclaims him; he deserves it too.
But what about our women, Britain's daughters, passing fair;
    The finest race of women on the Earth?
Have they been praised unsparingly? Have they received their share
    Of honour that should advertise their worth?

We see them in the canteens where they toil so laughingly,
    And feed the hungry soldier every day.
We see them on the 'buses where they tender chaffingly
    The humble fares along the jolting way.
We find them donning breeches, milking cows and making cheese;
    How charming is the agricultural maid!
She lets the men go fighting, and she tries so hard to please,
    And hides her fear whene'er she feels afraid.

The chauffeuse is the neatest and the sweetest little girl,
    Bedecked in livery of olive green.
She manages a motor-van or makes your senses whirl
    When taking out a pullman-limousine.
The girl of no vocation's doing all her good by stealth;
    It drains her purse alarmingly 'tis true;

But be she poor or be she rich she's thinking of the health
    Of Tommy – and that everlasting stew!

Impossible it is for me to mention all the work
    That our belovèd women find to do.
Suffice it then to say that they are never known to shirk,
    Though novelty has flown, and romance too.
But of the valiant daughters of this dear old troubled land
    The nurses 'tis a Tommy ne'er forgets.
God bless you and reward you, sisters of the Healing Hand;
    A life of honour, yours, with no regrets.

                             Colin Mitchell

Munition Girls

    Shells are but prayers for slaughter, cast in steel,
    A strange religion calls its devotees
        Cloistered with band and wheel
        To tell such beads as these!

    A twofold duty for a twofold need
    Summons the woman, in the self-same breath,
        To nurse, and yet to speed
        The loom of wounds and death.

    And Peace, the angel, as I see her move
    'Mong these new purlieus, pale from half-despair,
        Shudders, yet must approve
        The eager labour here.

    And from her eyes the passion-mist will clear,
    And from her face will wash the blood-red stain,
        If at the end she hear
        The pæan, 'War is slain!'

The Deserters

Where are the maids that used to lay my table
    And cook my meals and (sometimes) scrub the floor?
Florrie and Maud and Emily and Mabel,
    All, all are gone to prosecute the War;

In reeking vaults and mountain dells
They tend their sheep and fill their shells,
While my wife answers all the bells
And no one shines my Sam Browne any more.

Where is Elizabeth, whose eyes were argent?
How like a home *her* hospital must be,
Winnie's a 'Waac', and bound to be a Sergeant
Judging by how she dominated me
(Only I hope she never stoops
To talk like that to lady troops):
And Maud, who dropped so many soups –
What does she do with bombs and T.N.T.?

Our car stands starving in the dusty garage,
But Mabel drives a whacking Limousine;
And when they sprinkle us with bits of barrage
We know that much of it was made by Jean;
Our income slowly disappears,
While they get more than Brigadiers –
No wonder now the agent sneers,
'You *can't* get girls to come to Turnham Green.'

Do they look back and hope that we are happy,
With no one left to fuss about our food;
And when some foreman is extremely snappy
Recall with tears my courtlier attitude?
Rather, I ween, with mirthful hoots
They think of Master cleaning boots,
And thank their stars, the little brutes,
They bear no more the yoke of housemaid-hood.

And what will happen when the Bosch goes under,
And all these women fling their swords away?
Will the dear maids come back to us, I wonder?
Shall I be able to afford their pay?
And will they want Munitions rates?
Ah, who can read the ruthless Fates?
Meanwhile we wash the dirty plates
And do our whack as willingly as they.

                                        A.P. Herbert

The War Baby

Bye, Baby Bunting,
Daddy's gone Hun-hunting,
Brother's in the Navy,
Sister's making gravy,
Uncle's working on the land
Aunt is a munition hand,
Grandpa minds the hens and cocks,
Grandmamma is knitting socks,
Mummy's starting work afresh,
And has to leave you at the crèche.

[Pansy ran a Knitting Party]

Pansy ran a Knitting Party.
　　Oh! the things they knat.
Pansy's meetings never ended
And results were simply splendid,
　　I can swear to that,
Since for weeks we used the socks she sent
To take the place of wire entanglement.

Hampden Gordon

The Song of a Sock

Knitted in the tram-car,
    Knitted in the street,
Knitted by the fireside,
    Knitted in the heat;
Knitted in Australia,
    Where the Wattle grows,
Sent to you in France dear,
    Just to warm your toes.

Knitted by the seaside,
    Knitted in the train,
Knitted in the sunshine,
    Knitted in the rain.
Knitted here and knitted there
    With the glad refrain,
May the one who wears them
    Come back to us again.

[The Flag-Day Girl is dressed in white]

The Flag-Day Girl is dressed in white
    In sunshine or in sleet.
She is a most attractive sight
    When viewed across the street;

But don't you go too near that charming seller
Unless your name if Ritz P. Rockëfeller.

Hampden Gordon

For a Horse Flag Day
(Dedicated to the 'Blue Cross')

Buy a Flag!
Give your copper, give your silver, give your gold if you can:
To help the wounded horses is to help the cause of man –
    Buy a Flag! Buy a Flag! Buy a Flag!

Buy a Flag!
They, created to a freedom wide and wingèd as the wind,
Freely serve the higher brother of the master-hand and mind –
    Buy a Flag! Buy a Flag!

Buy a Flag!
Man has broken them to harness, but they give their wills to serve,
Responsive to a kindliness in every thew and nerve –
    Buy a Flag! Buy a Flag!

Buy a Flag!
They are suffering in our service, yet are patient, brave, and true;
Come, do your best for the horses, they have done so much for you! –
    Buy a Flag! Buy a Flag!

Buy a Flag!
Give your copper, give your silver, give your gold if you can:
By their strength and noble patience they have served the cause of man –
    Buy a Flag! Buy a Flag! Buy a Flag!

Jessie Annie Anderson

The Everlasting Flag

*Lines written by one who endures much agony of mind
on being required at frequent intervals to vend flags of a Saturday*

I've never seen the Dardanelles,
    I've never been to France,
I've never nursed in Egypt,
    Nor recruited in Penzance.

I've never helped in Africa
    To polish off De Wet,
I've never even tried to raise
    A 'Maisie' Bed as yet.

I do not write to papers, lines
    On Berlin on the Spree,
And suggestively white feathers,
    Do not emanate from me.
I've never warbled more than twice
    At territorial teas,
I haven't stumped up overmuch
    To send the navy peas.

I do not often mend the hose
    Of Bantams in distress,
(In fact I wish my own required
    The darning-needle less.)
But if you think I'm conscienceless
    You certainly are wrong,
For one department's left in which
    I always come out strong.

And though I truly am not one
    As generally brags,
I 'do my bit' – oh, cursèd fate,
    Selling those plaguey flags

    For:

There's the country's Indispensable
    Who snubs you with a stare,
And the gallant Major-Gen'ral
    With a pulverising glare.
There's the over-dressed young person
    Who's 'afraid she's got no change',
And the lady with the powerful tongue
    Who thinks it *very* strange
They haven't had a flag-day yet
    For (Blank) – could I arrange?

There's the worthy maiden-auntie
    Whose flag's been left at home,
And the rather stingy gentleman
    Who's almost heard to groan.
There's the naughty little villain
    Who thinks it very nice
To wear his flag well out of sight
    And hear you ask him twice,
And the 'strong and silent' personage
    Who freezes you to ice.

And though it sometimes happens
    That amidst the gloom may flash
A patriotic Christian who
    Doles smiles out with his cash,
When all is said and done I doubt
    I'd better wear a gag
Next time I'm pounced upon to vend
    The everlasting flag.

[The Women's Volunteer Reserve]

The Women's Volunteer Reserve
Parade the streets and do deserve
    Official recognition.
Myself, I strive to recognise
My Aunt in military guise,
    Amazing apparition!
But up till now I've met with no success.
I wish I could remember her address.

*　　*　　*

I want my puttees back.

Hampden Gordon

Route March Sentiments

I'm happy from the ankles up
    How happy I can't tell,
But, from the ankles down, alas!
    I do not feel so well.
A frieze of sticking-plaster winds
    Around each wounded heel,
And words of mine can not describe
    The feelings that they feel.
But from the ankles up my joy
    Is glowing and complete.
How sad it is that we must have
    Those gentle things called feet!

I. Grindlay

His 'Bit'

What have you done in the War, my son?
    Look in my face and say!
You have grasped no gun, nor a risk have run,
    In the heart of the red-hot fray.
You have ne'er a foe on the earth below,
    Nor a scar on that rose-leaf skin;
So what have you done in the War, my son?
    And how have you helped us win?

What have you done in the War, my son?
    Oh, you came on a darksome day,
And you turned a heart from the coward's part
    When it all but had crept away:
For the Hope and Cheer that can persevere
    Were your gift to that soul brought low;
And a Faith, half-dead, raised its faltering head
    At the sound of your triumph-crow.

What have you done in the War, my son?
    You have grown as the lilies do;
You have made sad eyes scan the far blue skies
    And rejoice in the sun with you;
You have day by day by the desert-way
    Been a well-spring of bubbling joy:

Say, what further task has the Realm to ask
    At the hands of my Baby-Boy?

These Little Ones!

Oh, guard them well, their heritage is goodly,
    They have a line of splendour to uphold,
Theirs are the names that shall be traced in glory
    On stainless pages with a pen of gold.
Oh, guard them well, their forebears are so wondrous,
    And they so young, so tender and so small,
God's angels o'er them smile in blessings ever,
    God from His Heaven looks down and loves them all.

Oh, guard them well, such storm-clouds dim their childhood,
    Such dark forebodings fill each mother's breast,
And yet they bloom like flowers amid the greyness,
    And in their smile the weary hearts find rest.
Oh, guard them well, for them the far horizon
    Holds such vast promise of a brighter day,
Of a new world – united – re-created,
    With strife and enmity all swept away.

Oh, guard them well – yours is the work unceasing,
    Yours is the vigil to be watched at home,
Yours the great guardianship that tireless ever
    Holds these dear hosts 'gainst dangers that may roam.
Women of England – keepers of rich treasure –
    Guide well these little feet in case they fall;
To you, with you, the children's weal is trusted,
    While God from Heaven looks down and loves them all.

                                        Augusta Hancock

National Service Lyrics
(or, square pegs in round holes)

('A Correspondent writes: "A City man, aged about fifty, with three sons officers in the Army, volunteered for National Service. He was asked to take over a milk round."' – *Evening News*)

Father's in the City, he is fifty-five and fat,
I think it is a pity they didn't think of that.

He's really rather clever
Though you'd never think it – never,
So he volunteered; he thought it was his duty,
   And he's got a situation
   In the Service of the Nation
Running errands for a 'Specialist in Beauty!'

Uncle Tom's an Architect, an F.R.I.B.A.,
And his profession, I expect, is not much catch to-day;
   But he thought it was a rum thing
   If he couldn't tackle something,
So he filled a form and sent it in on Friday.
   But he's not just overjoyed with
   Messrs Smith, whom he's employed with,
For his job's to sweep the shop and keep it tidy!

Uncle Jim, an Engineer, and rather proud of it,
Made up his mind to volunteer ('man must do his bit');
   But I fancy, poor old chappie,
   He is far from being happy
In a Government Department full of flappers,
   Where from 10 to 6 he lingers
   Getting ink upon his fingers,
Writing names upon interminable wrappers!

Cousin Fred's a ne'er-do-well, his strong point's not his brain,
He's never punctual at a meal and cannot catch a train;
   But he sent an application
   With his usual hesitation
And the answer made the others gnash their molars,
   For he's got a well-paid billet,
   Though I don't know how he'll fill it,
And his title is CONTROLLER OF CONTROLLERS!

How It Takes You

When the Zepps above us hover,
   They've a curious effect,
And make people take to cover
   In a way you don't expect.

Papa sits in the cellar
    With the Pommery and Schweppes,
For he says it helps a feller
    When he has to dodge the Zepps.

And the children in the store-room
    Play the deuce with the preserves,
And eat on till they've no more room,
    Just to fortify their nerves.

And uncle, though a dug-out,
    Has no notions all the same,
For he takes his flask and rug out
    To our best cucumber frame.

While aunty, *à la* Hubbard,
    To avoid a chance mishap,
Seeks for safety in the cupboard
    With the poodle and a wrap.

And Sis a sight to kill is,
    For when Zepps are in the wind,
She gets up and puts on frillies
    Of a most provoking kind.

Yes, when Zepps above are strafing,
    And the bombs begin to blaze,
You see all your friends behaving
    In a lot of funny ways.

[I know a blithe blossom in Blighty]

I know a blithe blossom in Blighty
Whom you (I'm afraid) would call flighty
    For when Zepps are about
    She always trips out
In a little black crêpe de chine nighty.

Model Dialogues for Air-Raids

(A few specimen conversations are here suggested as suitable for the aerial conditions to which we have been subjected. The idea is to discourage the Hun by ignoring those conditions or explaining them away. For similar conversations in actual life blank verse would not of course be obligatory.)

I

A.   Beautiful weather for the time of year!

B.   A perfect spell, indeed, of halcyon calm,
Most grateful here in Town, and, what is more,
A precious gift to our brave lads in France,
Whose need is sorer, being sick of mud.

A.   They have our first thoughts ever, and, if Heaven
Had not enough good weather to go round,
Gladly I'd sacrifice this present boon
And welcome howling blizzards, hail and flood,
So they, out there, might still be warm and dry.

II

C.   Have you observed the alien in our midst,
How strangely numerous he seems to-day,
Swarming like migrant swallows from the East?

D.   I take it they would fain elude the net
Spread by Conscription's hands to haul them in.
All day they lurk in cover Houndsditch way,
Dodging the copper, and emerge at night
To snatch a breath of Occidental air
And drink the ozone of our Underground.

III

E.   How glorious is the Milky Way just now!

F.   True. In addition to the regular stars
I saw a number flash and disappear.

E.   I too. A heavenly portent, let us hope,
Presaging triumph to our British arms.

IV

G. Methought I heard yestere'en a loudish noise
    Closely resembling the report of guns.

H. Ay, you conjectured right. Those sounds arose
    From anti-aircraft guns engaged in practice
    Against the unlikely advent of the Hun.
    One must be ready in a war like this
    To face the most remote contingencies.

G. Something descended on the next back-yard,
    Spoiling a dozen of my neighbour's tubers.

H. No doubt a live shell mixed among the blank;
    Such oversights from time to time occur
    Even in Potsdam, where the casual sausage
    Perishes freely in a *feu de joie.*

V

J. We missed you badly at our board last night.

K. The loss was mine. I could not get a cab.
    Whistling, as you're aware, is banned by law,
    And when I went in person on the quest
    The streets were void of taxis.

J.   And to what
    Do you attribute this unusual dearth?

K. The general rush to Halls of Mirth and Song,
    Never so popular. The War goes well,
    And London's millions needs must find a way
    To vent their exaltation – else they burst.

J. But could you not have travelled by the Tube?

K. I did essay the Tube, but it was stuffed.
    The atmosphere was solid as a cheese,
    And I was loath to penetrate the crowd
    Lest it should shove me from behind upon
    The electric rail.

J.   Can you account for that?

K. I should ascribe it to the harvest moon,
    That wakes romance in Metropolitan breasts,
    Drawing our young war-workers out of town
    To seek the glamour of the country lanes
    Under the silvery beams to lovers dear.

                                    Owen Seaman

Beasts and Superbeasts

(A German zoologist has discovered in German New Guinea a new kind of opossum
to which he proposes to give the name of *Dactylopsila Hindenburgi*.)

At the Annual convention of the Fishes, Birds and Beasts,
Which opened with the usual invigorating feasts,
The attention of the delegates of feather, fur and fin
Was focussed on a wonderful proposal from Berlin.

The document suggested that, to signalise the feats
Of the noble German armies and the splendid German fleets,
Certain highly honoured species, in virtue of their claims,
Should be privileged in future to adopt Germanic names.

To judge by the resultant din, the screams and roars and cries,
The birds were most ungrateful and the quadrupeds like-wise;
And the violence with which they 'voiced' their angry discontent
Was worthy of a thoroughbred Hungarian parliament.

The centipede declared he'd sooner lose a dozen legs
Than wear a patronymic defiled by human dregs;
And sentiments identical, in voices hoarse with woe,
Were emitted by the polecat and by the carrion crow.

The rattlesnake predicted that his rattle would be cracked
Before the name *Bernhardii* on to his tail was tacked;
And an elderly hyæna, famed for gluttony and greed,
Denounced the suffix *Klucki* as an insult to its breed.

Most impressive and pathetic was the anguish of the toad
When he found the name *Lissaueri* had on him been bestowed;
And a fine man-eating tiger said he'd sooner feed with SHAW
Than allow the title *Treitschkei* to desecrate his jaw.

But this memorable meeting was not destined to disperse
Without a tragedy too great for humble human verse;
For, on hearing that *Wilhelmi* had to his name been tied,
The skunk, in desperation, committed suicide.

C.L. Graves

FOUR

The New Armies go to France

*The Canadians, the New Armies begin to leave for France,
trench life*

As soon as war was declared, young men from Canada, Australia, New Zealand and South Africa volunteered to fight. Meanwhile, Kitchener's New Armies began to arrive in France in 1915. After crossing the Channel, they might experience a further period of intensive training at the Base Camp at Étaples before being transported in cattle trucks, marked 'HOMMES 40 CHEVAUX 8', to the railhead, from where they marched, heavily laden, often many miles to the line.

The usual routine was for men to spend four days in the front line and four days in reserve in billets behind the line, then, after two weeks or so, to have six days' rest away from the fighting area, although these times varied according to conditions. While in reserve, the troops carried out fatigues, carrying supplies up into the line or acting as covering parties; these times were often more exhausting than when they were in the front line.

The line itself consisted of three lines of trenches – front line, support and reserve – linked by communication trenches built on a zigzag pattern to break the trajectory of enemy fire; the trenches were often given the names of familiar streets from home. The front-line trench was protected by earthworks forming a parapet, further built up with earth-filled sandbags. Against the front wall a firestep was constructed to enable men to view no man's land, the strip of ground that separated the British and German trenches, which could be anything from 25 yards to half a mile wide. Immediately in front of the trench, barbed wire entanglements were laid. The floor of the dugout was covered with wooden duckboards, but shelter was primitive. Dugouts and fox holes, built into the wall of the trenches, were rarely elaborate constructions. This was different from the German lines, where more carefully constructed dugouts – often cut deep into the chalk downs – gave not only greater protection but also a sense of permanence. The British authorities discouraged this, for the men were meant to realise that they were holding their positions only temporarily and that the line would soon move on again.

The day began and ended with 'stand-to', when the men lined the parapet, for this was the time most vulnerable to enemy attack. The first task once daylight had come was the cleaning and inspection of rifles, after which the men were given a tot of rum. Some of the day was spent cleaning up or sleeping, and much of it was spent waiting for something to happen – the discomfort and tedium were endless. Most of the work was done at night as men went out under cover of darkness into no man's land to reconnoitre or to repair the wire. There was constant sniping, and shelling by 'Jack Johnsons' – heavy shells that were named after a celebrated black American boxer because they created a dense black smoke when they exploded – and 'Minnies', the formidable German trench mortar or *Minenwerfer*. Even in quiet parts of the line, a thousand-strong battalion could expect to lose thirty men a month from sniping, shelling or sickness.

The plague of the trenches was rats, which multiplied and grew fat on the unburied dead, though there were also the beauties of birds, particularly the skylark, and of trench flowers.

Canadians

With arrows on their quarters and with numbers on their hoofs,
With the trampling sound of twenty that re-echoes in the roofs,
Low of crest and dull of coat, wan and wild of eye,
Through our English village the Canadians go by.

Shying at a passing cart, swerving from a car,
Tossing up an anxious head to flaunt a showy star,
Racking at a Yankee gait, reaching at the rein,
Twenty raw Canadians are tasting life again!

Hollow-necked and hollow-flanked, lean of rib and hip,
Strained and sick and weary with the wallow of the ship,
Glad to smell the turf again, hear the robin's call,
Tread again the country road they lost at Montreal!

Fate may bring them dule and woe; better steeds than they
Sleep beside the English guns a hundred leagues away;
But till war hath need of them lightly lie their reins,
Softly fall the feet of them along the English lanes.

Will H. Ogilvie

To a Bad Correspondent in Camp

To Lieutenant John Samp,
    26th Regiment,
The Canadian Camp,
    East Sandlingborne, Kent
(Or anywhere else about England that the Regiment may have been sent).

Dear John, – All your kith
    And your kin (counting me)
Are dissatisfied with
    The scant treatment that we
Have received in the matter of letters since your transport in June put to sea.

One brief note as you sailed
    Thanking me for the socks,
And the picture-card mailed
    From the Liverpool docks,
With two sheets to your mother from Reading, haven't busted the old letter-box.

Now, if nothing is back
    Of your taciturn way
But congenital lack
    Of the right thing to say,
Here's a little set form for your letters which you're welcome to use day by day: –

DEAR MOTHER, [*Aunt, Cousin*] –
    I take a pen in hand
In more health than I was in
    When not so much tanned
By our open-air marches and drillings in this fine soldier-fashioning land.

For some twenty-four hours,
    You'll be happy to know,
We've had plenty of showers
    [*Blizzards, sunshine, or snow –*
The third item won't do for the nighttime, but with long English days it may go].

We're just back to our huts
    From ten hours in the trench,

[*Route march, at the butts,*
    Drilling, studying French]
And my brain [*tongue, hand, eye*] is so weary I could fall asleep here on the bench.

    This county of Kent
      [*The valley of Dee,*
The banks of the Trent,
    York, Salisbury,
You've a copious choice of encampment] is something I wish you could see.

    At each moment one stops
      With a gasp of surprise;
    The most exquisite hops
      [*Maidens, cowslip, pork-pies*] –
I gather them often by armfuls – furnish ever a feast for the eyes.

    Down the green shady lanes
      Of the neighbouring park
    Float the tremulous strains
      Of the cuckoo [*thrush, lark,*
Newt, medlar, tench, cairngorm, or lamprey], and my cares fly away as I hark.

    But this must be all,
      For the bugles of camp
    Blow [*any old call*]
      And I'm hearing the tramp
Of the guard taking [*any old duty*], so remain, Yours, etc., J. SAMP.

    With this bit of advice,
      Which, unless I'm deceived,
    Ought to have in a trice
      Your pen-palsy relieved,
I remain, your fond cousin, PRISCILLA. P.S. – We have really been peeved.

                               F.C. Walker

A Canadian to his Parents

    Mother and Dad, I understand
      At last why you've for ever been
    Telling me how that way-off land
      Of yours was Home; for since I've seen

The place that up to now was just a name
    I feel the same.

The college green, the village hall,
    St Paul's, The Abbey, how could I
Spell out your meaning, I whose all
    Was peaks that pricked a sun-down sky
And endless prairie lands that stretched below
    Their pathless snow?

But now I've trodden magic stairs
    Age-rounded in a Norman fane,
Beat time to bells that trembled prayers
    Down spangly banks of country lane,
Throbbed with the universal heart that beats
    In London streets.

I'd heard of world-old chains that bind
    So tight that she can scarcely stir,
Till tired Old England drops behind
    Live nations more awake than her,
Like us out West. I thought it all was true
    Before I knew.

But England's sure what she's about,
    And moves along in work and rest
Too big and set for brag and shout,
    And so I never might have guessed
All that she means unless I'd watched her ways
    These battle-days.

And now I've seen what makes me proud
    Our chaps have proved a soldier's right
To England; glad that I'm allowed
    My bit with her in field and fight;
And since I'm come to join them Over There
    I claim my share.

C. Conway Plumbe

The Catechism of the Kit

To-day's the kit inspection, and, Tommy, can you say,
If you're complete in each detail, such as your two shirts grey,
Your table knife, your dressing field, your trousers service dress,
Your haversack, your cardigan, your useful tin for mess,
Your helmets smoke and satchels, your spoon, your body band,
Your braces, soap cake, puttees, and towel Turkish hand?
Have you got your rations iron, lad? and then your laces pair,
Your shaving brush, your razor, and the comb to do your hair;
Your disc identity with cord, oil bottle and pull-through,
Your little goggles anti-gas, knife clasp, and hussif too,
Socks worsted, hold all, fork, brush tooth, and jacket service dress,
Cap comforter, your titles shoulder – two pairs, more or less,
Your boots ankle, your pay-book, and heavy coat great drab,
Your woollen drawers, your badge cap, and little ration bag?
Then, or course, your rifle's spotless, your bayonet sword is clean,
And your shrapnel helmet's not mis-used – for cooking in, I mean?
Your scabbard is not rusty, and your ground sheet's there as well,
And your water bottle's cleansed and free from any funny smell,
All your pouches ammunition are packed with S.A.A.?
Up you go! and the best o' luck – you're ready for the fray.

Walter M. Bryden

The Inspection

The word went round the regiment with electrical effect –
Upon the morrow would arrive a General to inspect,
A very mighty General, whose ribbons knew no end,
Upon whose critical report our future would depend.

We vowed we'd turn the regiment out in perfect record style,
If extra polish meant a trip to Potsdam or the Nile;
We wolfed our simple soldiers' tea – but not to go to town;
To five hard hours of furbishing the regiment settled down.

We blanco-ed head-ropes till they gleamed like freshly-fallen snow,
We polished buttons till they shone like stars set in a row;
Wherever anything of brass about our kit was seen,
With Soldier's Friend and elbow-grease we worked till it was clean.

We took our saddles from the pegs and rubbed the soap therein
Until they wore the satin sheen of some old violin;
We burnished sword-hilts, stirrups, bits, to see the metal wink,
And toiled o'er curb-chains till they flashed – a jewel every link.

Lights Out might sound and be obeyed; we toiled on in the dark,
For every buckle 'neath the moon appeared a silver spark
Till, wearied 'midst our saddlery and polishes we lay,
And dreamed of buttons overlooked till bugles brought the day.

Now never mind the General's praise (our horn let others blow),
What said the Major, whom we strove to dazzle with the show?
His fierce blue eye roved up and down, and then – what did he say?
'Was that your horse that coughed, MacTurk? I heard him yesterday.'

W. Kersley Holmes

Eye-wash

Whene'er I see some high brass-hatted man
    Inspect the Depôt with his ribboned train,
When all seems spick and absolutely span
    And no man spits and nothing gives him pain,
I think what blissful ignorance is theirs
    Who only see us on inspection days,
And wonder, could they catch us unawares,
    Would they be still so eloquent of praise?

They think the soldiers are a cleanly type,
    For all their brass is bright with elbow-fat,
Burnished their bayonets and oiled their hyp;
    Do they suppose they always look like that?
They see the quarters beautiful and gay,
    Yet never realise, with all their lore,
Those bright new beds were issued yesterday
    And will tomorrow be returned to store.

They doubtless say, 'Was ever drill so deft?
    Were ever rifles so precisely sloped?
Observe that section change direction left
    So much, much better than the best we hoped';

But little know with what grim enterprise
　　For week on week that clever-looking crew
Have practised up for their especial eyes
　　The sole manœvre they can safely do.

And I could tell where many a canker gnaws
　　Within the walls they fancy free from sin;
I know how officers infringe their laws,
　　I know the corners where the men climb in;
I know who broke the woodland fence to bits
　　And what platoon attacked the Shirley cow,
While the chill Staff, for all their frantic chits,
　　Know not the truth of that distressing row.

These are the things I think they should be taught,
　　But, since I know what ages must elapse,
What forms be filled, what signatures be sought,
　　Ere I have speech with such exalted chaps,
I here announce that they are much misled,
　　That they should see us when we think them far,
Should steal upon us, all unheralded,
　　And find what frauds, what awful frauds we are.

A.P. Herbert

The Draft

So it is done – the calling and the counting,
　　The solemn mustering, the ritual care,
The fevered messages, the tempers mounting
　　For some old rogue who never can be there;
No more the Adjutant explodes and splutters
　　Because the rifles are too few by four;
No longer now the Quartermaster mutters
　　It's time that bedding was returned to store;
But all is ship-shape, and, to cut it fine,
The draft has now departed down the line.

These were the men that we have trained from tyros;
　　We took them in, we dressed them for the wars;
For us they first arranged themselves in wry rows,
　　For us they formed their first unlovely fours;

We taught them cleanliness (by easy stages)
    And cursed them daily by platoons and squads,
And they, unmoved by months of mimic rages,
    Regarded us – most properly – as gods:
They were our very own and, being such,
For all our blasphemy we loved them much.

But strangers now will have them in their keeping,
    Unfeeling folk who understand them ill,
Nor know what energies, what fires unsleeping
    Inform the frames that seem so stupid still;
Who'll share their struggles and curtail their slumbers,
    And get conceited when the men do well,
Nor think of us who brought them up by numbers,
    Save in the seasons when they don't excel,
And then they'll say, 'The fellows should be strafed,
Whoever trained this blooming awful draft.'

But not the men: they will not slight so early
    The mild-eyed masters who reviled them first,
But, mindful still of marches out to Shirley,
    Wet walks at Hayes and romps round Chislehurst;
When in some ditch, untroubled yet though thinner,
    They talk good days and feelingly refer
Over their bully to the Depôt dinner,
    They'll speak (I hope) about 'the officer',
And say at least, as Sub-Lieutenants go,
He was the most intelligent they know.

And now is life bereft of half its beauty,
    Now the C.O., like some afflicted mare
Whose cherished colts have been detailed for duty,
    Paws the parade where late his yearlings were;
We shall not lie with them in East-bound vessels,
    Nor see new shores in sunlit sweeper-craft,
Nor (save in soul) be with them in their wrestles,
    Nor wear the ribbons that shall deck the draft;
Not in our praise will laureates be loud;
We must turn to and train another crowd.

                          A.P. Herbert

Night Duty in the Station

I

Slowly out of the siding the troop train draws away,
Into the dark it passes, heavily straining.
Shattering on the points the engine stutters.
Fires burn in every truck. Rich shadows play
Over the vivid faces . . . bunched figures. Some one mutters
'Rainin' again . . . it's raining.'

Slammings – a few shouts – quicker
Each truck the same moves on.
Weary rain eddies after
Drifts where the deep fires flicker.
Into the dark with laughter
The last truck wags . . . it is gone.

II

Horns that sound in the night when very few are keeping
Unwilling vigil, and the moonlit air
Is chill, and everything around is sleeping –
Horns that call on a long low note – ah, where
Were you calling me last?
The ghastly huntsman hunts no more, they say
The Arcadian fields are drugged with blood and clay.
And is Romance not past?

III

The station in this watch seems full of ghosts.
Above revolves an opalescent lift
Of smoke and moonlight in the roof. And hosts
Of pallid refugees and children, shift
About the barriers in a ceaseless drift.

Forms sleeping crowd beneath the rifle-rack,
Upon the bookstall, in the carts. They seem
All to be grey and burdened. Blue and black,
Khaki and red, are blended, as a dream

Into eternal grey, and from the back
They stagger from this darkness into light
And move and shout
And sing a little, and move on and out
Unready, and again, into the night.

IV

The windows in the Post Office are lit with olive gold.
Across the bridge serene and old
White barges beyond count
Lie down the cold canal
Where the lost shadows fall;
And a transparent city shines upon a magic mount.

Now fired with turkis blue and green
Where the first sunshine plays
The dawn tiptoes between
Waiting her signal from the woodland ways . . .

Carola Oman

The Route March
(With apologies to Dr Brown)

This route march is a blighted thing – God wot.
The sun –
How hot!
No breeze!
No pewter pot!
He is a blooming pool
Of grease –
'The Sarge',
And yet the fool
(He's large)
Pretends that he is not.
Not wet!
Foot-slogging over Belgian ways –
In summer blaze!
Ah! but I have a sign;
The sweat
Keeps dripping off this blessed nose of mine.

F.W. Harvey

A Halt on the March

Rifle and pack are laid aside,
Tunic and shirt are open wide,
No longer we stumble and curse in the dusty straggling line,
But deep we lie in the grass,
Watching the great clouds pass,
And the scent of the earth is like wine to us, beakers of cool green wine.

We smoke together and smile,
Good comrades, knowing no guile,
While a frail moon hangs in the blue, and the day goes down like a song.
No shadows mock our little life,
As they did in days before the strife,
But the twilight, the stars and the dawn are kind, and we suffer no wrong.

J.B. Priestley

The Squadron Takes the Ford

As we ride downhill at ease,
    Two and two,
Shines the river through the trees
    Into view,
    With a sparkle and a sheen
Caught in glimpses through the green;
And we check with one accord
    For the ford.

From the moving column floats
    Dusty haze,
Dust is in our thirsty throats:
    Summer's blaze
Glows on khaki, flames on steel,
Till we scorch from head to heel –
But the ford is full in sight,
    Cool and bright.

Trampled pebbles shining fly
    As we splash
Through the shallows, flinging high
    Foam and flash:

Jewels drip from hoof and flank
As we scramble up the bank,
While the troubled ripples clear
  In the rear.

W. Kersley Holmes

'In the Pink' – A Letter

Dearest Florrie, Came to anchor after 10 miles on a road
Which for stones would beat a quarry and for mud a bloomin' sink,
I am lying in a farmyard, where we're making our abode,
And I hope you're doing nicely, as this leaves me in the pink.

Well, we've marched for miles on cobbles, which is dreadful for the feet,
Past the fertile fields of France, which have a most peculiar stink;
And we've smoked that French tobacco, and it much resembles peat,
And we've tried a few French liquors which they leaves me in the pink.

We haven't seen a German, but we're getting pretty near:
And we haven't been in Trenches, but we're just upon the brink,
And when I write again, you need not be surprised to hear
We've been at 'em with the bayonet, and been dabbling in the pink.

Well, whatever comes, keep smiling, for, whatever comes, I'm true,
And so are all the Glosters and they're not the boys to shrink,
And when the Kaiser's busted, I'll be racing back to you,
And trust as [I] shall find you as this leaves me – in the pink.

Sign Posts

There's a line that runs from Nieuport down into Alsace Lorraine,
Its twists and turns are many, and each means a loss or gain;
Every yard can tell a story, every foot can claim its fee,
There the line will stay for ever from Lorraine up to the sea.

Places memorised by symbol, little things that caught the mind,
As at Loos 'twas but a lone tree which in mem'ry is enshrined;
Perhaps at Wipers 'twas a corner, shell-bespattered, held our sight,
Or a nightingale at Plug Street, sending music through the night.

Little things, yet each implanted when the nerves are tension high,
And in years to come remembered how, while gazing, death passed by;
So the line for all has sign posts, and a dug-out oft can hold
Little memories to haunt one as the future years unfold.

Though this line will be behind us as we push on to the Spree,
Yet to all it will be sacred, mud-encased though it may be;
In the future dim and distant they will tell the tale again –
The ghosts of those who held the line from Nieuport to Lorraine.

War

Take a wilderness of ruin,
    Spread with mud quite six feet deep;
In this mud now cut some channels,
    Then you have the line we keep.

Now you get some wire that's spiky,
    Throw it round outside your line;
Get some pickets, drive in tightly,
    And round these your wire entwine.

Get a lot of Huns and plant them
    In a ditch across the way;
Now you have war in the making
    As waged here from day to day.

Early morn the same old 'stand to'
    Daylight, sniping in full swing;
Forenoon, just the merry whizz-bang,
    Mid-day oft a truce doth bring.

Afternoon repeats the morning,
    Evening falls then work begins;
Each works in his muddy furrow
    Set with boards to catch your shins.

Choc-a-block with working parties,
    Or the rations coming up;
Four hours scramble, then to dug-out,
    Mud-encased, yet keen to sup.

Oft we're told, 'Remember Belgium'
In the years that are to be;
Crosses set by all her ditches
Are our pledge of memory.

Macfarlane's Dug-out
'This is the house that Mac built'

Since the breed that were our forebears first crouched within a cave,
And found their food and fought their foe with arrow and with stave,
And the things that really mattered unto men were four, or three:
Shelter, and sustenance; a maid; the simple right to be;
And Fear stalked through the forest and slid adown the glade –
There's been nothing like the dug-out that Macfarlane made!

When Mac first designed his dug-out, and commenced his claim to peg,
He thought of something spacious in which one might stretch a leg,
Might lie out at one's leisure, and sit up at one's ease,
And not be butted in the back by t'other fellow's knees;
Of such a goodly fashion were the plans the builder laid,
And even so the dug-out that Macfarlane made.

He shored it up with timber, and he roofed it in with tin.
Torn from the battered boxes that they bring the biscuits in –
(He even used the biscuits, but he begs I should not state
The number that he took for tiles, the number that he ate!) –
He shaped it, and secured it to withstand the tempest's shocks –
(I know he stopped one crevice with the latest gift of socks!) –
He trimmed it with his trenching-tool, and slapped it with his spade –
A marvel was the dug-out that Macfarlane made.

He lined the walls with sand-bags, and he laid the floor with wood,
And when his eye beheld it, he beheld it very good;
A broken bayonet in a chink to hold the candle-light;
A waterproof before the door to keep all weather-tight;
A little shelf for bully, butter, bread, and marmalade –
Then finished was the dug-out that Macfarlane made.

Except the Lord do build the house there is no good or gain;
Except the Lord keeps ward with us the watchman wakes in vain:
So when we'd passed the threshold, and partaken of Mac's tea,
And chalked upon the lintel, 'At the Back o' Bennachie',
Perchance a prayer soared skyward, although no word was said –
At least, God blessed the dug-out that Macfarlane made!

For when the night was dark with dread, and the day was red with death,
And the whimper of the speeding steel passed like a shuddering breath,
And the air was thick with wingèd war, riven shard, and shrieking shell,
And all the earth did spit and spume like the cauldron hot of Hell:
When the heart of man might falter, and his soul be sore afraid –
We just dived into the dug-out that Macfarlane made!

Deep is the sleep I've had therein, as free from sense of harm
As when my curly head was laid in the crook of my mother's arm;
My old great-coat for coverlet, curtain, and counterpane,
While patter, patter on the roof, came the shrapnel lead like rain;
And when a huge 'Jack Johnson' made us a sudden raid,
I was dug out from the dug-out that Macfarlane made!

If in the unseen scheme of things, as well may be, it chance
That I bequeath my body to the soil of sunny France,
I will not cavil though they leave me sleeping where I fell,
With just a little wooden cross my lowly tale to tell:
I do not ask for sepulture beneath some cypress shade –
Just a six by two feet 'dug-out' by Macfarlane made.

Joseph Lee

Music in a Dug-out

The hour is drowsed with things of sleep
That round my tottering senses creep
Like subtle wandering scents, so rare
They might ensweeten fairies' hair;

And I am walking in a glade
With gold and green and purple made
Unearthly beautiful:
And, oh, the air is very cool!

I see green lawns between the trees,
And cows and sheep upon the leas,
And, in the distance, hills;
And at my feet cool, mossy rills
Empurpled with the wavering shade
Of trees and bushes in the glade;
And ever I rejoice
And ever sings a voice.

I see – but, sudden the singing ceases,
Splintering my dream in pieces –

I see, in waving candle light
That cowers and flickers in a draft,
A low-roofed den – a hole of night –
That leaks to heaven by creaky shaft;
A table (where the candle stands
In bottle streaked with frozen strands
Of tallow drippings), strewn with tins
And cans, just tiny refuse bins
With swelling slops of tea and jam
And twisted greasy bits of ham;
And belts hung round the dingy walls
Like horses' harness in their stalls;
And in the corner gloom, alone –
A dusty, silent gramophone!

                                        R. Watson Kerr

Rats

I want to write a poem, yet I find I have no theme,
'Rats' are no subject for an elegy,
Yet they fill my waking moments, and when star-shells softly gleam,
'Tis the rats who spend the midnight hours with me.

On my table in the evening they will form 'Battalion mass',
They will open tins of bully with their teeth,
And should a cake be sent me by some friend at home, alas!
They will extricate it from its cardboard sheath.

They are bloated, fat and cunning, and they're marvels as to size,
And their teeth can penetrate a sniping plate,
I could tell you tales unnumbered, but you'd think I'm telling lies,
Of one old, grey whiskered buck-rat and his mate.

Just to show you, on my table lay a tin of sardines – sealed –
With the implement to open hanging near,
The old buck-rat espied them, to his missis loudly squealed,
'Bring quickly that tin-opener, Stinky dear!'

She fondly trotted up the pole, and brought him his desire,
He proceeded then with all his might and main,
He opened up that tin, and then – 'tis here you'll dub me 'Liar!' –
He closed it down, and sealed it up again.

Have you seen one, should a rival chance to spoil his love affair,
Bring a bomb, Mills, hand, and place it underneath
The portion of the trench where that said rival had his lair,
And then he'll pull the pin out with his teeth.

The Chats' Parade

When the soldier, fagged and weary,
In surroundings that are dreary,
    Aside lays his rifle and grenade,
Seeks solace in forgetful slumber,
From shell-crash and battle's thunder,
    'Tis then the 'chats' are mustered for parade.

At the double about his back
In a most irregular track
    They make for the parade-ground on his spine.
When there they will never keep still,
Undisciplined they stamp at will,
    And up and down they march in ragged line.

Round his ribs they do manœuvre,
Curses issue from the soldier,
    There's divisions by the score, he declares,
Doing artillery formation
Without his approbation,
    He wriggles and he twists and loudly swears.

Through long, dark night they carry on,
At charges they become 'tres [bon]',
    The soldier to disperse them madly tears
With savage fingers at his skin,
And prays for the morning glim,
    In darkness, though, the victory is theirs.

The morn at last breaks good and clear,
Light is this 'Army's' one great fear,
    They retired to warm flannel trenches.
But not too long there they linger,
For the soldier's thumb and finger,
    Routs them out with unregretful wrenches.

But no victory is there won,
For again reinforcements come,
    And in darkness of night again attack;
So on the fight goes – on and on,
They are almost like the Hun:
    Their foul deeds are performed behind the back.

                              J.M. Harkins

The All-Powerful

Poets from time of yore have sung,
With every rhyme in every tongue
Of beauty and the power of love;
Or earthly things, and things above.

Sonnets to ladies dedicated
(Often, I fear, much overrated);
They raved on this, they raved on that
From dukes to the domestic cat.

On blessed peace and glorious war:
On feats of daring steeped with gore;
And every kind of wondrous deeds
Which hist'ry or tradition breeds.

But I would humbly sing to praise
Something unhonored in these days;
The cure for broken legs and arms,
For sufferers from rheumatic qualms,

From wounds by bullet or the knife
Obtained in peace or deadly strife;
For broken heads or chilblained toes
And twenty thousand other woes;

For that incurable disease
A sup'rabundance of V.C.s;
For nervous breakdown, shrapnelitis,
Toothache, acute malingeritis;

For broken hearts, for busted clo'es;
For every sickness science knows;
All these and every other ill
Are cured by that all-searching PILL,

Choice gift to earth by powers divine –
I sing in praise of NUMBER NINE!

Stand-to!

I'd just crawled into me dug-out,
    And pulled me coat over me 'ead,
        When the Corpor-al
        He begins to bawl,
And these were the words he said:
    'Stand to –
Show a leg! – Get a move on, You! –
    Ye's can't lie and snore,
    Till the end o' the war –
Stand-to! – STAND-TO! STAND-TO!'

I was just a-dreamin' of 'Ome Sweet 'Ome,
   A-top of a fevver bed;
     And Sister Nell
     Had looked in to tell
Of tea, and toasted bread –
     'Stand-to!' –
Of a sudden a change of view –
     'Come on – you there –
     Take a sniff o' fresh air –
Stand-to! – STAND-TO! STAND-TO!'

Joseph Lee

At Dawn in France

Night on the plains, and the stars unfold
The cycle of night in splendour old;
The winds are hushed, on the fire-swept hill
All is silent, shadowy, still –
Silent, yet tense as a harp high-strung
By a master hand for deeds unsung.
Slowly across the shadowy night
Tremble the shimmering wings of light,
And men with vigil in their eyes
And a fever light that never dies –
Men from the city, hamlet, town,
Once white faces tanned to brown, –
Stand to the watch of the parapet
And watch, with rifles, bayonets set,
For the great unknown that comes to men
Swift as the light: sudden, then –

Dawn! the light from its shimmering wings
Lights up their faces with strange, strange things:
Strange thoughts of love, of death and life,
Serenity 'mid sanguine strife: –
Dreams of life where the feet of youth
Rush to the pinnacles of Truth;
Where early dreams with pinions fleet
Rush to find a love complete;
Of Love and Youth 'neath rosy bowers
Sensuous, mad with wine-filled hours,

Flushed with hope and joy's delight,
Weaving rapture from the night: –
Visions of death where the harp is still
And the sun sets swiftly behind youth's hill;
Where the song is hushed and the light is dead
And the man lies with the rememberèd;
Where Memory weaves a paradise,
A mother's face, her tender eyes,
Her suffering for the child she gave,
Her love unbroken by the grave;
Where shadows gather o'er the bliss,
The rapture of a bridal kiss: –
Yet dreams where Youth (sublimity!)
Doth thrill to give for Liberty
Its love, its hope, its radiant morn,
Doth thrill to die for the yet unborn,
To die, and pay the utmost price
And save its ideals thro' the sacrifice.

Thus at dawn do the watchers dream,
Of life and death, of love supreme:
Flushed with the dawn, hope in each breast,
Their faces turn to the starless west:
Thus at dawn do the watchers think
Resolute-hearted upon death's brink
With a strange, proud look on every face –
The SCORN of Death, the PRIDE of race.

John W. Streets

To Those Who Wait

Some sing of the glory of war,
Of heroes who die in the fight;
Of the shock of the battle, the roar of the guns,
When the enemies clash by night.

Some mourn the savagery of war,
The shame and the waste of it all;
And they pity the sinfulness of men
Who heard not the Master's call.

They may be right, and they may be wrong,
But what I'm going to sing
Is not the glory of the war –
But the weariness of the thing.

For most of the time there's nothing to do
But to sit and think of the past;
And one day comes and slowly dies –
Exactly like the last.

It's the waiting – seldom talked about –
Oh, it's rarely ever told –
That most of the bravery at the front –
Is waiting in the cold.

It's not the dread of the shrapnel's whine
That sickens a fighting soul;
But the beast in us comes out at times
When we're waiting in a hole.

In a hole that's damp and full of rats
The poisoned thoughts will come;
And there are thoughts of long dread days,
Of love, and friends and home.

Just sitting and waiting and thinking
As the dreary days go by
Takes a different kind of courage
From marching out to die.

                                      Don White

Tommy and Fritz

He hides behind his sand-bag,
    And I stand back o' mine;
And sometimes he bellows, 'Hullo, John Bull!'
    And I hollers, 'German swine!'
And sometimes we both lose our bloomin' rag
    And blaze all along the line.

Sometimes he whistles his 'Ymn of 'Ate,
    Or opens his mug to sing,
And when he gives us 'Die Wacht am Rhein'
    I give 'im 'God Save the King';
And then – we 'get up the wind' again,
    And the bullets begin to ping –
(If we're in luck our machine gun nips
    A working squad on the wing.)

Sometimes he shouts, 'Tommy, come over!'
    And we fellers bawl out, 'Fritz,
If yer wants a good warm breakfast,
    Walk up and we'll give you fits!'
And sometimes our great guns begin to growl,
    And blows his front line to bits.

And when our shrapnel has tore his wire,
    And his parapet shows a rent,
We over and pays him a friendly call
    With a bayonet – but no harm meant.
And he – well, when he's resuscitate,
    He returns us the compliment!

I stand behind my sand-bag,
    And he hides back o' his'en;
And, but for our bloomin' uniforms,
    We might both be convicts in pris'n;
And sometimes I loves him a little bit –
    And sometimes I 'ate like p'ison.

For sometimes I mutters 'Belgium',
    Or 'Lusitani–a',
And I slackens my bay'net in its sheath,
    And stiffens my lower jaw,
And 'An eye for an eye; a tooth for a tooth',
    Is all I know of the Law.

But sometimes when things is quiet,
    And the old kindly stars come out,
I stand up behind my sand-bag,
    And think, 'What's it all about?'

And – tho' I'm a damned sight better nor him,
    Yet sometimes I have a doubt,
That if you got under his hide you would see
A bloke with a heart just the same's you and me!

Joseph Lee

The Soldier's Dog

A little, vagrant cur,
    He had a noble heart;
He met us on the road,
    And chose the better part.

It may be Belgium's wrongs
    Beneath his weskit burned;
Or visions of a home
    The Huns had overturned.

And so he sought our camp,
    And followed to the trench,
For Englishmen to him
    Were much the same as French.

The soldier's dog, he shared
    The soldier's daily bread,
And howsoever short
    The rations, he was fed.

And in return he warred
    Against the soldier's pest,
The vermin great and small
    Which rob them of their rest.

Sometimes he would patrol
    Along the parapet,
To scent the creeping guile
    Of Huns on mischief set.

And had Hunny snake
    Through barbed fences crawled,
He would have had his bags,
    And bit him till he bawled.

Then why, oh why, when you
    Had made your footing sure
Did you mistake the road,
    Or fall to alien lure?

I cannot think that you
    Did willingly desert,
Still less that to Kultur
    You were a base pervert.

I fancy when the fight
    Is raging on the plain,
Beside the old platoon
    You will be found again.

Noon

It is midday: the deep trench glares . . .
A buzz and blaze of flies . . .
The hot wind puffs the giddy airs . . .
The great sun rakes the skies.

No sound in all the stagnant trench
Where forty standing men
Endure the sweat and grit and stench,
Like cattle in a pen.

Sometimes a sniper's bullet whirs
Or twangs the whining wire;
Sometimes a soldier sighs and stirs
As in hell's frying fire.

From out a high cool cloud descends
An aeroplane's far moan . . .
The sun strikes down, the thin cloud rends . . .
The black speck travels on.

And sweating, dizzied, isolate
In the hot trench beneath,

We bide the next shrewd move of fate
Be it of life or death.

Robert Nichols

To a Choir of Birds

Green are the trees, and green the summer grass,
    Beneath the sun, the tiniest leaf hangs still:
The flowers in languor droop, and tired men pass
    All somnolent, while death whines loud and shrill.
O fine, full-throated choir invisible,
    Whose sudden burst of rapture fills the ear!
Are ye insensible to mortal fear,
    That such a stream of melody ye spill,
While murk of battle drifts on Auber's hill,
And mankind dreams of slaughter? What wild glee
    Has filled your throbbing throats with sound, until
Its strains are poured from every bush and tree,
    And sad hearts swell with hope, and fierce eyes fill?
The world is stark with blood and hate – but ye –
    Sing on! Sing on! in careless ecstasy.

E.F. Wilkinson

Shelley in the Trenches

Impressions are like winds; you feel their cool
Swift kiss upon the brow, yet know not where
They sprang to birth: so like a pool
Rippled by winds from out their forest lair
My soul was stir'd to life; its twilight fled;
There passed across its solitude a dream
That wing'd with supreme ecstasy did seem;
That gave the kiss of life to long-lost dead.

A lark trill'd in the blue: and suddenly
Upon the wings of his immortal ode
My soul rushed singing to the ether sky
And found in visions, dreams, its real abode –
I fled with Shelley, with the lark afar,
Unto the realms where the eternal are.

John W. Streets

Love and War

In the line a soldier's fancy
Oft may turn to thoughts of love,
But 'tis hard to dream of Nancy
When the whizz-bangs sing above.

In the midst of some sweet picture
Vision of a love-swept mind,
Bang! 'A whizz-bang almost nicked yer!'
'Duck, yer blighter, are yer blind?'

Take the case of poor Bill 'Arris
Deep in love with Rosy Greet,
So forgot to grease his tootsies,
Stayed outside and got 'trench feet'.

Then remember old Tom Stoner,
Ponder of his awful fate.
Always writing to his Donah,
Lost his rum 'cos 'e was late.

Then again there's 'Arry 'Awkins,
Stopped to dream at Gordon Farm.
Got a 'blightie', found his Polly
Walking out on Johnson's arm.

Plenty more of such examples
I could give, had I but time.
War on tender feelings tramples,
H.E. breaks up thoughts sublime.

'Don't dream when you're near machine guns!'
Is a thing to bear in mind.
Think of love when not between Huns,
A sniper's quick, and love is blind.

To Minnie
Dedicated to the P.B.I.

In days gone by some aeons ago
That name my youthful pulses stirred,

I thrilled whene'er she whispered low,
Ran to her when her voice I heard.

Ah Minnie! how our feelings change,
For now I hear your voice with dread,
And hasten to get out of range
Ere you me on the landscape spread.

Your lightest whisper makes me thrill,
Your presence makes me hide my head,
Your voice can make me hasten still –
But 'tis away from you instead.

You fickle jade! you traitrous minx!
We once exchanged love's old sweet tales;
Now where effulgent star-shell winks
Your raucous screech my ear assails.

No place is sacred, I declare,
Your manners most immodest are,
You force your blatant presence where
Maidens should be particular.

You uninvited do intrude,
You force an entrance to my couch,
Though if I've warning you're about
I'll not be there, for that I'll vouch.

Name once most loved of all your sex,
Now hated with a loathing great,
When next my harassed soul you vex
You'll get some back at any rate.

At Stand Down

Above the trench I heard the night wind sigh,
Across the tattered sandbags moonbeams lay,
While Flanders stars shone overhead, and I
Alone with thoughts of you at close of day.

The cannon's angry roar had died away
And left the stillness of a Summer's night
For one sweet hour of peace that would not stay,
And I could rest before the coming fight.

And then I saw a star shoot in the West . . .
I wonder if beyond the silver sea
It found you somewhere in its loving quest –
And pressed a kiss upon your lips from me?

Raymond Heywood

The Night Hawks

Talk not to me of vain delights,
Of Regent Street or Piccadilly.
A newer London, rarer sights
I visit nightly willy-nilly.

When daylight wanes and dusk is falling
We start out clad in gum boots thigh
To wander through the gloom appalling,
Through crump holes deep in mud knee-high.

From Gordon Farm to Oxford Street
(These duck-boards are the very devil.)
Where strange concussions fill the air.
(I wish they'd keep the – CENSORED – things level).

Through Oxford Street we gaily slide,
And call at Batt. H.Q. to see
If there be aught that we can do
For them. (Well, just a spot for me!)

Then on through Regent Street, and thence
To Zouave Wood, where plain to see
That 'Spring is Coming', hence the change
From winter's gloom to verdancy.
    (For authority see D.R.O.)

Here Foresters make nightly play,
And in the mud hold revel high,

Recalling fancy stunts performed
At Shoreham, and at Bletchingley.

Should you but care to journey on
You'll reach, by various tortuous ways,
To Streets named Grafton, Conduit, Bond,
Where memory ever fondly strays.

And each in some peculiar way
Has charms not easy to define.
So thus the London which we knew
Remembered is along the line.

The Romance of Place-Names

('Many of the names now given to places in the battle-area will survive the war', *Daily Paper*. This should give a great chance to the Picardy Poet of the future.)

The leafy glades of 'Maida Vale'
 Are bright with bursting may,
And daffodils and violets pale
 Bedew 'The Milky Way;'
There's perfect peace in 'Regent Street',
 In 'Holborn' rural charm,
But nowhere smells the Spring so sweet
 As down by 'Stinking Farm'.

And as I rode through 'Dead Cow Lane',
 Beneath the dungeon keep
Of 'Wobbly House' that tops the plain,
 I saw a maiden peep;
Her glance was like the dappled doe's,
 She blushed with shy alarm,
As pink as any Rambler-rose
 That climbs at 'Stinking Farm'.

O maiden, if it be my fate
 To win so great a boon,
At 'Hell-fire Corner' I will wait
 Beneath the silver moon;

I'll swear no maid but thee I know
    As softly arm-in-arm
Along the 'Blarney Road' we go
    That leads to 'Stinking Farm'.

And we will wander, O my Queen,
    By many a mossy nook,
Where limpid waters flow between
    The banks of 'Beery Brook';
In 'Purgatory' we will roam
    Where blow the breezes warm,
If thou wilt come and make thy home,
    O sweet, at 'Stinking Farm'.

Edward de Stein

Sounds by Night

I hear the dull low thunder of the guns
Beyond the hills that doze uneasily,
A sullen doomful growl that ever runs
From end to end of the heavy freighted sky:
A friend of mine writes, squatted on the floor,
And scrapes by yellow spluttering candle light.
'Ah! hush!' he breathes, and gazes at the door
That creaks on rusty hinge, in pale affright.
(No words spoke he, nor I, for well we knew
What rueful things these sounds did tell.)
A pause – I hear the trees sway sighing thro'
The gloom, like dismal moan of hollow knell,
Then out across the dark, and startling me
Bursts forth a laugh, a shout of drunken glee!

R. Watson Kerr

The Song of the Reconnoitering Patrol

Oh! it's roaming in the gloaming
    When the birds have gone to roost;
When the evening hate's beginning,
    And Machine Guns do a boost;
When you're crawling on the ground,
    While the bullets flick around,
Oh! it's very jolly roaming in the gloaming.

Just roaming in the gloaming
    When the flares drop on your head.
And you wonder if your friends at home
    Will know that you are dead;
When before your straining eyes
    Countless Huns appear to rise,
It's a merry business roaming in the gloaming.

Oh! it's roaming in the gloaming
    On an old decaying cow,
When your head gets in its stomach
    And you're mixed up anyhow;
When enveloped by the smell,
    You can only whisper 'H——'.
It's a weary business roaming in the gloaming.

Just roaming in the gloaming
    When the rain begins to fall;
When you feel convinced you've lost your way
    And won't get home at all;
When you shiver and perspire,
    And trip over German wire,
Oh! it's then you're fond of roaming in the gloaming.

Oh! it's roaming in the gloaming
    When you're safely back at last;
When your sentries haven't shot you,
    And the rum is flowing fast;
When you write a grand report
    Saying more than all you ought,
That's quite the best of roaming in the gloaming.

[I oft go out at night-time]

I oft go out at night-time
    When all the sky's a-flare
And little lights of battle
    Are dancing in the air.

I use my pick and shovel
    To dig a little hole,
And there I sit till morning –
    A listening-patrol.

A silly little sickle
    Of moon is hung above;
Within a pond beside me
    The frogs are making love:

I see the German sap-head;
    A cow is lying there,
Its belly like a barrel,
    Its legs are in the air.

The big guns rip like thunder,
    The bullets whizz o'erhead,
But o'er the sea in England
    Good people lie abed.

And over there in England
    May every honest soul
Sleep sound while we sit watching
    On listening patrol.

                                    Patrick MacGill

A True Tale of the Listening Post
(Dedicated to R.E.K.)

Men are queer things right through – whatever make –
But Tommy Atkins really takes the cake.

                *   *   *

Which said, see in your mind (my point to prove)
Two soldiers, frozen and afraid to move,
On listening patrol. For four dead hours
Afraid to move or whisper, cough or sneeze,
Waiting in wonder whether 'twas the breeze
Moved in the grass, shaking the frozen flowers

Just then. Germans were out that night, we knew,
With bombs to throw, and so we lay, we two,
With rifle ready at shoulder, and . . . What's that
Twanging the wire (both heard the sound) – a rat?
Or the Bosche bomber creeping, creeping nigher
To hurl death into the trench behind us? Both
Turned barrels 'gainst the unknown, ready to fire,
Waiting to fire should ever it take form
Of human body. – Waiting, being loath
To shoot at nothing, making so alarm
And laughter in the trench we guarded. Here
Sounds a hoarse whisper against my ear:
Something it utters – 'What is it?' I hiss,
Soft as a serpent; and upon my oath
My comrade covering still the sound, said – this.
This, while the unknown stalked, and fear was chilly
Like ice around our hearts – 'I say old chap'
(My laughter followed like a thunder-clap)
'Couldn't I do some beef and piccalilli.'

*   *   *

Men are quaint things world over, willy nilly.
But R.E.K. – you take the – piccalilli.

F.W. Harvey

No Man's Land

No Man's Land is an eerie sight
At early dawn in the pale grey light.
Never a house and never a hedge
In No Man's Land from edge to edge,
And never a living soul walks there
To taste the fresh of the morning air; –
Only some lumps of rotting clay,
That were friends or foemen yesterday.

What are the bounds of No Man's Land?
You see them clearly on either hand,
A mound of rag-bags grey in the sun,
Or a furrow of brown where the earthworks run

From the Eastern hills to the Western sea,
Through field or forest o'er river and lea;
No man may pass them, but aim you well
And Death rides across on the bullet or shell.

But No Man's Land is a goblin sight
When patrols crawl over at dead o' night;
Boche or British, Belgian or French,
You dice with death when you cross the trench.
When the 'rapid', like fire-flies in the dark,
Flits down the parapet spark by spark,
And you drop for cover to keep your head
With your face on the breast of the four months' dead.

The man who ranges in No Man's Land
Is dogged by shadows on either hand
When the star-shell's flare, as it bursts o'erhead,
Scares the great grey rats that feed on the dead,
And the bursting bomb or the bayonet-snatch
May answer the click of your safety-catch,
For the lone patrol, with his life in his hand,
Is hunting for blood in No Man's Land.

James H. Knight-Adkin

On Patrol

There were dead men on the wire
Lying in the bloodied mire –
Staring wildly at the skies
With their cold and sightless eyes –
Stars grinned down with hideous faces,
And the moon was mocking them
With grimaces.

Raymond Heywood

FIVE

Out of the Line

Billets, letters from home, estaminets and concerts

Out of the line the men were billeted in barns or abandoned buildings. Here they could catch up on news from home and on sleep, although the drills and fatigues – taking materials up into the line – often made their rest even busier than their time in the trenches. They would visit communal baths – possibly old wooden vats filled with hot water – and be issued with clean uniforms, though it would not be long before the perennial problem of a soldier's life – lice, or 'chats' as they called them – would reassert themselves. Many hours were spent 'chatting', as they ran candle-flames up the seams of their clothes to burn the lice out, or picked them off one by one and burst them between their finger-nails.

There were visits to the local family-run estaminet or bar, where there might be an attractive young daughter of the house with whom they could flirt. Here they drank sometimes over-priced and almost always watered-down beer, or white wine, which they nicknamed plink-plonk after *vin blanc*, and ate egg and chips. Football matches or gymkhanas might be organised, and occasionally some kind of entertainment was laid on, either with visiting artistes or with shows put together by the men themselves. For some there were visits to local prostitutes, and venereal disease was soon a serious problem.

The Dawn
(Givenchy)

The dawn comes creeping o'er the plains,
The saffron clouds are streaked with red,
I hear the creaking limber chains,
I see the drivers raise their reins
And urge their weary mules ahead.

And men go up and men go down,
The marching hosts are grand to see
In shrapnel-shivered trench and town,
In spinneys where the leaves of brown
Are falling on the dewy lea.

Lonely and still the village lies,
The houses sleeping, the blinds all drawn.
The road is straight as the bullet flies,
And villagers fix their waking eyes
On the shrapnel smoke that shrouds the dawn.

Out of the battle, out of the night,
Into the dawn and the blush of day,
The road that takes us back from the fight,
The road we love, it is straight and white,
And it runs from the battle, away, away.

Patrick MacGill

Back in Billets

We're in billets again, and to-night, if you please,
I shall strap myself up in a Wolsey valise.
What's that, boy? Your boots give you infinite pain?
You can chuck them away: we're in billets again.

We're in billets again now and, barring alarms,
There'll be no occasion for standing to arms,
And you'll find if you'd many night-watches to keep
That the hour before daylight's the best hour for sleep.

We're feasting on chocolate, cake, currant buns,
To a faint German-band obbligato of guns,
For I've noticed, wherever the regiment may go,
That we always end up pretty close to the foe.

But we're safe out of reach of trench mortars and snipers
Five inches south-west of the 'Esses' in Ypres;
– Old Bob, who knows better, pronounces it Yper,
But don't argue the point now – you'll waken the sleeper.

Our host brings us beer up, our thirst for to quench,
So we'll drink him good fortune in English and French:
– Bob, who finds my Parisian accent a blemish,
Goes one better himself in a torrent of Flemish.

It's a fortnight on Friday since Christopher died,
And John's at Boulogne with a hole in his side,
While poor Harry's got lost, the Lord only knows where; –
May the Lord keep them all and ourselves in His care.

. . . Mustn't think we don't mind when a chap gets laid out,
They've taken the best of us, never a doubt;
But with life pretty busy and death rather near
We've no time for regret any more than for fear.

. . . Here's a health to our host, Isidore Deschildre,
Himself and his wife and their plentiful childer,
And the brave *aboyeur* who bays our return;
More power to his paws when he treads by the churn!

You may speak of the Ritz or the Curzon (Mayfair)
And maintain that they keep you in luxury there:
If you've laid for six weeks on a water-logged plain,
Here's the acme of comfort, in billets again.

Charles Scott-Moncrieff

Gonnehem

Of Gonnehem it shall be said
That we arrived there late and worn
With marching, and were given a bed
Of lovely straw. And then at morn
On rising from deep sleep saw dangle –
Shining in the sun to spangle,
The all-blue heaven – branch loads of red
Bright cherries which we bought to eat,
Dew-wet, dawn-cool, and sunny sweet.
There was a tiny court-yard, too,
Wherein one shady walnut grew.
Unruffled peace the farm encloses –
I wonder if beneath that tree,
The meditating hens still be.

Are the white walls now gay with roses?
Does the small fountain yet run free?
I wonder if that dog still dozes . . .
Some day we must go back to see.

F.W. Harvey

The Billet

A roof that hardly holds the rain;
Walls shaking to the hurricane;
Great doors upon their hinges creaking;
Great rats upon the rafters squeaking –
A midden in the courtyard reeking –
Yet oft I've sheltered, snug and warm,
Within that friendly old French farm!

To trudge in from the soaking trench –
The blasts that bite, the rains that drench –
To loosen off your ponderous pack,
To drop the harness from your back,
Deliberate pull each muddy boot
From each benumbed, frost-bitten foot;
To wrap your body in your blanket,
To mutter o'er a 'Lord be thankit!'
Sink out of sight below the straw,
Then – Owre the hills and far awa'!

*   *   *

Perchance to waken from your sleep,
And hear the big guns growling deep,
Turn on your side, but breathe a prayer
For beggars you have left up 'there'.

Then in the morn to stretch your legs,
And hear the hens cluck o'er their eggs;
And chanticleer's bestirring blare;
The whinnying of the Captain's mare;
Contented lowing of the kine,
Complacent grunting of the swine;
Chirping of birds beneath the eaves,
Whisper of winds among the leaves,
And – sound that soul of man rejoices –
The pleasant hum of women's voices –
With all the cheery dins that be
In a farmyard community;
While sunlight bursting thro' the thatch
Burns in the black barn, patch and patch.

By now your eyes and ears you ope –
The pipes are skirling, 'Johnnie Cope' –
And you arise to toil and trouble,
And certainly to 'double! double!' –
Of the day's drills, must grudged of all
That lagging hour called 'physical!'

Breakfast, of tea, and bread, and ham,
With just a colouring of jam;
Or, if you have the sous to pay,
A feast of *œufs* and *café-au-lait.*

Comes ten o'clock and we fall in,
With rifle cleaned, and shaven chin;
Once more we work the 'manual' through,
And then 'drill in platoons' we do
Till one, or maybe even two.
At last 'cook-house' the pipers play,
And so we dine as best we may.

And now a shout that never fails
To fetch us forth, 'Here come the mails!' –
While one rejoices, t'other rails
Because he has received no letter –
Next time the Fates may use him better!

Then comes an hour beneath a tree,
With 'Omar Khayyam' on your knee,
While wanton winds, in idle sport,
Bombard you after harmless sort
With apple blossoms from the bough –
Ah! here is Paradise enow!

'Tis now that mystic hour of night
When – parcels open – no respite
Is given to cake, sweetmeat, sardine;
Our zest would turn a gourmet green
With envy, could he only see
The meal out here, that's yclep 'tea'.

The night has come, and all are hearty,
Being exempt from a 'working party':
And so we gather round the fire
To chat, and presently conspire
To pass an hour with song and story –
The grave, the gay, ghostly or gory, –
A tale, let's say, both weird and fierce,
By Allan Poe or Ambrose Bierce,
Then Skerry – Peace be to his Shade! –
May play us Gounod's 'Serenade',
And, gazing thro' the broken beams,
Perchance we see the starry gleams.

*   *   *

But 'Lights-out!' sounds; 'Good nights' are said,
And so we bundle off to bed.

Sweet dreams infest each drowsy head
And kindly Ghosts that work no harm
Flit round about that old French farm!

Joseph Lee

The Camp in the Sands

Down in the hollow of the dunes one night
We made our bivouac; serene and bright
The autumn day drew to its early close.
While still the west was red, the moon arose
And flung the witchery of her silver lamp
Over the bustle of our hasty camp.
Beyond the crested dunes the windy sea
Murmured all night, now near, now distantly:
And eerily around us we could hark
The grass's widespread whisper in the dark,
As if the Little People of the Sands
Gathered about us in their stealthy bands.

Within the dip where our encampment lay
The lines of weary horses munched their hay
Or pawed the sand with quick, uneasy hoof;
A glowing cook-fire flickered red aloof,
From which a drift of soft blue smoke was blown;
The loudest voice soon sank to undertone,
Amidst the empty space 'twixt sand and sky,
Ruled by the moon that rose so splendidly.
All night around the camp our watch we kept,
Posted on crests of sandy billows; swept
From eve till dawn by the unbroken wind,
Our eyes towards the dark; our camp behind.

W. Kersley Holmes

Letters to Tommy

Oh, friends past our deserving,
    Discovered everywhere,
Who load us lucky fellows
    With things to eat and wear,
Your kindness knows no limit – you seem sincerely vexed
That ever you need ask us – 'What can we send you next?'

For packages of pastry,
    For cigarettes and sweets,
For cakes and scones and butter,
    For savoury bakemeats,

For garments that you knit us – we thank you thousandfold,
And if you ask, 'What else, now?' – why shouldn't you be told?

> When from parade returning,
>   We put our rifles by,
> There's spring in every footstep,
>   And hope in every eye;
> We hurry to our billets – yet, hungry and athirst,
> We don't stampede for dinner – we look for letters first.

> You'd laugh, or sigh, to notice
>   The pleasure fellows show
> To read their war addresses
>   In writing that they know –
> Oh, if you wish us kindly, who fight – or hope to fight –
> Don't wonder what to send us; we want you just to *write*.

W. Kersley Holmes

A Letter from Home

We sit in our tent and we're feeling forlorn,
It's raining outside and we're sorry we're born,
All the 'rookies' are sad and the trained men are quiet,
There's not a man there who is game for a riot.

But hark! down the lines a rough voice is calling,
'Tis the Orderly Corporal standing there bawling,
And the words that he shouts amoving have set us,
'Come out of your tents and fall in for your letters'.

There's one for Bill Stewart from his darling Polly,
And off to his tent he goes looking jolly.
And so it goes on till they're all given away,
Tho' there's many a chap who's forgotten to-day.

Then back they all go and you can't hear a sound
As they read them while sitting on the rough ground.
And those who have got none look on with sad eyes,
And envy the chaps who have captured a prize.

So while we do our bit to keep home fires burning,
Don't forget it's your letters for which we are yearning,
In billet or camp, and wherever we roam,
There's nothing we prize like 'a letter from home'.

Will Leslie

Letters Home
(This is Vers Libre, this is!)

Come, let me write to Melisande,
To Melisande whose moth-feet are even now
Passing, brogue-clad,
Over the valerian-coloured meadows . . .
The Postman will take the letter (with luck)
Up the street,
Up the little zig-zag village street,
Past old Ben's, the Butchers,
Who owes me two-and-fourpence;
And past the 'Yellow Unicorn'
Where Melisande is very probably
Getting off with that annoying fellow Bert.

P'raps I will write to Mother instead.

Hampden Gordon

The Dilemma
Verses on the Divers Charms of Two Young Wenches.

Erstwhile, in pedagogic garb,
I felt the urgings of the Muse,
But now I feel Love's stinging barb,
And, loving, know not where to choose.

For Julia's charms my heart entwine,
Alas! I own her kisses sweet –
Yet while I strive to make her mine,
Long for the arms of Marguerite.

Her unforgettable embrace
Makes throb my heart, my pulses beat,
Yet while I gaze on her fair face
I fly, in winged fancy fleet,

To where my Julia stands aglow
For me, her amorous dolt, to fly
From fettering wires and indents slow,
To lay me fettered to her eye.

Humble their birth, yet great their grace,
What though they thump the yeasty flour
When Julia lifts to me her face,
What man but envies me my hour?

And when, a-strolling at my ease,
I look to pass the time away,
At Marguerite a-shelling peas,
What dog but envies me my day?

Ah! pity me, poor luckless wight,
Thus envious envied, much bemused,
Yet, should I strive to set wrong right,
Who knows I were by one refused?

So deeply pledged to Marguerite,
So basely bound to Julia's nod,
My only hope's a shell to meet,
And hide my shame beneath the sod.

A Literary War Worker
(The favourite reading at the Front is, we are informed, the novelette
of the more sentimental kind.)

In these days of stress and tumult, when the frightfulness of war
Readjusts the private notions which were prejudiced before,
It behoves the present critic to express his deep regrets
For his strictures on the makers of the nation's novelettes.

He has sneered at them and found it far from easy to forgive
Their adeptness at the splitting of the frail infinitive;
He has sniggered at the love scenes, where, in sylvan spots apart,
Eva emptied over Ernest all the slop-pail of her heart.

But to-day the case is altered, now that somewhere that is French
'Tis the novelette brings comfort to the troops that man the trench;
Tommy, resting from his labours, is perusing with a zest
How Sir Blagdon hugged Belinda to his large expanse of breast.

Here's a luck to such romancing; may ideas be never short
To the British novelettist of the sentimental sort!
May whatever gods inspire him keep his fancy free and fit,
For he's Tommy's favourite reading; so he does his little bit!

T. Hodgkinson

The Sub.

He loves the Merry 'Tatler', he adores the Saucy 'Sketch',
The 'Bystander' also fills him with delight;
But the pages that he revels in, the evil-minded wretch,
Are the adverts of those things in pink and white.

They are advertised in crêpe de chine, and trimmed with silk and lace;
The pictures fairly make him long for leave;
And while he gloats upon their frills, he cannot find the grace
To read the pars of PHRYNETTE, BLANCHE and EVE.

Before the war, he'd hardly heard of lace and lingerie;
He didn't know the meaning of chemise,
But thanks to weekly papers, this astounding mystery
Has been solved by dainty VENN and dear LABISE.

Before the war, he only knew of corsets and of hats,
All other vogues invoked a ribald 'what-ho'.
But the last decree of Fashion is a dinky nightie, that's
Embroidered with his regimental motto.

It's this war that is responsible for teaching simple youth
All sorts of naughty Continental tricks;
And already he's decided, when it's over, that, in truth,
He'll buy mamma a pair of cami-knicks.

R[egimental] M[edical] O[fficer]

[There was an old dame at La Bassée]

There was an old dame at La Bassée
Who was quite undeniably passée
        When they said 'Mad'moiselle
        Vous êtes encore très belle,'
She replied 'Je suis très embarrassée.'

The Green Estaminet

The old men sit by the chimney-piece and drink the good red wine
And tell great tales of the *Soixante-Dix* to the men from the English line,
And Madame sits in her old arm-chair and sighs to herself all day –
So Madeleine serves the soldiers in the Green Estaminet.

For Madame wishes the War was won and speaks of a strange disease,
And Pierre is somewhere about Verdun, and Albert on the seas;
Le Patron, 'e is *soldat* too, but long time *prisonnier* –
So Madeleine serves the soldiers in the Green Estaminet.

She creeps downstairs when the black dawn scowls and helps at a neighbour's
    plough,
She rakes the midden and feeds the fowls and milks the lonely cow,
She mends the holes in the Padre's clothes and keeps his billet gay –
And she also serves the soldiers in the Green Estaminet.

The smoke grows thick and the wine flows free and the great round songs begin,
And Madeleine sings in her heart, maybe, and welcomes the whole world in;
But I know that life is a hard, hard thing and I know that her lips look gray,
Though she smiles as she serves the soldiers in the Green Estaminet.

But many a tired young English lad has learned his lesson there,
To smile and sing when the world looks bad, '*for, Monsieur, c'est la guerre*',
Has drunk her honour and made his vow to fight in the same good way
That Madeleine serves the soldiers in the Green Estaminet.

A big shell came on a windy night, and half of the old house went,
But half of the old house stands upright, and Mademoiselle's content;
The shells still fall in the Square sometimes, but Madeleine means to stay
So Madeleine serves the soldiers still in the Green Estaminet.

                                                            A.P. Herbert

The Penitent

As I lay in the trenches at Noove Chapelle,
Where the big guns barked like the Hounds o' Hell,
Sez I to mysel', sez I to mysel' –

Billy, me boy, here's the end o' you –
But if, by good luck, ye should chance to slip thro'
Ye'll bid all ye'r evil companions adieu;
Keep the Lord's ten Commands – and Lord Kitchener's two –
    Sez I to mysel' – at Noove Chapelle.

No more women, and no more wine,
No more hedgin' to get down the line,
No more hoggin' around like a swine,
    After Noove Chapelle – sez I to mysel'.

But only the good God in Heaven knows
The wayward way that a soldier goes,
And He must ha' left me to walk by mysel' –
    For three times I've fell, since Noove Chapelle.

Once at Bethune and twice at Estaires,
The devil gripped hould o' me unawares –
Yet often and often I've prayed me prayers,
    Since I prayed by mysel' at Noove Chapelle.

Well, the Lord above, who fashioned the French,
May bethink how bewitchin' is wine and a wench
To a chap that's been tied for three weeks to a trench,
    Around Noove Chapelle – that black border o' Hell.

And me throat was dry and the night was damp,
And the rum was raw – and red was the lamp! –
And – Billy, my boy, ye'r a bit o' a scamp,
    That's the truth to tell – tho' I sez it mysel'.

What's worritin' me isn't fear that they'll miss
Me out o' the ranks in the realms o' bliss;
It ain't hope o' Heaven, nor horror o' Hell,
But just breakin' the promise, 'twixt God and mysel',
    Made at Noove Chapelle.

Well, there's always a way that is open to men
When they gets the knock-out – that's get up again;
And, sure now, ould Satan ain't yet counted ten!
I'm game for another good bout wi' mysel' –
    As at Noove Chapelle.

                                        Joseph Lee

Concert

Mark i, Easy, Free and

To-night it's 'Free and Easy'
    And William's going to sing
His repertoire's as breezy
    As Robey, Earl of Bing.
Oh, Censor, do be careful,
    When we all shout for more,
What William may
    Produce by way
Of his umpteenth encore.

Mark ii, Refined
(Shall I try that vers libre stunt again? Certainly.)

A Rest-Camp.
Somewhere . . . Sometime . . .
And the Y.M. tent crowded . . . crowded . . .
And again, crowded.
Silence.
The tense silence of dense masses of tens of
Tense men in tents . . .
Then a Voice . . .
Oh dear me, what a Voice!
And the hoarse applause of scores of paws on paws;
Because
Of the sweet politeness of them,
And the great good nature of them,
And also because a man can only die once . . .
Generally speaking.

Mark iii, Fluffy

And is She really coming –
    The one with the long black tights?
'Me and My Girl' they are strumming –
    'Minds me of Empire nights,
And Margate . . . and the Follies . . .
    Lor lumme, can't she dance!
It's not *all* plum-and-apple
        Out in France.

Hampden Gordon

Going up the Line

O consolation and refreshment breathed
From the young Spring with apple-blossom wreathed,

Whose certain coming blesses
All life with token of immortality,
And from the ripe beauty and human tendernesses
And reconcilement and tranquillity
Which are the spirit of all things grown old.
    For now that I have seen
The curd-white hawthorn once again
    Break out on the new green,
And through the iron gates in the long blank wall
    Have viewed across a screen
Of rosy apple-blossom the grey spire
And low red roofs and humble chimney-stacks,
And stood in spacious courtyards of old farms,
And heard green virgin wheat sing to the breeze
And the drone of ancient worship rise and fall
In the dark church, and talked with simple folk
Of farm and village, dwelling near the earth,
Among earth's ancient elemental things:
    I can with heart made bold
Go back into the ways of ruin and death
With step unflagging and with quiet breath,
For drawn from the hidden Spirit's deepest well
I carry in my soul a power to quell
    All ills and terrors such as they can hold.

                                                Martin Armstrong

Back to the Trenches

        Unrest is in the trees
        And billowy clouds drive by:
        The curvèd moon rides high
        Like a ship midst stormy seas.

        Beneath her fitful light,
        To the trench's treachery
        And all Fate may decree,
        Fearless we march to-night.

        The reflected life of man
        'Neath the moon's reflected light,
        Riding its stormy night
        To the end no eye may scan.

                                                F.W. Harvey

SIX

Flanders, Gallipoli and the Mediterranean

The Second Battle of Ypres and first use of gas,
Gallipoli, Salonika, Egypt

As spring came, military operations began once more. In March 1915 the British attempted to break through the German line at Neuve Chapelle towards Aubers Ridge and the important railhead at Lille. They captured the village but were unable to advance further. The following month the Germans attacked at Ypres, and the Canadians suffered heavy casualties from the German use of a new and lethal weapon for which the defending troops were ill prepared – poisonous gas. Its use was greeted with outrage. A veteran later wrote that with the introduction of gas warfare a 'final stage seemed to be reached in the whole tendency of modern scientific warfare to depress and make of no effect individual bravery, enterprise, and skill'.

Meanwhile, Turkey had entered the war on the German side. In an attempt to break the stalemate on the Western Front, Winston Churchill, then First Lord of the Admiralty, proposed a second front against the Turks in the Dardanelles, with the intention of drawing enemy troops away from France and Belgium while at the same time opening up the Black Sea to allow free movement of supplies to and from Russia.

The campaign was doomed from the start. The Cabinet gave it only half-hearted support, premature, ill-conceived naval bombardment alerted the Turks, and the plans were so freely talked about that no surprise was possible. On 25 April 1915 the British landed at Cape Helles on the southern tip of the Gallipoli peninsular and at the isolated, undefended and precipitous Y beach 4 miles up the western coast. The Australian and New Zealand troops were to come ashore at the sandy bay of Gaba Tepe further north, but in the darkness they were swept by strong currents to a steeply cliffed inlet, later known as Anzac Cove. As opportunities were missed, there began months of desperate warfare where the terrain and conditions were as much the enemy as were the Turkish defenders. Casualties were appalling, the heat overwhelming, flies multiplied and dysentery was endemic. In the narrow foothold that the Allies had secured, there were no back areas to which tired men could escape. A second landing further north at Suvla Bay in August was no more successful than the first, and in November there were terrible storms, with torrential rain followed by a blizzard and sub-zero temperatures with which the weakened men, in their cotton drill clothes, could ill cope. Many drowned and others froze to death.

Meanwhile, attacks had been launched against the Turks in Mesopotamia. The British landed in Basra and advanced towards Baghdad, but there was inadequate strategic planning and a shortage of supplies. In November 1915 they were forced to retreat to Kut, where they were besieged for the next five months. Others serving in the Middle East and around the Mediterranean saw themselves as a forgotten army.

At the end of 1915 it was decided that Gallipoli should be evacuated. This began on 18 December and was completed on 8 January. After the failure of the landings it was brilliantly executed, for there was not a single loss of life – apart from the horses and mules, whose throats were cut so that they would not fall into Turkish hands. For many, the abandonment of the dead was the hardest part of the evacuation.

Despite its failure, the campaign saw the birth of independence of the antipodean nations, as the Australian and New Zealand Army Corps – the ANZACs – proved their courage and self-determination.

Lines Written in a Fire-Trench

'Tis midnight, and above the hollow trench,
Seen through a gaunt wood's battle-blasted trunks
And the stark rafters of a shattered grange,
The quiet sky hangs huge and thick with stars.
And through the vast gloom, murdering its peace,
Guns bellow and their shells rush swishing ere
They burst in death and thunder, or they fling
Wild jangling spirals round the screaming air.
Bullets whine by, and Maxims drub like drums,
And through the heaped confusion of all sounds
One great gun drives its single vibrant 'Broum'.
And scarce five score of paces from the wall
Of piled sand-bags and barb-toothed nets of wire,
(So near and yet what thousand leagues away)

The unseen foe both adds and listens to
The selfsame discord, eyed by the same stars.
Deep darkness hides the desolated land,
Save where a sudden flare sails up and bursts
In whitest glare above the wilderness,
And for one instant lights with lurid pallor
The tense, packed faces in the black redoubt.
Written in fire trench above 'Glencorse Wood', Westhoeck, 11 April, 1915.

W.S.S. Lyon

Poison

21st April 1919
(At Ypres, on April the 21st, 1915, the Huns made their first gas-attack.)*

Forget, and forgive them – you say:
    War's bitterness passes;
Wild rose wreaths the gun-pit to-day,
    Where the trench was, young grass is;
    Forget and forgive;
    Let them live.

Forgive them – you say – and forget;
    Since struggle is finished,
Shake hands, be at peace, square the debt,
    Let old hates be diminished;
    Abandon blockade:
    Let them trade.

Fools! Shall the pard change his skin
    Or cleanse one spot from it?
As the letcher returns to his sin
    So the cur to its vomit.
    Fools! Hath the Hun
    Earned place in the sun?

You who accuse that I fan
    War's spark from hate's ember,
Forgive and forget if you can;
    But I, I remember

---

* In fact, the first gas attack was on 22 April 1915.

Men who faced death,
   Choking for breath,

Four years back to a day –
   Men who fought cleanly.
Killed, say you? Murdered, *I* say,
   Murdered most meanly,
   Poisoned! . . . And yet,
   You can forget.

Gilbert Frankau

[There was a little Turk, and Baghdad was his home]

There was a little Turk, and Baghdad was his home,
There was a little Hun, and he lived in Bapaume,
Each said to the other, as they shivered with alarm,
'To find another home wouldn't do us any harm'.

Y Beach

Y Beach, the Scottish Borderer cried,
While panting up the steep hill side,
                Y Beach!
To call this thing a beach is stiff,
It's nothing but a bloody cliff:
                Why Beach?

Jack Churchill

For the Gallipoli Peninsula
History of the Great Fight
April 25th, 1915

Halt! Thy tread is on heroes' graves,
   English lads lie sleeping below,
Just rough wooden crosses at their heads,
   To let their comrades know.
They'd sleep no better for marble ones
   Or monuments so grand,
They sleep in tranquil contentment
   In that far off Turkish land.

I've often passed those little mounds,
    Where the deadly bullets me-ow,
And the air was full of shrapnel,
    'Tis called shrapnel gully now.
Whilst coming from the trenches,
    And glancing over there,
I've often seen many a khaki form
    Kneeling in silent prayer.

There's many a loving mother,
    Home in England dear,
Who is weeping and broken-hearted
    O'er her loved son lonely there.
There's many a true English girl
    Stricken with sudden pain,
Mourning for her fallen sweetheart
    Whom she'll never see again.

They know not where he lies,
    Nor how he fell.
That's why I'm writing these few lines
    The simple truth to tell.
Their graves are on Gallipoli,
    Up in the very heights,
Above the first great landing place,
    Scene of the first great fight.

Officers and men who fell
    In that first fierce rush of fame,
They lie there side by side,
    Their rank is now the same;
The city boy who left the pen,
    The country boy the plough,
They trained together in England,
    They sleep together now.

Sleep on! Fallen comrades,
    You'll ne'er be forgotten by
The boys who fought with you
    And the boys who saw you die.
Your graves may be neglected
    But fond memory will remain,

> The story of your gallant charge
>   Will ease the grief and pain.

> PS – That we know your kin are feeling,
>   Over there across the foam,
> And we'll tell the story of your fall,
>   Should we e'er reach Home Sweet Home.

J. Stewart

Fighting Hard
'The Australians are fighting hard in Gallipoli' – Cable.

Rolling out to fight for England, singing songs across the sea;
Rolling North to fight for England, and to fight for you and me;
Fighting hard for France and England, where the storms of Death are hurled;
Fighting hard for Australasia and the honour of the World!
       Fighting hard.

Fighting hard for Sunny Queensland – fighting for Bananaland,
Fighting hard for West Australia, and the mulga and the sand;
Fighting hard for Plain and Wool-Track, and the haze of western heat –
Fighting hard for South Australia and the bronze of Farrar's Wheat!
       Fighting hard.

Fighting hard for fair Victoria, and the mountain and the glen;
(And the Memory of Eureka – there were other tyrants then),
For the glorious Gippsland forests and the World's great Singing Star –
For the irrigation channels where the cabbage gardens are –
       Fighting hard.

Fighting hard for gale and earthquake, and the wind-swept ports between;
For the wild flax and manuka and the terraced hills of green.
Fighting hard for wooden homesteads, where the mighty kauris stand –
Fighting hard for fern and tussock! – Fighting hard for Maoriland!
       Fighting hard.

Fighting hard for little Tassy, where the apple orchards grow;
(And the Northern Territory just to give the place a show),
Fighting hard for Home and Empire, while the Commonwealth prevails –
And, in spite of all her blunders, dying hard for New South Wales.
       Dying hard.

Fighting for the Pride of Old Folk, and the people that you know;
And the girl you left behind you – (ah! the time is passing slow).
For the proud tears of a sister! come you back, or never come!
And the weary Elder Brother, looking after things at home –
Fighting hard! *You Lucky Devils!*
    Fighting hard.

Henry Lawson

Anzac Cove

There's a lonely stretch of hillocks.
    There's a beach asleep and drear.
There's a battered broken fort beside the sea.
There are sunken trampled graves,
    There's a little rotting pier,
And winding paths that wind unceasingly.

There's a torn and silent valley.
    There's a tiny rivulet
With some blood upon the stones beside its mouth.
There are lines of buried bones.
    There's an unpaid waiting debt.
There's a sound of gentle sobbing in the south.

Leon Gellert

Twitting the Turk

The Turk, he is an honest man,
    And fights us fair and true,
But we annoy him all we can
    As we are paid to do;
It's very hard to *keep* him riled;
We find him strangely reconciled
And things that once just made him wild
    He takes a liking to.

The bully tin no more insults,
    The Libby gives no grief,
That used to soar from catapults
    And biff the shocked Redif;
At first it gave him quite a turn,
The flight of that innocuous urn,

And then he spoiled the whole concern
   By gobbling up the beef.

Yet when the cruder kind of wheeze
   No longer irritates,
There's one that never fails to tease
   His friends across the Straits,
Where many a Moslem scans our slopes
(With now and then some cramp, one hopes,
From looking long through telescopes)
   And simply hates and hates.

We go and bathe, in shameless scores,
   Beneath his baleful een,
Disrobe, unscathed, on sacred shores
   And wallow in between;
Nor does a soldier there assume
His university costume,
And though it makes the Faithful fume
   It makes the Faithless clean.

Ay, all our arts have some reward,
   But this I think's the peach,
For man can bear the invader's horde,
   That riots in his reach,
That raids his roost in armèd swarms
Or swamps his citadels with storms,
But not their nude insulting forms
   A-bathing off his beach.

                          A.P. Herbert

A Dug-out Lament

It ain't the work and it ain't the Turk
   That causes us to swear,
But it's havin' to fight at dark midnight
   With the things in our underwear.
To-day there's a score – to-morrow lots more
   Of these rotters – it ain't too nice
To sit skin-bare in keen morning air
   Lookin' for bloomin' ——.

They're black an' grey an' brindle an' white,
    An' red an' big an' small,
They steeplechase around our knees –
    We cannot sleep at all! –
They're in our tunics, and in our shirts,
    They take a power of beating,
So for goodness sake, if you're sending us cake,
    Send also a tin of Keating.

T.A. Saxon

The Hospital Ship

There is a green-lit hospital ship,
Green, with a crimson cross,
Lazily swaying there in the bay,
Lazily bearing my friend away,
Leaving me dull-sensed loss.
Green-lit, red-lit hospital ship,
Numb is my heart, but you carelessly dip
There in the drift of the bay.

There is a green-lit hospital ship,
Dim as the distance grows,
Speedily steaming out of the bay,
Speedily bearing my friend away
Into the orange-rose.
Green-lit, red-lit hospital ship,
Dim are my eyes, but you heedlessly slip
Out of their sight from the bay.

*   *   *

There was a green-lit hospital ship,
Green, with a blood-red cross,
Lazily swaying there in the bay,
But it went out with the light of the day –
Out where the white seas toss.
Green-lit, red-lit hospital ship,
Cold are my hands and trembling my lip:
Did you make home from the bay?

W.H. Littlejohn

The Blizzard
Suvla, November 27, 1915

The night was dark as hell-mouth, the wind was bitter cold,
And there was little comfort in a sodden blanket rolled.
A foot or more of water, an inch or two of mud
Was what we had to walk in before came down – the flood.
It caught the shivering sentries along the parapet,
The front trench was abrim before they knew that they were wet,
Full seven feet deep the trenches were, the men were weighted down
With kit and ammunition, and mostly had to drown.
Behind was soon no better, a million tons of rain
Came swirling thro' the section by dug-out, sap and drain,
Headquarters, store and cook-house, bomb-shelter, splinter-proof,
Were all filled up with water, and in fell every roof.
Scummy and dark and icy, the torrent at a touch
Sucked in the greasy trench-walls that mocked the drowning clutch.
And now the land was covered, and now with choking breath
The wretched victims unawares stepped into hidden death.
Behind the up-flung parados – half buried in the slime,
Their fingers numb and useless – their rifles choked with grime.
Thro' thirty hours of darkness and twenty hours of day,
Foodless and drinkless (save the mark), a frozen handful lay.
My friends at home – at breakfast you saw a casual hint
Of half a quarter of the truth in seven lines of print.
But somewhere in the sullen sky that seemed to mock our woes
God saw my soldiers freeze and drown. It is enough. He knows.

F.W.D. Bendall

The Unburied

Now snowflakes thickly falling in the winter breeze
Have cloaked alike the hard, unbending ilex
And the grey, drooping branches of the olive trees,
    Transmuting into silver all their lead;
And, in between the winding lines, in No-Man's Land,
Have softly covered with a glittering shroud
      The unburied dead.

And in the silences of night, when winds are fair,
When shot and shard have ceased their wild surprising,

I hear a sound of music in the upper air,
   Rising and falling till it slowly dies –
It is the beating of the wings of migrant birds
Wafting the souls of these unburied heroes
     Into the skies.

Evacuation of Gallipoli

Not only muffled is our tread to cheat the foe.
We fear to rouse our honoured dead to hear us go.
Sleep sound, old friends – the keenest smart
Which, more than failure, wounds the heart
   Is thus to leave you – thus to part.
    Comrades, farewell!!

Alfred Leslie Guppy

Mudros after the Evacuation

I laughed to see the gulls that dipped to cling
To the torn edge of surge and blowing spray,
Where some gaunt battleship, a rolling king,
Still dreams of phantom battles in the bay.
I saw a cloud, a full-blown cotton flower
Drift vaguely like a wandering butterfly,
I laughed to think it bore no pregnant shower
Of blinding shrapnel scattered from the sky.
Life bore new hope. An army's great release
From a closed cage walled in by fire and sea,
From the hushed pause and swooping plunge of shells,
Sped in a night. Here children in strange peace,
Seek solitude to dull the tragedy
And needless horror of the Dardanelles.

Geoffrey Dearmer

The Graves of Gallipoli

The herdman wandering by the lonely rills
   Marks where they lie on the scarred mountain's flanks,
Remembering that wild morning when the hills
   Shook to the roar of guns and those wild ranks
    Surged upward from the sea.

None tends them. Flowers will come again in spring,
 And the torn hills and those poor mounds be green.
Some bird that sings in English woods may sing
  To English lads beneath – the wind will keep
   Its ancient lullaby.

Some flower that blooms beside the Southern foam
 May blossom where our dead Australians lie,
And comfort them with whispers of their home;
  And they will dream, beneath the alien sky,
   Of the Pacific Sea.

'Thrice happy they who fell beneath the walls,
 Under their father's eyes', the Trojan said,
'Not we who die in exile where who falls
  Must lie in foreign earth.' Alas! our dead
   Lie buried far away.

Yet where the brave man lies who fell in fight
 For his dear country, there his country is.
And we will mourn them proudly as of right –
  For meaner deaths be weeping and loud cries:
   They died pro patria!

Oh, sweet and seemly so to die, indeed,
 In the high flush of youth and strength and pride.
These are our martyrs, and their blood the seed
  Of nobler futures. 'Twas for us they died.
   Keep we their memory green.

This be their epitaph. 'Traveller, south or west,
 Go, say at home we heard the trumpet call,
And answered. Now beside the sea we rest.
  Our end was happy if our country thrives:
Much was demanded. Lo! our store was small –
   That which we had we gave – it was our lives.'

Gallipoli – In Memoriam

There is a barren and forbidding shore
    Where blue waves lap a narrow sand-strewn strand,
Where spirits shall keep guard for evermore
    O'er fifty thousand heroes of our land.
There winds and waters ever chant the fame
    And matchless valour of that dauntless band,
And generations yet shall laud their name
    Whose death enriched the glory of our land.

Steep rocky cliffs that wild goat feared to climb
    These valiant warriors scaled and met their foe,
Amid those rocks with bravery sublime
    They fought and fell. Now o'er the sands below –
Those golden sands that saw their life-blood drain –
    The restless ocean rolls at full of tide,
And sea waves sob and throb their sad refrain
    To Britain's heroes, lying side by side.

                        Will Leslie

Mesopotamian Alphabet

 was an Apple that grew so they say,
In the garden of Eden down Kurna way,
Till Eve came along and ate it one day,
And got thrown out of Mesopotamia.

 is the Biscuit that's made in Delhi,
It breaks your teeth and bruises your belly,
And grinds your intestines into a jelly,
In the land of Mesopotamia.

C is the poor old Indian Corps,
Which went to France and fought in the war,
Now it gathers the crops and fights no more
In the land of Mesopotamia.

D is the Digging we've all of us done
Since first we started to fight the Hun,
By now we've shifted ten thousand ton
Of matter in Mesopotamia.

was the Energy shown by the Staff
Before the much-advertised Hanna strafe,
Yet the nett result was the Turks had a laugh
At our Staff in Mesopotamia.

stands for 'Fritz' who flies in the sky,
To bring down the brute we've had many a try,
But the shells we shoot with all pass him by
And fall in Mesopotamia.

is the Grazing we do all the day,
We fervently hope that some day we may
Get issued again with a ration of hay,
'Though we're still in Mesopotamia.

are the Harems, which it appears
Have flourished in Baghdad for hundreds of years,
We propose to annex all the destitute dears –
When their husbands leave Mesopotamia.

is the Indian Government, but
About this I'm told I must keep my mouth shut,
For it's all due to them that we failed to reach Kut-
El-Amara in Mesopotamia.

is the Jam, with the label that lies,
And states that in Paris it won the First Prize,
But out here we use it for catching the flies
That swarm in Mesopotamia.

are the Kisses from lips sweet and fair,
Waiting for us around Leicester Square
When we wend our way home, after wasting a year
Or two in Mesopotamia.

is the Loot we hope we shall seize –
Wives and wine and bags of rupees,
When the Mayor of Baghdad hands over the keys
To the British in Mesopotamia.

M is the local Mosquito, whose bite
Keeps us awake all the hours of the night,
And makes all our faces a horrible sight
In the land of Mesopotamia.

N is the Navy that's tied to the shore,
They've lashings of beer, and provisions galore,
How I wish I had joined as a sailor before
I came out to Mesopotamia.

O are the orders we get from the Corps,
Thank goodness by now we are perfectly sure
If issued at three they'll be cancelled by four –
In this land of Mesopotamia.

P are the Postal officials who fail
To deliver each week more than half of our mail;
If they had their deserts they'd all be in jail
Instead of in Mesopotamia.

Q 's the Quinine which we take every day
To keep the Malarial fever away,
Which we're bound to get sooner or later, they say,
If we stop here in Mesopotamia.

R 's for the Rations they give us to eat,
For brekker there's biscuits, for dinner there's meat,
And if we've been good we get jam as a treat
For our tea in Mesopotamia.

S & T are supposed to supply
The Army with food, we all hope when they die
They will go to a spot as hot and as dry
As this rotten old Mesopotamia.

U is the Lake know as Um-el-Brahm
Which guards our left flank from all possible harm,
And waters old G——s barley farm
In the middle of Mesopotamia.

is the Victory won at Dijailah,
I heard it first from a pal who's a sailor
Who read it in Reuter on board his Mahola
On the Tigris in Mesopotamia.

stands for Wonder and pain
With which we regard the infirm and insane
Old *...... .... this campaign
We're waging in Mesopotamia.
[* CENSORED – ED.]

are the 'Xtras the Corps say we get,
But so far there isn't a unit I've met
That has drawn a single one of them yet
Since they landed in Mesopotamia.

is the Yearning we feel every day
For a passage to Basrah, and so to Bombay;
If we get there we'll see that we stop right away
From this wilderness Mesopotamia.

I've tried very hand, and at last I had hit
On a verse which this damnable letter would fit,
But the Censor deleted it – every bit
Save the last word 'Mesopotamia.'

Chahels is really a horrible spot
Where there isn't a drop of drink to be got,
Yet here we're going to be left till we rot
In the Middle of Mesopotamia.

Salonika in November

Up above the grey hills the wheeling birds are calling,
    Round about the cold grey hills in never-resting flight;
Far along the marshes a drifting mist is falling,
    Scattered tents and sandy plain melt into the night.

Round about the grey hills rumbles distant thunder,
    Echoes of the mighty guns firing night and day, –

Grey guns, long guns, that smite the hills asunder,
    Grumbling and rumbling, and telling of the fray.

Out among the islands twinkling lights are glowing,
    Distant little fairy lights, that gleam upon the bay;
All along the broken road grey transport wagons going
    Up to where the long grey guns roar and crash away.

Up above the cold grey hills the wheeling birds are crying,
    Brother calls to brother, as they pass in restless flight.
Lost souls, dead souls, voices of the dying,
    Circle o'er the hills of Greece and wail into the night.

Brian Hill

June in Egypt, 1916

June! – and, here,
Quivering heat,
Shimmering sand,
An aching land
Of sun's beat
And straggling, sere,
Wizened scrub;
Of mile on mile
Of nothingness
Scorched by the stress
Of some most vile
Beelzebub.
In this hell
Humankind
(You and I)
Live (and die)
Bent in mind
On killing well . . .
Over away
Across the plain
Of baking sand,
In an alien land
Ripe to be slain,
Ready to slay,
Other men

(Like you and me)
Scorch and endure,
Plan and procure,
Incessantly,
To kill again . . .
June, here;
This year.

June! – and there
The grasses stand
Green and tall,
And cuckoos call,
By Overstrand –
By Mundesley, where
The air breathes sweet
Of crisp dry turf
(O! wine-like smell
I love so well)
And salt from the surf;
Where lovers meet,
As I and a maid
(Divine with youth,
In her eyes
The light that cries
A splendid truth –
Unafraid)
Met long ago
(Before this hell)
Met and loved,
Loved, and proved
Love was well,
Long, long ago . . .
June, there;
Yester year.

El Qantara, 1916
Eliot Crawshay Williams

SEVEN

Conscription, Protest and Prisoners

Loos, Christmas 1915, protests at home and abroad,
the Derby Scheme, conscription and conscientious objection,
prisoners of war

After the failure of the earlier campaigns in 1915, the British attacked at Loos, south of Ypres, in September. The attack was a failure, partly because of shortage of shells and the poor quality of many of those that were sent; the German wire was largely uncut, and the British advanced into impenetrable defences. The scandal brought an end to the career of the British Commander-in-Chief, Sir John French, and the fall of Asquith's government. Haig was sent out to replace French, and Lloyd George became Prime Minister. The disaster led to the soldiers' song: 'If you want to find the ol' battalion, they're hanging on the ol' barbed wire.'

Failures in leadership meant that questions were now increasingly being asked about the conduct and purpose of the war. There was industrial unrest at home, and, although more than two million men had volunteered, a slowing down of recruitment and mounting casualties meant that more were needed. To begin with, those still eligible were given the opportunity to register voluntarily under the Derby Scheme, where they would then be called upon only if required, but at the end of December 1915 conscription was announced. By the summer of 1916 all men between 18 and 41 could expect to be called up – by April 1918 this would be 17 and 51 – and many previously turned down as medically unsound were re-examined and passed fit. Those who had moral objections to fighting – conscientious objectors, popularly known as 'COs' or 'conshies' – were allowed to plead their case in special courts, and might then be given work that did not involve fighting but that supported the war effort. Many joined the Friends' Ambulance Unit. Others believed that any support of the war was morally indefensible, and many of those who refused to participate were sent to prison. Here handwritten magazines were illicitly circulated among the prisoners, like the *Winchester Whisperer* put together by prisoners in Winchester Gaol.

Meanwhile there were other prisoners, as British troops fell into the hands of the Germans and spent the rest of the war in prison camps.

In the Morning
(Loos, 1915)

The firefly haunts were lighted yet,
    As we scaled the top of the parapet;
But the East grew pale to another fire,
    As our bayonets gleamed by the foeman's wire;
And the sky was tinged with gold and grey,
    And under our feet the dead men lay,
Stiff by the loop-holed barricade;
    Food of the bomb and the hand-grenade;
Still in the slushy pool and mud –
    Ah! the path we came was a path of blood,
        When we went to Loos in the morning.

A little grey church at the foot of a hill,
    With powdered glass on the window-sill.
The shell-scarred stone and the broken tile,
    Littered the chancel, nave and aisle –
Broken the altar and smashed the pyx,
    And the rubble covered the crucifix;
This we saw when the charge was done,
    And the gas-clouds paled in the rising sun,
        As we entered Loos in the morning.

The dead men lay on the shell-scarred plain,
    Where Death and the Autumn held their reign –
Like banded ghosts in the heavens grey
    The smoke of the powder paled away;
Where riven and rent the spinney trees
    Shivered and shook in the sullen breeze,
And there, where the trench through the graveyard wound,
    The dead men's bones stuck over the ground
        By the road to Loos in the morning.

The turret towers that stood in the air,
    Sheltered a foeman sniper there –
They found, who fell to the sniper's aim,
    A field of death on the field of fame;

And stiff in khaki the boys were laid
  To the sniper's toll at the barricade,
But the quick went clattering through the town,
  Shot at the sniper and brought him down,
    As we entered Loos in the morning.

The dead men lay on the cellar stair,
  Toll of the bomb that found them there,
In the street men fell as a bullock drops,
  Sniped from the fringe of Hulluch copse.
And the choking fumes of the deadly shell
  Curtained the place where our comrades fell,
This we saw when the charge was done,
  And the East blushed red to the rising sun
    In the town of Loos in the morning.

Patrick MacGill

After Loos

(Café Pierre Le Blanc, Nouex-les-Mines, Michaelmas Eve, 1915.)

Was it only yesterday
Lusty comrades marched away?
Now they're covered up with clay.

Seven glasses used to be
Called for six good mates and me –
Now we only call for three.

Little crosses neat and white,
Looking lonely every night,
Tell of comrades killed in fight.

Hearty fellows they have been,
And no more will they be seen
Drinking wine in Nouex-les-Mines.

Lithe and supple lads were they,
Marching merrily away –
Was it only yesterday?

Patrick MacGill

Christmas Truce

In France, maybe, war-weary men,
Thinking once more of home and peace,
Will bid this daily horror cease,
And call the truce of God again.

Will meet their enemy, and call
Him friend, and take him by the hand,
And, for the moment understand,
The bloody folly of it all.

But while in Flanders foe is friend,
Far from the shell-scarred battle-line
Old men will sit and sip their wine,
And talk about 'the bitter end'.

And reckon up the tale of dead,
And hate the foe they never saw,
And vow to carry on the war
Till the last drop of bleed be shed.

So they will stop the truce of Christ,
Will bid the battle re-begin;
And for the Elder Statesmen's sin
More young lives shall be sacrificed.

                                        W.N. Ewer

A Soldier's Testament

If I come to die
    In this inhuman strife,
I grudge it not, if I
    By laying down my life
Do aught at all to bring
    A day of charity,
When pride of lord or king
    Un-powerful shall be
To spend the nations' store,
    To spill the peoples' blood;

Whereafter evermore
    Humanity's full flood
Untroubled on shall roll
    In a rich tide of peace,
And the world's wondrous soul
    Uncrucified increase.
But if my life be given
    Merely that lords and kings
May say: 'We well have striven!
    See! where our banner flings
Its folds upon the breeze
    (Thanks, noble sirs, to you!).
See! how the lands and seas
    Have changed their pristine hue'.
If after I am dead
    On goes the same old game,
With monarchs seeing red
    And ministers aflame,
And nations drowning deep
    In quarrels not their own,
And peoples called to reap
    The woes they have not sown . . .
If all we who are slain
    Have died, despite our hope,
Only to twist again
    The old kaleidoscope –
Why then, by God! we're sold!
    Cheated and wronged! betrayed!
Our youth and lives and gold
    Wasted – the homes we'd made
Shattered – in folly blind,
    By treachery and spite,
By cowardice of mind
    And little men and light! . . .
If there be none to build
    Out of this ruined world
The temple we have willed
    With our flag there unfurled,
If rainbow none there shine
    Across these skies of woe,

If seed of yours and mine
    Through this same hell must go,
Then may my soul and those
    Of all who died in vain
(Be they of friends or foes)
    Rise and come back again
From peace that knows no end,
    From faith that knows not doubt,
To haunt and sear and rend
    The men that sent us out.

Bir el Mazar, Egypt
Eliot Crawshay Williams

The Cry

'Give us Peace!' cry the Peoples as they listen to their lords,
As they read the nimble speeches that are deadlier than swords.
'Give us Peace, though Peace be bitter with the memory of Woe
And the dead go past in millions, victor, vanquished, friend and foe.'
You have made your maps so proudly with their cruel crimson lines,
Secret schemes of shrieking conquest, treaties shaped of mad designs;
You have made us drunk with anger, you have poisoned us with lies
Till the Earth is desolation and a horror cleaves the skies.

Lo, your maps are madman-fancies! lo, your treaties curl in flame
If they be not drawn by Justice, if they spell a people's shame!
Lo, your lust of hate has shrivelled in the furnace of our pain!
You, who gave us war and torment, give the Peoples Peace again!
'Give us Peace! Our hearts are sickened with the terror of the strife;
Give the son back to the mother, and the husband to the wife!'
And the dead, the broken millions – let their supplication cease –
They are crying with living and the dying, 'Give us Peace!'

To any Diplomatist

Heading nought else, your subtle game you played,
Took tricks and lost them, reckoned up the score,
Balanced defeats with triumphs, less with more,
And plotted how the next point might be made:

How some sly move with counter moves to meet,
How by some crafty stratagem to gain
This empty point of honour, how obtain
That barren symbol of a foe's defeat.

Engrossed, you never cared to realise
The folly of the things for which you fought,
The hideous peril which your striving brought –
A witless struggle for a worthless prize!
God! Were you fiends or fools, who, in your game,
Heedless, have set the circling earth aflame?

W.N. Ewer

From the Youth of all Nations

Think not, my elders, to rejoice
    When from the nations' wreck we rise,
With a new thunder in our voice,
    And a new lightning in our eyes.

You called with patriotic sneers,
    And drums and sentimental songs.
We came from out the vernal years
    Thus bloodily to right your wrongs.

The sins of many centuries,
    Sealed by your indolence and fright,
Have earned us these our agonies:
    The thunderous appalling night,

When from the lurid darkness came
    The pains of poison and of shell,
The broken heart, the world's ill-fame,
    The lonely arrogance of hell.

Faintly, as from a game afar,
    Your wrangles and your patronage
Come drifting to the work of war
    Which you have made our heritage.

Oh, chide us not. Not ours the crime.
    Oh, praise us not. It is not won,
The fight which we shall make sublime
    Beneath an unaccustomed sun.

The simple world of childhood fades
    Beyond the Styx that all have passed;
This is a novel land of shades,
    Wherein no ancient glories last.

A land of desolation, blurred
    By mists of penitence and woe,
Where every hope must be deferred,
    And every river backward flow.

Not on this grey and ruined plain
    Shall we obedient recall
Your cities to rebuild again
    For their inevitable fall.

We kneel at no ancestral shrine.
    With admirable blasphemy
We desecrate the old divine,
    And dream a new eternity.

Destroy the history of men,
    The weary cycle of decay.
We shall not pass that way again,
    We tread a new untrodden way.

Though scattered wider yet our youth,
    On every sea and continent,
There shall come bitter with the truth
    A fraction of the sons you sent.

When slowly with averted head,
    Some darkly, some with halting feet,
And bowed with mourning for the dead
    We walk the cheering, fluttering street,

A music terrible, austere
    Shall rise from our returning ranks,
To change your merriment to fear,
    And slay upon your lips your thanks.

And on the brooding weary brows
    Of stronger sons, close enemies,
Are writ the ruin of your house,
    And swift usurping dynasties.

H.C. Harwood

Sonnet of a Son

Because I am young, therefore I must be killed;
Because I am strong, so must my strength be maimed;
Because I love this life (thus it is willed)
The joy of life from me a forfeit's claimed.
If I were old or weak, if foul disease
Had robbed me of all love of living – then
Life would be mine to use as I might please; –
Such the all-wise arbitraments of men!
Poor mad mankind that like some Herod calls
For one wide holocaust of youth and strength!
Bitter your wakening when the curtain falls
Upon your drunken drama, and at length
With vision uninflamed you then behold
A world of sick and halt and weak and old.

Eliot Crawshay Williams

A Veteran's View

'You want to fight if you've a chance?
    You must be mad! You must be drunk!
    Romance!!!
  War's run
By a crew of damned clerks, on a set of damned stools!
  War's won
By a lot of damned fools
    In a damned funk!!'

Charles T. Foxcroft

Socialist

(Any Nation)

'Leave me alone; I do not want your war:
War that means fools cutting each others' throats
While smug sleek diplomats in dulcet notes
Prate on of God (does it not ever jar?).
Yes, you may call me coward if you please,
Bellow that "we" are battling for the Right,
"We!" – you must seek some subtler sophistries,
There'd be no wars if *you* had but to fight.
Oh! that the world were not so darkly blind,
That men would see the poor fooled things they are,
And make that fawning dog Democracy
Turn on its master 'stead of on its kind.
Sirs, I've no quarrel – save with Some on High;
Leave me alone; to Hell with you, and War!'

Eliot Crawshay Williams

The Pity of It

When memory of Prussian foulness fails,
　　One thing will keep its fame
　　Of cruelty and shame –
The strike in Wales.

To the Nations

Let us get on with things!
Out of the way with this hampering war!
This idle, senseless waste of time!
Are there not a million evils unremedied?
Are there not men starving?
Women prostitute?
Children in misery?
Is not the mass ignorant?
Are not the rich indolent?
Is justice done?
Wins merit reward?
Has the worker the wage of his toil?
Mankind, lives it well?

In beautiful cities,
In wide streets,
Healthy houses?
Is disease conquered?
Are men and women strong, lovely, wise?
And art . . .
Music . . .
Is there no more to do that we should kill one another?

Come! to our work!
Out of the way with this pestilent war!
Let us get on with things!

El Arish

Eliot Crawshay Williams

Waste

Waste of Muscle, waste of Brain,
Waste of Patience, waste of Pain,
Waste of Manhood, waste of Health,
Waste of Beauty, waste of Wealth,
Waste of Blood, and waste of Tears,
Waste of Youth's most precious years,
Waste of ways the Saints have trod,
Waste of Glory, waste of God, –
War!

G.A. Studdert Kennedy

Wails to the Mail
(Married men of the latest armies will receive 104 pounds per annum
in addition to the usual separation allowance.)

Northcliffe, my Northcliffe,
In days that are dead
The bard was a scoffer
At much that you said,
A fervid opponent
Of 'Daily Mail' Bread.

The bard never dreamed
That it mattered a jot

If you trusted in soap
    Or put peas in your pot,
Or how many aeroplanes
    England had not.

And when you back Blatchford
    To bark at the Bosche,
Or when you puffed Willett
    As wiser than Josh –
Northcliffe, my Northcliffe,
    I own I said 'Tosh'.

Northcliffe, my Northcliffe,
    Now here at thy feet
The poet craves pardon
    Tho' vengeance be sweet
As peas that thou prizest
    In Carmelite Street,

Forgive me past trespasses,
    Hark to my trope,
To my words that are softer
    Than Lever's Soft Soap,
For only through thee
    Has a suppliant hope!

Northcliffe, my Northcliffe,
    Ah! greater than Mars
Or double-faced Janus
    Whose portal unbars
The flood-tide of battle
    Napoleon of 'Pars',

Whose words are uncensored,
    Whose leader compels
Greys, Asquiths, McKennas,
    And eke double L's,
With contraband cotton
    And scandal of shells,

Who rulest the Seas,
    And the Earth and the Air

And the manifold medals
   'Base' Officers wear,
Northcliffe, my Northcliffe,
   Now hark to my prayer!

When the 'Hide-the-Truth Press'
   And the 'Slack 23'
Have yielded sword, money,
   And trident to thee
And K.J. and Boosey
   And Pemberton B.

Remember, while paying
   The Derby man's rent,
His rates, his insurance,
   And more than he spent,
That others SAID NOTHING,
   GOT NOTHING, but WENT.

They were somewhere in France,
   While the Derby man bucked
To his wife, and in sheets
   Was connubially tucked . . .
But no one pays them
   For the homes that they chucked.

They were crouching to crumps
   While he cried at a Zepp,
He was dancing what time
   They were taught to 'Keep step',
And he gets a hundred
   Per an. PLUS the Sep-

aration allowance!
   By Carmelite House,
If a Man be worth anything
   More than a Mouse,
Northcliffe, my Northcliffe,
   THESE CHAPS HAVE A GROUSE.

               Gilbert Frankau

The Only Way

'Conscription will lead the way to the higher life.' – The Dean of Exeter.

Through the slow succeeding ages
Priests and prophets, saints and sages
Have waged a long, incessant strife,
Seeking for the higher life.
Hindus wrapt in contemplation,
Hebrews voicing revelation,
Greeks, Egyptians, and Chinese,
Moslems, Christians, and Parsees,
All have held the ancient quest,
All have sought to find the best;
All of them have gone astray –
None have found the narrow way.

Buddha lived, and preached, and died,
Christ was scourged and crucified,
Socrates and Plato taught,
St Francis prayed, Mahomet fought.
All their labour, all their pain,
All their strivings were in vain;
Vain the work of every master
From Bergson back to Zoroaster,
Vain the toil of every teacher
From Moses down to Friedrich Nietzsche.
No hope for many can ever be
In faith or in Philosophy.

Gloomy is the prospect then
For the stricken sons of men,
Doomed the lower life to live;
None has any help to give.
When, hark! there comes a voice from Devon!
The Dean has found the keys of heaven,
Has found the path that none could find,
Has seen where all the saints were blind.
Marlborough is come to bring salvation
And Higher Life to all the nation.
Sure and simple his prescription:
All mankind needs is – Conscription!

W.N. Ewer

The Last Rally

(Under England's supplementary Conscription Act, the last of the married men
joined her colours on June 24, 1916.)

In the midnight, in the rain,
That drenches every sooty roof and licks each window-pane,
The bugles blow for the last rally
Once again.

Through the horror of the night,
Where glimmers yet northwestward one ghostly strip of white,
Squelching with heavy boots through the untrodden plough-lands
The troops set out. Eyes right!

These are the last who go because they must,
Who toiled for years at something levelled now in dust;
Men of thirty, married, settled, who had built up walls of comfort
That crumbled at a thrust.

Now they have naked steel,
And the heavy, sopping rain that the clammy skin can feel,
And the leaden weight of rifle and the pack that grinds the entrails,
Wrestling with a half-cooked meal.

And there are oaths and blows,
The mud that sticks and flows,
The bad and smoky billet, and the aching legs at morning,
And the frost that numbs the toes;

And the senseless, changeless grind,
And the pettifogging mass of orders muddling every mind,
And the dull-red smudge of mutiny half rising up and burning,
Till they choke and stagger blind.

But for them no bugle flares;
No bright flags leap, no gay horizon glares;
They are conscripts, middle-aged, rheumatic, cautious, weary,
With slowly thinning hairs;

Only for one to-night
A woman weeps and moans and tries to smite

Her head against a table, and another rocks a cradle,
And another laughs with flashing eyes, sitting bolt upright.

John Gould Fletcher

Conscription and Conscience

'*In the meantime I would venture to appeal to the House, and to all sections in the House – whatever views they are disposed to take with regard to this matter* [i.e. *conscription*] *– to abstain from raising it here. We are at a very critical moment in the history of the war. We are watching with intense sympathy and hope the gallant and combined efforts of the Allied forces, and I do not think a greater disservice could be rendered to this country or to the Allied forces than at such a moment as this there should be any suggestion go forth to the world that there is any difference of opinion amongst us.*' – Mr Asquith in the House of Commons, September 28th.

'*It is with the greatest sense of responsibility that I take upon myself what may be the opprobrium of being unable to bind myself to the request made a few minutes ago by the Prime Minister. At a time like this people have got to do what they think is right, irrespective of pressure brought to bear upon them, from whatever source it may come. If I were convinced that the raising of the subject once more would in the very least degree prejudice the chances of the Allied forces in the great engagement in which we are now involved, I would not waste one minute of the time of the House in raising the subject . . . I maintain that the case which we put forward is not controversial.*' – Captain Guest, same place, same date.

'*Little as I know of Labour.*' – Ditto, ditto, ditto.

What, Asquith, *you* presume to use to *me*
This trivial cry of 'public policy'?
Appeals of that sort are no earthly go
Where I'm concerned; for I, the prophet, know
A lordlier guide, and in the heavens see I
The flaming scroll: 'Vox Guestii, Vox Dei'.
Yes, when my conscience shows her burning face,
Asquiths and such must take the lower place!
Proudly I answer to her clarion call
(For conscience will make martyrs of us all),
And my vast hunger for 'opprobrium'
Might strike an envious Von Tirpitz dumb!

*   *   *

But suppose, gallant Captain, that the State
Adopts your view (although a trifle late),

Suppose the sluggish powers-that-be begin
At last by force to rope the shirkers in;
Suppose, I put it, that you get your way
And we attain that glad millennial day
When your stout comrade, Colonel Arthur Lee,
Makes soldiering a sweated industry.
And suppose, then, some libertarian cur,
Some wretched working-man in Manchester,
In spite of all our peril, argues still
He does not think men should be forced to kill.
– What about that? . . . I am not certain, Guest,
But still I'm strongly tempted to suggest,
O Captain, my Captain, Captain Guest,
You'll find your conscience tells you it were best,
Sometimes, that in the public interest
The conscientious man should be suppressed.

Freedom on the Job!

Although our liberties are gone,
We've got a war for Freedom on!
In spite of each oppressive act,
The war for Freedom is a FACT:
So get it well into your head
That wars – for Freedom – *must* be fed
With conscript armies, vanish'd rights,
And all the Censorship's delights;
Whilst, though the people lose their freedom,
The profiteers are free to bleed 'em!
For things like that, you know, must be,
In a great war for liberty:
For which, because it's lost at home,
We have to fight, across the foam!

Lieutenant Tattoon, M.C.

The case of Lieutenant Tattoon, M.C.
    Is worthy of some remark.
He thought (and one should not think, you see)

That the War which was to make people free
　　Was now being fought in the dark.

For at first (he said) our aims were clear,
　　Men gave their lives with gladness
To save small nations from the fear
Of Tyrants who would domineer
　　And doom mankind to madness.

Our rulers had claimed – and rightly I ween –
　　That the Germans must be 'broken';
But afterwards, What that word might mean,
And what sort of peace was to supervene,
　　Were things which they left unspoken.

And no one knew whatever on Earth
　　Our present objective and aim were,
And whether the loss and deadly dearth
Of another Million of lives was worth
　　Some gains in Mesopotamia.

These were the thoughts of Lieutenant Tattoon. –
　　Of course it was very improper,
But he actually gave them expression, and soon
Found out he was trying to jump the Moon
　　And only coming a cropper!

For to say what you mean is all right as a rule
　　In a far oversea Dominion,
But at home or under the Prussian school
It is not safe – and a man is a fool
　　Even to have an opinion.

A Medical Board sat on him, in state
　　(No wonder they looked so solemn);
His sins were entered upon the slate
With every lapse detailed to date –
　　And they added up the Column.

He thought – which for a Lieutenant was rash;
　　He spoke, but should have kept silence;

He treated Imperial talk as trash,
And considered the honour before the cash
    Which might come to the British Islands.

'Twas insubordination, they said,
    And he surely must be crazy –
Yet there he stood, in mien well-bred;
Collected and calm, with clean-cut head,
    And looking as fit as a daisy.

An M.C. too – so what could they do?
    'Twas a most provoking and strange craze.
Yet to put him in prison a storm would brew
Of wrath – the mere proposal to mew
    A hero in Woking or Strangeways!

For half an hour (as once in Heaven)
    Silence fell on the folk assembled;
Till by one inspired the stillness was riven:
''Twas nervous shock'. The cue was given –
    And the whole Court gaily dissembled.

'Poor fellow!' they said, ''Twas nervous strain,
    He's a subject for our pity;
Let him to Hospital go, till his brain
Is healed, and there's no danger again
    That he will repeat that ditty.'

To a Shell-shock ward then he was sent,
    And there he was kindly treated
And even indulged to the top of his bent; –
But there ever since he has safely been pent,
    And his words have not been repeated.

                             Edward Carpenter

The Pacifist

Thou art the Disillusioner. Thy words
Are desolate winds and jagged spurs of rock,
Whereon they urge the frigate of our pride
To cast herself. How cruel is thy blade

To strip the sword of glory, leaving steel
Naked, and wounds, undecked of laurels, bare!
O still, small voice, the louder roars the whirl,
More clear thou comest, and more terrible!

E.H. Physick

To a Pacifist

Do you fail, even now, to realise
That not for this, our land we hold most dear
Alone, nor for the freedom that we prize;
Not for the love that wells in loyal eyes
To nerve our spirits; – not alone, you hear
For these; – but for yourself and for your breed, –
You, with your turgid soul and venomous tongue,
      You who have ever flung
      Gibes at our sacrifice, –
For you, too, must we suffer, must we bleed?

This thing is plain, altho' your lips deny;
When Honour calls, – for you we answer her;
When Death claims dues, – for you we go to die;
You thrive by virtue of our agony.
A saprophyte upon the sepulchre,
Lapping the spilt blood of the crucified,
This is your meed of thanks and recompense, –
      With pompous eloquence
      To prate interminably,
Sland'ring the sacred cause of those who died.

Geoffrey F. Fyson

To any Pacifist

You, who make clamour for a speedy peace,
Who bid us pause, and think, and count the cost,
And reckon up the lives and treasure lost
In this wild, senseless devil's orgy; Cease!
We may not listen to your treacherous word,
Unless we would be traitors to our dead,
And forfeit all for which their blood was shed,
And lose the prize for which we drew the sword.

We must fight on, whate'er the sacrifice,
Till we have reaped the fruits of victory;
We must fight on, however stern the price,
Till we have planted in Gallipoli,
On the grim, blood-stained slopes of Sedd-ul-Bahr,
The freedom-bringing banner of the Czar.

W.N. Ewer

The True Pacifist

Come at me with your scorn,
Strike me with your rod –
Though I be slain a thousand times,
I will not fight my God.

Witter Bynner

To the Followers of Christ among the Belligerent Nations

'Unum Corpus sumus in Christo.'

In Christ we all are one – we who believe,
And worship Him as Lord – and shall this War,
Wherever lies the blame, make us forget
That bless'd relationship? Shall gods like Thor,
And Mars, control our hearts to such extent
That Christ in us shall be o'erthrown? Oh, say!
If hated, shall we give back hate for hate?
If wronged, shall we with bitterness repay?
And so, because men's passions rage, let love
And all the highest duties be forgot? –
Discard the very things Christ values most,
And speak and act, as though we knew Him not?

Nay, God forbid! For we His children are –
His equal children, brothers all, in Christ;
And Christ hath said: 'As God is perfect, so
Be ye, His children'. Would it had sufficed –
His teaching so divine! And that we each
Had seen and clung to – years back – once for all –
His purpose and His will! – and lived our lives
In deeper heart-obedience to His call!

Too late, is it? Nay, nay! With broken heart,
And flooded eyes – that dare not look above,
Let us, confessing, smite upon our breast,
And beg for grace that we may learn to love!

H.J. Preece

A New Hymn

There's the blood of many martyrs on our banner;
　　There are heroes – named and nameless – dead, behind.
There are many fights before us,
There are dark clouds looming o'er us,
　　But we'll win, because our fight's for mankind.

We have fought the fight so long, and we are winning;
　　We have fought against the ignorant and blind.
But though death itself were in it,
We will fight the fight and win it,
　　For we must not lose the cause of humankind.

All the martyrs of the ages have been with us;
　　All have fought upon the battle-field of mind,
And their fight we will continue
With our muscle, brain, and sinew,
　　For, like theirs, our cause is that of humankind.

And at last we'll reach the goal for which we've striven,
　　And our dreams of earthly paradise we'll find;
Then with purpose high before us,
We will sing the stirring chorus
　　Of our glorious fight for freedom and mankind.

Song of the Friends Ambulance Unit
Tempo di Marcia.

Oh! the autumn sun on Jordans woods,
　　And the orchard's scarlet glow,
When Penn sleeps by the meeting-house,
　　And the beech-trees, shadows grow.

CHORUS.

But afar the world's need calls us,
  Can we stay lingering? No!
Then up, lads, now, and pack your kits!
From land and sea the Red Cross calls –
  In Christ's name let us go!

Oh! grass grows green in Ypres streets
  That once were fair to see;
The Sacré Cœur's a ruin now,
  But it's there that we would be.

The shrapnel screams o'er Nieuport Ville,
  The Eastern sky is bright
With flashes – driver, start her up!
  They're wanting you to-night.

The wards are full on Richmond Hill,
  And Uffculme's busy too.
Another convoy! Lend a hand,
  There's work for us to do.

'Neath the shadow of the Minster towers
  Lie the sick beds, row on row.
They need stout hearts and gentle hands,
  And it's there that we must go.

On the trains – in every stifling coach,
  In the ships' wards, crowded too –
From Rouen to the isles of Greece –
  We'll see the unit through!

CHORUS

For afar the world's need calls us,
  Can we stay lingering? No!
Then up, lads, now, and pack your kits!
From land and sea the Red Cross calls –
  In Christ's name let us go!

C.O.s in Prison

Who PUT them in Prison?
    'We' say the Court Martial –
    'Our judgement is partial, –
    Our job will be gone,
    And we can't carry on
    If we listen to conscience
    And that sort of nonsense.
    Away with their tale!
    Just clap them in jail, –
At the horrors we hear of the stoutest will quail!'

Who'll STARVE them, in prison?
    'Oh, we!' say the warders,
    'For such is our orders, –
    Reducing the ration
    Is now all the fashion,
    And ill-flavoured gruel
    Is left, – something cruel!
    Blackbeetles and Mice
    Spoil the oatmeal and rice,
And the "Objects" ob-*ject*, they're fearfully nice!'

Who sees them DIE?
    'Not *I*', says the Nation,
    'A pure fabrication!
    They've lost weight, we know –
    A few stones, or so, –
    And some have gone mad
    With the tortures they've had –
    But *if* some *have* died
    Such cases we hide –
And no one, you'll notice, for Murder is tried!'

Who'll HELP the C.O.s?
    'I can't', says the Church –
    'My 'scutcheon 'twould smirch, –
All war I abhor, it is not in my line,
But *this* war is diff'rent, it's holy, it's fine!

Now I can't quite explain, but you'll see, in a minute –
Although it's so holy, – why *I* am not in it;
The Government thought it would look very ill
The Cause notwithstanding, for *Clergy* to kill!
So this kind exemption of course I requite
By '*talking up*' fighting, – although I don't fight!
Thus you will perceive, though I feel for their woes,
That I can't say a word for the poor dear C.O.s!'

I Lived a Year in London

I lived a year in London,
    But I never saw St Paul's;
All famous stunts left undone,
    Nor visited the 'Halls'.
I lodged in Royal quarters,
    At Majesty's expense:
All round, the walls of Wormwood's halls
    Were reared for my defence.
        O, the Palace of Wormwood Scrubs!
        The snarling, the sneers, the snubs,
    And the long, dreary days spent in learning the ways
        Of the Palace at Wormwood Scrubs!

In shoddy grey they dressed me,
    I didn't dare refuse,
Though shape and fit distressed me,
    I wasn't asked to choose.
My outspread ears supported
    The largest size in caps:
My feet did cruise in shiplike shoes,
    While a breeze blew through the gaps.
        O, that court suit of Wormwood Scrubs!
        With its skin-chafing, irksome rubs,
    And the blush-raising shocks from its openwork socks
        As we wore 'em in Wormwood Scrubs!

In dignified retirement
    I ate three meals a day,
My very small requirement
    Was brought in on a tray.

But though I grieve to say it,
　　Nor gold nor silver plate,
But vulgar tin my food came in,
　　And I often had to wait.
　　　　O, the dinner at Wormwood Scrubs!
　　　　You people who dine at clubs,
　　Try just once, for a treat, with a spoon to eat meat,
　　　　And you'll fight shy of Wormwood Scrubs!

Each morn with others banded,
　　I walked the palace ground,
As etiquette demanded,
　　We circled round and round.
At time my dizzy senses
　　Were soothed by slumb'rous spell,
But when I woke I savage spoke
　　And I wished I were in – Well! –
　　　　It's no matter. At Wormwood Scrubs
　　　　There's snarling and sneers and snubs,
　　But if 'tweren't so bad, one would not be so glad
　　　　To bid farewell to Wormwood Scrubs!

Allan M. Laing

A Call from Prison

Comrades, let us on together in the course we have begun,
Fearless, tireless and unfaltering till our cause be won,
Let us ever keep before us as our guiding polar star,
Both in time of ease and plenty, and when warfare rages far,
Those ideas of Love and Freedom and the Brotherhood of Man,
Which alone can free the nations – bound since history began,
In the chains of fear and hatred, in the bonds of strife and sin –
Which alone can end war's triumph, and the better age bring in.
We are young in mind and body, strong in faith and high in hope,
Eager with the hosts of error and of prejudice to cope,
Mighty forces are against us, principalities and powers,
Ancient customs, wealthy systems, but the victory shall be ours,
For our cause is pure and holy, we are fighting for the right,
And the Truth shall surely conquer as the morning follows night,
Even now the dawn is breaking, faintly in the eastern sky,
Even now the light is spreading, and the ancient shadows fly.

Forward then, let nothing daunt us, danger, poverty nor scorn,
Forward, all we do or suffer brings more near that glorious morn
When the age-long feuds shall perish, and the sounds of war shall cease,
And one universal nation shall proclaim the reign of peace.

Winchester Gaol, 6 June 1917

Harold F. Bing

From Prison

Put out my eyes; but when you've done,
See if you can put out the sun!
Thrust me in gaol and turn the key –
Freedom shall win, nor fail with me.

Fetter these hands that wield the pen –
The sword most feared by knavish men;
Some hand, some pen renews the strife,
While throbs one heart for God and life.

What though my fire-touched lips were dumb,
Sealed in the darkness of the tomb?
Ten thousand voices thunder loud –
Shall mine be missed in such a crowd?

You think the Spring is dead, of course,
Its light, its song, its sap, its force,
Because your stupid hands prevail
To strangle one poor nightingale!

Father Tyrell

Compensation

What a beautiful gift is water
To a throat that is parched with thirst!
How inspiring a look that is kindly
To one who is deemed accursed!

The torrent that rushes so freely
Down many a mountain-side
Is not esteemed so greatly
As a drop when rain is denied.

The joy that it is to be living,
To be vigorous, sturdy and well,
Is felt with double keenness
After being infirm for a spell.

And those who have not lived in prison
Scarce know what it feels to be free:
To enjoy the full rapture of freedom
A prisoner first one must be.

To the captive the air seems more fragrant
After being immured in a gaol,
And before the pure pleasure of freedom
All other enjoyments pale.

                                        Ben Taylor

Prisoners of War

In the little empty worlds of the camps
      We live through the weary hours;
Endless monotony, endless strain
      Of silent endurance is ours,
When before the dead days' endless march
      The very spirit cowers.

Home and friends are so far away
      Foes and hate are so near,
We are back with the primitive things of life,
      Hunger and cold and fear.
We must keep steady in heart and brain –
      Brethren, pray for us here.

                                    M.G. Meugens

Rastatt

Within these cages day by day we pace
The bitter shortness of the meted span;
And this and that way variously we plan
Our poor excursions over the poor place,
Cribbed to extinction. Yet remains one grace.
For neither bars nor tented wire can ban

Full many a roving glance that dares to scan
The roomy hill, and wanders into space.
Yea, and remains for ever unrepealed
And unimpaired the free impetuous quest
Of mind's soaring eye, at length unsealed
To the full measure of a life possessed
Awhile, but never counted, now revealed
Inestimable, wonderful, unguessed.

A.A. Bowman

Loneliness

Oh where's the use to write?
What can I tell you, dear?
Just that I want you so
Who are not near.
Just that I miss the lamp whose blessèd light
Was God's own moon to shine upon my night,
And newly mourn each new day's lost delight:
Just – oh, it will not ease my pain –
That I am lonely
Until I see you once again,
You – you only.

F.W. Harvey

Thoughts of Home

Day follows night, and night returns to day
Through all the enchanting stages of the spring;
And exile lengthens out to months that fling
Their shadow further, and my life grows gray;
Grays even with the sun's increasing ray;
While forward still the heading heats do wing
Into the year, that softly rounds his ring
To midsummer, and June is on the way:
The perfect season, when the hawthorn blows
Down cream-white Scottish hedges, and the spent
Airs of the evening gently swaying close
Tired eyes upon it, heavy with its scent;
While on the Downs the beating sunlight glows,
And sends the wildering roses over Kent.

A.A. Bowman

Requiescat
(W.M. Shot, June 1917, Schwarmstedt Camp)

Were men but men, and Christians not at all:
Mere pagans, primitive and quick of sense
To feel the sun's great blind beneficence:
The kind hand of the breeze: – nay but to see
Only the brotherly blue that's over all,
And realise that calm immensity
So far-enfolding, softly-bright and still,
Feel only that: – Surely they would not kill!

Beside a new-digged grave beneath the trees
I kneel. The brotherly sky is over all.
It seems to me so strange wars do not cease.

F.W. Harvey

EIGHT

The Royal Navy

Life at sea, sinking of the Lusitania, *the Battle of Jutland*

For a hundred years, since the Battle of Trafalgar, Britain had enjoyed an unchallenged supremacy of the sea. With the pre-war building of Dreadnoughts and the widening of the Kiel Canal, Germany had increasingly threatened this position.

As an island, it was essential that Britain protect its coasts and trade routes, but its freedom of the seas came increasingly under attack from German U-boat submarines. Heavy loss of merchant shipping had disastrous effects on the supply of food and raw materials. Realising this, the Germans concentrated their U-boat attacks on these supply ships, hoping in this way to bring the British government to its knees. Merchant ships were undefended, and to begin with the Germans gave warning of attack, enabling the sailors to escape. After unrestricted U-boat warfare was launched in February 1917, such niceties were forgotten, and the destruction of British ships became so heavy that the country had food supplies for only a few weeks.

In May 1915 the passenger liner *Lusitania* was sunk with the loss of 1,198 lives, including 124 US citizens. The Germans claimed, with justification, that there were arms on board, but it was a disaster that would eventually lead to America coming into the war.

The most important naval engagement of the war, the Battle of Jutland, took place on 31 May 1916 off the coast of Denmark. After heavy fighting, with the loss of 6,000 British and 2,500 German lives, the German Fleet withdrew, leaving the British in control of the North Sea but without a decisive victory. Winston Churchill, who, until the failure of the Gallipoli campaign, had been First Lord of the Admiralty, criticised the conduct of the battle; this was leapt upon by *Punch*, which henceforth delighted in poking fun at him.

Less than a week later, HMS *Hampshire* was sunk off the Orkneys, and Lord Kitchener, the creator of the New Armies, was drowned.

The Sailing of the Fleet

A signal flutters at the Flagship's fore,
And a deep pulse
Stirs in the mighty hulls
Slow wheeling seaward, where, beyond the Bar,
Half veiled in gloom,
Those messengers of doom
The lean Destroyers are.

From the thronged piers
Faintly, the sound of cheers
Tossed by the winds afar . . .

With gathering speed
The grey, grim shapes proceed –
The Might of England – to uphold the Law
'Gainst blackest treachery.
And the same courage high
That fired those valiant hearts at Trafalgar,
Burning from age to age,
Our proudest heritage,
Pierces disquieting war-clouds like a star,
As, burdened with a Nation's hopes and fears,
The Battle Fleet of England sweeps to war.

                                        N.M.F. Corbett

The Four Sea Lords
(For the information of an ever-thirsty public.)

FIRST SEA LORD

This is the man whose work is War;
He plans it out in a room on shore –
He and his Staff (all brainy chaps)
With miniature flags and monster maps,
And a crew whose tackle is Hydrographic,
With charts for steering our ocean traffic.
But the task that most engrosses him
Is to keep his Fleet in fighting trim;
To see that his airmen learn the knack
Of plomping bombs on a Zeppelin's back;

To make his sailors good at gunnery,
And so to sink each floating hunnery.

SECOND SEA LORD

Here is the man who mans the Fleet
With jolly young tars that can't be beat;
He has them trained and taught the rules;
He looks to their hospitals, barracks, schools;
He notes what rumorous Osborne's doing,
And if it has mumps or measles brewing.
He fills each officer's vacant billet
(Provided the First Lord doesn't fill it);
And he casts a fatherly eye, betweens,
On that fine old corps, the Royal Marines.
This is the job that once was Jellicoe's,
But now he has one a bit more bellicose.

THIRD SEA LORD

Ships are the care of the Third Sea Lord,
And all Material kept on board.
'Tis he must see that the big guns boom
And the wheels go round in the engine-room;
'Tis he must find, for cloudy forays,
Aeroplanes and Astra Torres;
And, long ere anything's sent to sea,
Tot up the bill for you and me.

FOURTH SEA LORD

The Fourth Sea Lord has a deal to plan,
For he's, chief of all, the Transport man.
He finds the Fleet in coal and victuals
(Supplying the beer – if not the skittles);
He sees to the bad'uns that get imprisoned,
And settles what uniform's worn (or isn't) . . .
Even the stubbornest own the sway
Of the Lord of Food and the Lord of Pay!

R.P. Keigwin

Destroyers

On this primeval strip of western land,
With purple bays and tongues of shining sand,
Time, like an echoing tide,
Moves drowsily in idle ebb and flow;
The sunshine slumbers in the tangled grass
And homely folk with simple greeting pass,
As to their worship or their work they go.
Man, earth, and sea
Seem linked in elemental harmony,
And my insurgent sorrow finds release
In dreams of peace.

But silent, gray,
Out of the curtained haze,
Across the bay
Two fierce destroyers glide with bows afoam
And predatory gaze,
Like cormorants that seek a submerged prey.
An angel of destruction guards the door
And keeps the peace of our ancestral home;
Freedom to dream, to work, and to adore,
These vagrant days, nights of untroubled breath,
Are bought with death.

Henry Head

Mine Sweepers
(Over three hundred of Grimsby's fleet of trawlers are engaged in the hazardous task
of sweeping the seas for mines sown by the Germans.)

''Ware mine!'
'Starboard your helm!' . . . 'Full speed ahead!'
The squat craft duly swings: –
A hand's breath off, a thing of dread
The sullen breaker flings.

Carefully, slowly, patiently,
The men of Grimsby town
Grope their way on the rolling sea –
The storm-swept, treach'rous grey North Sea –
Keeping the death-rate down.

Cold is the wind as the Gates of Death,
Howling a dirge with its biting breath,
Tearing rude music from rigging taut –
The tune with deadly omen fraught:
'Look to yourselves, oh, sailors bold –
I am the one ye know of old!
I make my sport with such as ye –
The game that is played on every sea
With death as the loser's penalty!'

Valiantly, stoutly, manfully,
    The trawlers fight the gale;
Buoyant they ride on the rolling sea –
The storm-swept, treach'rous grey North Sea –
    Lashed by the North Wind's flail.

Cruel the waves of that ocean drear,
Whelming the heart with a palsying fear,
Hurling their might on the stagg'ring craft,
Crashing aboard of her fore and aft,
Buffeting, pounding, a dreadful force,
Sweeping her decks as she hugs her course.

Little they care, come wind or wave,
    The men of Grimsby Town;
There are mines to destroy and lives to save,
And they take the risk, these sailormen brave,
With a laugh and a joke, or a rollicking stave,
    As the gear goes plunging down.

          Honour the trawler's crew,
          For Fear they never knew!
          Now on their quest they go
          With measured tack and slow –
          Seeking the hidden fate
          Strewn with a devilish hate.

Death may come in a terrible form,
Death in a calm or death in a storm,
Death without warning, stark and grim,
Death with a tearing of limb from limb,

Death in a horrible, hideous guise: –
Such is the minesweepers' sacrifice!
Careless of terrors and scornful of ease,
Stolid and steadfast, they sweep the seas.

Cheerfully, simply, fearlessly,
    The men of Grimsby Town
Do their bit on the rolling sea –
The storm-swept, treach'rous grey North Sea –
Doing their duty unflinchingly
    Keeping the death-rate down.

H. Ingamells

Submarines

By paths unknown to Nelson's days,
    Our swift flotillas prowl below,
We go upon our various ways
    Where Drake and Howard might not go.
Unheard, intangible as air,
    Unseen, yet seeing all things plain,
While ships and wild-eyed seamen stare
    We pass and strike and pass again.

No sun upon our wake is seen,
    No night looks down upon our deeds,
But broken half-lights, strangely green,
    Gleam tangled in the swaying weeds.
Dim vistas loom before our eyes,
    Vast shapes across our vision flee,
And, round about our feet, there lies
    The twilit silence of the sea.

Beside our tracks, half-guessed at, dim,
    The creatures of the ocean browse,
Yet none so dreadful, none so grim,
    As those we carry in our bows.
The navies of forgotten kings
    Lie scattered on the ocean-bed;
We float among prodigious things,
    We, that are neither quick nor dead.

There, in their never-ending sleep,
    The sailors of a bygone day
Dream of the land they died to keep –
    A land more permanent than they.
And we, who have new ways of war,
    Strange means of death beyond their ken,
Oh, may we fight as fought before
    Our fathers, who begat us men!

So, where the tides and tempest rust
    The shattered argosies of Spain,
We praise the gods that now entrust
    This England to our charge again.
Then, with thanksgiving, as is meet
    From such as hold their lives in pawn,
We glimmer upwards, till we greet
    The grey relentless Channel dawn.

J.L. Crommelin Brown

You Never Can Tell

'It's a submarine!' the lookout cried,
    'A porpoise', said the mate.
'A set of mines hooked to a shark',
    The boatsmen were not late.

The skipper threw the safe away,
    The first luff's feet were cool.
The navigator cleared the stern
    Lashed to a sliding rule.

From the engine-room another,
    With a left-hand monkey-wrench,
And through the starboard mess-hall door
    Flew a sailor on a bench.

The boatswain piped a phoney call,
    And loudly he did bellow,
While high and dry on the pilot-house
    Stood Doc with his umbrella.

Some one hit a jingle,
  For the throttle opened wide,
The fish-boat quivered fore and aft,
  Went astern, and saved our hide.

Safety first is a landman's cry,
  I'm sure you will agree.
On the poggy trawler do your bit
  And believe just half you see.

Frank G. Bigelow

[Sing us a song of the Northern Seas]

Sing us a song of the Northern Seas –
(Where the ships patrol and the gunners freeze)
  Of sight and fights and Jack's delights –
    The pudding and beef and gravy;
Sing us a song to clearly show
That the boys in blue are the ones to go
And they wait like hounds for a skulking foe –
  Sing us a song of the Navy.

J.M. Ryan

Low Visibility

Our gentle pirate ancestors from off the Frisian Isles,
Kept station where we now patrol so many weary miles:
There were no International Laws of Hall or Halleck then,
They only knew the simple rule of 'Death to beaten men'.
And what they judged a lawful prize was any sail they saw
From Scarboro' to the sandy isles along the Saxon shore.
We differ from our ancestors' conception of a prize,
And we cruise about like Agag 'neath Sir Samuel Evans' eyes;
But on one eternal subject we would certainly agree:
It's seldom you can see a mile across the Northern sea,
For as the misty clouds came down and settled wet and cold,
The sodden halliards creaked and strained as to the swell they rolled.
Each yellow-bearded pirate knew beyond the veil of white
The prize of all the prizes must be passing out of sight;
And drearily they waited while metheglin in a skin
Was passed along the benches, and the oars came sliding in;

Then scramasax and battleaxe were polished up anew,
And they waited for the fog to lift, the same as me and you;
Though we're waiting on the bottom at the twenty fathom line,
We are burnishing torpedoes to a Sunday morning shine.
The sailor pauses as he quaffs his tot of Navy rum,
And listens to a noise that drowns the circulator's hum:
'D'y 'ear those blank propellers, Bill – *the blinking female dog* –
That's Tirpitz in the 'Indenburg gone past us in the fog!'

John G. Bower

The Auxiliary Cruiser

(H.M. Auxiliary Cruiser —— has been lost at sea with all hands. It is presumed that she struck a mine during the gale on the night of the 12th inst. The relatives have been informed. – *Admiralty Official.*)

The day closed in a wrath of cloud. The gale –
Like a fierce beast that shuns the light of day,
Skulking within the jungle till his prey
Steals forth at dusk to water at the well, –
Now leapt upon her, howling. Steep and swift,
The black sea boiled about her sky-flung bows,
And in the shrouds, the winds in mad carouse
Screamed: and in the sky's pall was no rift.

And it was cold. Oh, bitter cold it was,
The wind-whipped spray-drops froze before they fell
And tinkled on the iron decks like hail;
And every rope and block was cased in glass.
And ever wild and wilder grew the night.
Great seas lunged at her, bellowing in wrath,
Contemptuous, to sweep her from their path.
And not in all that waste one friendly light.

Alone, spray-blinded, through the clamorous murk,
By skill and courage besting the hungry sea,
Mocking the tempest's fury, staggered she.
The storm is foiled: now for the Devil's work!
The swinging bows crash down into the trough,
And with a sudden flame the sea is riven,
And a dull roar outroars the tempest even.
Her engine's pulse is stilled. It is enough.

Oh, have you ever seen a foundered horse –
His great heart broken by a task too great
For his endurance, but unbroken yet
His spirit – striving to complete his course?
Falling at last, eyes glazed and nostrils wide,
And have not ached with pity? Pity now
A brave ship shattered by a coward blow
That once had spurned the waters in her pride.

And can you picture – you who dwell secure
In sheltered houses, warm and filled with light, –
The loneliness and terror of that fight
In shrieking darkness? Feel with them (the sure
Foundation of their very world destroyed),
The sluggish lifting of the lifeless hull,
Wallowing ever deeper till, with a dull
Half-sob she plunges and the seas are void.

Yet – Oh be sure, they did not pass alone
Into the darkness all uncomforted;
For round them hovered England's mighty Dead
To greet them: and a pale poop lanthorn shone
Lighting them homeward, and a voice rang clear –
As when he cheered his own devoted band –
'Heaven's as near by sea as by the land',
Sir Humphrey Gilbert hailed them: 'Be of cheer!'

N.M.F. Corbett

To Fritz

I wish that I could be a Hun, to dive about the sea,
I wouldn't go for merchantmen, a man-of-war for me;
There are lots of proper targets for attacking, little Fritz,
But you seem to like the merchantmen, and blowing them to bits.
I suppose it must be easy fruit to get an Iron Cross
By strafing sail and cargo ships, but don't you feel the loss
Of the wonderful excitement when you face a man-of-war,
And tearing past you overhead the big propellers roar?
When you know that it's a case of 'May the fish run good and true',
For if they don't it's ten to one it's R.I.P. for you?

Although perhaps you can't be blamed – your motives may be pure –
You're rather new to submarines – in fact, an amateur;
But we'd like to take your job awhile and show you how it's done,
And leave you on the long patrol to wait your brother Hun.
You wouldn't like the job, my lad – the motors turning slow,
You wouldn't like the winter-time – storm and wind and snow,
You'd find it weary waiting, Fritz – unless your faith is strong –
Up and down on the long patrol – How long, O Lord, How long?
We don't patrol for merchant ships, there's none but neutrals there,
Up and down on the old patrol, you can hear the E-boat's prayer:
'Give us a ten-knot breeze, O Lord, with a clear and blazing sky,
And help our eyes at the periscope as the High Sea Fleet goes by.'

John G. Bower

The Armed Liner

The dull grey paint of war
Covering the shining brass and gleaming decks
That once re-echoed to the steps of youth.
That was before
The storms of destiny made ghastly wrecks
Of Peace, the Right and Truth.
Impromptu dances, coloured lights and laughter,
Lovers watching the phosphorescent waves;
Now gaping guns, a whistling shell; and after
So many wandering graves.

H. Smalley Sarson

The Lusitania

In a world that is neither night nor day,
    A quiet twilight land,
With fifty fathoms over you
And the surge of seas to cover you,
    You rest on the kindly sand.

Above, the earth is March or May,
    And skies are fair in spring,
But all the seasons are one with you,
Summer and winter have done with you,
    And wars, and everything.

Surely this is a goodly gift,
    To sleep so sound and sure
That neither spite nor weariness,
Passion, nor pain, nor dreariness
    Can touch you any more.

In drifting spume and flying scud,
    When the great tides shoreward sweep,
The seas that are all in all to you
Whisper and move and call to you,
    Whisper and call and weep.

J.L. Crommelin Brown

Below

'Great credit is due to the engine-room staff.' Admiral Beatty.

The man who's down below
    Sees nothing of the show;
He's only got to do his bit and wait:
    With his eye upon the dial,
    It's a devil of a trial
Blindly to bear the onsets of his fate.

Yes, he's buried in the deep,
    And he can't have even a peep
At the things that make the blood run fast and proud:
    His prison walls are thick,
    And a lesser man were sick
To know he could not mingle with the crowd.

So, his colour comes and goes,
    And he gives a thought to those
Who are trusting to his skill and honour bright;
    He reckons he is *there*,
    And he doesn't turn a hair,
Though he knows he's in the bowels of the fight.

By the churning of the screw
    He gets a kind o' clew
That they're jinking all they can the submarines;
    For below the water-line

He can tap the secret sign,
And he has a pretty inkling what it means.

He trusts the Bridge above,
And he thinks but little of
The dangers that beset him in his den;
The signals tell him some,
And he's sure there's more to come –
What, the worst? Well, it happens to all men!

And so, within his cage,
Oil-spray and pressure-gauge
And drone of turbine occupy his mind;
He doesn't see the show,
But this we surely know,
He's the bravest man of any you can find!

John Hogben

Wet Ships
'. . . And will remain on your Patrol till the 8th December . . .' (*Extract from Orders.*)

The North-East Wind came armed and shod from the ice-locked Baltic shore,
The seas rose up in the track he made, and the rollers raced before;
He sprang on the Wilhelmshaven ships that reeled across the tide.
'Do you cross the sea to-night with me?' the cold North-Easter cried –
Along the lines of anchored craft the Admiral's answer flashed,
And loud the proud North-Easter laughed, as the second anchors splashed.
'By God! you're right – you German men, with a three-day gale to blow,
It is better to wait by your harbour gate than follow where I go!'

Over the Bight to the open sea the great wind sang as he sheered:
'I rule – I rule the Northern waste – I speak, and the seas are cleared;
You nations all whose harbours ring the edge of my Northern sea,
At peace or war, when you hear my voice you shall know no Lord but me.'
Then into the wind in a cloud of foam and sheets of rattling spray
Head to the bleak and breaking seas in dingy black and grey,
Taking it every lurch and roll in tons of icy green
Came out to her two-year-old patrol – an English submarine.

The voice of the wind rose up and howled through squalls of driving white:
'You'll know my power, you English craft, before you make the Bight;

I rule – I rule this Northern Sea, that I raise and break to foam.
Whom do you call your Overlord that dares me in my home?
Over the crest of a lifting sea in bursting shells of spray,
She showed the flash of her rounded side, as over to port she lay,
Clanging her answer up the blast that made her wireless sing:
'*I serve the Lord of the Seven Seas. Ha! Splendour of God – the King!!*'

Twenty feet of her bow came out, dripping and smooth it sprang,
Over the valley of green below as her stamping engines rang;
Then down she fell till the waters rose to meet her straining rails –
'I serve my King, who sends me here to meet your winter gales'.
(Rank upon rank the seas swept on and broke to let her through,
While high above her reeling bridge their shattered remnants flew);
'*If you blow the stars from the sky to-night, your boast in your teeth I'll fling,*
I am your master – Overlord and – Dog of the English King!'

John G. Bower

The Battle off Jutland
May 31st, 1916

The silent fleet that braved the North Sea tempests,
The submarines, the snow and fog and spray,
Through sleepless nights and weary months of waiting,
Spoke with its guns to-day.

Sir David Beatty's cruisers did discover
The presence of a German force at sea;
Where by the verdict of the British nation
It had no right to be.

He first engaged a battle-cruiser squadron,
Which showed unusual eagerness to fight;
For in support their naval strength was gathered
To challenge Britain's might.

The only anxious thoughts that troubled Beatty
Were lest they should escape the British fleet;
Though fresh divisions soon his foes had doubled,
He scorned to bid retreat.

More fiercely raged the fight as other units
Out of the mists appeared on either side;
Great German battleships into the conflict
Were flung to turn the tide.

On either side proud ships were seen to stagger,
Then disappear beneath the waves in flame.
To Beatty by o'erwhelming foes imperiled
Our super-dreadnoughts came.

The 'Warspite', 'Valiant', 'Barham' and 'Malaya':
What cheers for hard pressed comrades bravely ring;
What deeper voices to that stern engagement
Their mighty weapons bring.

Another cloud loomed dark o'er the horizon,
Like growing storm, 'Twas Jellicoe's grand fleet;
Before its deadly hail and wrathful thunders
The German ships retreat.

Darkness shut down with mist upon the ocean:
Such dreadful night the sea had never known;
But in the wild mêlée the British triumph,
The foe is overthrown.

G.B. Warren

War Chant of the Harbour-Huns

In 1914

Our country's pride,
Sea-Huns we are;
Our time we bide –
Then woe betide
The British tar!

The foeman's fate
And doom are sealed;
Within our gate
We lie in wait.
Britain shall yield!

Hail to the Day!
Let them come forth –
Hun mines shall slay
Their hated prey
In righteous wrath!

Then shall we sail
To Britain's shore;
The fist of mail
Shall make her quail
And death outpour!

Till even she
Proclaim our worth,
And we shall be
Lords of the sea
And of the earth!

In 1916

By luck, again
Safe back to port!
The heaving main
Strewn with our slain,
The battle fought.

In peril's throes
Home course we shaped;
A mist arose
And from our foes
We just escaped.

Once more we hide
At anchor here,
While they with pride
The ocean ride
Both far and near.

The longed for Day –
A bubble burst!

Our land's dismay
We did allay,
Nor told the worst.

In victory's guise
Was failure clad;
So through deft lies
Our nation wise
Is falsely glad.

Once more, with hate,
Britain to brave
We watch and wait.
By cursed fate
She rules the wave.

How Tirpitz Won the Battle off Jutland

Von Tirpitz was an admiral, his beard flew bold and free,
He called up all his captains and 'My gallant lads', quoth he,
'The day has come, ten thousand "Hochs", and though I stay at home
My spirit will be with you. Now prepare to brave the foam!'

The captains tried with one accord to raise a pleasant grin,
Yet each one wondered when and how the trouble would begin;
Their ships they put in dry dock, had the barnacles removed,
While by the aid of countless 'steins' the outlook they improved.

'What ho, my merry mariners!' said Tirp. one day in May,
'Art ready now to sweep the sea and end Britannia's day?
Has each of you his Iron Cross, and flannel next his skin?'
With one accord they answered 'Ja!' 'Gut! now we can begin!'

So Tirpitz crept unto the gate, and peered out o'er the sea,
While gravely muttering in his beard, 'I'd rather you than me!'
'The coast is clear', he shouted back, 'make haste, 'The Day' is here!'
Then shut the gate behind them, and consoled himself with beer.

When on his homeward way he paused, this master of the gales,
And drove into his statue half a ton of six inch nails;
'Hoch! hoch!' quoth he, 'now I must go and write up my report
Of this, our greatest victory, and lessons it has taught.'

So he and Wolff sat down to think, and soon one came to see
The mighty German fleet had won a glorious victory,
So 'Wire the news around at once, the time is getting short,
The world must have our story ere our ships get back to port.'

Then back went Tirp. to Kiel again, and peeping through the gate
He saw some ships returning in a mighty flurried state,
'What's this?' he cried, behind his beard his face was turning pale,
And straightway to this statue went and drove another nail.

'Ho! ho! my gallant lads', quoth he, 'why make such frantic haste?
You come as though by devils chased, and little time to waste.'
The pale and shaky captains muttered through their chattering teeth,
'We've won a great big vic'try, all the foe is underneath.'

'If that is so,' quoth Tirpitz, 'why this frantic need to haste,
Why not remain and glut on joys of which you've had a taste,
Why leave the field of victory whose laurels wreath your hair?'
'Well, to be honest 'twas because the British fleet was there.'

'Oh well!' said Tirp., 'the glorious news is speeding on its way,
And 'twill be known the whole world o'er ere breaks another day;
If we can't win by ships and guns we can at least by tales.'
And then into his statue drove another ton of nails.

A British Boy

John Travers Cornwell, 1st Class Boy on H.M.S. *Chester*, 31st May 1916.
(See Admiral Jellicoe's dispatch, published in newspapers, 7th July 1916.)

> For God and king, for country and for right,
> The sons of Britain's far-extending sway
> Flock to the flag, the patriot's debt to pay
> For freedom's gift, against satanic might!

And thus, where all were heroes in the fight
Against a foe who long had sought 'the Day',
A boy stands nobly in the blinding spray
Of sea and shot – one more example bright!

Erstwhile some said the spirit of our race
Was dead through love of gold and gilded toys,
Unfit to hold the realms our fathers won.
The sailor child stands steadfast in his place,
His life-blood ebbing – type of British boys;
The Nelson breed is proud of such a son.

Thomas Hannan

Epigram, R.B.

Earth held thee not, whom now the gray seas hold,
By the blue Cyclades, and even the sea
Palls but the mortal, for men's hearts enfold,
Inviolate, the untamed youth of thee.

Frederic Manning

'Si Monumentum Requiris'
(Lord Kitchener)

If death must claim him, let the North Sea wave
    Hold him; though tombless he shall sleep content;
Proud, o'er the mists that cloak her Great Man's grave
    England, transfigured, stands – his Monument.

Charles T. Foxcroft

Winston's Last Phase

(Mr WINSTON CHURCHILL, in the *London Magazine*, declares that there is no strategic
cause impelling us to fight the German Fleet off the Danish coast, and implies that the
action was audacious but unnecessary.)

When Churchill ran the naval show
    He was extremely optimistic,
And, in referring to the foe,
    Inclined at times to be hubristic.

But when the limelight's genial beams
    No more their influence exerted,
The spirit of his naval dreams
    Incontinently was inverted.

And critics did not fail to note
    That while he ruled the British Navy
His motto was, 'All's well afloat',
    And only when he left it, '*Cave*!'

With a *beau geste* he left the House
    And flounced off to the Front in Flanders,
But soon returned to carp and grouse
    Against our land and sea commanders.

And now, resorting to the pen
    With pompous self-exalting prattle,
He dares to criticize the men
    Who fought and won the Jutland battle.

Prophet by turns of good and ill,
    Oh long may he remain a stranger
To office, who by tongue and quill
    Has proved himself a public danger!

                                                  C.L. Graves

Stories for Our Sons

Yes! Daddy knows right well, my lad,
    The story of the fleet
That met the Huns off Coney Isle
    In Hipper's great defeat.

I served a twelve-inch gun, my lad,
    Upon the gallant ARK,
And fought the fight without respite
    From early dawn till dark.

We left our base the year before,
    And steamed at forty knots,

Until we heard the cry of 'smoke'
    And saw them there in spots.

Aye, there they were at twenty yards,
    A thousand ships in line;
We opened first when 'mess-gear' went
    And sank them all by nine.

Yes! Daddy was right there, my lad,
    He served a five-inch gun,
And all alone killed Kaiser Bill,
    Before the war was won.

                                  Eugene E. Wilson

NINE

The Royal Flying Corps

Life, death and chivalry in the air

The Royal Flying Corps had been formed in May 1912 as an army corps. This was the first war in which aeroplanes would play a significant part, although, unlike in later wars, their principal purpose was not to attack enemy troops but to record their movements and the layout of their guns and positions.

From the time of the BEF landing in France, aircraft of the Royal Flying Corps had tracked the advance of German troops as they moved across Belgium and northern France. Once the line had been established along the Western Front, it was important to maintain supremacy of the air in order to prevent the Germans from carrying out similar sorties over the British lines. This was particularly important during the build-up to a major offensive, when the air was also dotted with observation balloons. During the early summer of 1916, as preparations were underway for the Battle of the Somme, the RFC was especially active, but the heaviest casualties came in April 1917, when 275 British aircraft were shot down in one month with 421 casualties, including 207 airmen killed. The short lifespan of pilots contributed to their particularly black form of humour. Many thought of them as modern chivalric knights, moving perilously but freely above the squalor of the trenches.

In April 1918 the Royal Flying Corps became the Royal Air Force with its own establishment and uniform.

A Recruiting Song of the Royal Flying Corps

I was standing at the corner
When I heard somebody say,
'Come and join the Flying Corps –
Come, step along this way'.

I threw my thirty-chest out,
 And put my cap on straight,
And walked into the office
 Along with Jack, my mate.

They offered me two bob a day,
 I said, 'I didn't think',
But when they murmured 'Four bob',
 I said, 'Come, have a drink.'
And now I spend my Sundays
 With Lizzie in the Lane.
I wonder when I'll get my first
 Or see an aeroplane.

I never was so well off
 In all my naturel:
You should see me in St James's,
 I am an awful swell.
And now I've been to Larkhill
 My education is complete.
'Form fours', ''Bout turn', 'Two deep',
 Oh! don't I do it neat!

You should see us hold our heads up
 When the others pass us by.
The girls they all run after us
 And, breathless, say, 'Oh, my!
Dear Tommy brave, I'll be your slave,
 If you will take me up.'
But hastily I answer,
 'I've an invitation out to sup.'

Jimmy

Jimmy gets his 'Wings' to-night,
 Let the bumper flow!
Jove! but he's a living wonder!
He will cleave the skies asunder!
British to the core, by thunder,
 Fearless of the foe!

Jimmy masters all machines
    With unerring skill.
He's the sturdiest of smiters,
And, by all the Bristol Fighters,
He will strafe the Hunnish blighters –
    Strafe them with a will!

Jimmy's booked for overseas,
    Eagerly he waits.
Then he'll give some demonstrations,
And some staggering sensations,
Followed up by decorations
    In the Palace gates!

Jimmy's just the jolliest sport
    One could wish to see!
Golden conquests lie before him;
Where's the Hun that dare ignore him?
Here's his health! for we adore him,
    Jimmy – R.F.C.!

A Song of the Air

This is the song of the Plane –
    The creaking, shrieking plane,
    The throbbing, sobbing plane,
And the moaning, groaning wires: –
    The engine – missing again!
    One cylinder never fires!
    Hey ho! for the Plane!

This is the song of the Man –
    The driving, striving man,
    The chosen, frozen man: –
The pilot, the man-at-the-wheel,
    Whose limit is all that he *can*,
    And beyond, if the need is real!
    Hey ho! for the Man!

This is the song of the Gun –
>The muttering, stuttering gun,
>The maddening, gladdening gun: –
That chuckles with evil glee
>At the last, long dive of the Hun,
>With its end in eternity!
>Hey ho! for the Gun!

This is the song of the Air –
>The lifting, drifting air,
>The eddying, steadying air,
The wine of its limitless space: –
>May it nerve us at last to dare
>Even death with undaunted face!
>Hey ho! for the Air!

>>>>>>Gordon Alchin

R.A.F.

With the first light, the morning flight
>Before the dawn-wind stirs,
Comes out to pass across the grass
>Jewelled with gossamers;
Then one by one at speed they run
>Until the lifting planes,
Earth-bound no more, tilt up, and soar
>To the wide air's domains.

Now in the swerves of spiral curves
>As the swift kestrels tower,
Each pilot swings blue-circled wings,
>And in the pride of power
Laughs at the wind he leaves behind,
>And eastward at full speed
Where the sun's rose, cloud-veiled, just shows,
>Heads his unbridled steed.

Now underneath, the white mist-wreath
>Clears off from field and lane;
Below and far, one long raw scar,
>The battle-line shows plain,

And there is need that he should read
   As in a book, by signs
Of dust or smoke, what night may cloak
   Within the foeman's lines.

So, tho' he hear the shells burst near,
   Or see the black-crossed foe
And feel the breath of hissing death
   About his temples go,
On his set ways he holds his gaze,
   Nor quits the airy field
Till brain and eyes have gained the prize
   Of secrets all revealed.

F.W.D. Bendall

The Dawn Patrol

Sometimes I fly at dawn above the sea,
Where, underneath, the restless waters flow –
   Silver, and cold, and slow.
Dim in the east there burns a new-born sun,
Whose rosy gleams along the ripples run,
   Save where the mist droops low,
Hiding the level loneliness from me.

And now appears beneath the milk-white haze
A little fleet of anchored ships, which lie
   In clustered company,
And seem as they are yet fast bound by sleep,
Although the day has long begun to peep,
   With red-inflamèd eye,
Along the still, deserted ocean ways.

The fresh, cold wind of dawn blows on my face
As in the sun's raw heart I swiftly fly,
   And watch the seas glide by.
Scarce human seem I, moving through the skies,
And far removed from warlike enterprise –
   Like some great gull on high
Whose white and gleaming wings beat on through space.

Then do I feel with God quite, quite alone,
High in the virgin morn, so white and still,
    And free from human ill:
My prayers transcend my feeble earth-bound plaints –
As though I sang among the happy Saints
    With many a holy thrill –
As though the glowing sun were God's bright Throne.

My flight is done. I cross the line of foam
That breaks around a town of grey and red,
    Whose streets and squares lie dead
Beneath the silent dawn – then am I proud
That England's peace to guard I am allowed;
    Then bow my humble head,
In thanks to Him Who brings me safely home.

Paul Brasher

A Perfect Day
By an Old Bird

When you're out on a long reconnaissance,
And seated alone in the air,
While the 'Archies' explode with a loud report,
And bullets are singeing your hair,
Then a couple of Halberstadts dive on your tail,
And both Lewis guns jamb from the start,
And you land with a crash in 'No Man's Land',
Then you and your 'Bus' have to part.

    Then you've got near the end of a Perfect Day;
    Near the end of your lifetime, too,
    For the bullets are hitting the ground all round,
    With an aim that is sure and true.
    You lie like a log in 'No Man's Land',
    And you pray for the sun to set,
    When you'll get to the end of this Perfect Day,
    And day you will ne'er forget.

Now this is a pilot's Perfect Day,
To see a 'dud' morning break,
When the rain pours down and the sky is grey,
And you've photographs to take,

And you think as you sip at your morning tea
Of a town that all pilots know,
And you hum as you sharpen your razor blade,
And pray that the rain won't go.

Then you come to the end of this 'Perfect Day',
And the end of a dinner, too;
Your head feels light, and your knees feel weak,
For you've painted Amiens blue.
Heidsieck has christened that perfect day,
And the Gobert has done its best.
But the morning after that Perfect Day,
You long for a perfect rest.

Cadet Marchant

Song of the Aeroplane

Up in the zenith, the fleecy clouds chasing,
    Monarch of air in my power supreme,
Looking with scornful eye on the Earth under,
    Swathed in the Sun's golden garment I gleam.
Follow who may thro' my cloud-splashed dominion,
    Uncharted, eternal, unbounded and free,
Cleaving my way across Heaven's fair bosom,
    Brave of the bravest, who travels with me?

Where I go gliding;
Silver clouds sliding,
Dipping and leaping,
My joyous way keeping,
Drooping and stooping,
Twirling and looping,
Brave of the bravest, who travels with me?

Turning and sweeping,
Warily creeping
Into the gloaming,
With night birds a-roaming,
Through the cloud swaying,
On the breeze laying,

Over the moorland dim,
Blithely I hum and skim
Brave of the bravest, who revels with me?

Into the battle's gloom,
Heedless the cannon's boom,
Scorning the shrapnel's shriek,
Cleaving the lyddite's reek,
Poised o'er the belching guns,
Never a foe but runs,
Straight drops my eager bomb,
Hark to its deadly hum.
Flames – and the crash of doom
Breaks in the gath'ring gloom,
Brave of the bravest, who battles with me?

Back through the starry-pierced sky I am speeding,
    O'er the fields where Death's harvest lies
Still and ungarnered, nor heed they the morrow,
    (O, but the tears, the moans and the sighs!)
Proudly to Earth once again I'm returning,
    Darkly to crouch till morning's fair light
Breaks, then again to the heavens go soaring,
    Brave of the bravest, to-morrow we'll fight.

Peace Song of the Aeroplanes

Upward and upward with quiver and whirr,
Onward and upward, our pulses astir,
Higher and higher to heaven's clear blue,
Clearing the rain-cloud we swiftly skim through.
Joyous and fleet as a bird on the wing,
'Faster and faster' we hear the wheels sing;
Swift through the air as a swallow we swoop,
Turn a clear somersault, looping the loop;
Onwards and upwards through limitless space,
Challenge the breezes to outstrip our pace;
Flecked with the sunbeam's bright ripple of mirth
Up to the sphere where the snowflakes have birth.
Bathing our planes in a shimmer of light,
Gliding along in the silver of night.

Earth far below us in mystery fades,
Ghost of a dream-world enwrapped in the shades;
Clear as a songbird's most glorious note
Peals of a church bell in harmony float,
Rising like incense to regions above,
Melting away in a vision of love.
Onward and onward, a speck in the sky,
Dimmer and dimmer to man's watching eye,
Moving through sunlight of brightness untold,
Losing ourselves in a river of gold.

[Here in the eye of the sun]

Here in the eye of the sun
I sit and wait for the Hun;
Twenty thousand feet on high
Out on the roof of the world am I,
I and my 'Pup' and my 'rattle gun'.

There he comes below,
The unsuspecting foe,
A reckless shaft from the gleaming sun.
I dive like death on the hated Hun;
Too late he turns to go.

Sideslip, spin or loop,
He can't evade my swoop;
In vain he's up to his knavish games . . .
A burst! and he plunges down in flames;
I give him the hunter's 'whoop'!

Alone again in space
I turn to the earth my face;
The armies fight below
As ants on the warpath go . . .

. . . But if man's works seem small to me and odd,
How mighty small these things must look to God.

Capt. ffrench

Reconnaissance

I journeyed to the east,
Rolled on the surgent airs of autumn days:
   Below, the earth lay creased
With myriad meadows in the morning haze.
   Far off, where lay the sea,
A silvered mirror beckoned to my bent,
   And, moving orderly,
The high cloud-armies marched magnificent.

   Some menace in the sky,
Some quick alarm did wake me as I sped:
   At once, unwarningly
Streamed out repeated death, from one that fled
   Headlong before my turn –
But, unavoiding of the answering blast,
   Checked sudden, fell astern –
And unmolested fared I to the last.

Gordon Alchin

Over the Lines

We were flying in formation and we kept our ruddy station,
   Though the wind was trying hard to sweep the sky.
And we watched the puffs of powder, heard the Archies booming louder
   And we didn't need to stop to reason why.

With the German lines below us, and a gale that seemed to throw us
   Into nowhere, as it would a schoolboy's kite,
We went skimming through the ether always keeping close together
   And we felt the joy of battle grip us tight.

Then from out of the horizon which we kept our eager eyes on
   Swept the Fokkers in their deadly fan-wise dash.
Soon the Vickers guns were cracking and a couple started backing,
   Whilst a third was sent down in a flaming flash.

How we blessed our Bristol Fighters, as we closed in with the blighters
   And we zoomed and banked and raced them through the air.
We abandoned our formation, but we won the situation,
   Won it easily, with four machines to spare.

Then Archie burst around us, and the beggar nearly found us,
  But we dived towards our lines without delay,
And we finished gay and merry on a binge of gin and sherry,
  For we knew we'd lived to see another day.

Semi-Detached

At a lofty elevation
Floating lazy in the sun,
What an ideal occupation
Keeping watch on brother Hun!

Though a 'sausage' is my villa
Far from angry whizz-bangs' scream,
I can watch the caterpillar,
And all things are what they seem.

In a contemplative manner
When the 'big push' is begun,
'Tis from here I'd love to see it,
From my place up in the sun.

Eyes in the Air

Our guns are a league behind us, our target a mile below,
And there's never a cloud to blind us from the haunts of our lurking foe –
Sunk pit whence his shrapnel tore us, support-trench crest-concealed,
As clear as the charts before us, his ramparts lie revealed.
His panicked watchers spy us, a droning threat in the void;
Their whistling shells outfly us – puff upon puff, deployed
Across the green beneath us, across the flanking gray,
In fume and fire to sheath us and baulk us of our prey.
    Before, beyond, above her,
        Their iron web is spun:
    Flicked but unsnared we hover,
        Edged planes against the sun:
    Eyes in the air above his lair,
        The hawks that guide the gun!

No word from earth may reach us, save, white against the ground,
The strips outspread to teach us whose ears are deaf to sound:
But down the winds that sear us, athwart our engine's shriek
We send – and know they hear us, the ranging guns we speak.
Our visored eyeballs show us their answering pennant, broke
Eight thousand feet below us, a whorl of flame-stabbed smoke –
The burst that hangs to guide us, while numbed gloved fingers tap
From wireless key beside us the circles of the map.
     Line – target – short or over –
       Come, plain as clock hands run,
     Words from the birds that hover,
       Unblinded, tail to sun;
     Words out of air to range them fair,
       From hawks that guide the gun!

Your dying shells have failed you, your landward guns are dumb:
Since earth hath naught availed you, these skies be open! Come,
Where, wild to meet and mate you, flame in their beaks for breath,
Black doves! the white hawks wait you on the wind-tossed boughs of death.
These boughs be cold without you, our hearts are hot for this,
Our wings shall beat about you, our scorching breath shall kiss;
Till, fraught with that we gave you, fulfilled of our desire,
You bank – too late to save you from biting beaks of fire –
     Turn sideways from your lover,
       Shudder and swerve and run,
     Tilt; stagger; and plunge over
       Ablaze against the sun:
     Doves dead in air, who clomb to dare
       The hawks that guide the gun!

Gilbert Frankau

Ten German Aeroplanes

Ten German aeroplanes coming from the Rhine,
One was shot down, and then there were nine.

Nine German aeroplanes sang the 'Hymn of Hate',
One burst his lungs up, and then there were eight.

Eight German aeroplanes travelling towards Heaven,
One lost his way there, and then there were seven.

Seven German aeroplanes in an awful fix,
One got fizzled up, and then there were six.

Six German aeroplanes trying how to dive,
One sank below the Thames, and then there were five.

Five German aeroplanes dodging round a store,
A British airman caught one, and then there were four.

Four German aeroplanes going out to sea,
One got 'drownded', and then there were three.

Three German aeroplanes, wobbling as they flew,
One over-wobbled, and then there were two.

Two German aeroplanes turned their tails to run
Home to the Fatherland, and then there was one.

One German aeroplane travelling all alone,
He gave himself up, and then there were none.

Two Pictures

Dawn . . .
    And the dewy plain
    Awakes to life and sound –
    Where on the flying-ground
    The ghostly hangars blaze with lights again.
The giant birds of prey
    Creep forth to a new day,
    And one by one
    As morning gilds the dome
    Leave the grey aerodrome –
    – The day's begun.

Dusk . . .
    And the vanish'd sun
    Still streaks the evening skies:
    Below, the prone Earth lies
    Darken'd, wherever warring Night has won.

The 'planes, returning, show
   Deep black in the afterglow,
   And one by one
   Drop down from the higher airs,
   – Down, down the invisible stairs –
     The day is done.

                        Gordon Alchin

Searchlights

You who have seen across the star-decked skies
The long white arms of searchlights slowly sweep,
Have you imagined what it is to creep
High in the darkness, cold and terror-wise,
For ever looked for by those cruel eyes
Which search with far-flung beams the shadowy deep,
And near the wings unending vigil keep
To haunt the lonely airman as he flies?

Have you imaged what it is to know
That if *one* finds you *all* their fierce desire
To see you fall will dog you as you go,
High in a sea of light and bursting fire,
Like some small bird, lit up and blinding white
Which slowly moves across the shell-torn night?

                        Paul Bewsher

Every Little While

Every little while I crash a Camel,
Every little while I hit a tree;
I'm always stalling – I'm always falling,
Because I want to fly a posh S.E.
Every little while my engine's conking,
Every little while I catch on fire.
All the time I've got my switch up
I've always got the wind up.
Every, every, every little while.

[Captain Riddell, R.F.C.]

Captain Riddell, R.F.C.
   Trying to land a bumble-bee
      Broke an under carriage Vee.

First he blamed the E.L.C.,
   Foiled in that the landing Tee . . .
      . . . what a dreadful liar he.

O.C. Squadron said 'Let's see
   That's the tenth machine that he
      Has destroyed most foolishly;
        I shall recommend he be
          Transferred to the A.S.C.'.

The moral of this tale is plain
   Speak the truth and shame the devil
If you're summoned to explain
   Always do so on the level.

The Last Lay of the Sopwith Camel Pilot

Beside a Belgian 'staminet when the smoke had cleared away,
Beneath a busted Camel, its former pilot lay,
His throat was cut by the bracing wires, the tank had hit his head,
And coughing a shower of dental work, these parting words he said:

   'Oh, I'm going to a better land,
   They binge there ev'ry night,
   The cocktails grow on bushes,
   So ev'ryone stays tight.
   They've torn up all the calendars,
   They've busted all the clocks,
   And little drops of whisky
   Come trickling through the rocks.'

The pilot breathed these last few gasps before he passed away,
'I'll tell you how it happened – my flippers didn't stay,
The motor wouldn't hit at all, the struts were far too few,
A shot went through the gas tank, and let the gas leak through.

'Oh, I'm going to a better land, where the motors always run,
Where the eggnog grows on the eggplant, and pilots grow a bun.
They've got no Sops, they've got no Spads, they've got no Flaming Fours,
And little frosted juleps are served at all the stores.

'Oh, I'm going to a better land,
They binge there ev'ry night,
The cocktails grow on bushes,
So ev'ryone stays tight.
They've torn up all the calendars
They've busted all the clocks,
And little drops of whisky
Come trickling through the rocks.'

The Dying Aviator

A handsome young airman lay dying,
　　　lay dying,
And as on the aer'drome he lay,
　　　he lay,
To the mechanics who round him came sighing,
　　　came sighing,
These last dying words he did say,
　　　he did say:
'Take the cylinder out of my kidneys,'
　　　'of his kidneys'
'The connecting rod out of my brain,'
　　　'of his brain,'
'The cam box from under my backbone,'
　　　'his backbone,'
'And assemble the engine again.'
　　　'again'.

Captain Albert Ball, V.C., D.S.O.

You may prate of dashing Majors, or of gallant, grim old stagers,
　　When you're sitting in the smoke-room of the Club;
You may laud the high endeavour of the warriors swift and clever,
　　From the Colonel to the smallest junior sub.

They are Britain's vowed defenders; they have added to her splendours,
  They are heroes in excelsis, one and all;
But the Trojan of our nation, who has soared to Fame's high station,
  Is the Nottinghamshire nugget – Albert Ball!

He has hewn a path to Glory; he shall shine in endless story;
  He has triumphed in the conquest of the air;
He has wrought a thousand wonders 'mid the tumults and the thunders
  Of a War with which no others can compare.
He was true to our traditions; he fulfilled the fiercest missions
  With a bravery that nothing can efface;
Bringing Bosches down in plenty, he, a youth of only twenty,
  Must be reckoned with the giants of the race!

He is gone – alas, for ever; yet his fame shall falter never,
  And his deeds of dazzling daring shall endure,
To inspire each generation with a glowing admiration
  For the ways of peerless pilots, swift and sure.
Though his innings here is finished, still with fervour undiminished
  We will praise him, first and foremost in the van;
And wherever men may muster, they shall magnify his lustre,
  For he proved himself a hero and – a man!

TEN

Verdun, the Battle of the Somme Begins

The opening of the 'Big Push'

Plans for a combined French and English assault in France in the summer of 1916 were thrown into disarray when the Germans attacked the French at Verdun in February that year. Their plan was not the capture of Verdun – it was to bleed the French white. The siege, which lasted until July, resulted in more than half a million dead and was the bloodiest battle in history. The French commander, Marshal Pétain, famously declared: 'Ils ne passèrent pas', but the scale of the tragedy was to lead to the French army mutinies of 1917.

Preparations for the Somme offensive went ahead, but it now became a largely British campaign, one in which the New Armies would play their first really significant role. Preparations were thorough and extensive, and optimism high. The northernmost point of the British front was the village of Gommecourt, where a diversionary attack was to be launched, and from there the battle line stretched south over the rolling chalk downs above the River Somme. The preliminary bombardment, in which nearly two million shells were fired, lasted initially for six days and could be heard in England. The scale of this artillery attack led the High Command to believe that the German defences had been destroyed and that the British would walk across no man's land with little opposition.

But some of those on the ground, particularly junior officers who would be leading the men, saw things differently. They could see that in many places the British wire remained uncut, and reports brought back by patrols told them that the German defenders had retreated deep into dugouts cut into the chalk.

Heavy rain delayed the attack for 48 hours. It was launched at 7.30 a.m. on the morning of 1 July, a beautiful summer's day. Shortly before zero hour, three huge mines were exploded beneath the German lines, but, though they suffered huge casualties, their defence was largely unbroken. As the British, each man with 66lb of kit and many carrying entrenching tools or ladders or carrier-pigeon boxes, began to move across no man's land behind an artillery barrage that had now slowly lifted and moved beyond the enemy front line, German machine-gunners came up from their dugouts and manned their parapets. The British were cut down in their thousands. In parts of the line the attackers did reach the German trenches, but the ferocity of the enemy defence meant that no man's land was sometimes impassable; communications were cut off and the planned support and supplies could not get across. As the day wore on, many British who had survived were forced to withdraw to their jump-off positions. By nightfall 19,240 British soldiers were dead, most of them within the first hour. At Serre, the Accrington Pals were all but wiped out. As well as the dead, 57,470 men were wounded or missing. It was the worst day in the history of the British army.

An unofficial truce that night meant that the British were able go out into no man's land to bring in some of their wounded, but many more were left where they had fallen, among the dead.

Verdun

'Verdun is ours!' the vaunting Teuton cries,
    And pours his serried ranks of frenzied hate
    Wave upon wave, carnage insatiate,
To make a highway for the Lord of Lies.
'Verdun is mine!' unflinching France replies;
    'In vain the tyrant thunders at the gate;
    For ruined homes and hearths laid desolate
The hand of Freedom beckons – and I rise.'

Joyous the lark shall soar above the green
    That clothes the fallen; glad the corn shall wave;
Old eyes shall glow, recalling what hath been,
    And how a new France blossomed from the grave.
Thou livest to all time, Verdun. Thy dead?
One hath them in His charge. Be comforted.

F.W. Platt

Before Action

Over the down the road goes winding,
    A ribbon of white in the corn –
The young, green corn. O, the joy of binding
    The sheaves some harvest morn!

But we are called to another reaping,
    A harvest that will not wait.
The sheaves will be green. O, the world of weeping
    Of those without the gate!

For the road we go they may not travel,
    Nor share our harvesting;
But watch and weep. O, to unravel
    The riddle of this thing!

Yet over the down the white road leading
    Calls; and who lags behind?
Stout are our hearts; but O, the bleeding
    Of hearts we may not bind!

Somme, July 1916
J.E. Stewart

Life and Death

If Death should come with his cold hasty kiss
    Along the trench or in the battle strife,
I'll ask of death no greater boon than this:
    That it shall be as wonderful as life.

Carroll Carstairs

Gommecourt

I

The wind, which heralded the blackening night,
Swirled in grey mists the sulphur-laden smoke.
From sleep, in sparkling intensity of light,
Crouched batteries like grumbling tigers woke
And stretched their iron symmetry; they hurled
Skyward with roar and boom each pregnant shell
Rumbling on tracks unseen. Such tyrants reign
The sullen masters of a mangled world,
Grim-mouthed in a womb of furnaced hell,
Wrought, forged, and hammered for the work of pain.

For six long days the common slayers played,
Till, fitfully, there boomed a heavier king,
Who, crouched in leaves and branches deftly laid,
And hid in dappled colour of the spring,
Vaunted tornadoes. Far from that covered lair,
Like hidden snares the sinuous trenches lay
'Mid fields where nodding poppies show their pride.
The tall star-pointed streamers leap and flare,
And turn the night's immensity to day;
Or rockets whistle in their upward ride.

II

The moment comes when thrice-embittered fire
Proclaims the prelude to the great attack.
In ruined heaps, torn saps and tangled wire
And battered parapets loom gaunt and black:
The flashes fade, the steady rattle dies,
A breathless hush brings forth a troubled day,
And men of sinew, knit to charge and stand,
Rise up. But he of words and blinded eyes
Applauds the puppets of his ghastly play,
With easy rhetoric and ready hand.

Unlike those men who waited for the word,
Clean soldiers from a country of the sea;
These were no thong-lashed band of goaded herd
Tricked by the easy speech of tyranny.
All the long week they fought encircling Fate,
While chaos clutched the throat and shuddered past,
As phantoms haunt a child, and softly creep
Round cots, so Death stood sentry at the Gate
And beckoned waiting terror, till at last
He vanished at the hurrying touch of sleep.

The beauty of the Earth seemed doubly sweet
With the stored sacraments the Summer yields –
Grass-sunken kine, and softly-hissing wheat,
Blue-misted flax, and drowsy poppy fields.
But with the vanished day Remembrance came
Vivid with dreams, and sweet with magic song,

Soft haunting echoes of a distant sea
As from another world. A belt of flame
Held the swift past, and made each moment long
With the tense horror of mortality.

That easy lording of the Universe
Who plotted days that stain the path of time,
For him was happy memory a curse,
And Man a scapegoat for a royal crime.
In lagging moments dearly sacrificed
Men sweated blood before eternity:
In cheerful agony, with jest and mirth,
They shared the bitter solitude of Christ
In a new Garden of Gethsemane,
Gethsemane walled in by crested earth.
They won the greater battle, when each soul
Lay naked to the needless wreck of Mars;
Yet, splendid in perfection, faced the goal
Beyond the sweeping army of the stars.
Necessity foretold that they must die
Mangled and helpless, crippled, maimed and blind,
And cursed with all the sacrilege of war –
To force a nation to retract a lie,
To prove the unchartered honour of Mankind,
To show how strong the silent passions are.

III

The daylight broke and brought the awaited cheer,
And suddenly the land is live with men.
In steady waves the infantry surge near;
The fire, a sweeping curtain, lifts again.
A battle-plan with humming engines swerves,
Gleams like a whirring dragon-fly, and dips,
Plunging cloud-shadowed in a breathless fall
To climb undaunted in far-reaching curves.
And, swaying in the clouds like anchored ships,
Swing grim balloons with eyes that fathom all.

But as the road-winged battle-planes outsoared
The shell-rocked skies, blue fields of cotton flowers,

When bombs like bolts of thunder leapt and roared,
And mighty moment faded into hours,
The curtain fire redoubled yet again:
And grey defence reversed their swift defeat
And rallied strongly; whilst the attacking waves,
Snared in a trench and severed from the main,
Were driven fighting in a forced retreat
Across the land that gaped with shell-turned graves.

IV

The troubled day sped on in weariness,
Till Night drugged Carnage in a drunken swoon.
Jet-black, with spangling stars athwart her dress
And pale in the shafted amber of the moon,
She moved triumphant as a young-eyed queen
In silent dignity: her shadowed face
Scarce veiled by gossamer clouds, that scurrying ran
Breathless in speed the high star-lanes between.
She passed unheeding 'neath the dome of space,
And scorned the petty tragedy of Man.
And one looked upwards, and in wonder saw
The vast star-soldiered army of the sky.
Unheard, the needless blasphemy of War
Shrank at that primal splendour sweeping by.
The moon's gold-shadowed craters bathed the ground –
(Pale queen, she hunted in her pathless rise
Lithe blackened raiders that bomb-laden creep)
But now the earth-walled comfort wrapped him round,
And soon in lulled forgetfulness he lies
Where soldiers clasping arms like children sleep.

Sleep held him as a mother holds her child:
Sleep, the soft calm that levels hopes and fears,
Now stilled his brain and scarfed his eyelids wild,
And sped the transient misery of tears,
Until the dawn's sure prophets cleft the night
With opal shafts, and streamers tinged with flame,
Swift merging riot of the turbaned East.
Through rustling gesture loomed the advancing light;
Through fitfully eddying winds, grey vanguards came
Rising in billowy mountains silver-fleeced.

And with the dawn came action, and again
The spiteful interplay of static war:
Dogged, with grim persistence Blood and Pain
Rose venomous to greet the Morning Star.
But others watched that lonely sentinel
Chase fleeting fellow-stars before the day;
Fresh men heard tides of thunder ebb and flow.
– Stumbling in sleep, scarce heeding shot or shell,
The men who fought at Gommecourt filed away:
The poppies nodded as they passed below.

They left the barren wilderness behind,
And Gommecourt gnarled and dauntless, till they came
To fields where trees unshattered took the wind,
Which tossed the crimson poppy heads to flame.
But one stood musing at a waking thought
That spurred his blood and dimmed his searching eyes –
The primal thought that stirs the seed to birth.
Here when the battling nations clashed and fought
The common grass still breathed of Paradise
And Love with silent lips was Lord of Earth.

Geoffrey Dearmer

German Boy

German boy with cold blue eyes,
In the cold and blue moonrise,
I who live and still shall know
Flowers that smell and winds that blow,
I who live to walk again,
Fired the shot that broke your brain.

By your hair all stiff with blood,
By your lips befouled with mud,
By your dreams that shall no more
Leave the nest and sing and soar,
By the children never born
From your body smashed and torn,
– When I too shall stand at last
In the deadland vast,

Shall you heap upon my soul
Agonies of coal?
Shall you bind my throat with cords,
Stab me through with swords?
Or shall you be gentler far
Than a bird or than a star?
Shall you know that I was bound
In the noose that choked you round?
Shall you say, 'The way was hid.
Lord, he knew not what he did'?
Shall your eyes that day be mild,
Like the Sacrifice, the Child?
. . . German boy with cold blue eyes,
In the cold and blue moonrise.

Louis Golding

The Bullet

Every bullet has its billet;
    Many bullets more than one:
God! Perhaps I killed a mother
    When I killed a mother's son.

Joseph Lee

Left Alone

Left alone among the dying!
All around are moaning, sighing,
Or are cursing, sobbing, crying
    In Death's crushing, hushing hand.
We are torn upon the wire,
We are scorched and burnt with fire,
Or lie choking in the mire
    Of the star-lit 'No Man's Land'.

Hear our prayers, O! gentle Jesus,
Send Thine angels down to ease us
From the pains of Hell that seize us,
    From our burning, yearning thirst.

We are broken, we are battered,
Bodies twisted, crushed and shattered
By the shells and bullets scattered
    On this strip of land accurst.

Round about are shadows creeping,
Formless Things which wake the sleeping,
Glaring eyes from shell-holes peeping,
    Mocking always at our pain.
Cold and wet our limbs are numbing,
Fevered brows are drumming, drumming –
Are the stretchers *never* coming?
    Are we numbered with the slain?

God in Heaven, canst Thou hear us?
Mary Mother! Dost Thou fear us?
Stretcher-bearers, are you near us?
    Give us water or we die!
But a grisly shadow's creeping
With his cruel scythe a-reaping
Weary souls which fall to sleeping
    In a choking, croaking sigh.

                              Dudley H. Harris

My Pal and I

I called his name and fear was in my calling.
I pressed his hand. I saw his tired smile.
I leaned above him for a quite while
And wondered at the crimson blood drops falling.

A wildness o'er my brain was surely stealing,
I even humm'd a stave of comic tune,
And yet he never moved. Beneath the moon
I lay beside him, dead to every feeling.

And oh! the tired dawn when I was waking
To find him cold behind me on the grass.
God heard my moan and watched me rise and pass
To hide the pity of a heart that's breaking.

                              A.N. Choyce

R.I.P.

Lay them together in this muddy shell-hole,
Cover them over with this muddy sheet.
Heed not their staring eyes, they gaze to starry skies
Wrap their red tartans around their poor feet.
Cover them quickly nor mutter a prayer,
Pile on the earth quick with never a pang,
Mark it another grave – haste, ev'ry second save –
Here on this rifle their tin helmets hang.

High soar the night flares – hush! swift to your fire-step:
Leave them to rest there out under the stars,
Boys of the city bred, men of the tartan dead,
Laid in the lone waste by sad dead Le Sars.

So do we leave you, lads, laid in the sheer waste,
Sleeping till summer shall flit o'er the foam,
Robed in her gold and blue, to clasp, caressing you
Close to her bosom, her own gathered home.

John Peterson

A Soldiers' Cemetery

Behind that long and lonely trenchèd line
To which men come and go, where brave men die,
There is a yet unmarked and unknown shrine,
A broken plot, a soldiers' cemet'ry.

There lie the flower of Youth, the men who scorned
To live (so died) when languished liberty:
Across their graves, flowerless and unadorned,
Still scream the shells of each artillery.

When war shall cease this lonely, unknown spot
Of many a pilgrimage will be the end,
And flowers will bloom in this now barren plot
And fame upon it through the years descend –
But many a heart upon each simple cross
Will hang the grief, the memory of its loss.

John W. Streets

[Went the day well?]

Went the day well?
    We died and never knew.
But well or ill,
    England, we died for you.

To my Chum

No more we'll share the same old barn,
The same old dug-out, same old yarn,
No more a tin of bully share,
Nor split our rum by a star-shell's flare,
    So long old lad.

What times we've had, both good and bad,
We've shared what shelter could be had,
The same crump-hole when the whizz-bangs shrieked,
The same old billet that always leaked,
    And now – you've 'stopped one'.

We'd weathered the storm two winters long,
We'd managed to grin when all went wrong,
Because together we fought and fed,
Our hearts were light; but now – you're dead
    And I am Mateless.

Well, old lad, here's peace to you,
And for me, well, there's my job to do,
For you and the others who lie at rest,
Assured may be that we'll do our best
    In vengeance.

Just one more cross by a strafed roadside,
With its G.R.C., and a name for guide,
But it's only myself that has lost a friend,
And though I may fight through to the end,
No dug-out or billet will be the same,
All pals can only be pals in name,
But we'll carry on till the end of the game
    Because you lie there.

Travail

A ghastly something there where feasts a glittering swarm of flies,
A slow, hot breeze, a curious sickening stench,
A bloated rat, some nameless filth, charred rags! – behind the trench
     Unending orderlies
With sun-baked forms on stretchers; – what's that tiger-tearing crunch?
Dropped from its rosy whisp of cloud – of which a sunset might be proud –
Their shrapnel's ripped right through that bunch
Of mules and motors! – How they pound
The white road past the lakes!
That's shrapnel swish – that's 'big stuff' where the ground
Swells up in sootlike snakes! –
     Now glance again
Towards those wrecked tanglements – no bodies now,
     (Gad, there's a thud,
     Nineteen inch guns) –
But you can see, where yesterday
'Twas much too hard to plough,
To-day – and not a single drop of rain –
For half a mile across the grey, parched plan,
     A swamp of red-brown mud!

*   *   *

Yet wan-faced women whisper, while they pray,
'We know this, and yet knowing, send our sons!'

Charles T. Foxcroft

From the Somme

    In other days I sang of simple things,
        Of summer dawn, and summer noon and night,
    The dewy grass, the dew-wet fairy rings,
        The lark's long golden flight.

    Deep in the forest I made melody
        While squirrels cracked their hazel nuts on high,
    Or I would cross the wet sand to the sea
        And sing to sea and sky.

When came the silvered silence of the night
  I stole to casements over scented lawns,
And softly sang of love and love's delight
   To mute white marble fauns.

Oft in the tavern parlour I would sing
  Of morning sun upon the mountain vine,
And, calling for a chorus, sweep the string
   In praise of good red wine.

I played with all the toys the gods provide,
  I sang my songs and made glad holiday.
Now I have cast my broken toys aside
   And flung my lute away.

A singer once, I now am fain to weep.
  Within my soul I feel strange music swell,
Vast chants of tragedy too deep – too deep
   For my poor lips to tell.

          Leslie Coulson

ELEVEN

Casualties of the Somme

The first wounded, the dead and the casualty lists, grief at home

In the wake of the initial assault of 1 July, medical services were stretched almost to breaking point. Those who could walk made their own way to Regimental Aid Posts, then on to Advanced Dressing Stations further behind the line. Men whose injuries were not serious would be patched up and returned to their units, but the more seriously wounded were transported by road or train to Casualty Clearing Stations and Base Hospitals.

Initially, reports reaching England suggested that the day had gone well and that advances were significant. Gradually, however, it became clear that this was not so. As the casualty lists published in newspapers grew longer and longer, and as War Office telegrams began to arrive at the homes of those who had died, the scale of the tragedy began to become apparent.

Walking Wounded

Still I see them coming, coming
    In their broken ragged line,
Walking wounded in the sunlight,
    Clothed in majesty divine.
For the fairest of the lilies
    That God's summer ever sees
Ne'er was robed in royal beauty
    Such as decks the least of these;
Tattered, torn and bloody khaki,
    Gleams of white flesh in the sun,
Robes symbolic of their glory
    And the great deeds they have done:

Purple robes and snowy linen
    Have for earthly kings sufficed,
But these bloody, sweaty tatters
    Were the robes of Jesus Christ.

                  T.D. Studdert Kennedy

The Messages

I cannot quite remember . . . There were five
Dropt dead beside me in the trench – and three
Whispered their dying messages to me . . .

Back from the trenches, more dead than alive,
Stone-deaf and dazed, and with a broken knee,
He hobbled slowly, muttering vacantly:

I cannot quite remember . . . There were five
Dropt dead beside me in the trench – and three
Whispered their dying messages to me . . .

Their friends are waiting, wondering how they thrive –
Waiting a word in silence patiently . . .
But what they said, or who their friends may be

I cannot quite remember . . . There were five
Dropt dead beside me in the trench – and three
Whispered their dying messages to me . . .

                  Wilfrid W. Gibson

Unloading Ambulance Train

Into the siding very wearily
She comes again:
Singing her endless song so drearily,
The midnight winds sink down to drift the rain.

So she comes home once more.

Is it an ancient chanty
Won from some classic shore?
The stretcher-bearers stand
Two on either hand.

They bend and lift and raise
Where the doors open wide
With yellow light ablaze.
Into the dark outside
Each stretcher passes. Here
(As if each on his bier
With sorrow they were bringing)
Is peace, and a low singing.

The ambulances load,
Move on and take the road.
Under the stars alone
Each stretcher passes out.
And the ambulances' moan
And the checker's distant shout
All round to the old sound
Of the lost chanty singing.
And the dark seamen swinging.
Far off some classic shore . . .

So she comes home once more.

Wimereux
Carola Oman

The Casualty Clearing Station

A bowl of daffodils,
A crimson-quilted bed,
Sheets and pillows white as snow –
White and gold and red –
And sisters moving to and fro,
With soft and silent tread.

So all my spirit fills
With pleasure infinite,
And all the feathered wings of rest
Seem flocking from the radiant West
To bear me thro' the night.

Gilbert Waterhouse

Quantum Mutatus

Cover him up! My nerve hath not the steel,
    Doctor, of yours! – And so you tended him?
    Your fingers dress'd each torn and shatter'd limb?
You swath'd that ruin'd face? Ye Gods! I feel,
Did we but know, we lesser men would kneel
    In reverence for the hands no terrors grim
    Can shake, the eye no horror can make dim.
– This lad hath taught me what it means to heal!
So young! So far from home! – Alas! 'twas best!
    Rejoice, poor boy, for that dividing sea,
And think thee in thy lonely death thrice blest!
    So shall a mourning mother-heart be free
To see thee still the baby at her breast,
        The pretty child that danc'd upon her knee.

                        E. Armine Wodehouse

The Casualty List

'Killed – Wounded – Missing. Officers and men,
    So many hundreds.' Numbers leave us cold.
    But when next day the tale again is told
In serried lines of printed names – Ah then!
The tragic meaning of it all grows plain.
    We know them not; yet picture in each one
    Some woman's husband, some fond mother's son,
Some maiden's lover, some child's father – slain!

The cost of war looms large before our eyes;
Our hearts beat quicker, tears unbidden rise.
Then thoughts fly upward, shape themselves in prayer.
'God of our fathers, for the stricken care!
The wounded do Thou heal, the lost restore;
Bind broken hearts, bid mourners weep no more;
Loved ones in peril guard by day and night;
And speed, O Lord, the triumph of the Right!'

[There are tear-dimmed eyes in the town today]

There are tear-dimmed eyes in the town today,
　　There are lips to be no more kissed,
There are bosoms that swell with an aching heart
　　When they think of a dear one missed.
But time will assuage their heartfelt grief;
　　Of their sons they will proudly tell
How in gallant charge in this world-wide war,
　　As 'Pals' they fought and fell!

T. Clayton

Broken Bodies

　　Not for the broken bodies,
　　　　When the War is over and done,
　　For the miserable eyes that never
　　　　Again shall see the sun;
　　Not for the broken bodies
　　　　Crawling over the land,
　　The patchwork limbs, the shoddies,
　　Not for the broken bodies,
　　　　Dear Lord, we crave your hand.

　　Not for the broken bodies,
　　　　We pray your dearest aid,
　　When the ghost of War for ever
　　　　Is levelled at last and laid;
　　Not for the broken bodies
　　　　That wrought their sorrowful parts
　　Our chiefest need of God is,
　　Not for the broken bodies,
　　　　Dear Lord – the broken hearts!

Louis Golding

The Widow

　　My heart is numb with sorrow;
　　　　The long days dawn and wane;
　　To me no sweet to-morrow
　　　　Will bring my man again.

Yet must my grief be hidden –
  Life makes insistent claim,
And women, anguish-ridden,
  Their rebel hearts must tame.

For while, my vigil keeping,
  I face the eternal law,
Here on my breast lies sleeping
  The son he never saw.

C.M. Mitchell

A Little War Tragedy

I must not bewail,
  Falter or grow pale,
Say I'm ill or sit wrapped in a shawl:
  He was not my brother,
  Nor acknowledged lover –
No one knew I cared for him at all.

Just by chance they said,
  'Have you heard he's dead?'
As they handed me a cup of tea:
  One among so many,
  Guess they had not any –
He was just the whole wide world to me.

Life must still go on,
  Work is to be done –
These things happen every day I know:
  I was nothing to him
  Have no right to rue him,
Save the right of having loved him so.

To A.M.
(Killed in Flanders)

Now you are dead, I dare not read
  That letter that you sent to me
Before you went: my heart would bleed
  If I that writing now should see.

For I should dream how, long ago,
    We walked those careless Oxford ways,
When Cherwell's banks were all aglow
    With hawthorn and with reddening mays.

And see, as once I used to see,
    St Mary's spire against the sky:
And hear you laugh and call to me
    As I came slowly up the High.

H. Rex Freston

Lost in France

He had the ploughman's strength
In the grasp of his hand.
He could see a crow
Three mile away.
And the trout beneath the stone.
He could hear the green oats growing,
And the sou'-west making rain;
And the wheel upon the hill
When it left the level road.
He could make a gate, and dig a pit,
And plow as straight as stone can fall.
And he is dead.

Ernest Rhys

Telling the Bees
(An old Gloucestershire superstition)

They dug no grave for our soldier lad, who fought and who died out there:
Bugle and drum for him were dumb, and the padre said no prayer;
The passing bell gave never a peal to warn that a soul was fled,
And we laid him not in the quiet spot where cluster his kin that are dead.

But I hear a foot on the pathway, above the low hum of the hive,
That at edge of dark, with the song of the lark, tells that the world is alive:
The master starts on his errand, his tread is heavy and slow,
Yet he cannot choose but tell the news – the bees have a right to know.

Bound by the ties of a happier day, they are one with us now in our worst;
On the very morn that my boy was born they were told the tidings the first:
With what pride they will hear of the end he made, and the ordeal that he trod –
Of the scream of shell, and the venom of hell, and the flame of the sword of God.

Wise little heralds, tell of my boy; in your golden tabard coats
Tell the bank where he slept, and the stream he leapt, where the spangled lily
    floats:
The tree he climbed shall lift her head, and the torrent he swam shall thrill,
And the tempest that bore his shouts before shall cry his message still.

G.E. Rees

To a Dog

Past happiness dissolves. It fades away,
    Ghost-like, in that dim attic of the mind
    To which the dreams of childhood are consigned.
Here, withered garlands hang in slow decay,
And trophies glimmer in the dying ray
    Of stars that once with heavenly glory shined.
    But you, old friend, are you still left behind
To tell the nearness of life's yesterday?

Ah, boon companion of my vanished boy,
    For you he lives; in every sylvan walk
    He waits; and you expect him everywhere.
How would you stir, what cries, what bounds of joy,
    If but his voice were heard in casual talk,
    If but his footstep sounded on the stair!

John Jay Chapman

The Dead Hero

I know where I can find him. I shall look
In every whispering glade and laughing brook,
In every passing wind I'll hear his sigh
And feel his tears fall on me from the sky
In drops the foolish living call the rain,
And in the sun I'll see his smile again,
And on the roses blowing in the South
I'll feel once more the soft touch of his mouth.

Elsie P. Cranmer

TWELVE

The Wounded in England

Military hospitals, VADs, convalescence

The more seriously wounded from the Somme fighting were brought back to England. They crossed by boat, some coming into Southampton, others to Dover from where they were taken by train through the Kent countryside to London. At Charing Cross station crowds gathered in the forecourt to see them arrive, and the wounded were then driven by ambulance to their destinations.

For many the war was over; their wounds were too serious for them to go back. Their initial response was often one of relief for, however serious their injuries, they were at least alive.

In the hospitals they were looked after by professional nurses, and by VADs, volunteer nurses who made up a substantial part of the nursing force. Some went to Roehampton Hospital, the centre for limbless servicemen.

For those whose injuries were less severe, their time in England came to an end. When they had been passed fit, they returned once more to France.

***

Ex Umbra

Morning.
A khaki line – a drizzling rain,
    The thunder of big guns pealing;
The shriek of shell – a cry of pain,
    And dark o'er my senses stealing.

Evening.
A salt sea breeze – a city's roar,
    The sense of a journey ending;
A shaded lamp in a corridor,
    And a sweet face o'er me bending.

J. Bourke

Evening – Kent

Sheep, like woolly clouds dropt from the sky,
   Drift through the quiet meads.
From over the seas, a little cry,
    — Europe bleeds!

Clouds, like woolly sheep, hardly stirr'd,
   Drift through the quiet skies.
From over the seas, a little word,
    — Europe dies!

Louis Golding

Charing Cross

The incoming tide beats up the river,
   With a breeze from the main,
And people await, with hearts a-quiver,
   The incoming train!

Day in, day out, through the grimy portals,
   The pale patients of Pain
Pass 'mid the tears and smiles of the mortals
   They gaze on again!

In War's red tide they were tossed and broken –
   Never shattered in vain!
They faced Death in Life's eyes in unspoken
   But noble disdain!

Now they are home, and hundreds await
   The incoming train;
Pride in the heroes their hearts doth elate
   Like a breeze from the main!

A Sister in a Military Hospital

Blue dress, blue tippet, trimmed with red,
White veil, coif-like about her head.
Starched apron, cuffs, and cool, kind hands,
Trained servants to her quick commands.

Swift feet that lag not to obey
In diligent service day by day.

A face that would have brought delight
To some pure-souled pre-Raphaelite;
Madonna of a moment, caught
Unwary in the toils of thought,
Stilled in her tireless energy,
Dark-eyed and hushed with sympathy.

Warm, eager as the south-west wind,
Straight as a larch and gaily kind
As pinewood fires on winter eves,
Wholesome and young as April leaves,
Four seasons blent in rare accord
– You have the Sister of our ward.

Winifred M. Letts

To a V.A.D. from a V.A.D.

When you start by oversleeping, and the bath is bagged three deep,
When you stagger to the window 'neath the blind to take a peep,
When you find the snow is snowing, and it's murky overhead,
When your room-mate has a day off, and lies snugly tucked in bed,
When your cap falls in the coal-box and you lose your collar stud,
When it's time to start, and then you find your shoes are thick in mud,
When you scramble in to breakfast, just too late to drink your tea –
Don't grouse, my dear; remember you're a 'War-time V.A.D.'.

When you start to scrub the lockers and the bowl falls on the floor,
When you finish them and then you find that they were done before,
When you haven't got a hanky and you want to blow your nose,
When the patients shriek with laughter 'cos a bed drops on your toes,
When you use the last Sapolio and can't get any more,
When you've lost the key belonging to the Linen Cupboard door,
When your head is fairly splitting, and you're feeling up a tree –
Don't grouse, my dear; remember you're a 'War-time V.A.D.'.

When the Doctor comes into the ward, and each stands to his bed,
When he asks you for a probe and you hand him gauze instead,

When the Sister 'strafes' you soundly 'cos Brown's kit is incomplete,
When you take a man some dinner, and upset it on the sheet,
When you make the beds and sweep the ward and rush with all your might,
When you stagger off duty and the wretched fire won't light,
When you think of those at home and long for luxury and ease –
Don't grouse, my dears; remember you're the 'War-time V.A.D.s'.

When your name's read out for night shift and they leave you on your own,
When you're suddenly in darkness and you hear the telephone,
When you crash into a coke-bin as you rush to take the call,
When they tell you there are Zepps, and that you mayn't have lights at all,
When you go into the kitchen and a rat runs through the door,
When it chases you into a chair, and both fall on the floor,
When you try to eat your food, mistaking paraffin for tea –
Don't grouse, my dear; remember you're a 'War-time V.A.D.'.

Leslie M. Goddard

To a V.A.D.

In days gone by, O, V.A.D., you treated us with scorn;
We waited on you hand and foot, till eventide from morn.
You never went out shopping but you had us on your strings,
To pay your bills, to stand you teas, and carry home your things.
We've often waited hours, but there, why harp upon that theme;
Whate'er the cynics may have said, o'er us you ruled supreme.

But times, alas, have changed since then; you're doing now your bit.
Don't think I'm laughing up my sleeve. It takes a lot of grit
For modern girls to work so hard and give up all their leisure,
Washing, scrubbing, making beds, as if it were a pleasure.
In these (and many other ways) you're piling up huge scores,
Now you are at our beck and call as we were once at yours.

We never see you bargain-hunting now in Regent Street,
(The fashions cannot modify your uniform so neat.)
You have not time for books today, nor chocs, nor motor rides;
Nor all the other pastimes that a state of peace provides.
You've dropped most of the little ways that mother found so shocking,
Although I see you still expose two (?) inches of silk stocking.

The prophets tell us things will nevermore be as they were,
In days to come, oh V.A.D., in days *après la guerre,*
They prate of sex and class and votes, of freedom and of land.
Don't heed them, dear, I beg of you; they do not understand
That once I've doffed my uniform there's but one thing I crave,
To come once more beneath your sway and be your willing slave.

A Bit of Bunting

By a Wounded Anzac

They have settled the ward for the evening,
    And straightened every bed;
We have drunk our bowls of cocoa,
    And they've covered the lights with red.
We are lying now till the morning –
    'Tis a terrible time to wait,
When the day seems twenty-four hours
    And the night seems forty-eight.
For the man to the right is restless,
    I can hear him mutter and moan,
And the boy in the bed beside me
    Is breaking his heart for home.
I doze a little at moments,
    Till I'm back with the heat and flies
In the sniper's line of fire,
    With the sunlight in my eyes.
It's curious, lying thinking
    When the clock strikes once and again,
How fate has formed us together
    In a regiment of pain;
How from far-off town and village,
    From the peace of the country sward,
We have answered the call of England –
    To meet again in a ward!

You have heard of the old pied piper
    Who came to the village street,
And played a tune to the children,
    A melody strange and sweet;

And with eyes aglow with laughter,
    And curls that shone in the sun,
They tramped to the sound of the music
    And followed him every one.
We all grow bitter at seasons –
    God knows we are battered and worn –
And we feel in our darkest moments
    That nothing more can be borne;
But say what you will about it,
    There is something in each man's breast
That would urge him to rise and follow,
    Though he hungered for peace and rest.
It is stronger than home and comfort,
    It is stronger than love and life,
Than the speechless grief of a mother
    Or the clinging arms of a wife;
For whenever the old flag shall summon,
    In the midst of his direst pain,
He would hear it out of the shadows,
    And it would never call in vain.

Do we wonder why we have done it
    When the pain is hardest to bear,
And the helpless years to come
    Press like a load of care?
Do we wonder why we have done it,
    When just at the break of day
We fancy we hear the sobbing
    Of the loved ones far away?
Over the mantel yonder,
    Between the glass and the wall,
They have wedged a piece of bunting –
    You can scarcely see it at all;
But my eyes go searching for it
    Before they cover the light,
For it's brought a message with it,
    And I read it every night;
For whether he's tired and weary,
    Or whether he's hurt and sad,
Or whether he's old and helpless,
    Or whether he is but a lad, –

As long as England is England,
    And as long as a man has his will,
He would rise from a bed of sickness
    To hobble after it still.

They say that the grandest picture
    In England, when war is done,
And we've dragged our own from the Germans,
    And fought and bled and won,
Will not be the row of medals
    That blaze on a general's breast,
Or the little letters of glory
    That follow a hero's name;
But the sight that will rouse the nation
    And stir our pulses yet,
The sight that the women of England
    Will count as a lasting debt,
Is the empty sleeve of a soldier
    Who has braved the surgeon's knife,
And the man who goes on crutches
    For the rest of his mortal life.

Wounded

    I am not brave
    As others seem to be;
    But, like a knave,
    I cringe in misery:

    I cannot face
    With smiles my wound's keen bite;
    And, oh, a furnace
    Is my bed at night!

    O God, my God,
    Give me the strength to see
    Thy hand on the rod
    That hotly scourges me!

                           R. Watson Kerr

The Band

Down the street comes the marching music,
  New-called soldiers go swinging by.
Hark! the roll of the drums' deep triumph;
  Thrill of the bugles proud and high;
Singing of war and pomp of battle,
  Glory and honour that shall not die.

Here in the ward are sick men lying,
  Ne'er to follow the drums again:
Young men broken in life's fair morning,
  Weary-hearted and spent with pain,
Turn to listen as through the window
  Swells the lilt of that mocking strain.

Silence, silence, oh, lying music!
  War is waste and a searing fire;
Youth and gladness and all things lovely
  Trodden out in the bloody mire.
Still the music comes calling, calling,
  'Glory! Glory! beyond desire!'

                                          Eva Dobell

To Melt a Stone

Kindly manager of Cox,
I am sadly on the rocks,
For a time my warring ceases,
My patella is in pieces;
Though in Hospital I lie,
I am not about to die;
Therefore let me overdraw
Just a very little more.
If you stick to your red tape
I must go without my grape,
And my life must sadly fret
With a cheaper cigarette.
So pray be not hard upon
A poor dejected subaltern,
This is all I have to say,
        'IMPECUNIOUS' R.F.A.

Alleged Answer from Cox's

Sir, the kindly heart of Cox
Cannot leave you on the rocks,
And he could not sleep in bed
Thinking you were underfed;
So if you will let us know
Just how far you want to go,
Your request will not be vain,
Written from your bed of pain.
We will make but one request –
Keep this locked within your breast,
For if others know, they'll say,
'Good old Cox is sure to pay,
Only take him the right way.'

In Hospital

When the war is done we'll recall the fun –
    The fun that conquered the pain –
For we'll owe a debt (and we'll not forget)
    To the jokes that kept us sane:
How the wounded could laugh and bandy their chaff
    And kick up the deuce of a row!
        It may be, in peace, when the sufferings cease,
        We'll be sadder, aye sadder, than now.
                A 3rd L[ondon] G[eneral] H[ospital] Orderly

The Cripple

He totters round and dangles those odd shapes
    That were his legs. His eyes are never dim.
He brags about his fame between the tapes,
    And laughs the loudest when they laugh at him.
Amid the fights of snow he takes a hand;
    Accepts his small defeats, and with a smile
He rises from the ground, and makes his stand
    With clumsiness, but battles hard the while.
So quick to see the pain in fellow men,
    He chides them; yea, and laughs them into youth.

And yet, when death was near to one, 'twas then
   About his kindly heart we learnt the truth.
Since nowadays of cheer there is a dearth,
    'Twas smiles or tears, and so he chose the mirth.

Leon Gellert

The Road that Brought me to Roehampton

Of course, to be without a leg, as everybody knows,
Has this advantage – nobody can tread upon your toes;
   And when a Theatre, or may be, a Cinema you're in,
   There's nobody who's clumsy who can kick you on the shin.
Again, you can't get chilblains, or trench feet when you're out,
And so you see how safely you can always get about.

   They are long long trails I've tramped on;
   There are lonely spots I've camped on;
   There are doorsteps I have stamped on;
   There are pianos I have vamped on;
     But the Trail I've struck,
     With the Best of Luck,
  Is the Road that brought me to Roehampton.

Now when your leg is separate, there's one thing to be said,
You can be half-dressed already when you're getting out of bed;
   But if you're on a muddy road, it may be just your luck
   To twist your foot right round, if in the mud you get it stuck.
And then you'll keep on walking round and round upon your track,
For you won't really know if you are going on or back.

   They are long long trails I've tramped on, etc.

When I obtain my wooden leg, I'll hop and skip and jump;
I never may be wealthy, being always on the stump;
   Yet I can always stump up, and at any time I beg
   To say that like some others I can always 'Swing the leg'.
So put your best foot forward – an easy thing to do –
Though it might be hard to say which is the better of the two!

   They are long long trails I've tramped on, etc.

Sivori Levey

My Motor-Bus Conductress

(A Tribute)

If a one-legg'd man jumps on a bus,
    He needs expert assistance;
He doesn't want a lot of fuss
    To go a little distance.
And starting from Roehampton Lane
    A Number Eighty-Five
Has got a Lady Bus Conductor
    Very much alive.
A little curl says 'Cheerio!'
    From underneath her hat,
She wears a uniform, and she
    Looks very smart in that.

My Lady Bus Conductress,
With sweet smile and 'Good Luck' tress,
    'The Green Man' at the turning
    Murmurs 'Mustard' or 'Chutney!'
But with her hand to hold me,
And her arm to enfold me,
    It's safely on and safely off –
    At Roehampton or at Putney.

At Roehampton Lane or Putney Heath,
    The Hill, or at the Station,
You see her hat and underneath
    Her smile of animation.
And when you come to Putney Bridge
    You're in the best of care,
Because that Lady Bus Conductor
    Always is 'all there!'
Her smiling eyes say 'Cheerio!'
    To all who sit or stand,
And getting on or getting off,
    She gives a helping hand.

My Lady Bus Conductress, etc.

And when you get up from your seat,
    She takes hold of your crutches;
And helps you down – it's quite a feat! –
    Majestic as a Duchess.
Roehampton House or Dover House,
    For officer or man,
That Lady Motor Bus Conductor
    Does the best she can.
Her agile hands say 'Cheerio!'
    There's 'Good Luck' in her eye;
There's no need for anxiety
    When she is standing by.

My Lady Bus Conductress, etc.

Sivori Levey

In a Tramcar

Rain, dark, and mud; the gaslights dim and shrunk;
    Dull full-fed faces ranged in double row,
Oozing respectability; and, drunk,
    Within his corner, mounting in a glow
Of mirth that is not mirth, he sat and sang
    Of Afton's green braes. His friend, mean, shoddy-clad,
And hunched and writhen, in a voice that rang
    Strange on those stolid masks, explained: 'This lad
(I dinna ken him; I'm just seeing him through)
    Got blinded at the war. He's no himsel''.
Then suddenly I saw his eyes were two
    Red smears. The conductress signed and rang the bell.
      They lumped him out into the triple night
      Of dark and mental mirk and blasted sight.

E. Albert

After Visiting an Asylum

I saw them sitting on a grassy bank –
Under the shade of mighty trees they were;
Yet those they saw not, with their dreadful stare,
Of naught expressive save the spirit's blank.

They sat companioned, yet they sat alone:
Nature and all the glory of the hour
They heeded not; and memory could not dower
Their minds with images; no future known,
They could not hope; of others nought they knew,
Therefore they conversed not; and while they slept
They were as conscious of the hours that crept
As when awake – and in my mind there grew
Horror before their fate who thus were caught
And prisoned in a hell beyond our thought.

Alexander Robertson

Gold Braid

Same old crossing, same old boat,
    Same old dust round Rouen way,
Some old nasty one-franc note,
    Same old 'Mercy, sivvoo play';
Same old scramble up the line,
    Same old 'orse-box, same old stror,
Same old weather, wet or fine,
    Same old blooming War.

    Ho Lor, it isn't a dream,
        It's just as it used to be, every bit;
    Same old whistle and same old bang,
        And me to stay 'ere till I'm 'it.

           *   *   *

'Twas up by Loos I got my first;
    I just dropped gently, crawled a yard
And rested sickish, with a thirst –
    The 'eat, I thought, and smoking 'ard . . .
Then someone offers me a drink,
    What poets call 'the cooling draft',
And seeing 'im I done a think:
    '*Blighty*', I thinks – and laughed.

I'm not a soldier natural,
　　No more than most of us to-day;
I runs a business with a pal
　　(Meaning the Missis) Fulham way;
Greengrocery – the cabbages
　　And fruit and things I take meself,
And she has daffs and crocuses
　　A-smiling on a shelf.

'Blighty', I thinks. The doctor knows;
　　'E talks of punctured damn-the-things.
It's me for Blighty. Down I goes;
　　I ain't a singer, but I sings;
'Oh, 'oo goes 'ome?' I sort of 'ums;
　　'Oh, 'oo's for dear old England's shores?'
And by-and-by Southampton comes –
　　'Blighty!' I says and roars.

I s'pose I thort I done my bit;
　　I s'pose I thort the War would stop;
I saw myself a-getting fit
　　With Missis at the little shop;
The same like as it used to be,
　　The same old markets, same old crowd,
The same old marrers, same old me,
　　But 'er as proud as proud.

*　　*　　*

The regiment is where it was,
　　I'm in the same old ninth platoon;
New faces most, and keen becos
　　They 'ope the thing is ending soon;
I ain't complaining, mind, but still,
　　When later on some newish bloke
Stops one and laughs, 'A blighty, Bill',
　　I'll wonder, 'Where's the joke?'

Same old trenches, same old view,
    Same old rats and just as tame,
Same old dug-outs, nothing new,
    Same old smell, the very same,
Same old bodies out in front,
    Same old *strafe* from 2 till 4,
Same old scratching, same old 'unt,
    Same old bloody War.

      Ho Lor, it isn't a dream,
        It's just as it used to be, every bit;
      Same old whistle and same old bang
      And me out again to be 'it.

                              A.A. Milne

THIRTEEN

Autumn and Winter 1916–1917

*The end of the Battle of the Somme, winter 1916–1917, the
maintenance of morale in the line, Winston Churchill*

The Battle of the Somme went on until 18 November, with steadily mounting
casualties and in increasingly impossible conditions of wet, mud and cold. By the
time it came to an end there were an estimated 420,000 British casualties, and
some of the objectives of 1 July were still in enemy hands. The maximum advance
was 7½ miles. It remains one of the most contentious battles of history.

Most saw the battle as the great watershed of the war. The poet David Jones
wrote that after July 1916 'things hardened into a more relentless, mechanical
affair [and] took on a more sinister aspect'. Many soldiers noted that the earlier
optimistic enthusiasm and companionship, where men had volunteered and
trained together, was never the same once the price of failure had become
apparent and unwilling conscripts had filled the gaps left by the heavy casualties
among the New Armies. Yet, despite it all, the spirit of the army remained
unbroken.

The winter that followed was one of the most severe in living memory.

>─┤─◄►─•─⊖─•─◄►─┤─◄

Before Ginchy
September, 1916

Yon poisonous clod,
    (Look! I could touch it with my stick!) that lies
      In the next ulcer of this shell-pock'd land
        To that which holds me now;
Yon carrion, with its devil-swarm of flies
      That scorn the protest of the limp, cold hand,
        Seeing half-rais'd to shield the matted brow;
          Those festering rags whose colour mocks the sod;

And, O ye gods, those eyes!
Those staring, staring eyes.

How can I gaze unmov'd on sights like these?
What hideous enervation bids me sit
Here in the shelter of this neighbour pit,
Untroubled, unperturbèd, at mine ease,
And idly, coldly scan
This fearsome relic of what once was man?

Alas! what icy spell hath set
The seal upon warm pity? Whence
This freezing up of every sense?
I think not I lack pitifulness; – I know
That my affections were not ever so;
My heart is not of stone! – And yet
There's something in the feeling of this place,
There's something in the breathing of this air,
Which lets me gaze upon that awful face
Quite passionless; which lets me meet that stare
Most quietly. – Nay, I could touch that hair,
And sicken not to feel it coil and cling
About my fingers. Did occasion press,
Lo! I could spurn it with my foot – that thing
Which lies so nigh! –
Spurn it light-heartedly and pass it by.
So cold, so hard, so seeming pitiless
Am I!
And yet not I alone; – they know full well,
These others, that strange blunting of the heart:
They know the working of that devil's-art,
Which drains a man's soul dry,
And kills out sensibility!

They know it too, and they can tell
That this distemper strange and fell,
This hideous blotting of the sense
Creeps on one like a pestilence!
It is some deadly Power of ill
Which overbears all human will!

Some awful influence of the sky,
  Some dreadful power of the place,
   Wherein we live and breathe and move,
   Which withers up the roots of Love
And dries the very springs of Grace.
It is the place! – *For, lo, we are in hell.*
  That is the reason why!

And things that curse and writhe, and things that die,
  And fearful, festering things that rot,
  – They have their place here. They are not
Like unfamiliar portents hurl'd
From out some monstrous, alien world.
This is their place, their native atmosphere,
  Their home; – they are in keeping here!

  And, being in hell,
All we, who breathe this tense, fierce air,
  – On us too, lies the spell,
Something of that soul-deadening blight we share;
  That even the eye is, in a sense, made one
   With what it looks upon;
  That even the brain, in some strange fashion wrought,
   Twists its familiar thought
    To forms and shapes uncouth;
  And even the heart – the heart that once did feel
The surge of tears and pity's warm appeal –
  Doth quite forget her ancient ruth,
Can look on piteous sights unmov'd,
As though, forsooth, poor fool! she had never lov'd.

   * * *

They say we change, we men that come out here!
  But do they know how great that change?
  And do they know how darkly strange
  Are those deep tidal waves that roll
  Within the currents of the soul,
  Down in the very founts of life,
   Out here?

How can they know it? – Mother, sister, wife,
    Friends, comrades, whoso else is dear,
    How can they know? – Yet, haply, half in fear,
  Seeing a long-time absent face once more,
  Something they note which was not there before,
  – Perchance, a certain habit of the eye,
  Perchance, an alter'd accent in the speech –
Showing he is not what he was of yore.
    Such little, curious signs they note. Yet each
      Doth in its little, nameless way
      Some portion of the truth betray.
        Such tokens do not lie!

    The change is there; the change is true!
And so, what wonder if the outward view
  Do to the eye of Love unroll
  Some hint of a transformèd soul?
– Some hint; for even Love dare peep
  No further in that troubled deep;
  And things there be too stern and dark
  To live in any outward mark
    The things that they alone can tell,
    Like Dante, who have walk'd in hell.

E. Armine Wodehouse

September 25th, 1916

I sat upon the fire-step – by my side
The adjutant – next him an F.O.O.
The trench was an old German one, reversed.
The parapet was made of many things
That should not have been there at all – the time
Was zero minus twenty: and the noise
That had been horrible enough before,
Grew to an unimaginable pitch.
It seemed as tho' I had no eyes, no mouth,
No sense of sight or taste, no power of speech
But only hearing – hearing multiplied
To the last limit of a dizzy brain.
The noise was everywhere about – but mostly
Above us: and was made of every sort

Of bang, crash, whistle, whine, thump, shriek and thud.
If every devil from the pit of hell,
Each with an unmelodious instrument,
Each vieing with the other in making noise,
Had flown above me in the tortured air,
One great infernal pandemonium,
I do not think they would have made a tenth
Of the long seismic polyphony that passed
Over our heads: I saw the adjutant's
Mouth open, and his lips move as in speech,
But no words came that I could hear, because
My hearing was entirely occupied.
The trench-wall rocked – then dust and clods of earth
Fell all about me – and I was aware
Of fat grey smoke-wreaths and an acrid smell.
And, dimly, as one hears a metronome,
In punctuating stabs of sharper sound
Thro' a great orchestrated symphony,
I heard the German counter-barrage burst
On the high ground about us, saw my watch
Marking three minutes past the zero-hour,
Sat for another unremembered space,
Wondering what would happen if a shell
Fell in the trench beside me: felt again
By some sixth sense rather than thro' my ears,
That there were fewer shells – that they had ceased.
Climbed on the parapet – and – north by east
From the torn hill of Ginchy Telegraph –
Saw – aye, and seeing cheered exultantly –
The long well-ordered lines of our advance
From Bouleaux Wood to distant Gueudecourt
Sweep from the valley underneath my feet
Up the long slopes to Morval and Les Bœufs.

F.W.D. Bendall

The German Dug-out

Forty feet down
A room dug out of the clay,
Roofed and strutted and tiled complete;
The floor still bears the mark of feet

(Feet that never will march again!)
The doorposts' edge is rubbed and black
(Shoulders that never will lift a pack
Stooping in through the wind and rain!)
Forty feet from the light of day,
Forty feet down.

A week ago
Sixteen men lived there,
Lived, and drank, and slept, and swore,
Smoked, and shivered, and cursed the war,
Wrote to their people at home maybe,
While the rafters shook to the thudding guns;
Husbands, fathers, and only sons,
Sixteen fellows like you and me
Lived in that cavern twelve foot square
A week ago.

Into the dark
Did a cry ring out on the air,
Or died they stiffly and unafraid
In the crash and flame of the hand-grenade?
We took the trench and its mounded dead,
And the tale of their end is buried deep,
A secret which sixteen corpses keep
With the sixteen souls which gasped and fled
Up forty steps of battered stair,
Into the dark.

Forty feet down,
Veiled from the decent sky,
The clay of them turns to its native clay,
And the stench is a blot in the face of day.
Men are a murderous breed, it seems,
And these, maybe, are quieter so;
Their spirits have gone where such things go;
Nor worms nor wars can trouble their dreams;
And their sixteen twisted bodies lie
Forty feet down.

J.L. Crommelin Brown

Mud

It's said that our fight with the Kaiser
    Is the wettest affray since the Flood,
At least every day makes us wiser
    In the infinite samples of mud.

We've mud on our knees and our faces,
    We've mud on our ears and our hair,
We've mud on our tunics and braces,
    On everything else that we wear.

We've mud on our sugar and coffee,
    We've mud on our beef and our bread,
We seem to be tramping through toffee,
    We've mud from our toes to our head.

We've mud that is dreadfully sticky
    (Its depth may be more than a foot),
We've mud that is chalky and tricky,
    We've mud that is liquefied soot.

At times we have mud that's like treacle,
    At times it is thinner than soup,
At times many men by a squeak'll
    Just fail to do 'looping the loop'.

No matter what else may befall us,
    No matter how smooth be our path,
When home the authorities call us,
    The first thing we'll need is a BATH.

Somewhere in France, November 1916.

Alfred Miller

A Song of Winter Weather

It isn't the foe that we fear;
It isn't the bullets that whine;
It isn't the business career
Of a shell, or the bust of a mine;

It isn't the snipers who seek
To nip our young hopes in the bud:
No, it isn't the guns,
And it isn't the Huns –
It's the MUD,
      MUD,
        MUD.

  It isn't the *mêlée* we mind.
  That often is rather good fun.
  It isn't the shrapnel we find
  Obtrusive when rained by the ton;
  It isn't the bounce of the bombs
  That gives us a positive pain:
  It's the strafing we get
  When the weather is wet –
  It's the RAIN,
      RAIN,
        RAIN.

It isn't because we lack grit
We shrink from the horrors of war.
We don't mind the battle a bit;
In fact that is what we are for;
It isn't the rum-jars and things
Make us wish we were back in the fold:
It's the fingers that freeze
In the boreal breeze –
It's the COLD,
      COLD,
        COLD.

  Oh, the rain, the mud, and the cold,
  The cold, the mud, and the rain;
  With weather at zero it's hard for a hero
  From language that's rude to refrain.
  With porridgy muck to the knees,
  With sky that's a-pouring a flood,
  Sure the worst of our foes
  Are the pains and the woes

                    Of the RAIN,
                            the COLD,
                                and the MUD.

                                            Robert W. Service

                            An Appeal

There are various types of courage, there are many kinds of fear,
There are many brands of whiskey, there are many makes of beer,
There is also rum, which sometimes in our need can help us much,
But 'tis whiskey – whiskey – whiskey! hands the courage which is 'Dutch'.

In moments when the front is still – no hustling whizzbangs fly –
In all the world you could not find a braver man than I!
Yet on patrol in No-Man's-Land, when I may have to stalk a
Benighted Hun, in moments tense I have recourse to 'Walker'.

'Tis Scotland's best which helps me rest, 'tis Mountain Dew which stays me
When Minnies rack my wearied soul, or blatant H.E. flays me,
'Twas by its aid that I endured Trones Wood and such-like places.
In times of stress my truest friend accelerates my paces.

Take what you will save only this – my evening tot of whiskey,
It gives me warmth, and helps to make a soaking much less risky,
Oh! G.O.C.s now hear our pleas respectfully presented,
Lend us your aid in this our plight, and we will be contented.

                        They Didn't Believe Me!

        Don't know how it happened quite,
        Sure the jar came up all right?
        Just as full as it should be,
        Wouldn't touch it, no, not me!
        Sergeants very seldom touch
        Rum, at least, not very much,
        Must have been the A.S.C.,
        Anyway, it wasn't me!

Yet when I told them that I hadn't touched the jar,
They didn't believe me, they didn't believe me;
They seem to know a sergeant's thirst,
I fear they all believe the worst.
It's the rottenest luck that there could be;
And when I tell them, and I'm certainly going to tell them
There'll be fatigues for them where'er I be,
They'll never believe me, they'll never believe that
The man who tapped the jar could not be me!

[The corp'rl and the privit they]

The corp'rl and the privit they
    Was standing in the road.
Do you suppose, the corp'rl said,
    That rum is 'à la mode?'
I doubt it! said the privit as
    He shouldered up his load.

'Now this 'ere war', the corp'rl said,
    'Has lasted long enuff.'
'Gorblime,' said the private with
    His voice exceeding gruff,
'Not 'arf it ain't!' and drew his nose
    Across his sheepskin cuff.

The privit to the sergeant said,
    'I wants my blooming rum.'
'No poo,' the sergeant curtly said,
    And sucked his jammy thumb.
'There's "soup in loo" for you to-night.'
    The privit said, 'By gum!'

Cigarettes

In careless fingers loosely swung,
Up their curling smokepuffs blow,
Lightly whirling wreaths are hung,
Blue and dreaming, circling slow.

Fire-points kindle, gleaming red,
Tiny fire-sparks scatter swift,
Specks of flamelight quickly sped
E'er the lazy smoke-veils lift.

Dreams they bring of hearth and home,
Loves forgotten, – all the things
Dearer now to men who roam –
Wakened by the magic rings.

Airy castles, wonder-built,
Shortlived memories that charm,
Hopes of future, fancy-gilt,
Visioned peace and victor's palm.

Wayward, fleeting thoughts will stray,
Words, warm with the weaving spell
Wrought by winding smoke-wreaths, may
On mind's store of treasure dwell.

Spirits rising care defy,
Laughter chimes with tale or joke,
Vanish worry, woe and sigh,
In the twirling fumes of smoke.

Cigarettes! Bear, in your wake,
Consolation, cheer and wit;
Woodbine, Player, Golden Flake,
Truly, you have done your bit!

Minor Worries

If the Hun lets off some gas –
                    Never mind.
If the Hun attacks in mass –
                    Never mind.
If your dugout's blown to bits,
Or the C.O.'s throwing fits,
Or a crump your rum jar hits –
                    Never mind.

If your trench is mud knee-high –
         Never mind.
You can't find a spot that's dry –
         Never mind.
If a sniper has you set,
Through dents in your parapet,
And your troubles fiercer get –
         Never mind.

If you're whizzbanged day and night –
         Never mind
Bully all you get to bite –
         Never mind.
If you're on a working party,
Let your grin be wide and hearty,
Though the sappers may be tarty –
         Never mind.

If machine guns join the muddle –
         Never mind.
Though you're lying in a puddle –
         Never mind.
If a duckboard barks your shin,
And the barbed wire rips your skin,
'Tis reward for all your sin –
         So never mind.

But this warning I'd attest –
         Have a care.
When your Div. is back at rest –
         Then beware.
When that long three months is over,
And you've lost your canteen cover,
Shoot yourself or find another –
         Have it there!

Have you all your drill forgotten? –
         Luckless wight.
Through those months so rain besotten –
         Day and night.

On the left you'll form platoon,
Willy nilly, six till noon,
Front line trench will seem a boon –
        Drill's a rite.

Oh! you poor unhappy thing –
        Be not sad.
Just remember when all's wrong –
        And you're mad,
Though your worries may be great,
They're but part, at any rate,
Of poor Fritz's awful fate –
        Buck up, lad!

To all 'Doubting Thomases'

Now listen ye of mournful mien, whose bleatings rend the air,
Who spread an air of gloom where'er you go,
That though of cleverness you have p'r'aps more than your fair share,
Yet most of us just hate your wail of woe.

One day 'tis 'this', and next day 'that', your bogies come at will,
Of fearful ills to come you rave and rant,
You said a year ago the war was lost – we're fighting still,
The job has been no easier for your cant.

In reverse you see disaster, and a victory spurs you on
To still greater efforts in the realms of doubt,
'We'll be lured into a trap', or 'We can ne'er hold what we've won',
And 'We'll all be starved to death' your constant shout.

'Tis true that mostly you are those who ne'er have known the joy
Of living in ten feet of mud and slime,
Or the ecstasy which thrills one, sheer delight without alloy,
When you're dodging crumps and Minnies all the time.

So in future cut the grousing, and for God's sake wear a grin,
The time is surely coming in a while,
When in spite of all your croakings the old Huns will be 'all in',
Cut the everlasting wail and smile, man, SMILE!

The Armoured(illo) Train

This is the Armoured(illo) Train.
His great advantages are plain;
A lumbering beast, yet still we note
That in his cumbrous overcoat
Mosquito bites he can defy
While spitting fire as he goes by;
So safety lurks beneath his weight
Of Armadillo-pattern plate.

St John Hamund

The Sentrypede

The Centipede, so folks repeat,
Has something like a hundred feet.
The Sentrypede has only two –
Enough for what he has to do;
But when he's done his Sentry-go
In ammunition boots, you know,
Each foot is in a sorry state,
And feels about a hundredweight!

St John Hamund

[The world wasn't made in a day]

The world wasn't made in a day,
And Eve didn't ride on a 'bus,
But most of the world's in a sandbag,
The rest of it's plastered on us.

[Little stacks of sandbags]

Little stacks of sandbags,
    Little lumps of clay;
Make our blooming trenches
    In which we work and play.

Merry little whizz-bang,
    Jolly little crump
Made our trench a picture,
    Wiggle, woggle, wump.

Why Not?

We've had a play in ragtime, and we've had a ragtime band,
We've had a ragtime army, and we've had a ragtime land;
But why not let us have what we have never had before?
Let's wade right in tomorrow and let's have a ragtime war.

Let's carry up our duckboards to a ragtime's jerky strains,
Let's whistle ragtime ditties while we're bashing out Hun brains,
Let's introduce this melody in all we say and do,
In our operation orders, and in all our lies to Q.

Let us write O.O.s to music, and the red-hats can decide
The witching hour of zero to a dainty Gaby Glide;
We'll take the fateful plunge, and when we venture o'er the top
We'll do it to a Turkey Trot or tuneful Boston Hop.

We'll drink our S.R.D. to tune, and even 'chatting up'
Becomes a melody in rhyme if done to 'Dixie Pup',
A bombing raid to 'Old Kentuck' would make a Fritzie smile,
He'd stop a bomb with pleasure to a ragtime's mystic guile.

Can you see our giddy 'Q' staff, as they go up the line,
Just walking round the trenches to the air 'Kentucky Mine',
Gaily prancing down the duckboards, as they tumble o'er a bucket
To the quiet seducing strains of 'My Dear Home in Old Kentucket'.

The Duck Board

It's a long way to Tipperary,
    Or so it always seems;
There's a long, long trail awinding
    Into the land of dreams.
And there's a long and narrow path
    Our Warriors know well,
For one way leads to Blighty,
    And the other way to – well!

    It's the Duck Board Glide,
    It's the Duck Board Slide,
        On a cold and frosty night;
    For it's over a mile
    In single file
        Out in the pale moon-light.
    It's nippy; slippy;
    Bumpy; jumpy;
        Shell-holes either side;
    And when machine guns cough
    You can all drop off
    That Duck Board Glide.

It's very dark and lonely,
    And you see, when on the top,
A Very Light; so in the trench
    You very light-ly drop.
But when you want to reach the line,
    That's done as best you may,
There's only one path that you have to take,
    It is the only way.

    It's the Duck Board Glide, etc.

When you were young, and went to Church,
     Or Chapel, it may be,
The *Padre* used to take some text
     To *strafe* you all with glee.
'The path is long and narrow
     Along which you ought to go!'
We did not know then what it was,
     But now, of course, we know.

          It's the Duck Board Glide, etc.

                                        Sivori Levey

Joseph Arthur Brown

The name of Joseph Arthur Brown
     By some profound mischance
Was sent right through to G.H.Q.
     As 'Killed in action, France.'

So when poor Joseph went to draw
     His bully beef and bread,
'You're not upon the strength, my son,'
     The Quartermaster said.

To Sergeant Baird then Joseph went
     And told his fortune harsh,
But Sergeant Baird on Joseph glared
     And pulled his great moustache.

'Have I not taught you discipline
     For three long years?' said he,
'If you are down as dead, young Brown,
     Why, dead you'll have to be.'

In vain the journal of his town
     Was bought by friends to please,
That he might see his eulogy
     In local Journalese;

For to the Captain Joseph went
    With teardrops in his eye,
And said, 'I know I'm dead, but oh!
    I am so young to die!'

And at the Captain's feet he knelt
    And clasped him by the knee.
But on his face no sign of grace
    Poor Joseph Brown could see.

'Then to *John Bull* I'll write,' he cried,
    'Since supplication fails.'
'But you are dead,' the Captain said,
    'And dead men tell no tales.'

So reckless passion seized upon
    The luckless Private Brown,
And with two blows upon the nose
    He knocked the Captain down.

'Mid cries of horror and surprise
    They led the lad away.
Before the Colonel grim and stern
    They brought him up next day.

But when the Colonel sentenced Brown
    (R.62703)
With thund'rous voice and language choice
    To thirty days F.P.,

Across the trembling prisoner's face
    A smile was seen to spread,
As he replied, with conscious pride,
    'You can't, 'cos I am dead.'

                          Edward de Stein

The Missing Leader

What is Master Winston doing?
What new paths is he pursuing?
What strange broth can he be brewing?

Is he painting, by commission,
Portraits of the Coalition
For the R.A. exhibition?

Is he Jacky-obin or anti?
Is he likely to 'go Fanti',
Or becoming shrewd and canty?

Is he in disguise at Kovel,
Living in a moujik's hovel,
Making a tremendous novel?

Does he run a photo-play show?
Or in *sæva indignatio*
Is he writing for HORATIO?

Fired by the divine afflatus
Does he weekly lacerate us,
Like a Juvenal *renatus*?

As the great financial purist,
Will he smite the sinecurist
Or emerge as a Futurist?

Is he regularly sending
HAIG and BEATTY screeds unending,
Good advice for censure blending?

Is he ploughing, is he hoeing?
Is he planting beet, or going
In for early 'tato-growing?

Is he writing verse or prosing,
Or intent upon disclosing
Gifts for musical composing?

Is he lecturing to flappers?
Is he tunnelling with sappers?
Has he joined the U-boat trappers?

Or, to petrify recorders
Of events within our borders,
Has he taken Holy Orders?

Is he well or ill or middling?
Is he fighting, is he fiddling? –
He can't be only thumb-twiddling.

These are merely dim surmises,
But experience advises
Us to look for weird surprises,
Somersaults, and strange disguises.

*   *   *

Thus we summed the situation
When SIR HEDWORTH MEUX' oration
Brought about a transformation.

Lo! the Blenheim Boanerges
On a sudden re-emerges
And, to calm the naval *gurges*,
FISHER'S restoration urges.

C.L. Graves

Leave

Days in 'Blighty'

Although officers were given leave every three months or so, men in the ranks could wait more than a year for a chance to get home. For those who had a long way to go once they had crossed the Channel – men who lived in the Highlands or in Cornwall, for example – much of their precious ten days was spent travelling, starting with a walk to the railhead, then tedious waiting for a train to the Channel port and more time wasted as they hung around for a boat to take them to England.

Although for some the homecoming was joyous, many soon realised that their experiences had separated them from those at home. The up-beat propaganda of the press and the apparent optimism of men's letters meant that their relatives had little chance to understand what they were truly undergoing, and they found themselves ill at ease and disoriented while they were at home. Although many dreaded the end of leave with its renewed parting, others were glad to get back to the front and to companions who understood what this war was really like.

A Song

(To W.N.W., an Adjutant)

Sing me a song of the Army,
    Of khaki and rifles and drums;
Sing me a ballad of heroes,
    Taking each day as it comes.
Sing of the colonel who bellows,
    Sing of the major who swears,
Sing of the slackers who don't care a jot,
    And the second lieutenant who dares.

Sing of the raptures of marching
  (I *may* interrupt, but don't grieve!);
But above all sit down now and tell me
  The glorious MYTH *about* LEAVE!

Lucas Cappe

The Wire that Failed

Sez I to my wife: 'As leave is tight,
Just send me a wire to-morrow night.
Say you're moving, or had a fire,
Or caught the measles, or – anyway wire!'
The telegram came at three to-day,
And it done no good, for I grieve to say
She's short of sense is that wife of mine –
Here's her telegram, line for line:
'Please grant leave to Private Bell,
I've got the measles and don't feel well.
The house is on fire – I'm filled with sorrow,
And if that's not enough, we're moving tomorrow!'

Four Words

There are four words, the sweetest words
  In all of human speech,
More sweet than are all songs of birds,
  Or Lyrics poets teach.
This life may be a vale of tears,
  A sad and dreary thing –
Four words, and trouble disappears
  And birds begin to sing.

Four words, and all the roses bloom,
  The sun begins to shine:
Four words, will dissipate the gloom,
  And water turn to wine.
Four words, will hush the saddest row,
  And cause you not to grieve –
Ah well, here goes, you've got them now:
  '*You're next for leave.*'

Louie Samuels

[If you're waking call me early, call me early, sergeant dear]

If you're waking call me early, call me early, sergeant dear,
For I'm very, very weary, and my warrant's come, I hear;
Oh! it's 'blightie' for a spell, and all my troubles are behind,
    And I've seven days before me
    (Hope the sea will not be stormy)
    Keep the war a'going sergeant,
    Train's at six, just bear in mind!

Of Harold, and his Fatal Taste for Souvenirs

Who lists to what I here relate, a tale both sad and movin' hears
Of Harold, who was taught too late to curb his itch for souvenirs;
It really was as though he deemed it heinous as a sin to rest
Inactive when the country teemed with objects of such interest;
And once his fancy caught a thing, he'd jump out straight and whisk it in –
A splinter from a Gotha's wing – a Very light – a biscuit-tin –
Shell-noses, clasp-knives, water-flasks, Bosche helmets, and a rifle too,
Old buttons, badges, Hun gas-masks, and every kind of trifle too.
His shell-cases just stood in stacks; he filled the entire bunk with them,
And leather jerkins, German packs – his quarters fairly stunk with them.
But protest was but wasted breath although you spent a day on it,
He'd threaten you with instant death and wave a rusty bayonet.
(Here comes a protest from my Muse: 'Have done with all this frolicking,
And if you tell the sequel, choose a metre not so rollicking.')

    Leave at last had Hiawatha
    (I beg pardon, I mean Harold),
    Leave to visit home and kindred;
    Safely was the Channel travelled,
    But, alas, at disembarking,
    As he staggered up the gangway –
    Hundredweights of kit about him,
    As he fumbled in his pocket
    For the little landing-ticket,
    Came a deafening explosion,
    Came a flash of blinding brightness,
    Harold was no more existent;

In his hurry he'd forgotten
He'd a Mills' bomb in his pocket
Where he rummaged for the ticket.
So he never reached his home and
Wife and children vainly stuck the
Holly in the Christmas pudding;
All in vain the children's stockings,
Waited slack and empty for the
Souvenirs from France to fill them.
'Twas the child of the Inspector
At the Customs house at Folkestone
Who as fate ordained enjoyed them,
For the kit that had survived him
Had been promptly confiscated.

A moral from this tale appears, which let us not poke fun at: 'All Beware,
beware of souvenirs, and if you can, have none at all.'

Virtue

Now you subs of tender years
For your morals, it appears,
(You must admit they're open much to question)
There is shortly going to be
A morality O.C.,
Who will see that vice does not spoil your digestion.

His H.Q. is going to be
Close by Leicester Square, and he
Will parade his Batt. for duty every night,
In his ranks we'll shortly see
P'raps a Bishop or M.P.,
Who will see that virtue's path you tread aright.

If on leave and pleasure bent
At Victoria, a gent
Will grab you as you're dodging off alone,
Will escort you to H.Q.,
When you'll quickly find that you
Are provided with an aged chaperone.

Your amusement will depend
On how much she'll let you spend,
And you'll dine at Lyons or an A.B.C.,
Should you dare to want a drink,
With a look she'll make you think
What an awful well of sin a sub can be.

You may smoke one cigarette,
Ere retiring you will get
All your orders for the morrow's pleasure feast,
Hand your cash in charge, and then
Off to bed as clock strikes ten,
Feeling that in former days you were a beast.

You will come to learn and love
Programmes as described above
For you must admit that you were most immoral,
You will find when leave's expired
That your fancies will have tired
For the glass that sparkles, and for lips of coral.

Mufti Once More

(Lines on a prospect of Three Weeks' Leave.)

What though the camphor's barrage lines
Have failed to stop the looting
And moths have marred my chaste designs,
Oh *ante-bellum* suiting!
Oh stylish weeds wherein I wooed
Evangeline and Ermyntrude,
Oh pair of spats that once astounded Tooting!

What though, I say, this fancy vest
A fearsome sight discloses,
Where wingèd things have found a nest
And snatched their impious dozes,
And battened on the sacred woof,
And made it bed and board and roof,
Wearing, I doubt not, gas-masks on their noses?

Conscious, at least, that long ago
    They took the town with splendour,
Shall I not put them on and blow
    The war-time mufti-vendor?
Though I look somewhat like a sieve,
Shall not men, seeing me, forgive?
    There are no shades to-day so sweet, so tender.

Shall they not also say, 'This proves
    How soon, how swiftly laughed he
At all our petty peace-time grooves,
    And challenged Fritz the crafty;
These were the 1914 cut;
In those dim days he was a nut;
    Just now, of course, they seem a trifle draughty?'

Yes, I am proud; my chest is filled
    With triumph, and I smack it;
What do I care for punctures drilled
    Straight through a service jacket?
These are my wounds – this well-loved tweed,
Laid on one side for England's need,
    Less like a tweed now than a tennis racquet.

Then up, my ancient suits and ties!
    In vain the tailors peddle;
In vain for me the sempstress plies
    Her spinning-wheel and treadle;
The voice of British Honour speaks
In these my perforated breeks,
    Each orifice becomes a blooming medal.

                    E.G.V. Knox

A Vision of Blighty

I do not ask, when back on Blighty's shore
    My frozen frame in liberty shall rest,
For pleasure to beguile the hours in store
    With long-drawn revel or with antique jest.
I do not ask to probe the tedious pomp
    And tinsel splendour of the last Revue;

The Fox-trot's mysteries, the giddy Romp,
    And all such folly I would fain eschew.
But, propt on cushions of my long desire,
    Deep-buried in the vastest of armchairs,
Let me recline what time the roaring fire
    Consumes itself and all my former cares.
I shall not think nor speak, nor laugh nor weep,
But simply sit and sleep and sleep and sleep.

J. Shirley

Ragtime

A minx in khaki struts the limelit boards:
With false moustache, set smirk and ogling eyes
And straddling legs and swinging hips she tries
To swagger it like a soldier, while the chords
Of rampant ragtime jangle, clash, and clatter;
And over the brassy blare and drumming din
She strains to squirt her squeaky notes and thin
Spirtle of sniggering lascivious patter.

Then out into the jostling Strand I turn,
And down a dark lane to the quiet river,
One stream of silver under the full moon,
And think of how cold searchlights flare and burn
Over dark trenches where men crouch and shiver,
Humming, to keep their hearts up, that same tune.

Wilfrid W. Gibson

At Afternoon Tea
Triolet

We have taken a trench
    Near Combles, I see,
Along with the French.
We have taken a trench.
(*Oh, the bodies, the stench!*)
Won't you have some more tea?
    We have taken a trench
Near Combles, I see.

F.W. Harvey

On Leave (1)

I wanter go back to the trenches;
    I wanter go back to the front;
I wanter go back to me rifle an' pack,
    An' 'ear me old straps creak and grunt;
I wanter get back to me blanket,
    An' sleep on me little old plank,
'Cos the cold, clammy sheets that the folks thinks is treats
    Make me shiver like rats in a tank.

I wanter get back from the war news,
    I wanter get back to the Hun;
I wanter retreat from the chaps in the street
    'Oo know 'ow the war should be run:
I wanter go where 'Tipperary'
    Ain't whistled from mornin' till night;
I wanter go back where the Zepps don't attack
    'Cos there ain't any babies to fight.

I wanter get back from the flappers
    'Oo rattle their boxes an' flags;
I wanter vamoose from the bloomin' revues
    An' the wearisome singin' of 'rags';
I wanter get back from the motors,
    An' miners with strikes on the brain,
I'm too muddled to think, an' I shan't sleep a wink
    Till I'm safe back in Flanders again.

                                                D. Large

On Leave (2)
(To R.H. and V.H.L.D.)

It was not the white cliff at the rim of the sea,
Nor Folkestone, with its roofs all bless'd with smoke;
Nor the shrill English children at the quay;
Not even the railway-bank alight with primrose fire,
Nor the little fields of Kent, and the woods, and the far church spire –
It was not these that spoke.

It was the red earth of Devon that called to me,
'*So you'm back, you li'l boy that us used to know!*'
It was the deep, dim lanes that wind to the sea,
And the Devon streams that turn and twist and run,
And the Devon hills that stretch themselves in the sun,
Like drowsy green cats watching the world below.

There were herons stalked the salty pools that day,
Where the sea comes laughing up to the very rails . . .
At Newton I saw Dartmoor far away.
By Paignton there was one I saw who ploughed,
With the red dust round him like a sunset cloud,
And beyond in the bay was Brixham with her sails.

How could I fail to mourn for you, the brave,
Who loved these things a little year before?
In each unshattered field I saw a grave,
And through the unceasing music of the sea
The scream of shells came back, came back to me.
It was a green peace that suddenly taught me war.

Out of the fight you found the shorter way
To those great silences where men may sleep.
We follow by the paths of every day,
Blind as God made us, hoping that the end
May hear that laughter between friend and friend
Such as through death the greater-hearted keep.

We are not weary yet. The fight draws out,
And sometimes we have sickened at the kill,
And sometimes in the night comes slinking doubt
To whisper that peace cometh not through Hell.
But yet we want to hear God's anger tell
The guns to cease their fury and be still.

We are not weary yet, though here the rain
Beats without shame upon the shattered dead.
And there I see the lazy waves again.

And in the weedy pools along the beach
The brown-legged boys, with their dear Devon speech,
Are happier than the gay gulls overhead.

Up the wet sand a spaniel sputters by,
Soused like a seal, and laughing at their feet;
There is a gull comes slanting down the sky,
Kisses the sea, and mews, and flies away.
And, like flat jewels set against the grey,
The roofs of Brixham glitter through the heat.

It was for this you died: this, through the earth,
Peace and the great men peace shall make,
And dogs and children and careless mirth . . .
Beauty be with you now – and of this land
In bloody travail for the world you planned,
God give you deep oblivion when you wake.

T.P. Cameron Wilson

A Day in Spring

But distant Spring sat waiting fair
    With wealth of flowers to be,
Half wond'ring if she scarcely dare
    To set a Spring-day free
With Winter still in power, and share
    The hours in rivalry.

I think she must have known that you
    And I were glad that day,
For in defiance, skies were blue
    And warm the sun's pale ray,
And distant lay the silvered view
    Of Trent's sweet winding way.

A gentle wind with zephyr sighs
    Caressed your glossy hair;
The river-light was in your eyes,
    Your face a happy lair
To catch the sunlight for your prize
    And keep it captive there.

We wandered through the leafless aisles
   That skirt the banks of Trent,
And oft, between the sudden whiles
   When sunshine came and went,
I saw your face with happy smiles
   And richest love all blent.

Those happy hours are ever set,
   Though all too brief and bright;
Within my book of 'Ne'er Forget' –
   The leaves where I indite
Sweet mem'ries, that will always wet
   The stars with tears at night.

                           Edmund Hennesley

Oxford Revisited

Last week, a prey to military duty,
   I turned my lagging footsteps to the West;
I have a natural taste for scenic beauty,
   And all my pent emotions may be guessed
     To find myself again
   At Didcot, loathliest junction of the plain.

But all things come upon the patient waiter,
   'Behold!' I cried, 'in yon contiguous blue
Beetle the antique spires of Alma Mater
   Almost exactly as they used to do
     In 1898,
   When I became an undergraduate.

'O joys whereto I went as to a bridal,
   With Youth's fair aureole clustering on a brow
That no amount of culture (herpecidal)
   Will coax the semblance of a crop from now,
     Once more I make ye mine;
   There is a train that leaves at half-past nine.

'In a rude land where life among the boys is
   One long glad round of cards and coffin juice,

And any sort of intellectual poise is
    The constant butt of well-expressed abuse,
        And it is no disgrace
    To put the table-knife inside one's face,

'I have remembered picnics on the Isis,
    Bonfires and bumps and BOFFIN'S cakes and tea,
Nor ever dreamed a European crisis
    Would make a British soldier out of me –
        The mute inglorious kind
    That push the beastly war on from behind.

'But here I am' (I mused) 'and quad and cloister
    Are beckoning to me with the old allure;
The lovely world of Youth shall be mine oyster
    Which I for one-and-ninepence can secure,
        Reaching on Memory's wing
    Parnassus' groves and Wisdom's fabled spring'.

But oh, the facts! How doomed to disillusion
    The dreams that cheat the mind's responsive eye!
Where are the undergrads in gay profusion
    Whose waistcoats made melodious the High,
        And the *jeunesse dorée*
    That shed the glamour of an elder day?

Can this be Oxford? And is that my college
    That vomits khaki through its sacred gate?
Are those the schools where once I aired my knowledge
    Where nurses pass and ambulances wait?
        Ah! sick ones, pale of face,
    I too have suffered tortures in that place!

In Tom his quad the Bloods no longer flourish;
    Balliol is bare of all but mild Hindoos;
The stalwart oars the Isis used to nourish
    Are in the trenches giving Fritz the Blues,
        And many a stout D.D.
    Is digging trenches with the V.T.C.

Why press the search when every hallowed close is
    Cluttered with youthful soldiers forming fours;
While the drum stutters and the bugler blows his
    Loud summons, and the hoarse bull-sergeant roars,
        While almost out of view
    The thrumming biplane cleaves the astonished blue?

It is a sight to stir the pulse of poet,
    These splendid youths with zeal and courage fired,
But as for Private Me, M.A. – why, blow it!
    The very sight of soldiers makes me tired;
        Learning – detached, apart –
    I sought, not War's reverberating art.

Vain search! But see! One ancient institution
    Still doing business at the same old stand;
'Tis Messrs Barclay's Bank, or I'm a Proosian,
    That erst dispensed my slender cash-in-hand;
        I'll borrow of their pelf
    And buy some War Loan to console myself.

                        C.H. Bretherton

On Christmas Leave

When I got into Chainey's bus
    Down at the station it began;
    I didn't seem a fighting-man
No more: the old hills made no fuss
At seeing me; the winding road
That troops an' transports never knowed,
    And the old station nag's click-clack
        Just took me back.

The Twelve Apostles' boughs were bare,
    Just as they was last time I came.
    Mother was looking just the same
And Father hadn't turned a hair.
I washed as usual at the pump;
My bed had got the same old lump;
    Dick lived next door – I near forgot
        I seen him shot.

Church wasn't changed on Christmas Day –
   Old Westmacott took round the plate;
   The old Major stood up stiff and straight,
And it seems somehow just like play
Saluting him, retired an' all.
Home – no, the War, I think – seems small . . .
   This evening I go back to France
     And take my chance.

W.W. Blair Fish

English Leave

Kneel then in the warm lamplight, O my Love,
Your dear dark head against my quiet breast,
And take me in your arms again and so
Hush my tired heart to rest;
And say that of all the glories you have won
My love's most dear and best.

Only to-night I want you all my own,
(Tomorrow I will laugh and bid you go,)
That if these fourteen days of heaven on earth
Are all the love-time we shall ever know
I may remember I am yours: My Dear,
Hold me still closer, still . . . and tell me so.

May Cannan

The Train for the Front

'Good-bye. You'll write and tell me how you are?'
   'Rather. It looks as if it will be wet.'
'Yes, so it does. I'm glad I've got the car.
   Here is your pipe, in case I should forget.'
'Oh, thanks; I think we'll soon be starting now.
   We're very late, unless my watch is fast.'
What? Yes, these engines make a beastly row;
   Good-bye, old girl, good-bye, we're off at last.'

*   *   *

And so they go the way all Britons tread,
Leaving the things that they feel most unsaid.

On Returning to the Front after Leave

Apart sweet women (for whom Heaven be blessed),
Comrades, you cannot think how thin and blue
Look the leftovers of mankind that rest,
Now that the cream has been skimmed off in you.
War has its horrors, but has this of good –
That its sure processes sort out and bind
Brave hearts in one intrepid brotherhood
And leave the shams and imbeciles behind.
Now turn we joyful to the great attacks,
Not only that we face in a fair field
Our valiant foe and all his deadly tools,
But also that we turn disdainful backs
On that poor world we scorn yet die to shield –
That world of cowards, hypocrites, and fools.

Alan Seeger

FIFTEEN

Spring and Early Summer 1917

*Calls for peace, the Battle of Arras, the retreat to the
Hindenberg Line, the old battlefields*

In December 1916 the Germans began to make moves towards a negotiated peace. The British believed that, if such discussions were to have any hope of creating a lasting peace, essential conditions of restitution, reparation and a guarantee against repetition must first be laid down. President Woodrow Wilson requested from both sides a statement of terms, meanwhile proposing an immediate gathering of peace delegates. Germany ignored his request to state their terms, but agreed to talks. On 30 December the British turned down the proposition, believing that the German proposals were empty and insincere.

Meanwhile, living conditions in Germany were very bad as a result of the allied blockade and the exceptionally hard winter. In July 1917 the Reichstag passed a peace resolution, which proposed that overtures should be made towards a negotiated end to the fighting, a move that angered their military high command. To the British, the resolution appeared to exonerate the Germans from any blame for the outbreak of the war, accusing the Allies of threats of conquest and domination in the face of Germany's need to defend its freedom and independence. The two sides were far apart and the proposals came to nothing, but there were many who despaired at the endlessness of hostilities.

The Allied advances of the Battle of the Somme had broken the strongly fortified German line, and so in mid-March the Germans began to retreat to a new defensive position, the Siegfried or Hindenburg Line, laying waste the country across which they moved. As the British and French came up out of their trenches and advanced in open warfare, stretches of the old Somme battlefields fell into their hands without a fight. In April the British attacked at Arras and the Canadians captured the strategically important ridge of Vimy.

[There was a little Hun, and at war he tried his hand]

There was a little Hun, and at war he tried his hand,
And while that Hun was winning war was fine you understand,
But when the others hit him back he shouted in alarm,
A little drop of peace wouldn't do me any harm.

More Peace-Talk in Berlin
To the War-Lord

'How beautiful upon the mountain-tops
    Their feet would sound, the messengers of Peace!'
So into neutral ears your unction drops,
    Hinting a pious hope that War may cease –
        War, with its dreadful waste
    Which never suited your pacific taste.

Strange you should turn so suddenly humane,
    So sick of ravage and the reek of gore!
Dare we assume that Verdun's long-drawn strain
    Makes you perspire at each Imperial pore?
        Or that your nerve's mislaid
    Through cardiac trouble caused by our Blockade?

You thought to finish on the high wave's crest;
    To say, 'These lands that 'neath our sceptre lie –
Such as we want we'll keep, and chuck the rest,
    And to the vanquished, having drained 'em dry,
        We will consent to give,
    Out of our clemency, the right to live.'

Then you came down a long, long way, and said,
    'For pure desire of Peace, and that alone,
We'll deem the dead past buried with its dead,
    Taking, in triumph's hour, a generous tone;
        Uplift the fallen foe
    And affably restore the *status quo*.'

Fool's talk and idle. In this Dance of Death
    The man who called the piper's tune must pay,

Nor can he stop at will for want of breath.
   Though War you chose, and chose its opening day,
     It lies not in your power
    To stay its course or fix its final hour.

Owen Seaman

The Kaiser's Cry for Peace

Thou shalt have peace enough when war is o'er,
   When nations gather at the conference
   Which Time shall hold to weigh thy great offence
Against the crimes of History's full store:
Thou then shalt stand in all thy guilt before
   The human virtues, dumb of all defence,
   Confronting Youth whom thy mad violence
Has hounded through death's youth-excluding door.
Cry not for Peace! Thou art her murderer!
   Thou'st violated nature with thy breath
     Of war – nature, mother of peace and light.
Thy god's the bloody god of massacre,
   The raging dragon, breathing blasting death,
    Blackening the dawn just breaking out of night.

William Dowsing

War Aims

There are our terms – concise, emphatic, plain;
Take them or leave them – we'll not compromise
Though all the flower of our young manhood dies.
'Tis all or nothing. We will still maintain
The contest till we have the victory,
Or till our final shilling and last man
Shall be expended. That's our simple plan,
Free of all guile or ambiguity.
Peace on our terms then – or no peace at all,
And we fight on, however high the cost.
What matter if more million lives be lost;
What matter if our race and Empire fall,
So Lothringen be called once more Lorraine
And Hartmannsweilerskopf be French again?

W.N. Ewer

The Woman who Shrieked against Peace

Abundant woman panting there,
    Whose breast is flecked with spots of grease
That splutter from your laboured hair,
        O dew-lapped woman, you who reek
            Of stout and steak and fish and chips,
        Why does the short indignant shriek
            Come toppling from your fleshy lips;
Because, poor smitten fool, I dare
    To breathe the outcast name of Peace?

And shall your flesh grow less to view,
    And shall your chubby arms grow thin,
And shall you miss your stout and stew,
        The bracelets which you wear so well,
            If blinded boys no more shall creep
        Along the scorching roads to Hell,
            If thick red blood no more shall steep
        Green fields in France, nor corpses smell;
            If Peace send down her blasting blight,
                O shall it spoil your sleep at night
And shall you lose your treble chin?

Louis Golding

Profit and Loss

Now William Hohenzollern, the King of all the Huns,
Had quite a lot of country and he also had six sons,
Of money too he'd plenty and a larder fully stocked –
In fact he'd all the wanted – so at grief and care he mocked.

Karl Baumberg lived in comfort with his frau and family,
His sons they numbered seven, and his daughters numbered three;
They'd just enough of everything and wished for nothing more,
(This happy time, you understand, was just before the war).

For reasons which they never knew Karl Baumberg's seven sons
Were quickly clad in suits of grey and labelled 'food for guns'.
Two rot in mud near Wipers, and another at Verdun,
The Somme accounted for a brace, and Passchendaele for one.

The one remaining to old Karl is minus both his arms,
His fighting days are finished, and he's sick of war's alarms;
He grinds his teeth with fury, while old Karl hunts round for food,
And his mother freely curses both the Kaiser and his brood.

His one remaining sister (death has claimed the other two)
Out of water and a horse bone tries to make a dish of stew.
Comes a mandate 'Our great Kaiser has another victory won,
Fly your flags and cheer, by order, for the victory of Verdun.'

Then old Karl, whose waking senses grasp a fact both strange and new,
That the victories are worthless if they bring no end in view,
And he curses Kaiser William who's the King of all the Huns,
But his frau is quietly sobbing for – the Kaiser has six sons.

Arras

I went and walked by Arras
In the dim uncertain night;
I went and walked by Arras
In the dazzling noonday light;
First I saw a fairy glamour,
Later, 'twas another sight.

Out by Arras in the night-time,
Star-shells in the starlit sky
Showered like wild silver raindrops
From a fountain scattered high,
Like the silver scales of fishes
In the tideway curving by.

Out by Arras in the night-time
There were glints of red and green
Like the glow of fairy camp-fires
In some hidden high wood seen,
Like the day-dawn of the night-land
Where no man has ever been.

Out by Arras in the day-time
There stretched broad the sun-parched sand:

Where together men and torture
Lived with foul death hand in hand,
Horror-stricken, God-forsaken,
There stretched far the war-cursed land.

And upon the stretches barren
Far I saw the thousands lie
That the wind of war had blasted,
Sweeping on without a sigh;
In the hollows, huddled hundreds
Who were not afraid to die.

John Peterson

Zero!

('Zero-hour' – commonly known as 'Zero' – is the hour fixed
for the opening of an Infantry attack.)

I woke at dawn and flung the window wide.
    Beneath the hedge the lazy river ran;
And dusky barges idled down the tide;
    In the laburnum-tree the birds began;
And it was May and half the world in flower;
    I saw the sun creep over an Eastward brow,
And thought 'It may be, this is Zero-hour;
    Somewhere the lads are "going over" now'.

Somewhere the guns speak sudden on the height
    And build for miles their battlement of fire;
Somewhere the men that shivered all the night
    Peer anxious forth and scramble through the wire,
Swarm slowly out to where the Maxims bark,
    And green and red the panic rockets rise;
And Hell is loosed, and shyly sings the lark,
    And the red sun climbs sadly up the skies.

Now they have won some sepulchered Gavrelle,
    Some shattered homes in their own dust concealed;
Now no Boche troubles them nor any shell,
    But almost quiet holds the thankful field,
Whilst men draw breath, and down the Arras Road
    Come the slow mules with battle's dreary stores,

And there is time to see the wounded stowed,
    And stretcher-squads besiege the doctors' doors.

Then belches Hell anew. And all day long
    The afflicted place drifts heavenward in dust;
All day the shells shriek out their devils' song;
    All day men cling close to the earth's charred crust;
Till, in the dusk, the Huns come on again,
    And, like some sluice, the watchers up the hill
Let loose the guns and flood the soil with slain,
    And they go back, but scourge the village still.

I see it all, I see the same brave souls
    To-night, to-morrow, though the half be gone,
Deafened and dazed, and hunted from their holes,
    Helpless and hunger-sick, but holding on.
I shall be happy all the long day here,
    But not till night shall they go up the steep,
And nervous now because the end is near,
    Totter at last to quietness and to sleep.

And men who find it easier to forget,
    In England here, among the daffodils,
That there in France are fields unflowered yet,
    And murderous May-days on the unlovely hills –
Let them go walking where the land is fair
    And watch the breaking of a morn in May,
And think, 'It may be Zero over there,
    But here is Peace' – and kneel a while, and pray.

A.P. Herbert

Open Warfare

Men said, 'At last! at last the open battle!
    Now shall we fight unfettered o'er the plain,
No more in catacombs be cooped like cattle,
    Nor travel always in a devious drain!'
They were in ecstasies. But I was damping;
    I like a trench, I have no lives to spare;
And in those catacombs, however cramping,
    You did at least know vaguely where you were.

Ah, happy days in deep well-ordered alleys,
　　Where, after dining, probably with wine,
One felt indifferent to hostile sallies,
　　And with a pipe meandered round the line;
You trudged along a trench until it ended;
　　It led at least to some familiar spot;
It might not be the place that you'd intended,
　　But then you might as well be there as not.

But what a wilderness we now inhabit
　　Since this confounded 'open' strife prevails!
It may be good; I do not wish to crab it,
　　But you should hear the language it entails,
Should see this waste of wide uncharted craters
　　Where it is vain to seek the companies,
Seeing the shell-holes are as like as taters
　　And no one knows where anybody is.

Oft in the darkness, palpitant and blowing,
　　Have I set out and lost the hang of things,
And ever thought, 'Where *can* the guide be going?'
　　But trusted long and rambled on in rings,
For ever climbing up some miry summit,
　　And halting there to curse the contrite guide,
For ever then descending like a plummet
　　Into a chasm on the other side.

Oft have I sat and wept, or sought to study
　　With hopeless gaze the uninstructive stars,
Hopeless because the very skies were muddy;
　　I only saw a red malicious Mars;
Or pulled my little compass out and pondered,
　　And set it sadly on my shrapnel hat,
Which, I suppose, was why the needle wandered,
　　Only, or course, I never thought of that.

And then perhaps some 5.9s start dropping,
　　As if there weren't sufficient holes about;
I flounder on, hysterical and sopping,
　　And come by chance to where I started out,

And say once more, while I have no objection
   To other people going to Berlin,
Give *me* a trench, a nice revetted section,
   And let me stay there till the Bosch gives in!

A.P. Herbert

Beaucourt Revisited

I wandered up to Beaucourt. I took the river track,
And saw the lines we lived in before the Boche went back.
But peace was now in Pottage, the front was far ahead,
The front was flying Eastward, and only left the dead.

And I thought 'How long we lay there, and watched across the wire,
While the guns roared round the valley and set the skies afire'.
But now there are homes in Hamel, and tents in the Vale of Hell
And a camp at Suicide Corner, where half the Regiment fell.

The new troops follow after and tread the land we won;
To them it is so much hillside, re-wrested from the Hun.
To us 'tis almost sacred, this dreary mile of mud;
The shell holes hold our history and half of them our blood.

Here at the head of Peche Street 'twas death to show your face,
To me it seemed like magic to linger in the place.
To me how many spirits hung round the Kentish Caves.
But the new men see no spirits – they only see the graves.

I found the half dug ditches we fashioned for the fight.
We lost a score of men there – young James was killed that night.
I saw the star shells staring, I heard the bullets hail,
But the new men pass unheeding – they never heard the tale.

I crossed the blood-red ribbon that once was No-Man's Land;
I saw a winter daybreak and a creeping minute hand:
And here the lads went over, and there was Harmsworth shot,
And here was William lying – but the new men knew them not.

And I said 'There is still the river and still the stiff stark trees
To treasure here our story, but there are only these'.
But under the white wood crosses the dead men answered low
'The new men know not Beaucourt, but we are here – we know'.

A.P. Herbert

Meditation in June, 1917

I

How can we reason still, how look afar,
    Who, these three years now, are
Drifting, poor flotsam hugely heaved and hurled
    In the birthday of a world,
Upon the waves of the creative sea?
    How gain lucidity
Or even keep the faith wherewith at first
    We met the storm that burst,
The singing hope of revolution's prime?
    For in that noble time
We saw the petty world dissolve away
    And fade into a day
Where dwelt new spirits of a better growth,
    Unchecked by spite and sloth.
We saw, and even now we seem to see,
    In fitful revelry,
Like hills obscured and hid by earthly mist,
    The hopes that first we kissed:
We see them, catch at them and lose again
    In apathy and pain
What maybe was (though it once seemed ours to hold)
    No more than fairy gold.

II

We pity those whom quick death overtakes,
    Though they will never see
How hope dissolves and founded loyalty shakes
    Traitorously, piteously.
They lose at most and death is voiceless still
    Nor whispers in their ears
When they are lying on the deep-scarred hill
    What our calm silence hears.
They lose all various life, they lose the day,
    The clouds, the winds, the rain,
The blossoms down an English road astray
    They will not see again;

Great is their loss but more tremendous things
    To us at home are given,
Doubts, fears and greeds and shameful waverings
    That hide the blood-red heaven.
They knew no doubt and fear was soon put by:
    Freely their souls could move
In deeds that gave new life to loyalty
    A sharper edge to love.
They are the conquerors, the happy dead,
    Who gave their lives away,
And now amid the trenches where they bled,
    Forgetful of the day,
Deaf, blind and unaware, sleep on and on,
    Nor open eyes to weep,
Know nought of what is ended or what begun
    But only and always sleep.

III

We said on the first day, we said and swore
    That self should be no more,
That we were risen, that we would wholly be
    For love and liberty;
And in the exhilaration of that oath
    We cast off spite and sloth
And laboured for an hour, till we began,
    Man after piteous man,
To lose the splendour, to forget the dream
    And leave our noble theme.
To find again our lusts and villainies
    And seek a baser prize;
This we have done and what is left undone
    Cries out beneath the sun.
How glad a dawn fades thus in foggy night,
    Where not a star shines bright!

IV

Is all then gone? That nobler morning mood
When pain appeared an honour and grief a gift

And what was difficult was also good?
Are all our wishes on the waves adrift?
The young, the eager-hearted, they are gone,
And we, the stay-at-homes, are tired and old,
Careless how carelessly our work is done,
Forgetful how that morning rose in gold
When all our hearts cried out in unison,
Triumphant in the new triumphal sun.
How dull a night succeeds! how dark and cold!
We will arise. Oh, not as then with singing,
But silence in our mouths and no word said,
Though wracks of that lost glory round us clinging
Shames us with broken oaths we swore the dead,
But steadfast in humility we rise,
Hoping no glory, having merited none,
Through the long night to toil with aching eyes
And pray that our humbler hearts may earn the sun.

Edward Shanks

In the Third Year of the War

'Would that the war were over, and again
We walked together in a Wiltshire lane.
The West shrills keenly through the Hackpen thorn:
From that high, lonely wood by Winterborne
Wet leaves are whirled far out across the vale.
We should find comfort in the downland gale;
Its glorious blast, so wild, yet angerless,
Blows sorrow from the heart and bitterness.'

*   *   *

So, like some wandering child, we stretch our hands
To shining phantom faces, and far lands
Of heart's desire.
                    O solace, vainly sought
To light the sad opacity of thought!
There is no charm in any outward thing
To ease the heart from smarting at the sting
Of friendship snapped, of dull frustrated days
Of hopes that perish in the desolate ways.

The wind of mirth and sympathy is spilled
Wherewith the vessel of our hearts was filled,
Lending bright influence to the wind and trees.
Our lives are empty now; and how for these
Can earth, that lives not, find reviving breath
To quicken the sterility of death?
The sun-rays still go wheeling o'er the hill;
But closed those eyes their passing used to fill
With sudden glory. Say! shall we return,
Where every sight can teach us but to mourn?
Shall we return, where every field and tree
Is radiant with the light of memory?
Here, by this hedgerow, Rupert musing lay:
This pool was Nigel's haunt at morning grey:
Down that hill-side Ned ran so cheerily
The day he left, and turned to call good-bye.
If once again we climb to Barbary,
None but the dead will keep us company:
Their printless feet will fall with ours, unseen;
And silent voices fill the listening dene.
'Dear land of noon-day light' we said before,
But now – 'Dear land of ghosts!' – for evermore.

*   *   *

The old, untroubled world is dead, where laughter
Was still more real than tears: and we, hereafter
Must live with grief for our reality.
We will return, then, not forgetfully,
To breathe an opiate in the upland wind,
And gain dull ease and vacant peace of mind.
We will return, but rather there to gain
More vital apprehension of our pain
In memory of the dead, and of our pride
In presence of the land for which they died:
Beyond the lonely wood once more to lie,
Where that remote green bastion fronts the sky;
To see beneath us plains and woodlands wide,
Encompassed round about and unified
In a great flood of light: once more to press
Our fingers in the turf's soft friendliness,

Fragrant with flowerets of thyme: and thence
Shall pass into our hearts a keener sense
Of what could those great hearts so greatly move,
England, their hope, their faith, their passion of love.

E. Hilton Young

Proverbs of the Pessimists

It's a long lane has no turning:
It's never 'too late' to mend:
The darkest hour is nearest the dawn,
And even *this* war must end.

SIXTEEN

Red Tape and Rivalry

Red tape, inter-corps rivalry, the Staff

Writers in trench magazines derived much fun from the endless red tape – particularly that involving the Quarter Master Sergeant or 'Q' – from inter-corps rivalry and from mocking the Staff. Meanwhile, the much put-upon PBI – the Poor Bloody Infantry – just grumbled.

Urgent or Ordinary

There was a time when first I donned the Khaki –
Oh, martial days in Brighton-by-the-Sea! –
When not the deepest draught of Omar's Saki
Could fire my ardent soul like dixie tea.
I dreamed of bloody spurs and bloodier sabre,
Of mentions – not too modest – in despatches;
I threw my foes, as Scotchmen toss the caber,
And sent my prisoners home in wholesale batches;
Led my platoons to storm the Prussian trenches,
Galloped my guns to enfilade his flank;
Was it H.M.'s own royal hand, or French's
That pinned the V.C. on my tunic? SWANK!

Those dreams are dead: now in my Wiper's dug-out
I only dream of Kirchner's naughtiest chromo;
The brazier smokes; no window lets the fug out;
And the Bosche shells; and 'Q' still issues bromo.
'For information' – 'Urgent' – 'Confidential' –
'Secret' – 'For necessary action, please' –
'The G.O.C. considers it essential' –
My soldier-soul must steel itself to these;

Must face, by dawn's dim light, by night's dull taper,
Disciplined, dour, gas-helmeted, and stern,
Brigades, battalions, batteries, of paper, –
The loud 'report', the treacherous 'return',
Division orders, billeting epistles,
Barbed 'Zeppelin' wires that baffle G.H.Q.,
And the dread 'Summary' whose blurred page bristles
With 'facts' no German general ever knew.
Let the Hun hate! We need no beer-roused passions
To keep our sword-blade bright, our powder dry,
The while we chase October's o'erdrawn rations
And hunt that missing pair of 'Gumboots, thigh'.

Gilbert Frankau

Requisitional
Or Hints to young Officers.

(We are still struggling with the final bits of red tape. A regiment now in training at a seaside place sent a requisition for 30 pickaxes. The official reply was that the proper way to requisition pickaxes was to call them 'Axes (Pick)'. – *Daily Chronicle.*)

When sending requisitions it is well to have a care
   That you're absolutely right in your appeal;
'Wheelbarrows' must be written – if you only want a pair
     'Barrows (Wheel)'.

It's a simple little process and, though puzzling for a bit,
   It doesn't take so *very* long to think
That an 'inkstand' should be designated when you order it –
     'Stand (Ink)'.

Suppose you want some paper and that 'foolscap' is the word
   Which you want to write, remember that the rule's
To reverse the whole expression and you'll put – it sounds absurd
     'Cap (Fools).'

To rag the War Department you will not attempt, I hope,
   Though I quite admit it *would* be tempting (very)
To ask for and to call the soldier's friend, the periscope,
     'Scope (Peri).'

W. Hodgson Burnet

An Ode to Q.

Listen reader, while I tell you
Stirring deeds both old and new,
Tales of battles during which we
Chits received from Batt. H.Q.

Fought we had a losing battle
All the day and all the night;
All communications broken,
Never was there such a plight.
Now the Hun comes o'er the sandbags
In one long unbroken mass –
Just in time – the welcome message
'Indent now for helmets gas.'

Shelled they'd been for three days solid
In a trench just two feet high;
Couldn't get retaliation
Matter not how they might try.
Binks's men had held the trenches,
(Binks is NOT his proper name),
Savagely he sent the message,
'Can't you stop their purple game?'
Anxiously they wait the answer,
What a brave but serried band.
Here it comes – Binks grabs the paper,
'Deficiencies not yet to hand!'

Have you ever heard the tale, lad,
How we took the trench at A?
Said the good old 92nd,
Here we are, and here we'll stay.
What a tale of awful trial,
Cut off was our food supply.
If we do not get some bully
– Bread or biscuits – we shall die.
The foe comes on in countless thousands
Bearing down with savage cry.
Jones receives a frantic message,
'Indent now for gum boots thigh'.

Thus you see, O gentle reader,
Why the O.C. Coys are grey.
These and other kindred worries
Are their portion day by day.

Our Fighting Men

R.E.

We all admire the Sapper,
    He is so full of brain;
He makes the most tremendous sumps
    That keep out all the rain;
And happy should I be if I
    Could find a dug-out half as dry.

He works both day and night
    With fierce and furrowed brow –
Or, rather, watches others work
    And tells them why and how;
And, with a muffled kind of sob,
    Gives someone else the hardest job.

R.F.A.

The Gunner's on a higher plane –
    His hours are 10 to 3,
He takes a day off when there's rain,
    Because he cannot see.

You find him seated on a knoll,
    Dreaming of range and fuse,
And wishing that the Div. Amm. Col.
    Were like the widow's cruse.

He loves his little weekly hate,
    And once he's fairly set,
He rarely puts much more than eight
    Rounds through the parapet.

Signals

The Signal man wears blue and white
    Most gorgeous on his arm,
And causes heaps of fun at night
    By spreading Gas Alarm.

He bags your wire – a thing I'd hate
    To do behind your back,
And when you gently remonstrate
    He murmurs, 'A(c) A(c) A(c)'.

A.S.C.

Some men I know have billets fine
And motor cars galore,
They live – oh miles behind the line . . .
The Army Service Corps.
They often go to A——s
To pass the time away;
Their life must be one constant grind
To earn their extra pay.

Rhymes without Reason
By P.B.I.

Foreword

Arise, My MUSE, and from the muddied trench
Let us give utterance to malicious thought,
Shouting aloud the things we never ought
Even to dream of: come, you shameless Wench,
With tongue in cheek let us set out to strafe
Gunners and Sappers, and the Gilded Staff.

I

Gunners are a race apart,
Hard of head and hard of heart.
Like the gods they sit and view
All that other people do:

Like the Sisters Three of Fate,
They do not discriminate.
Our Support Line, or the Hun's,
– What's the difference to the Guns?
Retaliation do you seek?
Ring them up, and – wait a week!
They will certainly reply
In the distant by-and-bye.
Should a shell explode amiss
Each will swear it was not his:
For he's never, never shot
Anywhere about that spot,
And, what's more, his Guns could not.

II

Sappers are wonderfully clever by birth,
And though they're not meek, they inherit the Earth.
Should your trenches prove leaky, they'll work with a will
To make all the water flow up the next hill.
(And when I say 'work', I should really explain
That we find the Labour, while they find the Brain.)
They build nice, deep dug-outs as quick as can be,
But quicker still mark them 'RESERVED FOR R.E.':
And, strangely, this speed of theirs seems to decline
As the scene of their labours draws near the Front Line.

III

Realising Men must laugh,
Some Wise Men devised the Staff:
Dressed them up in little dabs
Of rich variegated tabs:
Taught them how to win the War
On A.F.Z. 354:
Let them lead the Simple Life
Far from all our vulgar strife:
Nightly gave them downy beds
For their weary, aching heads:
Lest their relatives might grieve
Often, often gave them leave,

Decorations, too, galore:
What on earth could man wish more?
Yet, alas, or so says Rumour,
He forgot a sense of Humour!

Afterword

And now, Old Girl, we've fairly had our whack,
Be off, before they start to strafe us back!
Come, let us plod across the weary Plain,
Until we sight TENTH AVENUE again:
On, up the interminable C.T.,
Watched by the greater part of Germany:
And, as we go, mark each familiar spot
Where fresh work has been done – or p'r'aps not:
On, past the footboards no one seems to mend,
Till even VENDIN ALLEY finds an end,
And wading through a Minnie-hole (brand-new),
We gingerly descend to C.H.Q.,
Our journey ended in a Rabbit-hutch –
'How goes the Battle? Have they Minnied much?'

Professional Jealousy

By a Gloster

God made the bees,
    The bees make the honey;
The Glosters do the work
    And the R.E.s get the money.

The Sapper's Reply

Who eats the honey,
    Is it Glosters or the bee?
The bee gets no cash
    From the bally infantry.

Who pinches sandbags
    Required for parapet,

Drops them in the mud
    To save his feet from wet?

When dugout, sap or bridge
    Is required by infantry,
The Gloster bends his knee
    To the better paid R.E.

Who taught him how to bomb,
    Revet and to demolish,
To build a house or knock it down,
    The Germans for to dish?

Why should the Gloster grouse
    At the R.E. and his pay?
When the Glosters wants to know a thing
    The R.E. shows the way.

The Infantryman

The gunner rides on horseback, he lives in luxury,
The sapper has his dug-out as cushy as can be,
The flying man's a sportsman, but his home's a long way back,
In painted tent or straw-spread barn or cosy little shack;
Gunner and sapper and flying man (and each to his job, say I)
Have tickled the Hun with mine or gun or bombed him from on high,
But the quiet work, and the dirty work, since ever the War began
Is the work that never shows at all, the work of the infantryman.

The guns can pound the villages and smash the trenches in,
And the Hun is fain for home again when the T.M.B.s begin,
And the Vickers gun is a useful one to sweep a parapet,
But the real work is the work that's done with bomb and bayonet.
Load him down from heel to crown with tools and grub and kit,
He's always there where the fighting is – he's there unless he's hit;
Over the mud and the blasted earth he goes where the living can;
He's in at the death while he yet has breath, the British infantryman!

Trudge and slip on the shell-hole's lip, and fall in the clinging mire –
Steady in front, go steady! Close up there! Mind the wire!

Double behind where the pathways wind! Jump clear of the ditch, jump clear!
Lost touch at the back? Oh, halt in front! and duck when the shells come near!
Carrying parties all night long, all day in a muddy trench,
With your feet in the wet and your head in the rain and the sodden khaki's
    stench!
Then over the top in the morning, and onward all you can –
This is the work that wins the War, the work of the infantryman.

                                                        E.F. Clarke

Ballad of Army Pay

In general, if you want a man to do a dangerous job: –
Say, swim the Channel, climb St Paul's, or break into and rob
The Bank of England, why, you find his wages must be higher
Than if you merely wanted him to light the kitchen fire.
But in the British Army, it's just the other way,
And the maximum of danger means the minimum of pay.

You put some men inside a trench, and call them infantrie,
And make them face ten kinds of hell, and face it cheerfully;
And live in holes like rats, with other rats, and lice, and toads,
And in their leisure time, assist the R.E.s with their loads.
Then, when they've done it all, you give 'em each a bob a day!
For the maximum of danger means the minimum of pay.

We won't run down the A.S.C., nor yet the R.T.O.,
They ration and direct us on the way we've got to go.
They're very useful people, and it's pretty plain to see
We couldn't do without 'em, nor yet the A.P.C.,
But comparing risks and wages, – I think they all will say
That the maximum of danger means the minimum of pay.

There are men who make munitions – and seventy bob a week;
They never see a lousy trench nor hear a big shell shriek;
And others *sing* about the war at high-class music-halls
Getting heaps and heaps of money and encores from the stalls.
They 'keep the home fires burning' and bright by night and day,
While the maximum of danger means the minimum of pay.

I wonder if it's harder to make big shells at a bench,
Than to face the screaming beggars when they're crumping up a trench;

I wonder if it's harder to sing in mellow tones
Of danger, than to face it – say, in a wood like Trones;
Is discipline skilled labour, or something children play?
Should the maximum of danger mean the minimum of pay?

F.W. Harvey

To the P.B.I.

An appreciation

Gone is the Summer, and gone are the flies,
Gone the green hedges that gladdened our eyes;
Around us the landscape is reeking with rain,
Gone is all comfort – 'tis Winter again.

So here's to the lads of the P.B.I.,
Who live in a ditch that never is dry;
Who grin through discomfort and danger alike,
Go 'over the top' when a chance comes to strike;
Though they're living in Hell they are cheery and gay,
And draw as their stipend just one bob per day.

Back once more to the boots, gum, thigh,
In a pulverised trench where the mud's knee-high;
To the duck-board slide on a cold wet night,
When you pray for a star-shell to give you light;
When your clothes are wet, and the rum jar's dry,
Then you want all your cheeriness, P.B.I.

They take what may come with a grouse just skin-deep,
In a rat-worried dug-out on mud try to sleep;
Do you wonder they make all the atmosphere hum,
When some arm-chair old lunatic grudges them rum;
And they read in the papers that 'James So-and-Such
Thinks that our soldiers are drinking too much'.

Leave the Tommy alone Mr James So-and-Such.
There are vices much nearer home waiting your touch;
Take yourself now for instance, examine and see
If your own priggish virtue is all it should be;
Give those of a larger life chance to enjoy
A charity wider than that you employ.

Don't let Tommy's vices shatter your sleep,
When you write to the 'Times' stick to 'Little Bo-Peep',
As a subject she's really much more in your line
Than licentious soldiery, women, and wine.
So here's to the lads who can live and can die,
Backbone of the Empire, the old P.B.I.

Arma Virumque Cano

No Prayers of Peace for me; no maiden's sigh.
Give me the Chants of War, the Viking's Song;
Battle for me; nor care I for how long
This war goes on. Tell me, where bullets fly;
Where noble men and brave may bleed and die;
Where skilful parry foils the sword-thrust strong.
Such are the tales I love. (I may be wrong –
A warrior, and no carpet knight am I.)

The D.S.O., the M.C. grace my breast;
My brow is bound with laurels and with lace;
I love this war. Perhaps you think that that
Is strange. Well I am different from the rest
Of you poor blighters. I live at the Base,
And use the Brain inside my nice, red, hat.

To James

(On his appointment to the Staff.)

It does not make me laugh and whoop
    (Though certainly the choice *is* droll)
To hear that you are asked to stoop
To join that great malignant group;
    I hasten to condole.
Not for your frame I fear – ah, no,
For, far as creature comforts go,
They lack but little here below:
    I shudder for your soul.

I know that when the seas are rude
    And people's parcels long delayed,
No hint of trouble shall intrude
Where your select and frequent food
    Is delicately laid;
That, though the sweet Imbrosial hens
Abruptly perish in their pens,
Your eggs will not, like other men's,
    Be absent on parade.

I know the neighbourhood is rich
    In sandbagged shelters, cutely packed,
Yet if there be some special niche,
The perfect kind of cranny which
    We hitherto have lacked,
Where man may shun the shells of man
(And also Asiatic Anne),
'Twill be but part of some huge plan
    For keeping you intact.

I fear for you no foeman's knife,
    But fear to see on that fresh face
The lofty look of one whose life
Is quite remote from earthly strife
    (Though that will be the case);
I dread the perilous abyss
Of being *sui generis*,
And looking with some prejudice
    On any other race.

I fear, yet hope, that after all,
    If e'er you tread, supremely vast,
The lowly drain wherein we crawl,
You'll have the kindness to recall
    Some fragment of the past;
For some wee while confess the sin
Of merely earthly origin,
And not refuse a genial grin
    For fear of losing caste.

                          A.P. Herbert

The Sacred Documents

Major Augustus Edward Grace
    Was D.A.A.G. Corps,
And kept the Sacred Documents
    In pigeon-holes galore,
And knew that on his shoulders lay
    The burden of the war.

No officer on all the Staff
    Was diligent as he;
'Twas but a little fault he had
    That caused the tragedy.
A trifle absent-minded Grace
    Was sometimes apt to be.

One morning – I remember well,
    The day was wild and wet –
(The horror of that dreadful time!
    It makes me tremble yet) –
With 'A oblique stroke four five two'
    Grace lit his cigarette!

That evening from the Army came
    A note for Major Grace;
    'Ref. A oblique stroke four five two,
Line three, delete "his face".'
But 'A oblique stroke four five two'
    Had vanished into space!

We sought the Sacred Document
    Through half a hundred files,
At first with natural confidence
    And deprecating smiles,
Like cats that for the first time tread
    The dim nocturnal tiles.

But when we sought, and sought in vain,
    Slowly a nameless dread
Began to seize us, and the hairs
    Stood up upon each head

As in each other's startled eyes
   The dreadful thought we read.

The Sacred Document was lost!
   We heard the furies mock,
The D.A.A. and Q.M.G.
   In secret sold his stock.
And when the Corps Commander knew
   He fainted with the shock.

That night, when in our beds we lay,
   We saw – as in a trance –
A Britain humbled to the dust,
   A dominated France.
But ah! for human vanity
   Beneath the light of chance!

A bomb was dropped at dawn and left
   The offices a wreck,
And of the Sacred Documents
   Was found no single speck.
And yet – and Yet – and YET the war
   Went on without a check!

Edward de Stein

Headquarters

A league and a league from the trenches – from the traversed maze of the lines,
Where daylong the sniper watches and daylong the bullet whines,
And the cratered earth is in travail with mines and with countermines –

Here, where haply some woman dreamed, (are those her roses that bloom
In the garden beyond the windows of my littered working-room?)
We have decked the map for our masters as a bride is decked for the groom.

Fair, on each lettered numbered square – cross-road and mound and wire,
Loophole, redoubt and emplacement – lie the targets their mouths desire;
Gay with purples and browns and blues, have we traced them their arcs of fire.

And ever the type-keys clatter; and ever our keen wires bring
Word from the watchers a-crouch below, word from the watchers a-wing;
And ever we hear the distant growl of our hid guns thundering.

Hear it hardly, and turn again to our maps, where the trench-lines crawl,
Red on the gray and each with a sign for the ranging shrapnel's fall –
Snakes that our masters shall scotch at dawn, as is written here on the wall.

For the weeks of our waiting draw to a close . . . There is scarcely a leaf astir
In the garden beyond my windows, where the twilight shadows blur
The blaze of some woman's roses . . .
                              'Bombardment orders, sir.'
                                          Gilbert Frankau

A Staff Captain's Lament

'Twas near the close of 'Z' day
    When a lull fell o'er the fight,
The strain on the Staff had been great all day
    But was greater still that night.

'Beer Emma' sat wearily marking
    Fresh colours on his map,
While the G.O.C. and Signals
    Took a surreptitious nap.

The whole Red Line was captured,
    And most of the Green Line too,
And the points where the Boche still lingered
    Had now to be marked in Blue.

Fresh lines of Black and Yellow
    Now started to appear,
Shewing still further objectives
    In the open ground in rear.

A certain grim elation
    'Beer Emma' could scarce restrain,
For the Brigade had been advancing
    And would soon advance again.

First; to clear the blue bit
    He'd need a Tank or two,
With a score or so of bombers
    To see the thing go through.

Then on to the new objectives
    One regiment for each,
With the others to bring assistance
    At the points which the first can't reach.

The 'Esses C' worked sadly,
    No gleam of elation here,
For the work of a mere Staff Captain –
    Well, it isn't all skittles and beer.

All his water's expended,
    None of his rations remain,
And the dumps he's already moved forward
    Will have to move forward again.

It's far enough to the Red Line;
    It's further still to the Green,
And he's jolly well *got* to dump there
    Though there's no sort of road between.

The bombers will need ammunition,
    The throats of the men will be dry,
There are tracks where a mule *can't* be taken,
    Tho' God knows the fellows will try.

And mixed with the dump calculations
    In the wretched Staff Captain's head,
There's the daily return of the wounded,
    The horrible toll of the dead.

None of the Soldier's elation;
    Small share of the Victor's pride;
Just a butt for 'Q' of Division:
    You may not believe it – I've tried.

SEVENTEEN

Third Battle of Ypres (Passchendaele)

The missing and the dead, burials and the horrors of no man's land, rain, winter 1917, fatigues and carrying parties, horses and mules, bombing behind the lines, the end of the Battle of Passchendaele

The third Battle of Ypres, known as the Battle of Passchendaele, was planned for the summer of 1917 with the objective of breaking through the German lines north-east of Ypres. Haig believed that the heavy casualties suffered by the enemy at Verdun and on the Somme had weakened the German willingness to fight, and that with careful planning a new attack would overwhelm them and bring an end to the years of stalemate on the Western Front.

One thing that Haig could not plan was the weather. The heavy preliminary bombardment, which could again be heard in southern England, destroyed the drainage system that had redeemed the flat, waterlogged countryside round Ypres, and then – the day after the British went over the top on 31 July – the rain started to fall. The attacking forces faced a growing quagmire and strong enemy defences. The Germans had built small concrete redoubts, nicknamed by the Tyneside soldiers 'Tyne cots' since they reminded them of cottages at home: some of these have survived to this day and give their name to Tyne Cot, the largest British cemetery on the Western Front.

The battle, which lasted for three months, was fought in some of the worst conditions of the war. As the front line inched its way forward, wooden tracks and duckboards were laid across the morass, but one slip or false step meant that men and horses could drown in liquid mud. Going in and out of the line, or bringing up supplies, was carried out under heavy shellfire, for the German guns had the roads and tracks ranged precisely. The exposed road leading out of Ypres towards Menin, along which men and horses must travel, acquired a fearful reputation. At the beginning of November the battle came to an end with an advance of 5 miles and the capture of the village of Passchendaele.

By this stage in the war, German aircraft were bombing the rest areas behind the lines. There seemed nowhere to escape. The French armies mutinied, ground down by the losses at Verdun, but British morale held.

The Sound of Flanders Guns

Let me go far away, so far I shall not hear
The deep, insistent throbbing of the guns; they beat
For ever day and night – my tired heart and brain
Can find no rest, but beat and throb in unison.

A long, long journey, punctured through and through
With restless darts of pain, for ever loud above
The din of traffic and the busy travellers' talk,
I hear them muttering still, on and for ever on;
Oh, shall I never reach the Haven where I would be.

What could be fairer than this little village, set
Between its rocky sentinels, that watching stand
On either side, their bases lapped by seas of emerald,
Capped by great rolling hills, whose sides appear
Cushioned in velvet, for some giant king's repose?

Thinking, Here must be Peace, I raise my weary eyes
And scan the far horizon; there I see appear
A long grey shape, so silent, grim and stern:
Our sea-hounds prowl, guarding our English homes.
A goodly sight, indeed, but still it seems to me
I hear the echoes of the Flanders guns again.

I hear them in the plash of wave, the sea-birds' call,
And in the little church upon the windy hill,
Above the children's voices, shrilling loud and clear,
Above the parson's voice, they sound so in my ear
That 'Peace on earth, goodwill to men' appears
But as some faint, almost forgotten dream.

And some will hear them to their dying hour,
Grim legacy of days of waiting pain; will hear
Above the clarion voice of Victory, and the happy talk
Of re-united friends, the gladsome laugh of children
And hum of peaceful cities, still that baleful sound
Will be the under-current of their daily lives,
One tarnished thread, that, running through and through,
Will soil life's fairest fabric. We shall sometimes feel

Deep in our hearts a silent stab of pain, and hear
The low deep throbbing of the Flanders guns again.

Mary Beazley

The Burning Question

Three Tommies sat in a trench one day
Discussing the war in the usual way,
They talked of the mud, and they talked of the Hun,
Of what was to do and what had been done;
They talked about rum, and – 'tis hard to believe –
They even found time to speak about leave,
But the point which they argued from post back to pillar
Was whether Notts County could beat Aston Villa.

The night sped away and zero drew nigh,
Equipment made ready, all lips getting dry,
And watches consulted with each passing minute
Till five more to go, that 'twould find them all in it;
The word came along down the line to 'get ready!'
The sergeants admonishing all to keep steady,
But out rang a voice getting shriller and shriller:
'I tell yer Notts County can beat Aston Villa!'

The Earth shook and swayed, and the barrage was on
As they leapt o'er the top with a rush, and were gone
Away into Hunland, through mud and through wire,
Stabbing and dragging themselves through the mire.
No time to heed those who are falling en route
Till, stopped by a strong point, they lay down to shoot,
Then through the din came a voice: 'Say, Jack Miller!
I tell yer Notts County can beat Aston Villa.'

The strong point has gone, and forward they press
Towards their objective, in number grown less.
They reach it at last, and prepare to resist
The counter-attack which will come through the mist
Of the rain falling steadily; dig and hang on,
The word for support back to H.Q. has gone,
The air, charged with moment, grows stiller and stiller –
'Notts County's no earthly beside Aston Villa.'

Two 'Blighties', a struggle through mud to get back
To the old A.D.S. down a rough duckboard track;
A hasty field dressing, a ride in a car
A wait in a C.C.S., then there they are:
Packed side by side in a clean Red Cross train,
Happy in hopes to see Blighty again.
Still, through the bandages, muffled, 'Jack Miller,
I bet you Notts County can beat Aston Villa!'

Between the Lines

When consciousness came back, he found he lay
Between the opposing fires, but could not tell
On which hand were his friends; and either way
For him to turn was chancy – bullet and shell
Whistling and shrieking over him, as the glare
Of searchlights scoured the darkness to blind day.
He scrambled to his hands and knees ascare,
Dragging his wounded foot through puddled clay,
And tumbled in a hole a shell had scooped
At random in a turnip-field between
The unseen trenches where the foes lay cooped
Through that unending battle of unseen,
Dead-locked, league-stretching armies; and quite spent
He rolled upon his back within the pit,
And lay secure, thinking of all it meant –
His lying in that little hole, sore hit,
But living, while across the starry sky
Shrapnel and shell went screeching overhead –
Of all it meant that he, Tom Dodd, should lie
Among the Belgian turnips, while his bed . . .
If it were he, indeed, who'd climbed each night,
Fagged from the day's work, up the narrow stair,
And slipt his clothes off in the candle-light,
Too tired to fold them neatly in a chair
The way his mother'd taught him – too dog-tired
After the long day's serving in the shop,
Inquiring what each customer required,
Politely talking weather, fit to drop . . .

And now for fourteen days and nights, at least,
He hadn't had his clothes off, and had lain
In muddy trenches, napping like a beast
With one eye open, under sun and rain
And that unceasing hell-fire . . .
                                        It was strange
How things turned out – the chances! You'd just got
To take your luck in life, you couldn't change
Your luck.
               And so here he was lying shot
Who just six months ago had thought to spend
His days behind a counter. Still, perhaps . . .
And now, God only knew how he would end!

He'd like to know how many of the chaps
Had won back to the trench alive, when he
Had fallen wounded and been left for dead,
If any! . . .
               This was different, certainly,
From selling knots of tape and reels of thread
And knots of tape and reels of thread and knots
Of tape and reels of thread and knots of tape,
Day in, day out, and answering 'Have you got's
And 'Do you keep's till there seemed no escape
From everlasting serving in a shop,
Inquiring what each customer required,
Politely talking weather, fit to drop,
With swollen ankles, tired . . .
                                        But he was tired
Now. Every bone was aching, and had ached
For fourteen days and nights in that wet trench –
Just duller when he slept than when he waked –
Crouching for shelter from the steady drench
Of shell and shrapnel . . .
                                   That old trench, it seemed
Almost like home to him. He'd slept and fed
And sung and smoked in it, while shrapnel screamed
And shells went whining harmless overhead –
Harmless, at least, as far as he . . .
                                        But Dick –
Dick hadn't found them harmless yesterday,

At breakfast, when he'd said he couldn't stick
Eating dry bread, and crawled out the back way,
And brought them butter in a lordly dish –
Butter enough for all, and held it high
Yellow and fresh and clean as you would wish –
When plump upon the plate from out the sky
A shell fell bursting . . . where the butter went,
God only knew! . . .
                    And Dick . . . He dared not think
Of what had come to Dick . . . or what it meant –
The shrieking and the whistling and the stink
He'd lived in fourteen days and nights. 'Twas luck
That he still lived . . . And queer how little then
He seemed to care that Dick . . . perhaps 'twas pluck
That hardened him – a man among the men –
Perhaps . . . Yet, only think things out a bit,
And he was rabbit-livered, blue with funk!
And he'd liked Dick . . . and yet when Dick was hit,
He hadn't turned a hair. The meanest skunk
He should have thought would feel it when his mate
Was blown to smithereens – Dick, proud as punch,
Grinning like sin, and holding up the plate –
But he had gone on munching his dry hunch,
Unwinking, till he swallowed the last crumb.

Perhaps 'twas just because he dared not let
His mind run upon Dick, who'd been his chum.
He dared not now, though he could not forget.

Dick took his luck. And, life or death, 'twas luck
From first to last; and you'd just got to trust
Your luck and grin. It wasn't so much pluck
As knowing that you'd got to, when needs must,
And better to die grinning . . .
                            Quiet now
Had fallen on the night. On either hand
The guns were quiet. Cool upon his brow
The quiet darkness brooded, as he scanned
The starry sky. He'd never seen before
So many stars. Although of course, he'd known
That there were stars, somehow before the war

He'd never realised them – so thick-sown,
Millions and millions. Serving in the shop,
Stars didn't count for much; and then at nights
Strolling the pavements, dull and fit to drop,
You didn't see much but the city lights.
He'd never in his life seen so much sky
As he'd seen this last fortnight. It was queer
The things war taught you. He'd a mind to try
To count the stars – they shone so bright and clear.
One, two, three, four . . . Ah, God, but he was tired . . .
Five, six, seven, eight . . .

                       Yes, it was number eight.
And what was the next thing that she required?
(Too bad of customers to come so late,
At closing-time!) Again within the shop
He handled knots of tape and reels of thread,
Politely talking weather, fit to drop . . .

When once again the whole sky overhead
Flared blind with searchlights, and the shriek of shell
And scream of shrapnel roused him. Drowsily
He stared about him, wondering. Then he fell
Into deep dreamless slumber.

                  *   *   *

                       He could see
Two dark eyes peeping at him, ere he knew
He was awake, and it again was day –
An August morning, burning to clear blue.
The frightened rabbit scuttled . . .

                         Far away,
A sound of firing . . . Up there, in the sky
Big dragon-flies hung hovering . . . Snowballs burst
About them . . .

              Flies and snowballs! With a cry
He crouched to watch the airmen pass – the first
That he'd seen under fire. Lord, that was pluck –
Shells bursting all about them – and what nerve!
They took their chance, and trusted to their luck.
At such a dizzy height to dip and swerve,

Dodging the shell-fire . . .

        Hell! but one was hit,

And tumbling like a pigeon, plump . . .

           Thank Heaven,

It righted, and then turned; and after it

The whole flock followed safe – four, five, six, seven,

Yes, they were all there safe. He hoped they'd win

Back to their lines in safety. They deserved,

Even if they were Germans . . . 'Twas no sin

To wish them luck. Think how that beggar swerved

Just in the nick of time!

        He, too, must try

To win back to the lines, though, likely as not,

He'd take the wrong turn: but he couldn't lie

Forever in that hungry hole and rot,

He'd got to take his luck, to take his chance

Of being sniped by foes or friends. He'd be

With any luck in Germany or France

Or Kingdom-come, next morning . . .

        Drearily

The blazing day burnt over him. Shot and shell

Whistling and whining ceaselessly. But light

Faded at last, and as the darkness fell

He rose, and crawled away into the night.

         Wilfrid W. Gibson

Missing

'He was last seen going over the parapet into the German trenches.'

What did you find after war's fierce alarms,
    When the kind earth gave you a resting place,
And comforting night gathered you in her arms,
    With light dew falling on your upturned face?

Did your heart beat, remembering what had been?
    Did you still hear around you, as you lay,
The wings of airmen sweeping by unseen,
    The thunder of the guns at close of day?

All nature stoops to guard your lonely bed;
    Sunshine and rain fall with their calming breath;

You need no pall, so young and newly dead,
   Where the Lost Legion triumphs over death.

When with the morrow's dawn the bugle blew,
   For the first time it summoned you in vain;
The Last Post does not sound for such as you;
   But God's Reveillé wakens you again.

Geraldine Robertson Glasgow

Trampled Clay

We crept into the gas-polluted night,
A little band allotted for fatigue;
And yard by yard we searched a quarter league
Of ground new won by blood and strife and might;
Of ground dear lost, dear gained, and dearer held,
Where shell on shell still burst among the felled.

We went to seek the dead; with rough respect
To roll their mangled bodies down the shade
Of crater-lips that shrieking shells had made.
O, Mary, Mother, in white samite decked!
Beyond the chaos of our earthly strife,
What of the waiting mother, sister, wife?

The dreamer lay with blood-gout on his lips,
The strenuist with virile limbs stretched wide,
His leaded 'cosh' still lying at his side,
His bombing-jacket corded to his hips.
(At home the English journals said that we
Had gained another easy victory.)

We left them covered with an earthy shroud;
'Dust to the dust', without a single prayer
Save, mayhap, one that Pity murmured there.
But Pity's voice is never very loud,
And we are used to seeing comrades die,
And leaving them, perforce, just where they lie.

Thy Hand doth clothe the lily, warm the day;
Sol's cloth of gold most tenderly is drawn

Across the opalescent robes of Dawn;
Yet see, O, God! this mass of trampled clay,
These gaping wounds, these bodies shrapnel-torn.
Vengeance is Thine! Let vengeance now be sworn.

Colin Mitchell

Aftermath

With steady, silent tread,
Bearing aloft their dead, –
One at the foot, one at the head, –
The stretcher-bearers go;
Out of the dark they come
Stumbling and staggering, some
Bearing, maybe, a chum,
Pair after pair they go.

Vague silhouetted ghosts
Remnants of martyr'd hosts;
Think on the blatant toasts
Raised to 'King Glory';
Tread lightly, – that's the way,
Wake not the dead, lest they
Have other words to say of the same story!

D. Howard Tripp

Before Battle

I heard them sing of home last night,
A song of Devon they loved so well,
As they were marching to the fight –
Along the Flanders road to hell . . .

I scarce can think 'twas yesterday
Those laughing lads could laugh and sing,
For now their dear boy lips are grey,
And Devon has made her offering.

Their song is dead, but that sweet strain
Still gathering charms unknown before,

Will make a music in my brain,
And haunt my heart for evermore.

Raymond Heywood

Comrades

Those whom I've known, admired, ardently friended
Lie silent there wrapp'd in a soldier's shroud;
Death broke their dreams, their aspirations ended,
These sanguine youth, noble, brave and proud.

Slowly they bear them 'neath the dim star light
Unto their rest – the soldiers' cemetery:
The chaplain chants a low, brief litany;
The nightingale flings rapture on the night.

Back to their Mother Earth this night return
Unnumbered youth along the far-flung line;
But 'tis for these my eyes with feeling burn,
That Memory doth erect a fadeless shrine –
For these I've known, admired, ardently friended
Stood by when Death their love, their youth swift ended.

John W. Streets

The Soldier

'Tis strange to look on a man that is dead
    As he lies in the shell-swept hell,
And to think that the poor black battered corpse
    Once lived like you and was well.

'Tis stranger far when you come to think
    That *you* may be soon like him . . .
And it's Fear that tugs at your trembling soul,
    A Fear that is weird and grim!

Hamish Mann

Worm

Thou thing –
Slimy and crawling
Oozing along.

Not brown,
As men's eyes see
But reddish green,
And moist.
Death meaning nought
To thee.
Who livest
And breedest
During many aeons
Billions more yellow horrors
Like thyself.
Oh, Hell!

From the Line

Have you seen men come from the Line,
Tottering, doddering, as if bad wine
Had drugged their very souls;
Their garments rent with holes
And caked with mud
And streaked with blood
Of others, or their own;
Haggard, weary-limbed and chilled to the bone,
Trudging aimless, hopeless, on
With listless eyes and faces drawn
Taut with woe?

Have you seen them aimless go
Bowed down with muddy pack
And muddy rifle slung on back,
And soaking overcoat,
Staring on with eyes that note
Nothing but the mire
Quenched of every fire?

Have you seen men when they come
From shell-holes filled with scum
Of mud and blood and flesh,
Where there's nothing fresh
Like grass, or trees, or flowers,
And the numbing year-like hours

Lag on – drag on,
And the hopeless dawn
Brings naught but death, and rain –
The rain a fiend of pain
That scourges without end,
And Death, a smiling friend?

Have you seen men when they come from hell?
If not, – ah, well
Speak not with easy eloquence
That seems like sense
Of 'War and its Necessity'!
And do not rant, I pray,
On 'War's Magnificent Nobility'!

If you've seen men come from the Line
You'll know it's Peace that is divine!
If you've not seen the things I've sung –
Let silence bind your tongue,
But, make all wars to cease,
And work, and work for Everlasting peace!

R. Watson Kerr

After the Battle

So they are satisfied with our Brigade,
   And it remains to parcel out the bays!
And we shall have the usual Thanks Parade,
   The beaming General, and the soapy praise.

You will come up in your capacious car
   To find your heroes sulking in the rain,
To tell us how magnificent we are,
   And how you hope we'll do the same again.

And we, who knew your old abusive tongue,
   Who heard you hector us a week before,
We who have bled to boost you up a rung –
   A K.C.B. perhaps, perhaps a Corps — ;

We who must mourn those spaces in the Mess,
    And somehow fill the hollows in the heart,
We do not want your Sermon on Success,
    Your greasy benisons on Being Smart.

We only want to take our wounds away
    To some shy village where the tumult ends,
And drowsing in the sunshine many a day,
    Forget our aches, forget that we had friends.

Weary we are of blood and noise and pain;
    This was a week we shall not soon forget;
And if, indeed, we have to fight again,
    We little wish to think about it yet.

We have done well; we like to hear it said.
    Say it, and then, for God's sake, say no more.
Fight, if you must, fresh battles far ahead,
    But keep them dark behind your château door!

A.P. Herbert

Statesmen Debonair

O ye statesmen debonair,
With the partings in your hair;
Statesmen, ye who do your bit
In the arm-chairs where you sit;
You with top-hats on your head
Even when you lie in bed;
O superbly happy, ye,
Traders in Humanity;
    Every time you smile, sweet friends,
    A moan goes up, a plague descends.
    Every time you show your teeth,
    A hundred swords desert the sheath.
    Every time you pare your nails,
    The manhood of a city fails.
    Every time you dip your pen,
    You slaughter ten platoons of men.
    For every glass of port you hold
    Blood is spilt ten thousandfold . . .

O ye statesmen debonair,
With the partings in your hair;
O ye statesmen pink and white,
Sleep like little lambs to-night.

Louis Golding

The New Trade

In the market-place they have made
    A dolorous new trade.
Now you will see in the fierce naphtha-light,
    Piled hideously to sight,
Dead limbs of men bronzed in the over-seas,
    Bomb-wrenched from elbows and knees;
Torn feet, that would, unwearied by harsh loads,
    Have tramped steep moorlands roads;
Torn hands that would have moulded exquisitely
    Rare things for God to see.
And there are eyes there – blue like blue doves' wings,
    Black like the Libyan kings,
Grey as before-dawn rivers, willow-stirred,
    Brown as a singing-bird;
But all stare from the dark into the dark,
    Reproachful, tense, and stark,
Eyes heaped on trays and in broad baskets there,
    Feet, hands, and ropes of hair.
In the market-places . . . and women buy . . .
    . . . Naphtha glares . . . hawkers cry . . .
Fat men rub hands . . .
      O God, O just God, send
    Plague, lightnings . . .
      Make an end!

Louis Golding

Rain

Ah! when it rains all day
And the sky is a mist
That creeps by chillily
Where sun once kissed,

Like death pale shroud,
My soul cries out aloud
In hopeless misery.

I cannot read nor write
A line for gloom,
My life lags, drenched of light
To cheer its tomb;
Chill and wet,
Comfortless I fret
In hopeless night!

And naught to hear but rain
Battering the ground!
O numbing pain!
O maddening sound!
Drowned in sky
Trees drip, drip, and sigh
And drip, drip, again.

R. Watson Kerr

A Vignette

On stark and tortured wire
Where refuse of war lies
Tangled in mire –
When God is flinging
Rain down the skies –
Sit three little birds, singing.

R. Watson Kerr

The Flanders Rain

Watching the rain dry up,
Watching the rain dry up,
We stick and slip in Flanders mud
Till camouflaged just like a spud,
Watching the rain dry up.
Plastered from hoof to crown;
And when we've watched all the rain dry up,
We watch all the rain come down.

The Song of the Mud

This is the song of the mud,
The pale yellow glistening mud that covers the hills like satin;
The grey gleaming silvery mud that is spread like enamel over the valleys;
The frothing, squirting, spurting, liquid mud that gurgles along the road beds;
The thick elastic mud that is kneaded and pounded and squeezed under the
    hoofs of the horses;
The invincible, inexhaustible mud of the war zone.

This is the song of the mud, the uniform of the poilu.
His coat is of mud, his great dragging flapping coat, that is too big for him and
    too heavy;
His coat that once was blue and now is grey and stiff with the mud that cakes to it.
This is the mud that clothes him.
His trousers and boots are of mud,
And his skin is of mud;
And there is mud in his beard.
His head is crowned with a helmet of mud.
He wears it well.
He wears it as a king wears the ermine that bores him.
He has set a new style in clothing;
He has introduced the chic of mud.

This is the song of the mud that wriggles its way into battle.
The impertinent, the intrusive, the ubiquitous, the unwelcome,
The slimy inveterate nuisance,
That fills the trenches,
That mixes in with the food of the soldiers,
That spoils the working of motors and crawls into their secret parts,
That spreads itself over the guns,
That sucks the guns down and holds them fast in its slimy voluminous lips,
That has no respect for destruction and muzzles the bursting of shells;
And slowly, softly, easily,
Soaks up the fire, the noise; soaks up the energy and the courage;
Soaks up the power of armies;
Soaks up the battle.
Just soaks it up and thus stops it.

This is the hymn of mud – the obscene, the filthy, the putrid,
The vast liquid grave of our armies.

It has drowned our men.
Its monstrous distended belly reeks with the undigested dead.
Our men have gone into it, sinking slowly, and struggling and slowly disappearing.
Our fine men, our brave, strong, young men;
Our glowing red, shouting, brawny men.
Slowly, inch by inch, they have gone down into it,
Into its darkness, its thickness, its silence.
Slowly, irresistibly, it drew them down, sucked them down,
And they were drowned in thick, bitter, heaving mud.
Now it hides them, Oh, so many of them!
Under its smooth glistening surface it is hiding them blandly.
There is not a trace of them.
There is no mark where they went down.
The mute enormous mouth of the mud has closed over them.

This is the song of the mud,
The beautiful glistening golden mud that covers the hills like satin;
The mysterious gleaming silvery mud that is spread like enamel over the valleys.
Mud, the disguise of the war zone;
Mud, the mantle of battles;
Mud, the smooth fluid grave of our soldiers:
This is the song of the mud.

Mary Borden

Mad

Neck-deep in mud,
He mowed and raved –
He who had braved
The field of blood –

And as a lad
Just out of school
Yelled: 'April fool!'
And laughed like mad.

Wilfred W. Gibson

Carrying-Party
Time 10.30 p.m. Place, Communication Trenches.

Wire over'ead!
Mud underfoot:

    Gawd, I'm into a hole,
      Pullin' the sole
  Right off'en me boot –
I wish I was dead!

Wire over'ead –
(My load weighs like lead)
    The night's black as 'ell;
      I'm into a ditch –
        Ye son of a bitch!
   'Twas here Nelson fell –
   Bang! There goes a shell –
I wish I was dead!

Wire over'ead –
    Look out for the bridge!
      Hear ole Sergeant grunt,
       'Halt! you there in front!
    They've lost touch at the ridge' –
I wish *I* was dead!

Wire over'ead!
   Wire underfoot! –
      There's Tim come to grief –
      Christ! – he's dumping the beef.
   Pull 'im out by the root:
I wish I was dead –
(To home blokes are in bed) –
Wish Gawd I was dead!
     (Stumbles and grumbles on.)

                       Joseph Lee

The Fatal Wooden Track

In a place not far from Ypres,
Just a little further back,
By the name of Warrington Road, sir,
Better known as the Wooden Track.

If you went through the whole of Belgium,
Or along to the Somme and back,

There is no place so full of terror
As that awful Wooden Track.

'Tis vivid in our memory,
As here we try to tell,
There is no place to compare it
Not even that place called Hell.

So oft is it a driver's duty
Of the columns further back
To carry ammunition
Along that fatal track.

And when they get the order
To be ready sharp at nine,
You will see the drivers mounted
And ready for the line.

But still it is their duty,
As everyone should know,
And though death should await them,
Forward they will go.

For our guns are always calling
For shells both night and day,
And as they near the place, sir,
They think of home and pray.

They pray to God in Heaven
To bring them safely back,
And give them strength and courage,
When once they are on the track.

'Tis now that they need that courage
As they gallop up that track,
Though the shells may fall like hail, sir,
There is no turning back.

Though tragic in its splendour
Is the scene that meets the eye,

The bravest and the best, sir,
Have gone there, alas! to die.

'Tis a scene of sterling courage
Most awful to behold,
And the bravest men amongst us
Felt their very blood run cold.

Seen from an Aid-Post

There are many roads in Flanders, where the horses slide and fall,
There are roads of mud and pavé that lead nowhere at all,
They are roads that finish at our trench; the Germans hold the rest.
But of all the roads in Flanders, there is one I know the best.
It's a great road, a straight road, a road that runs between
Two rows of broken poplars, that were young and strong and green.

You can trace it from old Poperinghe, through Vlamertinghe and Wipers;
(It's a focus for Hun whizz-bangs and a paradise for snipers);
Pass the solid Ramparts and the muddy moat you're then in,
The road I want to sing about – the road that leads to Menin.
It's a great road, a straight road, a road that runs between
Two rows of broken poplars, that were young and strong and green.

It's a road that's cursed by smokers, for you dare not show a light;
It's a road that's shunned by daytime and is mainly used at night;
But at dusk the silent troops come up, and limbers bring their loads
Of ammunition to the guns that guard the Salient's roads.
It's a great road, a straight road, a road that runs between
Two rows of broken poplars, that were young and strong and green.

And for hours and days together I have listened to the sound
Of German shrapnel overhead while I was underground
In a damp and cheerless cellar, continually trying
To dress the wounded warriors, while comforting the dying
On that muddy road, that bloody road, that road that runs between
Two rows of broken poplars, that were young and strong and green.
                                        R[egimental] M[edical] O[fficer]

Gun-Teams

Their rugs are sodden, their heads are down, their tails are turned to the storm.
(Would you know them, you that groomed them in the sleek fat days of peace,
When the tiles rang to their pawings in the lighted stalls, and warm,
Now the foul clay cakes on britching strap and clogs the quick-release?)

The blown rain stings, there is never a star, the tracks are rivers of slime.
(You must harness-up by guesswork with a failing torch for light,
Instep-deep in unmade standings; for it's active-service time,
And our resting weeks are over, and we move the guns to-night.)

The iron tyres slither, the traces sag, their blind hooves stumble and slide;
They are war-worn, they are weary, soaked with sweat and sopped with rain:
(You must hold them, you must help them, swing your lead and centre wide
Where the greasy granite *pavé* peters out to squelching drain.)

There is shrapnel bursting a mile in front on the road that the guns must take:
(You are thoughtful, you are nervous, you are shifting in your seat,
As you watch the ragged feathers flicker orange, flame and break)
But the teams are pulling steady down the battered village street.

You have shod them cold, and their coats are long, and their bellies gray with the
     mud;
They had done with gloss and polish, but the fighting heart's unbroke . . .
We, who saw them hobbling after us down white roads flecked with blood,
Patient, wondering why we left them, till we lost them in the smoke;

Who have felt them shiver between our knees, when the shells rain black from
     the skies;
When the bursting terrors find us and the lines stampede as one;
Who have watched the pierced limbs quiver and the pain in stricken eyes –
Know the worth of humble servants, foolish-faithful to their gun.

Gilbert Frankau

Transport
(Courcelles)

The moon swims in milkiness,
The road glimmers curving down into the wooded valley

And with a clashing and creaking of tackle and axles
The train of limbers passes me, and the mules
Splash me with mud, thrusting me from the road into puddles,
Straining at the tackle with a bitter patience,
Passing me . . .
And into a patch of moonlight,
With beautiful curved necks and manes,
Heads reined back, and nostrils dilated,
Impatient of restraint,
Pass two grey stallions,
Such as Oenetia bred;
Beautiful as the horses of Hippolytus
Carven on some antique frieze.
And my heart rejoices seeing their strength in play,
The mere animal life of them,
Lusting,
As a thing passionate and proud.

Then again the limbers and grotesque mules.

Frederic Manning

Dumb Heroes

There's a D.S.O. for the Colonel,
    A Military Cross for the Sub,
A medal or two, when we all get through,
    And a bottle of wine with our grub.

There's a stripe of gold for the wounded,
    A rest by the bright sea-shore,
And a service is read as we bury our dead,
    Then our country has one hero more.

And what of our poor dumb heroes
    That are sent without choice to the fight,
That strain at the load on the shell-swept road
    As they take up the rations at night.

They are shelling on Hell Fire Corner,
    There's shrapnel just burst in the Square,
And their bullets drum as the transports come
    With the food for the soldiers there.

The halt till the shelling is over,
    The rush through the line of fire,
The glowing light in the dead of night,
    And the terrible sights in the mire.

It's the daily work of the horses
    And they answer the spur and rein,
With quickened breath, 'mid the toll of death,
    Through the mud, and the holes, and the rain.

There's a fresh treated wound in the chestnut,
    The black mare's neck has a mark,
The brown mule's new mate won't keep the same gait
    As the one killed last night in the dark.

But they walk with the spirit of heroes,
    They care not for medals or cross,
But for duty alone, into perils unknown,
    They go, never counting the loss.

There's a swift painless death for the hopeless,
    With a grave in a shell-hole or field,
There's a hospital base for the casualty case,
    And a Vet. for those easily healed.

But there's never a shadow of glory,
    A cheer, or a speech, in their praise,
While patient and true they carry us through
    With the limbers in shot-riven ways.

So here's to 'Dumb Heroes' of Britain,
    Who serve her as nobly and true,
As the best of her boys, 'mid the roar of the guns
    And the best of her boys on the blue.

They are shell-shocked, they're bruised, and they're broken,
    They are wounded and torn as they fall,
But they're true and they're brave to the very grave,
    And they're heroes, one and all.

T.A. Girling

My Beautiful
The Trooper to his Steed

Before the sun has shown himself, for your complacent sake,
Obedient to the bugle, I reluctantly awake;
Though hurricanes may whistle and though drenching torrents fall,
I've got to sacrifice my ease and stumble to your stall.

Is man creation's master, O my beautiful, my bay?
Yet I must do you courtesies with each returning day:
You stand – impatient frequently – impassive at the best,
While like a lazy potentate you're brushed and combed and dressed.

With rake and spade and haik and graip I serve you in the gloom;
For you I wheel the barrow, and for you I wield the broom;
That you may look your handsomest, I fling my tunic off,
And labour with a dandy-brush – you sybarite, you toff!

Sometimes, of course, my beautiful, you stand quite meekly by,
While others wait upon your wants – no wonder, so would I;
My very humble servant, eh? – my faithful, patient slave?
Just keep you waiting for your oats, and see how you behave!

*   *   *

I'm only chaffing you, old hoss, you needn't mind my fun –
You pay me back a thousandfold for anything I've done.
I slip my saddle on your back – swing up myself, my own –
And every monarch on the earth is welcome to his throne!

W. Kersley Holmes

Horse-Bathing Parade

A few clouds float across the grand blue sky,
The glorious sun has mounted zenith-high,
Mile upon mile of sand, flat, golden, clean,
And bright, stretch north and south, and fringed with green,
The rough dunes fitly close the landward view.
All else is sea; somewhere in misty blue
The distant coast seems melting into air –
Earth, sky, and ocean, all commingling there –

And one bold, lonely rock, whose guardian light
Glistens afar by day, a spire snow-white.
Here, where the ceaseless blue-green rollers dash
Their symmetry to dazzling foam and flash,
We ride our horses, silken flanks ashine,
Spattered and soaked with flying drops of brine,
The sunny water tosses round their knees,
Their smooth tails shimmer in the singing breeze.
White streaks of foam sway round us, to and fro,
With shadows swaying on the sand below;
The horses snort and start to see the foam,
And hear the breaking roar of waves that come,
Or, pawing, splash the brine, and so we stand,
And hear the surf rush hissing up the sand.

W. Kersley Holmes

The Air Raid

Above in the still and starlit sky
Smiles the full moon serene;
When a sound we hear that all men fear –
The pulse of the bomb machine.

The Hun rides on his raid tonight,
Death runs wild and free;
And terror wakes and cold fear shakes
The hearts of the soldiery.

Silent, ghostly cottages
Huddle beneath the skies,
And the frantic glare of rockets there
Glows fitfully and dies.

Silent are the moonlit streets,
Men seek the shadows there;
The awful breath of winnowing death
Is pulsing through the air.

Great God! To feel the helplessness
And the shame of naked fear!
To sit and wait in impotent hate
As the hawk of Hell draws near.

Suddenly the whirring stops
And thin high whistles sound;
There's blinding flash, a final crash,
And then silence all around.

And a little man in blue lies low
Under the moon's pale light;
In a pool of red he is lying, dead,
In the silence of the night.

Don White

The Shell

Shrieking its message the flying death
    Cursed the resisting air,
Then buried its nose by a battered church
    A skeleton gaunt and bare.

The brains of science, the money of fools
    Had fashioned an iron slave
Destined to kill, yet the futile end
    Was a child's uprooted grave.

H. Smalley Sarson

A Flemish Village

Gone is the spire that slept for centuries,
Whose image in the water, calm and low,
Was mingled with the lilies green and snow,
And lost itself in river mysteries.
The church lies broken near the fallen spire;
For here, among these old and human things,
Death swept along the street with feet of fire,
And went upon his way with moaning wings.
Above the cluster of these homes forlorn,
Where giant fleeces of the shells are rolled,
O'er pavements by the kneeling herdsmen worn,
The wounded saints look out to see their fold.

And silence follows fast, no evening peace,
But leaden stillness, when the thunder wanes,

Haunting the slender branches of the trees,
And settling low upon the listless plains.

Herbert Asquith

To Belgium
Lines written when travelling from Poperinghe to Étaples, December, 1917

Belgium, I do not see thee with the eyes
    Of poets, chaunting pæans upon thy state –
I view thee from a cattle-truck – a guise
    Of locomotion really out of date.

Nor do I scan thee like some writing chap,
    Who seeks to turn thy tragedies to pence;
Thy storied past don't interest me a scrap –
    My miseries are in the present tense!

Belgium, when no relief is in my reach,
    Thou robb'st me shamefully. No pig would touch
The fruit thou sellest at three-halfpence each;
    Then threepence halfpenny for *John Bull* – too much!

And eggs at half-a-franc which – well, 'tis war;
    Perchance my protest sounds a trifle flighty.
Belgium! I will forgive thee all – and more –
    If thou wilt only sell me (cheap) *one* 'Blighty'!

W. Clifford Poulten

EIGHTEEN

America Joins the War

Another 'Call to Arms', 'Somewhere in France'

For two-and-a-half years the United States, under President Wilson, had taken a neutral stance in the war. This position had been weakened by the sinking of the passenger ship the *Lusitania*, with the loss of American civilian lives, but Germany bowed to American pressure and abandoned unrestricted U-boat activity. However, early in 1917 the Germans renewed all-out U-boat warfare in order to bring Britain to its knees, and American ships were again sunk. On 3 February the United States severed diplomatic relations with Germany. Meanwhile, in January 1917 a telegram had been intercepted revealing German plans to incite Mexico into military action against the United States; in exchange for this support Mexico would receive from the victorious Germans the US territories of New Mexico, Texas and Arizona. On 6 April 1917, the United States formally declared war on Germany.

It took time for America to prepare for a war from which it had so resolutely distanced itself – it would be early 1918 before the Dough Boys, as they were called, arrived in France in any numbers – but the call for volunteers was reminiscent of England in 1914. The Selective Service Act of May 1917 authorised the President to raise a volunteer infantry force of four divisions, and all men between 21 and 30 were required to register for military service. By September nearly twenty-four million had done so; about two million would serve overseas. They began to arrive in France in significant numbers in the spring of 1918.

The Newt-ral

The Newt-ral has an artful eye
Swift any danger to espy;
A very wise amphibian he,
Preserving strict newt-rality.
His pattern is peculiar, too,
With stripes of variegated hue;
And when he's marked with stars as well,
There is no need his name to tell!

St John Hamund

My American Cousins

Because they speak the tongue that's mine,
    Rich in the treasure that belongs
To them as well as me, and twine
    Their heart-strings in our English songs,
I knew they'd scorn those German threats
        And sham regrets.

Because their country's name is scrolled
    With Liberty's; because her fate,
Like England's own, must be unrolled
    In Freedom still, they had to hate
The thought of bowing down before
        A Lord of War.

And now they'll lavish in the strife
    The gold they've scorned to love too well,
And fleets to bring the food that's life,
    And guns of death, and steel and shell;

Defeat or triumph, stand or fall,
    They'll share their all.

They're out for business; now's their Day;
    They took their time, but finished right;
The heat got slowly comes to stay;
    Patient for peace means firm in fight;
And so their country still shall be
    Land of the Free.

C. Conway Plumbe

The American Advance

The Eagle's bared his talons and has soared across the tide,
Shrilling forth in high defiance to the Prussian and his pride,
And the Eagle's legions gather – gather in the land of France,
For the hand of fate has signaled an American advance!

There's a sound – a rising murmur – hark! it swells into a roar –
'Tis a mighty nation wakened into action – into war;
Night and day the sound grows stronger, and the work fires gleam and dance,
For the country of the Eagle backs the American advance.

By the millions lads are marching – by the millions they will come.
Lo! the strains of peace are silenced by the roll of martial drum.
Leaps again the flame that smouldered deep within the people's soul,
And for Freedom that's endangered heroes pay a hero's toll.

Scornful sits the haughty war lord in a kingdom of the dead,
And with ears stopped by his ego, hears not yonder ominous tread.
Coldly on a suffering nation he has turned a murderer's glance.
God in heaven, speed the soldiers in the American advance!

Like the whirlwind and the fire sweeping o'er some doomèd town,
May they sweep o'er hellish forces – courage crushing 'kultur' down.
Let none idly stand indifferent, eyeing them with looks askance,
For the gods themselves are longing for the American advance.

In the name of all that's holy, in the nobleness of right,
They will charge, these Western vikings, toward the forces of the Night,
And eternal laws will hold them, dauntless through all battle shock,
For their fight is based on mercy, which is an eternal rock.

O ye boys of hopes and ideals! O ye modern minute-men!
Ne'er before has such call sounded in the ages of our ken.
Well ye've answered, grim preparing, leaving nothing unto chance.
Now in rightness and in justice – oh, Americans – ADVANCE!

Clelland J. Ball

Slacker, Think it Over!

Slacker, you sit in your easy-chair,
Thanking the Lord you're not over there,
Where the cannons roar and the brave men die,
And, dying, perhaps unburied lie;
You may have purchased a bond or two
And imagine that is enough to do.

But some day, after the war is done
And victory by the brave is won,
You'll see men sneer as they pass you by,
And you'll wish you had not been afraid to die,
For what is the life of a coward worth
When he hasn't a friend on the lonely earth?

But the world may consent to forget some day,
And when it has done so, what will you say
To the grandson sitting upon your knee,
As he shows you his book, saying, 'Grandpa, see!
Here is where in the great world war
We lost a thousand soldiers or more'.

And when he turns and looks up at you,
Saying, 'Tell me, grandpa, what did *you* do?'
Slacker, you'll sit in your big arm-chair,
Wishing that you had been over there,
And you'd give you life for the right to say,
'I fought for God and the U.S.A.'

Ralph J. Hall

The Crusader

Sailing for France! My heart beats high to-day:
    I've reached the crossroads, and have made the choice,

I've donned the new, and cast the old away;
    Yes, DIEU LE VOLT, I, too have heard the voice.

Brave spirit of the past, thy words are true,
    Guide thou my sword, for I have donned the new.

Arthur Sprague

To the Recruitin' Sergeant

'Oh, this army life's the candy for the guy that wants it soft,
    And the uniforms is free and so's the eats.
Just sign your name right here, please. We'll take you 'round the earth.
    For the wise ones, it's the life that can't be beat.'

But! Did you ever cross the 'briny' in a transport?
    Was you among the guys that went to France?
Did you ever sleep belowdecks when the 'subs' was all around
    And your life-belt was your one and only chance?

Did you ever go a-tourin' in a third-class English train,
    With the girls a-wavin' howdy from the street,
And land somewhere at midnight with our legs all tied in knots,
    And have to march three miles before you eat?

Did you ever come a-crawlin' from a leaky, soakin' tent,
    When the sergeant called sometime before the dawn,
And help to guy a mess-tent that was blowin' all to smash,
    And all your next day's rations soaked and gone?

Did you ever cross the Channel in an antique side-wheel tub,
    And freeze all night upon a heavin' deck,
And land 'Somewhere in France' next day unshaven and unshorn,
    And the old high-water mark around our neck?

Did you ever spend a fortnight in an alleged restin'-camp,
    And listen to a thousand tales or more,
About the Somme and Vimy Ridge, the Marne, and other scraps,
    And wonder why in hell you came to war?

Did you ever ride a 'rattler' on the old Chemin de Fer
    In a car marked 'Eight Chevaux or Forty Hommes',

And finally hit the trenches with your guts up in your throat,
    When you heard the Lewis barkin' and the bombs?

Did you ever see the star-shells flamin' ghastly in the sky?
    Did the shrapnel ever dent your tin chapeau?
Did you ever pass your canteen just to help your 'buddy' die,
    When the gas come down and caught the 'Blighter' slow?

'Oh, this army life's the candy for the guy that wants it soft,
    And the uniforms is free and so's the eats.
Just sign your name right here, please. We'll take you 'round the earth.
    For the wise ones, it's the life that can't be beat.'

George C. Dawson

Somewhere in France (1)

Some streets that are crooked, and houses of stone,
A very small room that the peasants call home,
A cow in the stable and *soldats* above,
With many war weapons you've often heard of;
Some little old women with great shoes of wood,
Old men who would go to the front if they could,
Tame geese on the highway in columns of file,
The dirt in the gutter all scraped in a pile;

Some girls who will give you a smile when you're blue,
A town hall, a square, and a large fountain, too,
A brook running by with its water so clear,
That comes from the hill situated right near;
Some trees, an old church with its bells in the tower,
Which ring out for those who desire the hour,
A very small boy with a patch on his pants,
Is my first impression of 'Somewhere in France'.

Stuart Cutler

Somewhere

It's a sizable place, this Somewhere –
    As big as the whole battle zone.
We eat it, we sleep it, we breathe it,
    It causes us many a groan.

We left from the port of Somewhere
  And we traveled Somewhere on sea
'Til we landed again at Somewhere,
  And it sounds mighty funny to me.

We boarded trains Somewhere for Somewhere,
  And we're camping Somewhere for a spell.
It's so that when one mentions Somewhere
  We're almost tempted to yell.

There's a Somewhere in France and in England,
  And Somewhere else at the front.
It was Somewhere the boys were in battle –
  Just Somewhere bearing the brunt.

It's Somewhere the censor is cutting
  Somewhere from the letters we write;
It seems we've been Somewhere forever.
  At its mention we're ready to fight.

At night we no longer have nightmares;
  We dream one continuous trip
From Somewhere back home to Somewhere.
  When we sleep into Somewhere we slip.

Geography's gone to the races,
  The faces of maps all are changed.
Somewhere in Somewhere by Somewhere
  And our minds are completely deranged.

Ye gods! Is the world mad completely?
  Will sanity e'er reign again?
Will we ever get back from Somewhere to earth?
  If so, O Lord, tell us when.

                                        Earle H. Tostevin

Passed as Censored

Received your parcel to-day, Mae.
    Gee! but those Meccas was prime!

And ain't you the swell little knitter!
    That sweater come through just in time.
The gum made me think of the movies;
    The candy's the first that I've had
Since that Sunday we walked to the Breakers
    And you thought I thought you was mad.

Well, how's things now at the office?
    Give my regards to the Boss.
And, say, Mae, you needn't worry –
    I haven't written to Floss.
What's happened to Willie Fitzgibbons?
    I hope he ain't seein' you home.
It seems about time he got drafted;
    That guy's got no sense in his dome.

As for me, Mae, I'm working my head off.
    They drills us from morning to night.
The officers calls it 'intensive',
    And they come pretty near bein' right.
But we're gettin' good eats all the time, Mae,
    And the boys are in dandy shape, too.
When they give us a chance at the Kaiser
    I'll hand him a wallop for you.

And say, Mae, drop me a line, please.
    I'll write you again in a while,
But we haven't got much time for writing
    And letters ain't much in my style.
Here's hoping that this find you well, Mae,
    As I am, who love you, you know,
And thank you again for the parcel.
    Good night. Taps has started to blow.

                        Harold Amory

Der Tag

When eau de cologne comes from limberger cheese,
    When the jelly fish swallows the whale;
When kangaroos roost on gooseberry trees
    And grasshoppers feed upon quail;

When the laws of gravity cease to exist
    And the rivers all run up hill;
When young Americans no more enlist
    To shoot at 'All Highest Bill';

When bumblebees whistle 'Die Wacht Am Rhine';
    When feathers are found upon frogs,
When the mule is blessed with a voice divine
    And humming birds prey upon hogs;

When submarines swim through the air at night;
    When powder won't burn in our guns –
Then maybe our allies will give up the fight
    And the world will be ruled by the Huns.

                                          Eugene E. Wilson

NINETEEN

The Final Year

England in 1918, hardships, the German assault of
21 March 1918, near defeat and anxiety, the reversal,
thoughts on post-war, the Kaiser abdicates

By the beginning of 1918 anxiety, exhaustion and shortage of food were taking their toll on those at home. But worse was to come, for early on the morning of 21 March the Germans launched a massive assault against the British and French on the Western Front. They chose this moment for several reasons: the strong Allied blockade meant that many German civilians were suffering to the point of starvation; following the collapse of the army after the revolution, Russia had sued for a separate peace, which meant that the German High Command could now move its men from the Eastern to the Western Front; and it knew that if it were to have any chance of defeating the French and British it would need to attack before the Americans arrived in France in large numbers.

Using new shock tactics, the Germans broke through the Allied line and forced the armies into retreat and disarray as they advanced up to 40 miles. As they pushed on towards the vital railhead of Amiens, crossing the ravaged countryside of 1917 and the old battlefields of the Somme, the situation became desperate. As trench warfare gave way to open fighting, the Allies were threatened with defeat. On 26 March, all the Allied forces came under a single command when General Foch was appointed military supremo.

On 11 April Haig issued a Special Order of the Day: 'Three weeks ago to-day the enemy began his terrific attacks against us on a fifty-mile front. His objects are to separate us from the French, to take the Channel Ports and destroy the British Army [. . .] Many among us now are tired. To them I would say that Victory will belong to the side which holds out the longest [. . .] There is no other course open to us but to fight it out. Every position must be held to the last man: there must be no retirement. With our backs to the wall and believing in the justice of our cause each one of us must fight on to the end.'

It was a turning point. The British and French rallied and counter-attacked with brilliantly carried-out strategy, and although the Germans attempted further assaults, their energy was spent. Then, in a series of fierce battles during what became known as the Last Hundred Days, the experienced, war-weathered Allied troops began remorselessly to push them back across the old battlefields. On 8 August they broke through the German lines and advanced 7 miles; the German Commander, Ludendorff, described this as 'the black day of the German Army'. Fighting was to continue for another three months, but the German High Command knew that it was all over.

The end, when it came, was more speedy than anyone had expected. With unrest and revolution spreading at home, caused partly by the effectiveness of the Allied naval blockade, early in November the Germans requested an armistice. On 9 November the Kaiser abdicated and fled to Holland. At dawn on the morning of 11 November the 3rd Canadian Division entered Mons, the town where the British war had begun. Hostilities ceased at 11 a.m.

But, though retreating, the German army in the field had not been defeated. This was to have huge significance in the years to come as the idea grew that they had been 'stabbed in the back' by those who had betrayed them at home.

[How doth the little busy wife]

How doth the little busy wife
Improve each shining hour?
She shops and cooks and works all day,
The best within her power.

How carefully she cuts the bread,
How thin she spreads the jam!
That's all she has for breakfast now,
Instead of eggs and ham.

In dealing with the tradesmen, she
Is frightened at the prices,
For meat and fish have both gone up,
And butter too, and rice has.

Each thing seems dearer ev'ry week,
It's really most distressing,
Why can't we live on love and air?
It would be such a blessing!

Nina Macdonald

Chairman Rhymes

(Regular advertisements for Chairman cigarettes appeared in the *Daily Chronicle*.)

The doctors say our national waste
Is largely due to too much taste.
We ought at once to form the habit
Of thinking something else is rabbit,
And never, when the meat is coarse,
Demand if it is cow or horse.
So long as hunger's satisfied,
Let's keep our palates to decide
Between a CHAIRMAN and the rest,
Which cigarette we find the best.

I bow before the butcher-man,
I grovel to the grocer,
I swallow all the saucy airs
With which they answer 'No, sir!'
But what a change, to go next door
And there with head erect,
To buy some CHAIRMAN cigarettes
And a little self-respect!

Food Control

Monday – we'll say is our 'Heatless Day',
    One cinder, one flicker, one coal.
Tuesday – well – this is our 'Meatless Day',
    One oyster, one herring, one sole.
Wednesday – oh, this is our 'Wheatless Day',
    One seed cake, one pancake, one scone.
Thursday – we must have a 'Sweetless Day',
    One pickle, one lemon, one bone.
Friday – will make a good 'Eatless Day',
    One cheerful and glorious fast.
Saturday – call it a 'Treatless Day',
    For all reciprocity's past.
But Sunday – may Ole Clynes forgive us, we pray,
    If we should all happen to feel
A little more hungry than usual to-day
    And once again eat a square meal.

Economy ad Insaniam

A thrifty old lady of Hull,
Whose intellect seemed rather dull,
When reading at night,
To economise light,
Put luminous paint on her skull.

The Soul of a Nation

The little things of which we lately chattered –
The dearth of taxis or the dawn of spring;
Themes we discussed as though they really mattered,
Like rationed meat or raiders on the wing; –

How thin it seems to-day, this vacant prattle,
Drowned by the thunder rolling in the West,
Voice of the great arbitrament of battle
That puts our temper to the final test.

Thither our eyes are turned, our hearts are straining,
Where those we love, whose courage laughs at fear,
Amid the storm of steel around them raining,
Go to their death for all we hold most dear.

New-born of this supremest hour of trial,
In quiet confidence shall be our strength,
Fixed on a faith that will not take denial
Nor doubt that we have found our soul at length.

O England, staunch of nerve and strong of sinew,
Best when you face the odds and stand at bay,
Now show a watching world what stuff is in you!
Now make your soldiers proud of you to-day!

Owen Seaman

Watch and Pray!

There's a hush upon the city, and its jarring voices cease;
All its thoughts are bent in silence on the strife beyond the seas.

It is watching, it is waiting, and it cannot choose but dwell,
On the dust-brown lines in Picardy that front the hordes of Hell.
Spring is pulsing in our gardens but we hardly feel its breath;
Through the song of thrush and linnet throbs the choral ode of Death;
And we walk like men who wander in some dream's mysterious maze,
Half-instinctive, half-unconscious, through the old familiar ways,
Hope with doubt and fear contending, while our hearts are strained and tense,
As we count the fateful minutes in the anguish of suspense;
As a prayer is breathed to Heaven from the million lips that say,
'God of Battles shield our England and her soldier sons this day!'

[What of our comrades in the forward post?]

What of our comrades in the forward post?
The fog of war but deepened with the day.
We knew that in that troubled ocean lay
Unchartered shoals, blind rocks, and treacherous coast.
And what of yonder never-ending host
Of wan, unwounded Portuguese? Ah, stay,
Pale sergeant. Do you bleed? You came that way?
What is the tidings? Is the front line lost?
'Nothing is known of posts that lie before
Levantie. At the cross-roads hellish fire
Has cut them off who shouldered the first load.'
Can they live through it? 'They can not retire,
Nor can you reinforce. I know no more
But this. No living thing comes down that road.'

.   .   .   .   .

Never wound cortège more exceeding slow,
Nor mourners to more melancholy tones,
Than that wan wending, musicked by the moans
Of wounded men, whom pity bade us show
That much of tenderness. Nor friend nor foe
Spoke in the heavy language of these groans,
But stark mankind, whose utter anguish owns
A common nature, in a common woe.
Full many a mile of weary footing sore,
By miry side tracks, not unkindly led;

And each unwounded man his burden bore
On stretcher or in blanket, ransacked bed,
Duck-board uprooted, hand-cart, unhinged door.
We left behind the dying and the dead.

Hour followed hour, and slowly on we wound,
Till wan day turned to front the gradual west;
And with day's waning waned the dream of rest
For the worn bearers, whom the twilight found
Voyaging no-man's gray, wide-watered ground,
Their shoulders bowed and aching backs distressed;
Isthmused between deep pools, and sorely pressed
To foot the flanks of many a slippery mound;
While floundering convoys, till the light was gone,
Across the perilous space their drivers nurse,
Limber and gun, by frightened horses drawn,
Whose plunging swerve that bogged their burdens worse,
Provoked Teutonic fury, well laid on
With sounding whipcord and sonorous curse.

And darkness fell, and a great void of space,
As if to bar our further going on,
Unfeatured, huge, gloomed o'er us. No light shone.
Strength, too, scarce held sufficient now to trace
The squalid reaches of this dismal place;
And silence settled near and far upon
That vacancy at length – our last guide gone.
Night hid each from his comrade, face from face.
As is a voyage through the uncharted waste
Of sea, unpiloted by any star,
Alone, unmooned, uncomforted, unplanned;
So forward still in silent pain we paced,
Nor light of moon nor pharos gleamed from far
Across the boding gloom of that lost land.

We came to Aubers at the dead of night,
And found the semblance of that circled hell,
Which Dante once, damnation's pains to tell,
Paced out in darkness, agony and fright.

In that blank lazarette no kindly light
On bending form of nurse or surgeon fell,
But darkness and barred doors proclaimed too well
The piteous end of long-endured plight.
No room was there in stable or in stall,
Nor roof to shelter cattle while they eat,
Where wounded men could shelter from the blight
Of the foul dew that drizzling covered all.
But in the open and the squelching street
We left them to endure the drenching night.

.   .   .   .   .

The last march opened with the sudden blaze
Of howitzers upon the face of night,
Waving us onward ere the laggard light
Of morning broke down transport-crowded ways.
Next to the first was this the bitterest phase
Of our humiliation. Yet 'tis right
To chronicle some kindness, and requite
Our armed custodians with this word of praise.
By Fournes, by Haubourdin, the endless reel
Of marching men ran out its windings slow,
Till near day's end, nigh broken on the wheel
Of hunger, and scarce longer fit to go,
Within the moated Citadel of Lille
The sharper pang gave place to deeper woe.

A.A. Bowman

During the Battle

O the terror of the Battle at this ending of the days!
   O the thunder of the wings through the gloom!
O the thousand thousand companies that strew the sombre ways
      To achieve this final doom!

Where the flames disrupt the night and the hell-fumes flee,
   'Mid the darkness and the splitting of the skies,
Only your young white wistful face I see,
      My brother, only your eyes!

Louis Golding

The Tide

To the Royal Naval Division

This is a last year's map;
   I know it all so well,
Stream and gully and trench and sap,
   Hamel and all that hell;
See where the old lines wind;
   It seems but yesterday
We left them many a league behind
   And put the map away.

'Never again', we said,
   'Shall we sit in the Kentish Caves;
Never again will the night-mules tread
   Over the Beaucourt graves;
They shall have Peace', we dreamed –
   'Peace and the quiet sun',
And over the hills the French folk streamed
   To live in the land we won.

But the Bosch has Beaucourt now;
   It is all as it used to be –
Airmen peppering Thiepval brow,
   Death at the Danger Tree;
The tired men bring their tools
   And dig in the old holes there;
The great shells spout in the Ancre pools,
   And lights go up from Serre.

And the regiment came, they say,
   Back to the selfsame land
And fought like men in the same old way
   Where the cookers used to stand;
And I know not what they thought
   As they passed the Puisieux road,
And over the ground where Freyberg fought
   The tide of the grey men flowed.

But I think they did not grieve,
   Though they left by the old Bosch line

Many a cross they loathed to leave,
    Many a mate of mine;
I know that their eyes were brave,
    I know that their lips were stern,
For these went back at the seventh wave,
    But they wait for the tide to turn.

A.P. Herbert

The German Graves

I wonder are there roses still
    In Ablain St Nazaire,
And crosses girt with daffodil
    In that old garden there.
I wonder if the long grass waves
    With wild-flowers just the same
Where Germans made their soldiers' graves
    Before the English came?

The English set those crosses straight
    And kept the legends clean;
The English made the wicket-gate
    And left the garden green;
And now who knows what regiments dwell
    In Ablain St Nazaire?
But I would have them guard as well
    The graves we guarded there.

So do not tear those fences up
    And drive your wagons through,
Or trample rose and buttercup
    As careless feet may do;
For I have friends where Germans tread
    In graves across the line,
And as I do towards their dead
    So may they do to mine.

And when at last the Prussians pass
    Among those mounds and see
The reverent cornflowers crowd the grass
    Because of you and me,

They'll give perhaps one humble thought
    To all the 'English fools'
Who fought as never men have fought
    But somehow kept the rules.

A.P. Herbert

The Turn of the Tide
By the Kaiser

When King Canute sat by the sea
    To stop the waves – but shirked it,
He can't have known – it seems to me –
The tide would turn at half-past three
    Or else he might have worked it.

And so it was that old Canute,
    His kingly honour pawning,
Allowed the waves to reach his boot
And then proclaimed in accents cute
    He meant it as a warning.

But kings should fly their flag with pride,
    Nor ever deign to strike it.
And if they watch the turn of tide
They'll still be on the winning side
    Although they may not like it.

So now for Socialists I yearn
    Which really is a rum thing.
With democratic zeal I burn
(Until the tide again shall turn
    And then I'll give them something!)

Edward de Stein

Victory Assured!
(Prime Minister at the Guildhall)

At no distant date Britons, Allies, Colonials see: –
Final Victory on Land and Victory on Sea:
The Mesopotamia struggle will be at an end:
The Huns for *ever* vanquished and friend
    Shakes hand with *friend.*

Work hard at Munitions and spare your wealth:
Be careful with food and take care of your health:
Let every Soldier, Sailor, and *Civilian* do his best,
A glorious time *is coming*, when all shall have rest.

F.H. French

When I Come Home

When I come home, dear folk o' mine,
We'll drink a cup of olden wine;
And yet, however rich it be,
No wine will taste so good to me
As English air. How I shall thrill
To drink it in on Hampstead Hill
        When I come home!

When I come home, and leave behind
Dark things I would not call to mind,
I'll taste good ale and home-made bread,
And see white sheets and pillows spread.
And there is one who'll softly creep
To kiss me, ere I fall asleep,
And tuck me 'neath the counterpane,
And I shall be a boy again,
        When I come home!

When I come home from dark to light,
And tread the roadways long and white,
And tramp the lanes I tramped of yore,
And see the village greens once more,
The tranquil farms, the meadows free,
The friendly trees that nod to me,
And hear the lark beneath the sun,
'Twill be good pay for what I've done,
        When I come home!

Leslie Coulson

To Certain Persons
('I would rather see England free than sober')

Did you think (fools!) I hated men?
    If so you thought, go think again.

And thought you that when I wrote 'If
    We Return' that we'd return to sniff
Over the drinkers of ale, the smokers
    Of 'baccy, the human vulgar jokers,
Best of what God and good green earth
    Have made; that I meant *lemonade*,
And not a valiant great birth
    Of Freedom, of men unafraid
Claiming a man's just right to eat,
    Drink, live and love, and breathe the sweet
Air of old England? Now as then
    I stand for men – just men, the men
Who saved from violence that skin
    Of yours: – God pardon them the sin!

*   *   *

Do I loathe drunkenness? I do, –
    Just half as much as cant, and you!

F.W. Harvey

The Call

There's an office back in London, and the dusty sunlight falls
    With its swarms of dancing motes across the floor,
On the piles of books and papers and the drab distempered walls
    And the bowlers on their pegs behind the door.
There's an office-stool in London where a fellow used to sit
    (But the chap that used to sit there's oversea);
There's a job they're keeping open till that fellow's done his bit,
    And the one that job is waiting for is – Me!

And it may be black ingratitude, but oh, Good Lord, I know
    I could never stick the office-life again,
With the coats and cuffs and collars and the long hours crawling slow
    And the quick lunch and the same old morning train;
I have looked on Life and Death and seen the naked soul of man,
    And the heart of things is other than it seemed,
And the world is somehow larger than the good old office plan,
    And the ways of earth are wider than I dreamed.

There's a chap in the Canadians – a clinking good chap too –
    And he hails from back o' nowhere in B.C.,
And he says it's sure some country, and I wonder if it's true,
    And I rather fancy that's the place for me.
There's a trail I mean to follow and a camp I mean to share
    Out beyond the survey, up in Cassiar,
For there's something wakened in me that I never knew was there
And they'll have to find some other chap to fill that vacant chair
    When the boys come marching homeward from the War.

C. Fox-Smith

Peace Problems

    What will they do, when the Boys have got back?
    What's to become of the Wren and the Waac?
    Will *they* carry on, while we tired heroes slack?
        I wonder.

    Ah! Shall I then marry the girl I adore?
    (Who earns same as I did – perhaps a bit more)
    Will one income keep two – perhaps three – maybe four?
        God help us!

    But what *shall* I do, when I've got my discharge?
    When I've stepped off the deck of the cross-channel barge
    And behave for a spell like a loonie at large?
        I wonder.

    Shall I lecture Girl Guides from my Field Service Book
    Till they quake at my 'Shun' and they quail at my look?
        No, I shan't then.

    But what *can* I do, when the war is 'finee'?
    Where is that job that is waiting for me?
    Will she give up my stool when they make her 'M.P.'?
        I wonder.

    Could I slog at a desk? Could I stick on the land?
    Shall I punch cows in Texas? or mine on the Rand?
    Is there any old job that I think I could stand?
        There isn't.

Shall I lecture or write of the battles I've won –
How I got the C.B.? or is that overdone?
Or – would Dad like to pension his brave soldier son?
        No, he wouldn't.

Then what the – I've got it! I'll be a Cook's Guide
And thrill wond'ring tourists with rapture and pride
As I point out the spots where I fought and I died!
        Well, why not?

From a Full Heart

In days of peace my fellow-men
    Rightly regarded me as more like
A Bishop than a Major-Gen.,
    And nothing since has made me warlike;
But when this age-long struggle ends
    And I have seen the Allies dish up
The goose of HINDENBURG – oh, friends!
    I shall out-bish the mildest Bishop.

When the War is over and the KAISER'S out of print,
I'm going to buy some tortoises and watch the beggars sprint;
When the War is over and the sword at last we sheathe,
I'm going to keep a jelly-fish and listen to it breathe.

I never really longed for gore,
    And any taste for red corpuscles
That lingered with me left before
    The German troops had entered Brussels.
In early days the Colonel's 'Shun!'
    Froze me; and, as the War grew older,
The noise of someone else's gun
    Left me considerably colder.

When the War is over and the battle has been won,
I'm going to buy a barnacle and take it for a run;
When the War is over and the German Fleet we sink,
I'm going to keep a silk-worm's egg and listen to it think.

The Captains and the Kings depart –
    It may be so, but not lieutenants;
Dawn after weary dawn I start
    The never-ending round of penance;
One rock amid the welter stands
    On which my gaze is fixed intently –
An after-life in quiet lands
    Lived very lazily and gently.

When the War is over and we've done the Belgians proud,
I'm going to keep a chrysalis and read to it aloud;
When the War is over and we've finished up the show,
I'm going to plant a lemon-pip and listen to it grow.

Oh, I'm tired of the noise and the turmoil of battle,
And I'm even upset by the lowing of cattle,
And the clang of the bluebells is death to my liver,
And the roar of the dandelion gives me a shiver,
And a glacier, in movement, is much too exciting,
And I'm nervous, when standing on one, of alighting –
Give me Peace; that is all, that is all that I seek . . .
    Say, starting on Saturday week.

A.A. Milne

The General*

Last night, as I was washing up,
And just had rinsed the final cup,
All of a sudden, 'midst the steam,
I fell asleep and dreamed a dream.
I saw myself an old, old man,
Nearing the end of mortal span,
Bent, bald and toothless, lean and spare,
Hunched in an ancient beehive chair.
Before me stood a little lad
Alive with questions. 'Please, Granddad,
Did Daddy fight, and Uncle Joe,
In the Great War of long ago?'

---

* A General was also a general cook-housekeeper.

I nodded as I made reply:
'Your Dad was in the H.L.I.,
And Uncle Joseph sailed to sea,
Commander of a T.B.D.,
And Uncle Jack was Major too ——'
'And what', he asked me, 'what were you?'
I stroked the little golden head;
'I was a General,' I said.
'Come, and I'll tell you something more
Of what I did in the Great War.'
At once the wonder-waiting eyes
Were opened in a mild surmise;
Smiling, I helped the little man
To mount my knee, and so began:
'When first the War broke out, you see,
Grandma became a V.A.D.;
Your Aunties spent laborious days
In working at Y.M.C.A.'s;
The servants vanished. Cook was found
Doing the conscript baker's round;
The housemaid, Jane, in shortened skirt
(She always was a brazen flirt),
Forsook her dusters, brooms and pails
To carry on with endless mails.
The parlourmaid became a vet.,
The tweeny a conductorette,
And both the others found their missions
In manufacturing munitions.
I was a City man. I knew
No useful trade. What could I do?
Your Granddad, boy, was not the sort
To yield to fate, he was a sport.
I set to work; I rose at six,
Summer and winter; chopped the sticks,
Kindled the fire, made early tea
For Aunties and the V.A.D.
I cooked the porridge, eggs and ham,
Set out the marmalade and jam,
And packed the workers off, well fed,
Well warmed, well brushed, well valeted.
I spent the morning in a rush

With dustpan, pail and scrubbing-brush;
Then with a string-bag sallied out
To net the cabbage or the sprout,
Or in the neighbouring butcher's shop
Select the juiciest steak or chop.
So when the sun had sought the West,
And brought my toilers home to rest,
Savours more sweet than scent of roses
Greeted their eager-sniffing noses –
Savours of dishes most divine
Prepare and cooked by skill of mine.
I was a General. Now you know
How Generals helped to down the foe.'
The little chap slipped off my knee
And gazed in solemn awe at me,
Stood at attention, stiff and mute,
And gave his very best salute.

G.K. Menzies

Herr Hohenzollern

(The papers announce that the KAISER wishes in future to be known
simply as a private gentleman.)

Says WILLIAM: 'Time has made of me
    A sadder man and wiser;
Henceforth my object is to be
    No more the German Kaiser,
But just a private gentleman.'
    Ah, WILLIAM, vain endeavour,
'Private?' As private as you can.
But 'gentleman?' No, never.

In Memory of Kaiser Bill (The Butcher)

Who lost his Crown, November 9th 1918
Aged 59 years.

Oh! how we shall miss him
    The villain was known so well.
He's booked his seat for Early Doors
    To the warmest place in Hell!

C. Clifford

Cousins German

Our family affairs seem rather bad.
There's Cousin William: all the papers say
He's to be hanged or somehow put away;
And Cousin Constantine they say's as bad;
And now – these awful things in Petrograd!
Poor Cousin Nicholas has lost his job,
Kicked from his palace by a vulgar mob,
And everybody here seems strangely glad.

It makes one anxious: not so long ago
His people were as loyal as mine to me.
Now suddenly they turn and bid him go,
Saying they have no use for royalty.
The English once before grew sick of kings.
What if —— Enough of such unpleasant things.

W.N. Ewer

TWENTY

Armistice and the Price of War

Joy and sadness, the survivors, reconciliation and hatred, the
return of the dead and the grief of the living, victory celebrations,
the Peace Treaty, the Tomb of the Unknown Warrior, war memorials,
In Memoriam

As the news of the armistice was received, crowds gathered to celebrate the end of the fighting. For many it was too late; relief was overborne by the grief of their loss. While some urged reconciliation, others had suffered too much to be willing to forget. And the dead seemed ever present; it was said that if they were to march four abreast, twenty-four hours a day, it would take them more than a week to pass a single point.

It took a long time for demobilisation to be completed, and many returning soldiers found it impossible to settle. They were physically and mentally exhausted, and needed time to come to terms not only with what they had experienced, but also with the new life they faced in a nation in mourning for those who would never return. Many had gone straight from school to war, and had never known peace as adults. The promises of 'a land fit for heroes' soon rang hollow. Many at home had grown rich while others were fighting and dying for the freedom they now enjoyed, but there was high unemployment among ex-soldiers and a growing sense of disillusionment and resentment against those who seemed unable or unwilling to understand what they had suffered.

The Treaty of Versailles, signalling a formal end to the war, was signed on 28 June 1919. Three weeks later there was a Victory March through the streets of London. At 11 a.m. on the anniversary of the armistice, 11 November, all traffic was stilled and the people fell silent as they paused to remember. Work was already underway all over the country to build memorials – though many believed that such memorials were meaningless and an insult to those who had died. Sir Edwin Lutyens designed an empty tomb – a cenotaph – commemorating all the dead of the war. This was unveiled in Whitehall on 11 November 1920, on the same day that the body of an unknown warrior was buried in Westminster Abbey.

In the days immediately before, the bodies of six unknown soldiers had been exhumed from the battlefields of the Aisne, the Somme, Arras and Ypres and brought to an army hut close to Arras. Here they were laid side by side, covered with Union Flags. A Brigadier General and Lieutenant Colonel from the Directorate of War Grave Registration went alone into the chapel, where the General, with closed eyes, placed his outstretched hand on one of the bodies. This was then sealed in a coffin, which was taken at once to Boulogne and placed inside a second, oak coffin made from a tree felled at Hampton Court. On 10 November a company of French infantry kept guard over the body in the chapel of Boulogne Castle, before it was taken, under French escort, to board the British destroyer, HMS *Verdun*, for its passage across the Channel; the ship's bell now hangs near the grave in the Abbey. With an escort of six other destroyers, it was met midway by HMS *Vendetta*, flying a white ensign at half-mast. As they came in to Dover, a field-marshal's salute of nineteen guns was sounded from the ramparts of Dover Castle.

On the morning of 11 November, the coffin was placed on a gun-carriage of the Royal Horse Artillery and taken past huge, silent crowds to Whitehall, where the King unveiled the Cenotaph. From there the cortège travelled to the North Door of Westminster Abbey. Here twelve pall bearers – admirals, field-marshals, generals and an air marshal – carried the coffin past a guard of honour of 100 holders of the Victoria Cross to be interred just inside the West Door. The grave was filled with 100 sandbags of earth brought from the battlefields, and was then covered with a marble slab and surrounded by Flanders poppies. The inscription read in part: 'Beneath this stone rests the body of a British warrior unknown by name or rank brought from France to lie among the most illustrious of the land . . . They buried him among the Kings.' Since then, even the most formal State procession entering the Abbey must step to one side to avoid walking on the Tomb of the Unknown Warrior.

><·<·>·<·O·<·>·<·>·<

The Armistice
In an Office, in Paris

The news came through over the telephone:
All the terms had been signed: the War was won:
And all the fighting and the agony,
And all the labour of the years were done.
One girl clicked sudden at her typewriter
And whispered, 'Jerry's safe', and sat and stared:

One said, 'It's over, over, it's the end:
The War is over: ended': and a third,
'I can't remember life without the war'.
And one came in and said, 'Look here, they say
We can all go at five to celebrate,
As long as two stay on, just for to-day'.

It was quiet in the big empty room
Among the typewriters and little piles
Of index cards: one said, 'We'd better just
Finish the day's reports and do the files'.
And said, 'It's awf'lly like *Recessional,*
Now that the tumult has all died away'.
The other said, 'Thank God we saw it through;
I wonder what they'll do at home to-day'.
And said, 'You know it will be quiet to-night
Up at the Front: first time in all these years,
And no one will be killed there any more',
And stopped, to hide her tears.
She said, 'I've told you; he was killed in June'.
The other said, 'My dear, I know; I know . . .
It's over for me too . . . my Man was killed,
Wounded . . . and died . . . at Ypres . . . three years ago . . .
And he's my Man, and I want him,' she said,
And knew that peace could not give back her Dead.

May Cannan

Bacchanal
(November, 1918)

Into the twilight of Trafalgar Square
They pour from every quarter, banging drums
And tootling penny trumpets – to a blare
Of tin mouth-organs, while a sailor strums
A solitary banjo, lads and girls
Locked in embraces, in a wild dishevel
Of flags and streaming hair, with curdling skirls
Surge in a frenzied, reeling, panic revel.

Lads who so long have looked death in the face,
Girls who so long have tended death's machines,

Released from the long terror shriek and prance:
And watching them, I see the outrageous dance,
The frantic torches and the tambourines
Tumultuous on the midnight hills of Thrace.

Wilfrid W. Gibson

For a Girl
Paris, November 11 1918

Go cheering down the boulevards
And shout and wave your flags,
Go dancing down the boulevards
In all your gladdest rags:
And raise your cheers and wave your flags
And kiss the passer-by,
But let me break my heart in peace
For all the best men die.
    It was 'When the War is over
    Our dreams will all come true,
    When the War is over
    I'll come back to you';
    And the War is over, over,
    And they never can come true.

Go cheering down the boulevards
In all your brave array,
Go singing down the boulevards
To celebrate the day:
But for God's sake let me stay at home
And break my heart and cry,
I've loved and worked, and I'll be glad,
But all the best men die.
    It was 'When the War is over
    Our dreams will all come true,
    When the War is over
    I'll come back to you';
    And the War is over, over,
    And they never can come true.

May Cannan

Tears

Silence o'erwhelms the melody of Night,
Then slowly drips on to the woods that sigh
For their past vivid vernal ecstasy.
The branches and the leaves let in the light
In patterns, woven 'gainst the paler sky
– Create mysterious Gothic tracery,
Between those high dark pillars, – that affright
Poor weary mortals who are wand'ring by.

* * *

Silence drips on the woods like sad faint rain,
Making each frail tired sigh, a sob of pain:
Each drop that falls, a hollow painted tear
Such as are shed by Pierrots, when they fear
Black clouds may crush their silver lord to death.
The world is waxen; and the wind's least breath
Would make a hurricane of sound. The earth
Smells of the hoarded sunlight that gave birth
To the gold-glowing radiance of that leaf,
Which falls to bury from our sight its grief.

Osbert Sitwell

Victory

Who are ye that come with eyes red and weeping
     In a long, long line and silent every one?
See overhead the flag of triumph sweeping –
     'We are the mothers, and each has lost a son.'

Cries of the crowd who greet their god of glory!
     What of these who crouch there silent in the street? –
'We are outraged women – 'tis a common story,
     Quietly we lie beneath your armies' feet.'

Red flags of conquest, banners great and golden! –
     Who are these silent ones upon our track?
'We in our thousands, perished unbeholden,
     We are the women: pray you, look not back.'

Margaret Sackville

To an Only Son

'For we brought nothing into this world,
And it is certain that we can carry nothing out.'

'They bring their love with them.' Old saying.

When first you came
You were so weak, so helpless, and so bare
In this great world
You had so small a share,
But you brought Love with you, and all our fears
Have changed to hopes through the long, happy years.

And now you go
Back to th' Eternal Love Who sent you here,
You take with you
All that we hold most dear,
Your love for us – now grown so large a thing,
And ours for you, past all imagining.

A little while
Without your living presence we must stay –
The love you brought
Death cannot take away,
Still living – still our own, Love cannot die!
The proof, the pledge of Immortality!

The Return

Last night, within our little town,
    The Dead came marching through;
In a long line, like living men,
    Just as they used to do.

Only, so long a line it seemed
    You'd think the Judgment Day
Had dawned, to see them slowly pass,
    With faces turned one way.

They walked no longer foe and foe
    But brother bound to brother;
Poor men, common men they walked
    Friendly to one another.

Just as in life they might have done
    Who stabbed and slew instead . . .
So quietly and evenly they walked
    These million gentle dead.

Margaret Sackville

Peace – The Dead Speak
Rondeau

Will ye forget now all is done,
And men may bear to feel the sun,
Nor see that friendly face with dread
To guess the friends who will be dead
Ere all his golden sand has run
To heap a sunset – since nor gun
Nor bomb tells now to any one
The thing wherefor our blood was shed . . .
    Will ye forget?

We died (whatever lie be spun)
Less for 'old England' than, each one,
For the New England which shall shed
Her sorrows, walking diamonded
With love to praise Love's sweetest Son . . .
    Will ye forget?

F.W. Harvey

The Survivors

    We who come back,
Nerveless and maimed, from the wild sacrifice
Of the World's youth, stretch'd quivering on the rack
Of Nature pitiless to all its pain,
    Will never look again
With the old gay, uncomprehending eyes
Upon the former founts of our delight,

Morning and eve and night,
Sunshine and shadow, melody, love and mirth.
War tutored us too well. We know their worth,
We who come back!

These will recall
Our martyred Innocence, the indelible stain
Of blood on our hands. Tho' leaves of coronal
Be heap'd upon our brows, 'twill not redress
The eternal bitterness
That surges with the memory of our slain,
Our brothers by the bond of suffering.
And tho' the Spring
Lights with new loves the eyes that once were wet
For loss of them, *WE* never shall forget,
We who come back!

Geoffrey F. Fyson

Who Won the War?

Who won the war?
   'I', said the Politician.
   'I made a mess of ammunition,
   And of the Dardanelles Expedition.
I won the war.'

Who won the war?
   'I', said the Conscientious Objector.
   'I didn't give a damn for England, and would like to have wrecked her.
   Now I'll be released before the man that's been my protector.
I won the war.'

Who won the war?
   'I', said the Profiteer.
   'I made everything dear.
   I want to send Armies to Russia and keep it up at least another year.
I won the war.'

Who won the war?
   'I', said the American President.
   'To raise a colossal Army I meant;

But I hadn't time to complete the experiment.
I won the war.'

Who won the war?
    'I', said the A.S.C.
    'I stuck to my lorry or my gee,
    And always had a loaf in two, when the troops were lucky to get one in three.
I won the war.'

Who won the war?
    'I', said Marshall Foch.
    'I stood no kind of josh.
    Apply to me for information on how to carry out the order 'At the Boche, slosh!'
I won the war.'

Who won the war?
    Said the Tommy, 'I thought I won it,
    But all these 'ere gents seem to ha' done it.
    So I s'pose I must be wrong again.
'Owever, let me get 'ome and put these damn clothes on the fire,
And they can keep their old war!'

All the Tricksters and the Schemers fell a-scheming and a-tricking,
When they thought from the war they had got their last fat picking;
But when Tommy gets back home they will get a good sound ——
And that will be the end of a Perfect War!

                              W. Clifford Poulten

The Offside Leader

This is the wish, as he told it to me,
Of Driver Macpherson of Battery B.

I want no praise, nor ribbons to wear.
I've done my bit and I've had my share
Of filth and fighting and blood and tears
And doubt and death in the last four years.
My team and I were among the first
Contemptible few when the war-clouds burst.
We sweated our gun through the dust and heat,
We hauled her back in the Big Retreat

With weary horses and short of shell,
Turning our back on them. That was Hell.
That was at Mons; but we came back there
With shine on the horses and shells to spare!
And much I've suffered and much I've seen
From Mons to Mons on the miles between,
But I want no praise nor ribbons to wear –
All I ask for my fighting share
Is this: that England should give to me
My offside leader in Battery B.

She was a round-ribbed blaze-faced brown,
Shy as a country girl in town,
Scared of the gangway and scared on the quay,
Lathered in sweat at a sight of the sea,
But brave as a lion and strong as a bull
With the mud at the hub in an uphill pull.
She learned her job as the best ones do,
And we hadn't been over a week or two
Before she would stand like a rooted oak
While the bullets whined and the shrapnel broke
And a mile of the ridges rocked in glee
As the shells went over from Battery B.

One by one our team went down
But the gods were good to the blaze-faced brown.
We swayed with the battles back and forth,
Lugging the limbers south and north.
Round us the world was red with flame
As we gained or gave in the changing game;
And, forward and backward, losses or gains,
There were empty saddles and idle chains,
For Death took some on the galloping track
And beckoned some from the bivouac,
Till at last were left but my mare and me
Of all that went over with Battery B.

My mates have gone and left me alone;
Their horses are heaps of ash and bone;
Of all that went out in courage and speed
There is left but the little brown mare in the lead,

The little brown mare with the blaze on her face
That would die of shame at a slack in her trace,
That would swing the team at the least command,
That would charge a house at the slap of a hand,
That would turn from a shell to nuzzle my knee –
The offside leader of Battery B.

I look for no praise, and no ribbons to wear.
If I've done my bit it was only my share,
For a man has his pride and the strength of his Cause
And the love of his home – they are unwritten laws.
But what of the horses that served at our side,
That in faith as of children fought with us and died?
If I, through it all have been true to my task
I ask for no honours; this only I ask:
The gift of one gunner. I know of a place
Where I'd leave a brown mare with a blaze on her face –
'Mid low leafy limetrees in cocksfoot and clover
To dream with the dragon-flies glistening over.

Will H. Ogilvie

To my Mate

Old comrade, are you living; do you hear me, can you see?
If they print this stuff in Blighty, will you guess it comes from me?
I was just a wee bit balmy, don't you reckon, all the while?
And perhaps the life in Flanders didn't help to fix that tile.
As the R.S.M. expressed it, 'Who's the freak in Number Nine
That looks as if his wits were umpteen kilos from the Line?'
So the Regimental copped it at the Cambrai do, I hear,
And the freak is safe in civvies with a pension, like a peer.
And for all his dud deportment and the Regimental's scorn
He could work his blooming ticket with the smartest soldier born.
I never wrote, I own it, and I've not so much as tried
To find if you're in England yet or on the other side;
But I never knew your number and I lost your home address
With my pack and all inside it, when they marked me C.C.S.
But I haven't quite forgot you, and my only souvenir
That I wouldn't sell for sixpence is the thought of you, old dear.
We were mates to some good purpose in a world of boundless bad,
And to scheme each other's welfare was the one good thing we had.

We were some queer brace of partners; Fate was surely on the spree
When she yoked in double harness such a pair as you and me.
You'd a craze for searching bodies – I could never stick the smell;
You'd a deep respect for Scripture and for words you couldn't spell.
You were gentler than a woman when you dressed a wounded limb,
And at grab – an old cat-mother isn't half so quick and slim.
I think I see you sitting in our dug-out at Bapaume
Where you found your German wrist-watch – did you ever get that home? –
With a sandbag on your napper and your feet inside a pair
While I punched a tin of 'Sweetened' that you'd raised from God knows where.

I see you sternly frowning with my glasses on your nose
While you proved from Revelation when the war was bound to close,
Till you smelt the old pot cooking and your brows relaxed their frown,
And you sat and purred with pleasure as you spooned the custard down.
Well, it's over now and ended; we shall never tramp again
Down the slimy, sodden mule-track in the darkness and the rain;
You would always come behind me on the duckboards, if you could,
To help me, if I stumbled with my load of wire or wood.
I can hear you in the darkness, when you saw that I was done –
'There's a tin of strawberry pozzy in my pack – step up, old son!'

I've got the same old billet, in the same old office chair,
And France seems just as wild a dream as Blighty seemed out there.
But I don't get on with civvies – they know too much for me;
They've read the war-news twice a day, not once a month, like we.
They'll swallow bags of bunkum and let it down, like pie,
But they think you daft, or shell-shocked, if you speak what ain't a lie.
They love you if you spruce 'em well and give 'em lots of buck –
Of the Prussian Guards you've strangled, and the squealing Huns you've stuck;
They ar'n't half sweet on bayonet-scraps and blood and all that tosh,
And they'd earn a D.C. Medal-mint at shouting down the Bosche.
But they've never heard the rat-tat of the gun that can't be seen,
They've never watched the sheaves go down, and walked behind to glean;
They've made their 'Great Advances' with pins on paper maps,
They've made their 'Splendid Pushes' with the 'latest' on their laps.
But it ain't worth while to tell 'em; you might talk till all was blue,
But you'd never make 'em compree what a bloke out there goes through.

George Willis

Reconciliation

When all the stress and all the toil is over,
And my lover lies sleeping by your lover,
With alien earth on hands and brows and feet,
    Then we may meet.

Moving sorrowfully with uneven paces,
The bright sun shining on our ravaged faces,
There, very quietly, without sound or speech,
    Each shall greet each.

We who are bound by the same grief for ever,
When all our sons are dead may talk together,
Each asking pardon from the other one
    For her dead son.

With such low, tender words the heart may fashion,
Broken and few, of pity and compassion,
Knowing that we disturb at every tread
    Our mutual dead.

Margaret Sackville

The Reason
(2nd November 1918)

You ask me why I loathe these German beasts
So much that I have dedicated self –
Brains, heart, and soul – to one black creed of hate,
Now and hereafter, both in war and peace.
You say I had a sense of humour once,
And kindliness, and Christian charity . . .
Perhaps I had – *before my pal came back.*
To-night he sleeps (thank God for morphia!)
And I shan't wake to hear him screaming out,
'Don't! I *will* work. Don't tie me up again.
Gilbert, for Christ's sake, keep these fiends away.'

I don't know *all* the things they did to him.
I only know that when I saw him last –

Helping a wounded Boche in Guillemont,
The day the Ulstermen took Lousy Wood –
He was a husky, cheerful, six-foot man,
(One of those glorious fools who didn't wait
To get commissions; but just joined the ranks);
That now, he's like some tortured starveling cat,
Who crawls about my house on twisted limbs,
Looking at me with *one* lack-lustre eye,
(His *wound* was in the knee-cap, not the head),
Twitching and tongue-tied; nothing like a man.
I don't know *half* the things they did to him.
But I have listened to his screams; and learned
Too much for man to know this side of Hell.

You see, *he wouldn't work* – the glorious fool:
Although their surgeons cut the bullet out –
('Chloroform? *Dummes Luder!* Strap him down.
I don't waste chloroform on English pigs.') –
And did their Prussian best to patch him up
For service in munitions or the mines . . .
He wouldn't make munitions; said he knew
The Hague Convention, International Law . . .
They triced him by the thumbs for that – eight hours,
Hands to the roof-beam, toes just off the ground;
And when they cut him down, he couldn't speak.
So – as he lay – they kicked him in the face . . .
I think that's how he lost his other eye.

I don't know where to find them on the map,
Those mines he sees o' nights. But there is snow,
Snow and black fir-trees. If a chap won't work –
(Remember, first he said he *wouldn't* work;
But Hunger and the Horsewhip soon cured that!) –
They make him take his clothes off; tie him up
Close to the red-hot stove, until the sweat
Pours off his body; then they hack him out,
Naked and bleeding. It is very cold
Up there among the fir-trees and the snow . . .

Sometimes I wish they hadn't sent him back,
Sometimes I feel he would be happier dead –

Cold-butchered by some *Unteroffizier*
In those latrines which they call prison-camps.
But he's come back; and I've learnt how to hate.

Hate! Not an individual loathing felt
For this one gaoler or the *Kommandant*
(With pardon and trade orders for the rest)
But absolute revulsion, merciless,
Inexorable, reasoned, and approved –
A plain man's hatred of the Unclean Folk.

Poor Jack – he's moaning – I must go to him.

Gilbert Frankau

Peace
June 28th 1919

From the tennis lawn you can hear the guns going,
    Twenty miles away,
Telling the people of the home counties
    That the peace was signed to-day.
To-night there'll be feasting in the city;
    They will drink deep and eat –
Keep peace the way you planned you would keep it
    (If we got the Boche beat).
Oh, your plan and your word, they are broken,
    For you neither dine nor dance;
And there's no peace so quiet, so lasting,
    As the peace you keep in France.

You'll be needing no Covenant of Nations
    To hold your peace intact.
It does not hang on the close guarding
    Of a frail and wordy pact.
When ours screams, shattered and driven,
    Dust down the storming years,
Yours will stand stark, like a grey fortress,
    Blind to the storm's tears.

Our peace . . . your peace . . . I see neither.
    They are a dream, and a dream.

I only see you laughing on the tennis lawn;
    And brown and alive you seem,
As you stoop over the tall red foxglove,
    (It flowers again this year)
And imprison within a freckled bell
    A bee, wild with fear . . .

*   *   *

Oh, you cannot hear the noisy guns going:
    You sleep too far away.
It is nothing to you, who have your own peace,
    That our peace was signed to-day.

Rose Macaulay

Return

This was the way that, when the war was over,
we were to pass together. You, its lover,
would make my love your land, you said, no less,
its shining levels and their loneliness,
the reedy windings of the silent stream,
your boyhood's playmate, and your childhood's dream.

The war is over now: and we can pass
this way together. Every blade of grass
is you: you are the ripples on the river:
you are the breeze in which they leap and quiver.
I find you in the evening shadows falling
athwart the fen, you in the wildfowl calling:
and all the immanent vision cannot save
my thoughts from wandering to your unknown grave.

St Ives, 1919
E. Hilton Young

The Victory March

By batteries and battalions the slow line swings along:
    Come out and shout with heartfelt joy,
Come out and make a Song
    That nothing ever shall destroy.

A song we never shall forget,
    Seething with fierce, unbounded gladness;
Tainted with no regret,
    Dulled with no touch of sadness.
Come out, you happy ones, whose men are come safe through the fight,
Thank God again you have them at your side.
Come out, you Broken-hearted,
Whose loved ones are departed:
Thank God with all your strength to-night,
That they for England died.

Patrick Miles

The Unknown Warrior

Through the silent streets they bore him
Proudly carried up on high.
No one going, no one coming,
To deter him from his triumph;
Silent was his passing by.

He wore no medals on his breast,
And his head no crown adorned;
But his eyes with tears were flowing
Weeping for his living brother,
Maimed, unreverenced, and scorned.

John Waring

Unknown
(November 1920)

Here, where our Kings are crowned;
    Here, where the brasses keep
Scroll of the names that resound,
Let one brass nameless be found,
    One unknown Englishman sleep.
Here, where we cherish in stone
    Those who or ruled us or led –
Statesmen and poets known –
Carve we a tomb and a throne
    'To One of our Warrior-Dead.'

Needless to carve us his name:
    Needless to know if he died
By Yser, by Tigris, or Thame,
Of the steel or the gas or the flame,
    At hazard of sky or of tide!
Since he died for us and our Race
    And the Fine undying Things,
Of his right (and not by their grace)
He has earned him his resting-place
    With our poets, our priests, and our Kings.

And even though his be the least
    Of all whose spirits went West
From the fight we fought with the Beast,
Yet neither a King nor a priest
    Shall grudge him his honoured rest;
But an Empire stand at his grave,
    And an Emperor-King bare head,
When we tomb with our lords of the waste and the wave,
In the heart of a Nation he died to save,
    One Man of our Million Dead.

Here let him sleep; for a sign
    Of high deeds wrought to an end
By the lowly folk and the fine
Whose lives were outspilled like wine
    For England – England, their friend.
Here let us cherish in stone,
    Not one man's worth, nor his name,
But a million heroes . . . Unknown?
Nay! their fame is as trumpets blown,
    Their fame is all England's fame.

And this England they saved shall endure,
    She shall neither dwindle nor pass,
Her feet shall be virile and sure;
She shall stamp on the creed impure –
    The creed of class-against-class.
Neither in haste nor in hate,
    Neither with tumult nor guns,
But duly in quiet debate

Shall she deal with the fate of her State,
　　Shall she order the claims of her sons.

Wherefore, if any to-day
　　Plot treason to ruin this land,
Here – by our unknown clay –
Let him kneel; and, kneeling, pray;
　　And praying, understand
The Cause for which one man died –
　　The Cause which is neither Bread
Nor Gold nor Conquest nor Creed nor Pride;
But the Cause of all Englishmen side-by-side,
　　The Cause of our Warrior Dead.

Gilbert Frankau

The War Memorial

Old Brown's speech I remember. Slow and wise.
Slow-wagging forefinger; slow-blinking eyes.
'The very thing we want' (said Brown)
'To make memorial for the dead
Is something useful for the town.
Some cosy reading-room?' (Brown said).
Jones smiled and nodded where he sat.
'Ay, we'd be comfortable in that.'
He coughed, empurpled; hoiked at phlegm.
Tears filled my eyes. I had seen *them*,
Swift, fair and eager . . . David . . . Yellow broom . . .
Suddenly I left the room
And them all gaping . . .

Godfrey Elton

Stranraer War Memorial

Erect the Memorial where all may see,
　　Let it have a fitting place;
For the men who died that we might be free
　　Were the flower of our race.

Give it pride of place in the old grey town,
　　Let it shine in the light of Heaven;

Oh! proud are we of our glorious dead,
　　For us their lives were given.

Raise it aloft in God's acre wide,
　　In the place where their forebears sleep –
Where men bow the head to honour the dead,
　　And the women kneel to weep.

The children shall hush their laughter
　　When they trace, with loving pride,
The name of a dear, dead daddy
　　Or soldier brother who died.

Let its column rise in the silence, sweet,
　　Far from the revellers' din;
Though their graves are afar, their names shall be
　　In the midst of their kith and kin.

On the market square, or the churchyard green,
　　Let our boys' memorial rise,
Where all who pass shall linger to read
　　How great was the sacrifice.

Mary Reid

In Flanders, Poppies Red

PLEASE READ THIS. Can you help this Ex-service Man by buying this Poetry. PRICE TWOPENCE. So please patronise an Ex-Soldier, Out of Work. NO PENSION. NO DOLE. I am a Genuine Discharged Soldier NOT AN IMPOSTER. I am compelled to sell these to keep myself, wife and children. Sold entirely by unemployed Ex-service men.

Out there in France on a battle's front,
　　Where poppies bloom so red,
They grow in silent tribute
　　On the graves of heroes dead.

Dead for Britain's honour,
　　They freely gave their lives.
And left behind to grieve them
　　Are fathers, mothers, wives.

England is proud in her sorrows,
    Proud of the blood that runs
Through the hearts of her soldiers and sailors
    Who gallantly kept back the Huns.

Ready when called for duty,
    Aye, ready to face the foe,
Some are now facing starvation,
    All through no fault of their own.

Is this the land for heroes
    Gained at such cost of life,
Where nothing reigns but poverty
    And want and strife!

I'm only one of many more,
    Admired while strong and well,
But now I'm broken in the War,
    No words can my feelings tell.

Because of England's promises,
    We did our best out there,
And now for those who have returned
    There is no work to spare.

To gain an honest living
    I try so very hard;
I ask you can you help me now
    By buying this small card?

Only an Officer

Only an officer! Only a chap
Who carried on till the final scrap,
Only a fellow who didn't shirk –
Homeless, penniless, out of work,
Asking only a start in life,
A job that will keep himself and his wife,
'And thank the Lord that we haven't a kid.'
Thus men pay for the deeds men did!

Only an officer! Only a chap
Wounded and gassed in a bit of a scrap,
Only a fellow who didn't shirk –
Shaky and maimed and unfit for work,
Asking only enough in life
To keep a home for himself and his wife,
'And she'll work if she can, but, of course, there's the kid.'
Thus men pay for the deeds men did!

Only our officers! Only the chaps
That war-time uses and peace-time scraps,
Only the fellows a bit too proud
To beg a dole from the charity-crowd,
Carrying on in civilian life,
Carrying on – with a smile for the wife,
'But it's breaking his heart because of the kid!'
Thus men starve for the deeds men did!

Gilbert Frankau

The Unemployed

'You might have died heroically: France
And Flanders surely gave you just the chance.
You'd have escaped this marching thro' the street,
This sordid seeking after bread and meat,
This aimless hunt for work. Work! Why, the war
Was held at great expense to manage for
The extra and unwanted carcases
Of men whose mere existences makes our ease
Uncertain. As your ranks go shuffling by,
The Premier can't enjoy tranquillity.
Would you have us give you work and food, instead
Of spending money on our gallant dead?

'As you have marched, misled by Bolshie tricks,
You must have noticed many a crucifix,
Raised that the people never may forget
Those who went out to pay our honor's debt:

Their glorious courage who would dare deny?
And they, at least, had the good sense to die;
Gass'd, shot, dismember'd, buried, blown to bits,
They don't come back and cry, where Dives sits,
'Work! Work! Give us this day our daily bread!'
Why are not you, like them, heroic dead?

'At the packed meeting in the village hall,
Where we have met for the Memorial,
We choose the Crucifix: not the Risen Lord,
Nor Baby Jesus, life still unexplored;
Not the young Carpenter of Nazareth;
Nor Christ speaking of Love before his Death;
Nor the familiar Friend of Bethany –
But Jesus, dead, on the accursèd tree:
We lie more tranquil in our easy bed
If God be, like our gallant heroes, dead.'

'Give us this day our daily bread!' I saw
The long procession trying to get to Law;
And as I looked I wondered – over there
Walked one man with a more familiar air;
Something remember'd in the way he stood
Flashed to my mind —

There is an empty rood!
The dead Christ has come down, even as he said,
And is walking with the men we wish were dead.
Not in the crib, no, nor on Mary's knee;
Nor at feast or fast; nor on the sacred Tree;
Not with the Saints, nor where the monstrance lifts
Its mystic promise of supernal gifts –
Not there can we find God, until, unless,
We see him in that man whose rags are less
Than the robe he wore when, in the palace-court,
They flogged him at the column for their sport.
The God whom we have imagined safely dead
Is marching down the Strand, shouting for bread.

R. Ellis Roberts

In Memoriam

RENNIE. – In loving memory of my dear son, Lance Corpl. Alex. Rennie, killed at Dardanelles, July 12th, 1915.

> Could we only have seen him once again,
>> If he had only come home to die,
> To kiss the face we loved so well,
>> And whisper, 'Alex., good-bye.'

– Inserted by his Mother (Mrs Rennie), Brother, and Sister. Backrampart.

BRUNSKILL. – In loving remembrance of Pte Arthur Brunskill (15738), 11th East Lancs. Regt. ('Pals'), who was killed in action on July 1st or 2nd, 1916, aged 22 years.

> May the heavenly winds blow softly,
>> O'er that sweet and hallowed spot;
> Though the sea divides his grave from us,
>> He will never be forgot.

– From Mother and Father, 20 Princess-street, Burnley.

DUCKWORTH. In loving memory of my dear son, Sergt. Wilfred Duckworth, 1st East Lancs., who was killed in action in France, July 1st, 1916.

> Take the soul that died for duty,
>> In Thy tender loving hand;
> Crown his life with heavenly beauty,
>> Life laid down for Motherland.

Always in our thoughts.
– From Mother, Brother, Sisters, and Janey, 21 Rumley-road, Burnley.

MAKIN. In loving memory of our dear son, Pte. Herbert Makin (1st East Lancashire Regiment), killed in France, July 1st, 1916.

> Can a mother ever forget the son she loved so dear!
>> Oh, no! the voice that now is still keeps ringing in our ears,
> Mother cease your weeping, angels round me smile,
>> We are only parted, just for a little while.

– From his sorrowing Mother, Sister, Mary, Hannah, Harry, and little Tom, and Herbert and Thomas, and Nellie, 6 Marquis-street, Accrington.

LOMAX. In loving memory of our dear son, Private George R. Lomax, RMLI, RND, who was presumed dead November 13th, 1916; aged 18 years.

> We think of him in silence,
> We make no outward show,
> For hearts that mourn sincerely,
> Mourn silently and low.

– From Father, Mother, Brother Allan, 5 Lang-street, Accrington.

MCCULLOCH – In fond remembrance of our dear sons, William and David McCulloch, RN, who died on March 9th, 1917.

> Four years ago a message came
>   From God, who thought it best
> To take them from this weary world
>   And give them peace and rest.
> It was God's will it should be so,
>   By His command we all must go.

– Inserted by their loving Father and Mother, Sisters and Brothers. Auchneight Dáiry, Drummore.

MURRAY. – In loving memory of our son and brother, Pte. John Murray, 1st Gordon Highlanders, who was killed at Infantry Hill, France, on 16th June, 1917, aged 19 years.

> The fairest flowers are first to fall,
>   The best are first to fade,
> The sweetest, dearest, best of all
>   Within their graves are laid.
>
> O, Lord, how wondrous are thy ways,
>   To pass the frail and old
> And take the young and beautiful –
>   The choicest of the fold.

– Inserted by his loving Father and Mother, Sister and Brothers. 48 Fisher St., Stranraer.

HOWARTH. In loving memory of Driver William Howarth, who died in France on November 10th, 1918.

> Time does not change our thoughts of him;
> Love and dear memories linger still;
> Sunshine passes, shadows fall;
> But true remembrance outlasts all.

– From his dear Mother and Brothers, Milton and Arthur, 88, Made-street, Church.

The Cenotaph: Armistice Day

To house the unburied spirits of our Dead
    We built this Tomb, and brought our simple flowers
    That they might, lying with Death a few short hours,
Utter our grief: for all our hearts were sad.
Mute and immovable, and with bowed head
    We stood: two minutes passed: worlds rose, dreams, fears,
    Chaos and quiet, old pain and sudden tears,
But we remembered, and for this, were glad.
Then someone moved; men breathed again: the earth
    Flung off her trance, and shuddered wearily.
Traffic and turmoil had a swift rebirth,
    And dim confusion shook the morning sky.
But we could not forget. There was no dearth
    Of thoughts for Those we loved, as we passed by.

A.L. Boden

TWENTY-ONE

The Return to France

Searching for graves, the next war

Early in the war – because of the scale of the casualties and the logistical problems of repatriating thousands of bodies while fighting continued – a decision had been made that the bodies of all the dead would be buried in the countries where they had fallen. Officers and men who had fought together would lie together, side by side in individual graves, without distinction. An organisation – now known as the Commonwealth War Graves Commission – was set up to oversee this burial.

After the war, the battlefields were gradually cleared and the fallen were reinterred in permanent cemeteries built to replace the many wayside burial sites. The land on which these stood was given to Britain in perpetuity. In each cemetery was a Cross of Sacrifice, a Stone of Remembrance inscribed 'Their name liveth for evermore', and simple, uniform headstones. On these were engraved the soldier's name, number, regiment, regimental emblem, age and date of death. If the family wished, they could pay to have an inscription of their choice engraved at the base of the stone: because of the problems this raised with poor families, this payment later became voluntary.

On the headstones of the many unidentified bodies were the words 'A soldier of the Great War known unto God'. The names of all those with no known grave were carved on stone panels in cemeteries or on the walls of the two great memorials to the fallen – the Menin Gate at Ypres and at Thiepval on the Somme. On the Menin Gate Memorial, which was unveiled on 24 July 1927, are inscribed the names of 54,900 men missing in the Ypres Salient; to this day the Last Post is sounded there every night at eight o'clock. That at Thiepval has the names of the 73,357 British and South African missing of the Somme; the Canadians and ANZACs have their own memorials. It was unveiled on Monday 1 August 1932, and was the last large-scale memorial to be dedicated. On that day the 3.30 a.m. edition of the *Daily Telegraph* reported the result of elections in Germany with the headline: 'HERR HITLER'S HOPES DASHED FOR EVER.'

Soon after hostilities ceased, relatives and survivors began to make pilgrimages to France, to search for the graves of those who had died and to retread the old battlefields. There were suggestions that parts of the front – in particular the town of Ypres – should remain as they were to form permanent shrines to the

fallen and as a reminder of the destruction wrought by war, but local people did
not agree. Gradually their towns and villages were rebuilt, and normal life began
to return to the devastated countryside.

The Battle-fields

You never saw the Summer dance and sing
And wreathe her steps with laughter, toss her larks,
And strew her crimson poppies, and make rise
Across the meadows in her train a cry
Of happy colors – O, you never knew
How birds can make a business of their singing,
How the golden music can rain down
From sunny heaven like a hail-storm all
Day long – you never saw the naked life
Of Summer, till you saw her in her wrath
And gladness, young-eyed, golden-irised, loud
And wild and lovely-drunken, running, prancing,
Clambering across these fields of death.

Old pits and craters where the solid earth
Rocked up and smoked like water are the beds
Of blowing lilies; huge, dull-yellowing piles
Of steel, the dead-ends of the work of death,
Are choirs for thrushes and gay trellises
For rose and morning-glory; and you see
The tissue petals trailing down the holes
Men huddled in to die like poisoned rats.
You see black, crazy strings of barbed-wire fences
Legging down the hillside like old men
Amuck, tripped up and clambered on and loved
Down into earth by mountains of wild-grape
And ivy. And you see vast obscene tanks,
Gigantic bugs without antennæ, bugs
Named Lottie and named Liesel, cracked and blasted,
Pouring out their iron guts among
The daisies, and you see the daisies laugh;

And long-tailed pies that fly like aeroplanes
Float from their turrets, gentle in the blue.

Whole cities were sown in this earth like seed.
The wealth and eagerness of all mankind
Was here, like mountain thunder, coursing through
These ghostly paths, that hie so privately
Beneath the glossy crowds of bee-loved clover.
They were here for murder, death-determined.
But the shepherd trails his willing sheep
To crop that clover; and the clicking hoe
And sliding shovel talk as surely forth
As crickets when a summer storm is past.

These villages, close-nesting like the hives
Of bees, were crushed to blood and powder by
The speeding hoof of war. Their temples fallen
And their homes a pit for gravel, they,
The many neighbours, are a lonely few
Lost pioneers. But they had pitched their tents
And tacked their paper shanties in the desert,
And the hens are clucking, and the beans
Are blossoming with white and brick-red blossoms,
And the vine, the purple clematis,
Is royal at the door. On holidays
They lay their tools down, and with sunny wine
From the old cellar-pits, and kindling mirth
From depths incredible, they eat their bread
In laughter, they fling jokes at the old war,
And pour soup in the bugle, and sing loud,
And pound the drum, and call out all the girls,
And march, and dance, and fill the darkened streets
With love and music till the moon goes out.

In all death's garden but one plot is dead,
One cold, bleak acre swept-up for our tears,
The turf, the pebbles, regular and still –
The tired, white little crosses marking time!
But they are feeble, and their watch is brief.
To-day remembering a name, to-morrow
They will mourn the death of memory;

Another morrow they are gone; time's wind
Has blown the sweet-briar roses over them.

Earth does not mind the madness of her children –
She has room. From one gaunt womb she could
Pour back those cities, and fill all these fields
With men and women aching at their toil,
And droll-faced children trudging with a pail
To greet them. This raw miracle of life
Is ruthless, reckless, sure. Plunge in your hands
To fashion it; be ruthless, reckless, sure.
Fear is the only danger. And the death
Of dreams dreamed weakly is the only death
Of man – the prayers sighed outward from the earth,
The songs that feed the poet with his wish,
Beatitudes tramped under armies, thoughts
Too mother-tender, or too childly wise,
To stand out in the weather of the world,
And deeds untimely kind, and deed-like words
Of Love's apostles, who would pilgrim down
The black volcanic valley of all time
With hymns and waving palms, their sweet white banners
Lost and perishing, like breath of brooks,
Like strings of thin mist when the mountains burn.
In them man's spirit in its power dies.
The rest is Nature's life – and she will live,
And laugh on dancing to the doomless future,
Slave to no thought softer than her own.

Max Eastman

The Menin Road, March 1919

Over the flat dim land I see you moving
Methodically; under a dark wide sky
Full of low clouds. You are gone far from our loving.
No fret of ours or grief can touch you now.
The road speaks nothing to our longing now.
The winds are dumb to us and pass us by.

The nameless tracks, the faded grass
Spread out as far as we can see.

The homeless shadows glance and pass
By shattered wood and naked tree.
Splintered and stark they rise alone
Against so wonderful a blue
Of distance – an intensity
At once so steadfast and so true
I wonder are you wholly gone?

Carola Oman

The Wood

I fear this beautiful, unholy place!
But O, what frights me among elder-boughs
June-blossoming: wild roses? Evil's here.
But how is evil here? What evil comes
Out of June meadows into the wood's calm?
Is it with Earth the wrong lies? Or with me?
Did elders bloom like this, on a wood's edge,
Close to pale foxgloves, neighbored with a briar,
When, long ago – how long I know not – hate,
First fear, or first injustice, bred in me?
Is this hid horror here, hid Memory?

J.C. Chadwick

Behind the Line

Treasure not so the forlorn days
When dun clouds flooded the naked plains
    With foul, remorseless rains;
    Thread not those memory ways
Where by the dripping alien farms,
Starved orchards with their shrivelled arms,
The bitter mouldering wind would whine
At the brisk mules clattering towards the Line.

Remember not with so sharp skill
Each chasm in the clouds that with strange fire
    Lit pyramid-fosse and spire
    Miles on miles from our hill;
In the magic glass, aye, then their lure
Like heaven's houses gleaming pure

Might soothe the long-imprisoned sight
And put the seething storm to flight.

Enact not you so like a wheel
The round of evenings in sandbagged rooms
    Where candles flicked the glooms;
    The jests old time could steal
From ugly destiny, on whose brink
The poor fools grappled fear with drink,
And snubbed the hungry, raving guns
With endless tunes on gramophones.

About you spreads the world anew,
The old fields all for your sense rejoice,
    Music has found her ancient voice,
    From the hills there's heaven on earth to view;
And kindly Mirth will raise his glass
To bid you with dull Care go pass –
And still you wander muttering on
Over the shades of shadows gone.

Somewhere in France (2)

'Somewhere in France' – we know not where – he lies,
'Mid shuddering earth and under anguished skies!
We may not visit him, but this we say:
Though our steps err, his shall not miss their way.
From the exhaustion of War's fierce embrace
He, nothing doubting, went to his own place.
To him has come, if not the crown and palm,
The kiss of Peace – a vast, sufficing calm!

So fine a spirit, daring, yet serene, –
He may not, surely, lapse from what has been:
Greater, not less, his wondering mind must be;
Ampler the splendid vision he must see.
'Tis unbelievable he fades away, –
An exhalation at the dawn of day!

Nor dare we deem that he has but returned
Into the Oversoul, to be discerned

Hereafter in the bosom of the rose,
In petal of the lily, or in those
Far jewelled sunset skies that glow and pale,
Or in the rich note of the nightingale.
Nay, though all beauty may recall to mind
What we in his fair life were wont to find,
In sun his nature, and in morn his fire,
In sea his force, in love his pure desire;
He shall escape absorption, and shall still
Preserve a faculty to know and will.

Such is my hope, slow climbing to a faith:
(We know not Life, how should we then know Death?)
From our small limits, and withholdings free,
Somewhere he dwells and keeps high company;
Yet tainted not with so supreme a bliss
As to forget he knew a world like this.

John Hogben

At Thiepval

Oh, nevermore shall a bud awake
On your tortured boughs at the call of Spring,
   But for your sake
   New life shall break
From the seeds that Victory shall fling
In earth of the soldier's slumbering.

For a hopeful Spring shall come at last,
A summer of sunlight sweet and pure,
   When the fiery blast
   With its blight's o'er past,
And the shade of the green young trees shall lure
The heirs of peace to a rest secure.

But ye shall stand as witnesses
Of the fight with a rude invading foe,
   Of its fiery stress
   And blood-bitterness,
Meet testament of the brave below
Who died for the peace the young trees know.

J. E. Stewart

A Father at the Grave of his Son

Steady, heart, for here's my journey's end – earth's end, for me
And this the door which closes once, and opens never –
These few unsodden clods of clay,
A shelter and a shade
To him who was, and is, my son.
To me a grave, to him the rainbow's end.
Though Death make cowards of the living,
They know him not, the dead.

He the arrow, I the bow
Which launched his flight towards infinity.
That form of willow,
Those eyes more eager than the dawn,
With all their freshness and surprise!
To him was duty pleasure, pleasure joy,
And joy was gratitude.

And with him many parts I've played,
A perch for childhood clinging,
His boyhood's anchor, in youth a shield,
And to his manhood's dawn
An answering call.
And now am I an echo stilled,
A silent bell, a wave without a shore.

In him died out my name and line,
Ancestry's sum of heritage
Back to the rim of Time.

And now he has the whole Picardian plain for a grave,
A fitting place to die
Where man has died for man,
To dream, to rest, and greet the morn.

A treader of the skies,
With brother falcons of the shield,
He made new worlds his own,
Soared beyond the condor's ken,
And shamed the eagle's flight.

He fought not treacherous foes on earth,
But in his venture toward the sun,
Met those for once ennobled by their deeds,
Who challenged, fought or fell, or died with him.

He knew not death, for as he fell,
He loosed from him that body which had served its day,
As wakes a sleeper from his dreams
And lays his cloak aside.
Then, eager went as eager came,
Up sped his soul and up, and ever up, a meteor in uncharted space,
A light to heavens new,
A banneret of valour 'gainst the setting sun.

And he has missed the heartache,
Life's jealousies and pain, and sympathies deceived.
Away then, Sorrow, beguiling sister of Despair,
I'll rest awhile with Sadness
In her twilight hour of balm,
And let grief's embers die.
For I've a treasury of memories so rich and dear
'Twould beggar all the son-less men of earth to buy!

Since memory's but the bridge of time,
I'll build it true and high,
To carry me across the skies
When comes my journey far,
And never fear but I'll know well
Where waits my boy for me –
At the rainbow's western end!

France, September 1919
Wade Chance

Soldiers' headstones

L/20675 Private Alfred James Clark
1st Queen's Own (Royal West Kent Regiment)
9 October 1915 Age 18
FAREWELL BELOVED SO YOUNG AND BRAVE
FOR KING AND COUNTRY HIS LIFE HE GAVE
Carnoy Military Cemetery, Somme H.3

847 Private A. G. Whittle
11th Bttn Australian Infantry
2 May 1915 Age 28
TOO FAR AWAY YOUR GRAVE TO SEE
BUT NOT TOO FAR TO THINK OF THEE
Lone Pine Cemetery, Anzac I.G.1

2167 Private Clifford Lionel Holton
5th Bttn Australian Infantry
13 August 1915 Age 19
AN ANZAC BRAVE
IN AN ANZAC GRAVE
Lone Pine Cemetery, Anzac III B.54

476 Private William Norman Arthur-Mason
19th Bttn Australian Infantry
19 September 1915 Age 19
HE DID HIS DUTY SIMPLY, BRAVELY
AND IN THE DOING DIED
Shrapnel Valley Cemetery I, Anzac F.8

Perfect Epilogue
Armistice Day 1933

It's when the leaves are fallen I think of you,
And the long boulevards where the ghosts walk now,
And Paris is dark again save for one great star
That's caught and held in the dark arms of a bough

And wonder, among them are two a girl and boy
Silent, because their love was greater than song,
Who whisper 'farewell' and whisper 'if it's for ever';
And did not know, poor ghosts, for ever could be so long.

It's when the leaves are fallen I think of you,
And if you're lonely too, who went with the great host;
And know that Time's no mender of hearts but only
Still the divider of Light and Darkness, Ghost.

May Cannan

Valete

This is a tale not relished by our time,
Soft with the thing that men call Victory.
You will not hear it round the midnight floor,
But only in the quiet, evening lane,
Or by the hearths of those that once were young
And stoop to feel the warmth of ashening fires,
Forgetting and remembering again.

They whisper that a thousand years ago,
A thousand years – unless this night just gone –
There was a road between the poplar trees
Long sleepless from the tramp of soldiery.
And as they marched, why! everybody sang
His dearest tunes, and, strangely, all of these
Together mingling, though in many a tongue,
Turned to an anthem, rapturous and free.

And this is true – that as their number passed,
Suddenly there was no more singing:
Only the silence, racked by crunching feet;
The level throb of drums, and worn studs ringing.

No emblem fluttered, not a hand was kissed,
And we that saw them found no word to say,
But stood there till the marching ebbed and died,
And all that distant company became
A vale of crosses wavering in the mist
A thousand years ago. – Or was it yesterday?

1933
William Box

TWENTY-TWO

L'Envoi

The Other Side

Being a letter from Major Average of the Royal Field Artillery in Flanders, acknowledging a presentation copy of a book of war-verse, written by a former subaltern of his battery – now in England.

Just got your letter and the poems. Thanks.
You always were a brainy sort of chap:
Though pretty useless as a subaltern –
Too much imagination, not enough
Of that rare quality, sound common-sense.
And so you've managed to get on the Staff:
Influence, I suppose: a Captain, too!
How do tabs suit you? Are they blue or green?

About your book. I've read it carefully,
So has Macfaddyen; (you remember him,
The light-haired chap who joined us after Loos?);
And candidly, we don't think much of it.
The piece about the horses isn't bad;
But all the rest, excuse the word, are tripe –
The same old tripe we've read a thousand times.

My grief, but we're fed up to the back teeth
With war-books, war-verse, all the eye-wash stuff
That seems to please the idiots at home.
You know the kind of thing, or used to know:
'Heroes who laugh while Fritz is strafing them' –
(I don't remember that *you* found it fun,
The day they shelled us out of Blauwport Farm!)
'After the fight. Our cheery wounded. Note
The smile of victory: it won't come off' –
(Of course they smile; so'd you, if you'd escaped,
And saw three months of hospital ahead . . .
They don't smile, much, when they're shipped back to France!)

'Out for the Great Adventure' – (twenty-five
Fat, smirking wasters in some O.T.C.,
Who just avoided the Conscription Act!)
'A strenuous woman-worker for the Cause' –
(Miss Trixie Toogood of the Gaiety,
Who helped to pauperise a few Belgiques
In the great cause of self-advertisement!) . . .

Lord knows, the newspapers are bad enough;
But they've got some excuse – the censorship –
Helping to keep their readers' spirits up –
Giving the public what it wants: (besides,
One mustn't blame the press, the press has done
More than its share to help us win this war –
More than some other people I could name):
But what's the good of war-books, if they fail
To give civilian-readers an idea
Of what life *is* like in the firing-line . . .

You might have done that much; from you, at least,
I thought we'd get an inkling of the truth.
But no; you rant and rattle, beat your drum,
And blow your two-penny trumpet like the rest:
'Red battle's glory', 'Honour's utmost task',
'Gay jesting faces of undaunted boys', . . .
The same old Boy's-Own-Paper balderdash!

Mind you, I don't deny that they exist,
These abstract virtues that you gas about –
(*We shouldn't stop out here long, otherwise!*) –
Honour and humour, and that sort of thing;
(Though heaven knows where you found the glory touch,
Unless you picked it up at G.H.Q.);
But if you'd common-sense, you'd understand
That humour's just the Saxon cloak for fear,
Our English substitute for '*Vive la France!*'
Or else a trick to keep the folk at home
From being scared to death – as we are scared;
That honour . . . damn it, honour's the one thing
No soldier yaps about, except of course
A soldier-*poet* – three-and-sixpence net.

Honest to God, it makes me sick and tired
To think that you, who lived a year with us,
Should be content to write such tommy-rot.
I feel as though I'd sent a runner back
With news that we were being strafed like Hell . . .
And he'd reported: 'Everything OK.'
Something's the matter: either you can't *see*,
Or else you see, and cannot write. That's worse.

Hang it, you can't have clean forgotten things
You went to bed with, woke with, smelt and felt,
All those long months of boredom streaked with fear:
Mud, cold, fatigue, sweat, nerve-strain, sleeplessness,
The men's excreta viscid in the rain,
And stiff-legged horses lying by the road,
Their bloated bellies shimmering, green with flies . . .

Have you forgotten? you who dine to-night
In comfort at the Carlton or Savoy.
(Lord, but I'd like a dart at that myself –
Oysters, *crème* something, sole *vin blanc*, a bird,
And one cold bottle of the very best –
A girl to share it: afterwards, a show –
Lee White and Alfred Lester, Nelson Keys;
Supper to follow.

                    Our Brigade's in rest –
The usual farm. I've got the only bed.
The men are fairly comfy – three good barns.
Thank God, they didn't have to bivouac
After this last month in the Salient) . . .

You *have* forgotten; or you couldn't write
This sort of stuff – all cant, no guts in it,
Hardly a single picture true to life.

Well, here's a picture for you: Montauban –
Last year – the flattened village on our left –
On our right flank, the razed Briqueterie,
Their five-nines pounding bits to dustier bits –
Behind, a cratered slope, with batteries

Crashing and flashing, violet in the dusk,
And prematuring every now and then –
In front, the ragged Bois de Bernafay,
Boche whizz-bangs bursting white among its trees.
You had been doing F.O.O. that day;
(The Staff knows why we had an F.O.O.:
One couldn't flag-wag through Trônes Wood; the wires
Went down as fast as one could put them up
And messages by runner took three hours.)
I'd got the wind up rather; you were late,
And they'd been shelling like the very deuce.
However, back you came. I see you now,
Staggering into 'mess' – a broken trench,
Two chalk-walls roofed with corrugated iron,
And, round the traverse, Driver Noakes's stove
Stinking and smoking while we ate our grub.
Your face was blue-white, streaked with dirt; your eyes
Had shrunk into your head, as though afraid
To watch more horrors; you were sodden-wet
With greasy coal-black mud – and other things.
Sweating and shivering, speechless, there you stood.
I gave you whisky, made you talk. You said:
'Major, another signaller's been killed.'
'Who?'
          'Gunner Andrews, blast them. O my Christ!
His head – split open – when his brains oozed out,
They looked like bloody sweetbreads, in the muck.'

And you're the chap who writes this clap-trap verse!

Lord, if I'd half *your* brains, I'd write a book:
None of your sentimental platitudes,
But something real, vital; that should strip
The glamour from this outrage we call war,
Showing it naked, hideous, stupid, vile –
One vast abomination. So that they
Who, coming after, till the ransomed fields
Where our lean corpses rotted in the ooze,
Reading my written words, should understand
This stark stupendous horror, visualise
The unutterable foulness of it all . . .

I'd show them, not your glamorous 'glorious game',
Which men play 'jesting' 'for their honour's sake' –
(A kind of Military Tournament,
With just a hint of danger – bound in cloth!)
But War, – as war is now, and always was:
A dirty, loathsome, servile murder-job: –
Men, lousy, sleepless, ulcerous, afraid,
Toiling their hearts out in the pulling slime
That wrenches gum-boot down from bleeding heel
And cakes in itching arm-pits, navel, ears:
Men stunned to brainlessness, and gibbering:
Men driving men to death and worse than death:
Men maimed and blinded: men against machines –
Flesh versus iron, concrete, flame and wire:
Men choking out their souls in poison-gas:
Men squelched into the slime by trampling feet:
Men, disembowelled by guns five miles away,
Cursing, with their last breath, the living God
Because He made them, in His image, men . . .
So – were your talent mine – I'd write of war
For those who, coming after, know it not.

And if posterity should ask of me
What high, what base emotions keyed weak flesh
To face such torments, I would answer: '*You!*'
Not for themselves, O daughter, grandsons, sons,
Your tortured forebears wrought this miracle;
Not for themselves, *accomplished utterly*
This loathliest task of murderous servitude;
But just because they realised that thus,
And only thus, by sacrifice, might they
Secure a world worth living in – *for you.*'

Good-night, my soldier poet. *Dormez bien!*

                                        Gilbert Frankau

Notes

CHAPTER ONE: THE OUTBREAK OF WAR

The Kaiser and Belgium, *Daily Chronicle*, 8 August 1914.

England to Belgium, *Swords and Ploughshares*.

The Old Soldiers, *Collected Poems*.

March up to the Colours, *Accrington Observer and Times*, 19 September 1914.

The Skunk, *The War Men-agerie*.

The Sloth, *ibid*.

Cricket Field or Battle Field?, *Daily Chronicle*, 1 September 1914.

First Week in the Army, *Peeko Journal*, no. 16 [May 1916]. The poem is signed 'Nemo'.

Pro Patria, *The Spires of Oxford*.

The Volunteers, *Punch*, vol. 148, 3 February 1915. The poem is signed 'R.C.L.'.

[A subaltern known as Colquhoun], *Fifth Gloucester Gazette*, no. 5, August 1915. The limerick is signed 'H.S.K.'.

The Barrack Room, *Ballads of Field and Billet*.

[Have you seen the Pals, sir?] Written in an autograph book belonging to Miss Alice Holliday of 42 Primrose Street, Accrington, the girlfriend of Pte Percy Martin of the Accrington Pals. The original manuscript disappeared some years ago; a line appears to have been omitted from the final stanza when it was transcribed.

The Call to Arms, *Saturday Westminster Gazette*, vol. 44, no. 6612, 15 August 1914. Reprinted in *The Spires of Oxford* with the title 'The Call to Arms in Our Street'.

On Trek, *Collected Poems*.

The House by the Highway, *Poems*.

The Last Evening, *ibid*.

CHAPTER TWO: EARLY MONTHS

[There was a strange Man of Coblenz], *The Book of William*.

Retreat, *The Night Sister*. Lars Porsena of Clusium was an Etruscan king who ruled central Italy *c.* 500 BC. The last Roman king, Lucius Tarquinius, had been deposed and Rome declared a republic; Tarquinius appealed to Porsena to help overthrow the revolutionaries and restore the throne. The story was the subject of a popular poem, 'Horatio' by Thomas Babington Macaulay, from which Charles T. Foxcroft quotes.

The Mouth-Organ, *Ballads of Battle*. As a note to the name Jimmy Morgan, Joseph Lee writes: 'Though for obvious reasons of rhyme I have here ventured to appropriate the classic name "Jimmy Morgan", nevertheless the best mouth-organist in D Company, if not in the battalion, is 2203 Private William Brough. He informs me that his present instrument is something the worse for wear.' 'Unter den Linden' is the best-known and most elegant street in Berlin, named from the linden or lime trees that line the roadway. 'Highland laddie, Highland laddie; whar hae you been a' the day?' is the regimental march of the Black Watch.

Singing 'Tipperary', *Ballads of Field and Billet.*

Another 'Scrap of Paper', *Punch*, vol. 147, 7 October 1914.

The Freedom of the Press, *ibid.*, vol. 147, 9 December 1914. Joseph Joffre (1852–1931) was Chief of the French General Staff until December 1916.

News from the Front, *Dead Horse Corner Gazette*, no. 3, June 1916. The poem was reprinted in a number of other trench magazines, e.g. *Kamp Knews*, no. 22, Christmas 1917.

[There once was a Man, Kaiser Will], *The Book of William.*

Where are the Russians?, *Accrington Observer and Times*, 19 September 1914.

The German Herr, *The War Men-agerie.*

The Traitor, *Punch*, vol. 147, 14 October 1914.

Ten Little Germans, *Craigleith Hospital Chronicle*, vol. 2, no. 9, August 1915. The poem is signed 'H.R.'.

[There once was a Ruler enraged], *The Book of William.*

Kaiser Bill, *Craigleith Hospital Chronicle*, vol. 1, no. 3, February 1915. The poem is signed 'Stop Gap'. Alexander Von Kluck (1846–1934) commanded the German First Army and led the German attack through Belgium in 1914; Field Marshal Sir John French (1852–1925) commanded the BEF during the early part of the war until he was replaced by Douglas Haig in December 1915; Grand Admiral Alfred Von Tirpitz (1849–1930) oversaw the building of the German naval fleet before the war, and was responsible for the German policy of unrestricted U-boat warfare. The Kiel Canal, built 1887–95, allowed German naval movement from their Baltic bases to the open sea; its widening in the years before the war was seen as an act of bellicosity. Davy Jones was a sailor's term for the sea, here the sea as a grave. Admiral Sir Frederick Sturdee (1859–1925) commanded the force that destroyed the German naval squadron commanded by Admiral Von Spee in the Battle of the Falklands in December 1914.

Ypres Cathedral, *New Statesman*, vol. 5, no. 128, 18 September 1915. Reprinted in *Ypres and Other Poems.*

Ypres, *Contemporary Review*. The poem is subscribed 'Ypres, October 1915'.

The Refugees, *Ypres and Other Poems.*

To the Kaiser – Confidentially, *Fifth Gloucester Gazette*, no. 10, 12 March 1916. Reprinted in *A Gloucestershire Lad*, where Harvey put 'Sir' into lower case, apart from the final 'Sir Kaiser'.

All Souls, 1914, *An Annual of New Poetry: 1917.*

The School at War – 1914, *Eton Lyrics*. 1,031 Etonians were killed or died of wounds in the First World War.

'Punch' in the Enemy's Trenches, *Punch*, vol. 148, 13 January 1915.

CHAPTER THREE: AUTUMN 1914 IN ENGLAND

The Women, *The Lady*, 3 September 1914.

Deportment for Women, *Punch*, vol. 148, 20 January 1916. For 'The Day' see Glossary under *Der Tag*. The Nut was a fop or dandy.

Khaki, *Ripples from the Ranks of the QMAAC.*

Leave your Change, *Accrington Observer and Times*, 3 October 1914, repeated on 10 October. The newspaper has the headline: 'LEAVE YOUR CHANGE FOR THE NATIONAL FUND.'

Britain's Daughters, *Trampled Clay.*

Munition Girls, *Glasgow Herald*, 29 February 1916. The poem is signed 'W.W.'.

The Deserters, *Punch*, vol. 154, 9 January 1918. Reprinted in *The Bomber Gipsy* with changes. A Sam Browne was the belt and cross-strap worn by officers.

The War Baby, *Craigleith Hospital Chronicle*, vol. 5, no. 29, June 1917.

[Pansy ran a Knitting Party], *Our Girls in Wartime.*

The Song of a Sock, *Rising Sun*, no. 9, 25 January 1917. The poem is signed 'Leongatha', which is a town south-east of Melbourne.

[The Flag-Day Girl is dressed in white], *Our Girls in Wartime.*

For a Horse Flag Day, *A Book of Poems for The Blue Cross Fund.*

The Everlasting Flag, *Craigleith Hospital Chronicle*, vol. 5, no. 30, September 1917. The poem is signed 'M.J.B.'. Christiaan Rudolph de Wet (1854–1922) was Commander in Chief of the Orange Free State forces during the Boer War, famed for the development of guerrila tactics. Bantams were battalions of volunteers below the regulation height of 5′3″. Many of the men were later integrated into regular battalions, and the Bantam battalions made up to strength with ordinary soldiers.

[The Women's Volunteer Reserve], *Our Girls in Wartime.* The Women's Volunteer Reserve, or WVR, was formed in March 1915 to assist other women's organisations, and for miscellaneous tasks such as canteen work and hospital gardening.

Route March Sentiments, *Ripples from the Ranks of the QMAAC.*

His 'Bit', *The Lady*, vol. 66, no. 1699, 6 September 1917. The poem is signed 'Q.S-H.'.

These Little Ones!, *ibid.*, vol. 66, no. 1690, 5 July 1917.

National Service Lyrics. Unidentified newspaper cutting in private scrapbook.

How It Takes You, *Craigleith Hospital Chronicle*, vol. 4, no. 23, December 1916. The poem is signed 'Edgar'.

[I know a blithe blossom in Blighty], *The Moonraker.*

Model Dialogues for Air-Raids, *Punch*, vol. 153, 10 October 1917, reprinted in *From the Home Front.*

Beasts and Superbeasts, *Punch*, vol. 148, 3 February 1915. Frederich von Bernhardi (1849–1930) was the author of *Germany and the Next War* (1914); Heinrich von Treitschkei (1834–96) was the author of a popular multi-volume history of nineteenth-century Germany. Writing in 1916 in *My London Mission*, Prince Karl Max Lichnowsky, Kaiser Wilhelm's Ambassador to London at the outbreak of war, criticised his country for its responsibility in bringing about the war, and spoke of 'the spirit of Treitschkei and Bernhardi, which glorifies war as an end in itself and does not loathe it as an evil' (see Wilson, *The Myriad Faces of War*, pp. 20, 22); General Alexander von Kluck commanded the German First Army that invaded Belgium in 1914; Ernst Lissauer was the author of the poem 'Hasslied', or 'Hymn of Hate', originally published in *Jugend* in 1914. In this he said that Germany's real enemy was neither France nor Russia, but England: 'He crouches behind the dark grey flood, | Full of envy, of rage, or craft, of gall, | Cut off by waves that are thicker than blood . . . | We will never forego our hate, | We have but one single hate, | We love as one, we hate as one, | We have one foe, and one alone – ENGLAND!' (trans. Barbara Henderson in the *New York Times*. See Charles F. Horne, ed., *Source Records of the Great War*, vol. 1, National Alumni, Indianapolis, 1923). Wilhelm is the Kaiser; *Punch* carried on a prolonged, but generally amiable, vendetta against the playwright George Bernard Shaw.

CHAPTER FOUR: THE NEW ARMIES GO TO FRANCE

Canadians, *The 'Country Life' Anthology of Verse*.

To a Bad Correspondent in Camp, *Punch*, vol. 149, 1 December 1915.

A Canadian to his Parents, *ibid.*, vol. 149, 1 September 1915.

The Catechism of the Kit, *Blighty*, no. 14, 29 August 1916. A 'pull-through' is a cord, with an oiled rag at one end and a weight at the other, that was pulled through a rifle barrel in order to clean it. A 'hussif' is a men's sewing kit.

The Inspection, *Ballads of Field and Billet*. 'Soldier's Friend' was metal polish used for cleaning brass.

Eye-wash, *Punch*, vol. 150, 26 April 1916.

The Draft, *Half-Hours at Helles*. A 'tyro' is a recruit.

Night Duty in the Station, *The Menin Road*.

The Route March, *Fifth Gloucester Gazette*, no. 2, 5 May 1915. Thomas Edward Brown (1830–97) was the author of the poem 'My Garden', with its opening line: 'A garden is a lovesome thing, God wot!'

A Halt on the March, *The Chapman of Rhymes*.

The Squadron Takes the Ford, *Ballads of Field and Billet*.

'In the Pink' – A Letter, *Fifth Gloucester Gazette*, no. 1, 12 April 1915.

Sign Posts, *'New Church' Times*, 22 May 1916.

War, *Wipers Times*, vol. 1, no. 2, 26 February 1916.

Macfarlane's Dug-out, *Ballads of Battle*. At the end of stanza 6, Joseph Lee has made a note: 'It may interest the reader to know that these lines are being written during a very considerable bombardment, in which one misses the friendly proximity of just such a dug-out as Macfarlane's.' At the end of the poem is a 'Postscript. – In the trenches, as will be readily understood, one has no continual abiding place. Consequently the dug-out of the picture is not the dug-out of the poem, and when I last looked in upon Macfarlane, he was swinging contentedly in a hammock of his own construction. It unfortunately falls to me to add a postscript of sadder import. Since the Advance of 25th September [1915, the opening of the Battle of Loos], my comrade has been counted among the missing.'

Music in a Dug-out, *War Daubs*.

Rats, *BEF Times*, vol. 1, no. 2, 25 December 1916.

The Chats' Parade, *Aussie*, no. 3, 8 March 1918. The second line of stanza 4 ends in 'bien', an error overlooked in the makeshift circumstances of its original publication.

The All-Powerful, *Rising Sun*, no. 13, 8 February 1917. The poem is signed 'X.Y.Z.'. Number Nine was an aperient administered to the men, used also as a stock remedy for all doubtful ailments or ills caused by malingering.

Stand-to!, *Ballads of Battle.*

At Dawn in France, *The Undying Splendour.*

To Those Who Wait, *Beaumont Bull*, no. 1, 11 February 1918.

Tommy and Fritz, *Ballads of Battle. Die Wacht am Rhein* translates as 'The line stands here' and was the title of a popular German patriotic song whose chorus was 'Land of our Fathers, have no fear. | Your watch is true, the line stands here'.

The Soldier's Dog, *Fifth Gloucester Gazette*, no. 6, September 1915.

Noon, *Ardours and Endurances.*

To a Choir of Birds, *More Songs by the Fighting Men.*

Shelley in the Trenches, *The Undying Splendour.* The poem is dated 2 May 1916.

Love and War, *Wipers Times*, vol. 3, no. 2, 6 March 1916. Stanza 1, l. 3, has 'too' in place of ''tis'.

To Minnie, *Somme-Times*, vol. 1, no. 1, 31 July 1916.

At Stand Down, *The Greater Love.*

The Night Hawks, *Wipers Times*, vol. 1, no. 1, 12 February 1916. The poem is signed 'By a Pioneer'. 'Foresters' are The Sherwood Foresters (Nottinghamshire and Derbyshire Regiment).

The Romance of Place-Names, *Punch*, vol. 155, 2 October 1918. Reprinted in *The Poets in Picardy*, where it is entitled 'Stinking Farm: By a Picardy Poet of the Future', and the subtitle is altered to read: 'This may be rather embarrassing for the Picardy Poet of the future.'

Sounds by Night, *War Daubs.* The poem is subscribed 'France 1917'.

The Song of the Reconnoitering Patrol, *Fifth Gloucester Gazette*, no. 4, 12 July 1915.

[I oft go out at night-time], *Soldier Songs.*

A True Tale of the Listening Post, *Fifth Gloucester Gazette*, no. 5, September 1915. R.E.K. was Raymond E. Knight, who died of wounds in July 1916.

No Man's Land, *Spectator*, vol. 116, no. 4580, 8 April 1916.

On Patrol, *The Greater Love.*

CHAPTER FIVE: OUT OF THE LINE

The Dawn, *Soldier Songs.*

Back in Billets, *The Muse in Arms.* The poem is dated February 1915. A Wolsey valise is a warm vest named after its well-known manufacturer.

Gonnehem, *Fifth Gloucester Gazette*, no. 5, August 1915. Reprinted in *A Gloucestershire Lad at Home and Abroad.*

The Billet, *Ballads of Battle.* Joseph Lee has added the note to 'Johnnie Cope': 'There is something slightly sardonic in the fact that the old Jacobite rant, "Hey, Johnnie Cope, are ye waukin' yet?" which was used for the berousing and belabouring of the Whigs, should now do duty as Reveille to a Highland regiment. So, at least, it seems to one at seven o'clock of a cold winter's morning!' Edgar Allan Poe (1809–49) wrote mystery and horror poems and short stories; Ambrose Bierce (1842–1914), described as the Master of the Macabre, was the author of *The Devil's Dictionary.*

The Camp in the Sands, *Ballads of Field and Billet.*

Letters to Tommy, *ibid.*

A Letter from Home, *Craigleith Hospital Chronicle*, vol. 4, no. 23, December 1916.

Letters Home, *Rhymes of the Red Triangle.*

The Dilemma, *Fifth Gloucester Gazette*, no. 7, October 1915.

A Literary War Worker, *Punch*, vol. 149, 24 November 1915.

The Sub., *BEF Times*, vol. 1, no. 5, 10 April 1917.

[There was an old dame at La Bassée], *The Dump*, vol. 2, Christmas 1916.

The Green Estaminet, *Punch*, vol. 154, 17 April 1918.

The Penitent, *Ballads of Battle*. Noove Chapelle was Neuve Chapelle, a battle fought on the Western Front in March 1915; Lord Kitchener's two commandments relate to a document given to all embarking troops, in which he said: 'In this new experience you may find temptations both in wine and women. You must entirely resist both temptations, and, while treating all women with perfect courtesy, you should avoid any intimacy.'

Concert, *Rhymes of the Red Triangle*. George Robey (1869–1954), described as the Prime Minister of Mirth, played in the hugely popular revue 'The Bing Boys Are Here', a show that contained the song 'If you were the only girl in the world'.

Going up the Line, *New Statesman*, vol. 14, no. 350, 20 December 1919.

Back to the Trenches, *Fifth Gloucester Gazette*, no. 5, August 1915.

CHAPTER SIX: FLANDERS, GALLIPOLI AND THE MEDITERRANEAN

Lines Written in a Fire-Trench, *Easter at Ypres*, 1915.

Poison, *The Poetical Works*, sub-titled 'Poems of War and Peace'.

[There was a little Turk, and Baghdad was his home], *BEF Times*, vol. 1, no. 4, 5 March 1917.

Y Beach, published in Alan Moorehead, *Gallipoli*, where he states that it appeared in an Army broadsheet.

For the Gallipoli Peninsula, *Summerdown Camp Journal*, no. 16, 22 January 1916.

Fighting Hard, *My Army, O, My Army.*

Anzac Cove, *Songs of a Campaign.*

Twitting the Turk, *Punch*, vol. 169, 1 September 1915. Reprinted in *Half-Hours at Helles*. Libby was a make of tinned dried milk.

A Dug-out Lament, *Rising Sun*, no. 12, 5 February 1917. The poem is dated November 1915, and there is a note that it is from the Anzac Book MSS. 'Keating's powder does the trick | Kills all Bugs and Fleas off quick.'

The Hospital Ship, *The Muse in Arms.*

The Blizzard, *Front Line Lyrics.*

The Unburied, *The Anzac Book*. The poem is signed 'M.R., N.Z. Headquarters'.

Evacuation of Gallipoli, taken from the collection of war poems, *The Digger Poets of the 1st AIF*, made by Kevin F. Tye for his Master's Degree in Australian Literature, University of Sydney, 1988; Australian War Memorial Archives, Canberra. Published in *From Gallipoli to Gaza.*

Mudros after the Evacuation, *Poems.*

The Graves of Gallipoli, *The Anzac Book*. The poem is signed 'L.L.'.

Gallipoli – In Memoriam, *Craigleith Hospital Chronicle*, vol. 3, no. 15, March 1916.

Mesopotamian Alphabet, *BEF Times*, 20 January 1917. Above the alphabet is the note: 'The following has been sent us from the Indian Army by one of our old divisional friends.' 'S&T' is probably Supply and Transport.

Salonika in November, *Youth's Heritage*.

June in Egypt, 1916, *Clouds and the Sun*.

CHAPTER SEVEN: CONSCRIPTION, PROTEST AND PRISONERS

In the Morning, *Soldier Songs*. At Hulloch Copse the British broke through the German lines, but were unable to exploit their success.

After Loos, *ibid.*

Christmas Truce, *Satire and Sentiment*.

A Soldier's Testament, *The Gutter and the Stars*.

The Cry. The poem is signed 'W.K.S.', and was copied into an autograph book belonging to Helen B. Woods of the Heytesbury Soldiers' Club, by 513 J. Tilley of No. 5 Camp, Sutton Veny, on 10 November 1917. Tilley was part of the AIF. Department of Documents, Imperial War Museum.

To any Diplomatist, *Poems Written during the Great War*. Dated February 1916. Originally published in *The Herald*.

From the Youth of all Nations, *Oxford Poetry 1914–1916*.

Sonnet of a Son, *The Gutter and the Stars*. The poem is dated 1915.

A Veteran's View, *The Night Sister*.

Socialist, *Clouds and the Sun*. The poem is dated 1915.

The Pity of It, *Punch*, vol. 149, 8 September 1915.

To the Nations, *The Gutter and the Stars*.

Waste, *The Unutterable Beauty*. The poem is subscribed 'Mudros, January 1916'.

Wails to the Mail, *'New Church' Times*, vol. 1, no. 4, 29 May 1916. The poem is dated 22 May 1916. Reprinted in *Poems*, where stanza 3, line 5, begins with '——ua', completing the name 'Joshua'. Lord Northcliffe (1865–1921) was the hugely influential publisher of *The Times*, *Daily Mail* and *Daily Mirror*. A fierce critic of Kitchener and Asquith, he supported David Lloyd George. Robert Blatchford (1851–1943) was a left-wing journalist who worked under the name of Nunquam. Sir Edward Grey (1862–1933) was British Foreign Secretary at the outbreak of the war and until December 1916. He spoke the famous words: 'The lamps are going out all over Europe: we shall not see them lit again in our lifetime'; Herbert Asquith (1852–1928) was British Prime Minister at the outbreak of war until his resignation in December 1916; Reginald McKenna (1863–1943) was moved from being Home Secretary to Chancellor of the Exchequer at the outbreak of war. He was opposed to conscription, and resigned from office when Lloyd George replaced Asquith as Prime Minister in December 1916; 'double L's' is David Lloyd George (1863–1945), who served with the Asquith administration, until he succeeded in ousting him from office in December 1916 and replacing him as Prime Minister; K.J. is probably Kennedy Jones, one of Northcliffe's trusted employees, who oversaw the relaunch of the *Mirror* in 1903.

The Only Way, *Five Souls.* The poem is dated June 1915. Henri Bergson (1859–1941), the noted French philosopher. Zoroaster (*c.* 630–*c.* 550 BC), the Persian philosopher otherwise known as Zarathustra. Friedrich Nietzsche (1844–1900), German philosopher, author of *Thus Spoke Zarathustra* and famed for his phrase 'God is dead', which pointed to the impending crisis in European thought following the erosion of its traditional foundations.

The Last Rally, *A Treasury of War Poetry.* Originally published in *Century Magazine.*

Conscription and Conscience, *New Statesman*, vol. 5, no. 130, 2 October 1915. The poem is signed 'S.'.

Freedom on the Job!, *The Tribunal*, 4 October 1917. The poem is signed 'Simple Simon'.

Lieutenant Tattoon, M.C., *Three Ballads (an Intermezzo in War-time).* Reprinted in *The Tribunal*, 29 November 1917, where it was signed 'E.C.'. Lieutenant Tattoon is Siegfried Sassoon, who had sent Carpenter a copy of his 'Statement against the continuation of the war – 1917', which said in part: 'I believe that this war, upon which I entered as a war of defence and liberation, has now become a war of aggression and conquest . . . I am not protesting against the conduct of the war, but against the political errors and insincerities for which the fighting men are being sacrificed.' Sassoon was diagnosed as suffering from neurasthenia, and sent to Craiglockhart Hospital, a move that helped to defuse the embarrassment caused by his protest.

The Pacifist, *The Ploughshare.*

To a Pacifist, *The Survivors.*

To any Pacifist, *Five Souls.* The poem is dated December 1916.

The True Pacifist, *The Ploughshare*, vol. 1, no. 6, July 1916.

To the Followers of Christ among the Belligerent Nations, *Evangelical Christendom*, March–April 1915. Reprinted in *Goodwill*, vol. 2, no. 1, 1 January 1916. The sub-title comes from Romans 12: 5: 'We are one body in Christ.'

A New Hymn, *News Sheet*, no. 9.

Song of the Friends Ambulance Unit, *The Swallow*, vol. 1, no. 4, June 1917. 'Penn' is William Penn (1644–1718). An early Quaker, he promoted the settlement of international differences by arbitration rather than by war. Richmond Hill is the site of the Star and Garter Home.

C.O.s in Prison, *The Tribunal*, 25 October 1917. The poem purports to be 'By the Mother of one of them'.

I Lived a Year in London, *Carols of a Convict.* To be sung to the tune of 'The Low-back'd Car'.

A Call from Prison, *The Tribunal*, 22 November 1917.

From Prison, *New Crusader*, 25 January 1918. Reprinted in *The Tribunal*, 14 March 1918.

Compensation, *Winchester Whisperer, Fortnightly from His Majesty's Prison, Winchester*, no. 6, 21 December 1918. Clandestine manuscript prison magazine, circulated among the prisoners. Library of Friends' House.

Prisoners of War, *Country Life*, vol. 44, no. 1126, 3 August 1918.

Rastatt, *Sonnets from a Prison Camp.* The poem is subscribed 'Rastatt, 7 May [1918]'. In the Foreword, Bowman says: 'It is no mere poetical exaggeration to say that in the first days of captivity at least, the writing of the sonnets was a labour that "stood between my soul and madness" . . . I wish to express my indebtedness to Captain Hohnholz, Commandant of the Prison-Camp at Hesepe, to whose kindness I owe it that I am able to offer the sonnets as they stand for publication. Offizier-Gefangenenlager, Hesepe, 17 August 1918.'

Loneliness, *Gloucestershire Friends*.

Thoughts of Home, *Sonnets from a Prison Camp*. The poem is dated 21 May [1918].

Requiescat, *Ducks*. 'W.M.' was shot while trying to escape. Harvey wrote of him: 'He was one of the gentlest and bravest souls I ever knew' (quoted in Anthony Boden, *F.W. Harvey: Soldier, Poet* (Sutton, 1988), p. 171).

CHAPTER EIGHT: THE ROYAL NAVY

The Sailing of the Fleet, *A Naval Motley*.

The Four Sea Lords, *Punch*, vol. 147, 9 December 1914. Osborne is the Royal Naval College, Osborne, Isle of Wight. An 'Astra Torres' was a French-designed airship.

Destroyers, *Destroyers*. Originally published in *Yale Review*.

Mine Sweepers, *Spectator*, vol. 115, no. 4526, 27 March 1915. The poem is subscribed 'Grimsby 8 March'.

Submarines, *Craigleith Hospital Chronicle*, vol. 1, no. 5, April 1915. Reprinted in *Dies Heroica*.

You Never Can Tell, *Songs from the Trenches*.

[Sing us a song of the Northern Seas], *Aussie*, no. 4, 4 April 1918.

Low Visibility, *Songs of the Submarine*. The poem is signed 'Klaxon'. William Edward Hall's *International Law* (1880); Henry Halleck's *International Law, or, Rules Regulating the Intercourse of States in Peace of War* (1861). Agag was the King of the Amalekites, whom Saul spared (1 Samuel 15: 8–9). The Rt Hon. Sir Samuel Evans (1859–1919) was Solicitor General 1908–10. A scramasax is a Frankish hunting knife.

The Auxiliary Cruiser, *A Treasury of War Poetry*. Sir Humphrey Gilbert (1537–83), explorer and soldier. According to the *ODNB*: 'about midnight on 9 September 1583, and having encountered a fierce storm around the Azores, the *Squirrel*, with Gilbert on board, was engulfed by sea . . . Gilbert was last seen standing on deck with a book in his hand. His final words, shouted over to the *Golden Hind*, were "We are as near to heaven by sea as by land"'.

To Fritz, *Songs of the Submarine*. The poem is signed 'Klaxon'.

The Armed Liner, *From Field & Hospital*.

The Lusitania, *Craigleith Hospital Chronicle*, vol. 2, no. 8, July 1915. Reprinted in *Dies Heroica*.

Below, *Craigleith Hospital Chronicle*, vol. 2, no. 12, November 1915. Admiral David Beatty (1871–1936) commanded the Grand Fleet's Battle Cruiser Squadron from 1913, and took over as Commander of the Grand Fleet in November 1916 after Jellicoe was appointed First Sea Lord. He was the first to engage the Germans in the Battle of Jutland.

Wet Ships, *Songs of the Submarine*. The poem is signed 'Klaxon'.

The Battle off Jutland, *For the Sceptre of the Sea*. Admiral Sir John Jellicoe (1859–1935) was appointed Commander of the Grand Fleet at the outbreak of war. He became First Sea Lord in November 1916.

War Chant of the Harbour-Huns, *Fifth Gloucester Gazette*, no. 15, October 1916. The poem is signed 'M.L.G.'.

How Tirpitz Won the Battle Off Jutland, *Kemmel Times*, vol. 1, no. 1, 3 July 1916.

A British Boy, *Craigleith Hospital Chronicle*, vol. 4, no. 19, August 1916.

Epigram, R.B., *Eidola*.

'Si Monumentum Requiris', *The Night Sister*. The title comes from 'Lector, si Monumentum Requiris, circumspice', translates as 'Reader, if you seek a memorial, look around you', which is inscribed to Sir Christopher Wren inside St Paul's Cathedral.

Winston's Last Phase, *Punch*, vol. 151, 18 October 1916. After the failure of the Gallipoli campaign, Churchill was removed from his position as First Lord of the Admiralty and given the post of Chancellor of the Duchy of Lancaster. He resigned from parliament and rejoined the army, serving on the Western Front and rising to the rank of colonel.

Stories for Our Sons, *Comrades of the Mist*. Originally published in *Arklight*, the weekly newspaper of the US ship *Arkansas*, attached to the Sixth Battle Squadron of the Grand Fleet. Admiral Franz von Hipper (1863–1932) was responsible for the naval bombardment of Scarborough early in the war. He opened hostilities against Beatty at Jutland in June 1916 and oversaw the surrender of the German Fleet in 1918.

CHAPTER NINE: THE ROYAL FLYING CORPS

A Recruiting Song of the Royal Flying Corps, *Tommy's Tunes*. Dating from 1915–16, an air-mechanic's song. 'Thirty chest' meant thirty-inch measurement; two bob (shillings) a day was the pay of a second-class air mechanic; four bob was that of a first-class mechanic, and 'first' refers to promotion from second to first class. Larkhill was at one time a training ground for drill, etc.

Jimmy, *The Fledgling*, vol. 1, no. 5, October 1917. The poem is signed 'G.R.S.'.

A Song of the Air, *Oxford and Flanders*.

R.A.F., *Front Line Lyrics*.

The Dawn Patrol, *More Songs by the Fighting Men*.

A Perfect Day, *The Fledgling*, vol. 1, no. 1, June 1917. A Halberstadt was a type of German aircraft. Heidsieck is a make of champagne.

Song of the Aeroplane, *K[ite]. B[alloon]. Tonic*, no. 24, 12 December 1915. The poem is signed 'H.L.M.'.

Peace Song of the Aeroplanes, *Fifth Gloucester Gazette*, no. 12, May 1916. The poem is signed 'M.L.G.' and is no. 1 in a group of three poems entitled 'Kings of the Air'.

[Here in the eye of the sun], manuscript poem in the RAF Museum (DC71/15/7). The poem is subscribed: 'St André au Bois, France, June 1918'. A Pup was a single-seater Sopwith biplane.

Reconnaissance, *The Muse in Arms*.

Over the Lines, *Airman's Song Book*. Sung by the RFC squadrons, France, 1917–18, to the tune of 'I'll be off to Tipperary in the morning'. A Fokker was a German monoplane with a machine gun that fired through the propeller; it inflicted heavy casualties on Allied aeroplanes in 1915–16.

Semi-Detached, *'New Church' Times*, vol. 1, no. 4, 29 May 1916.

Eyes in the Air, *The Guns*. Originally published in *Land & Water*, vol. 66, no. 2802, 20 January 1916, under the heading 'A Song of the Guns'.

Ten German Aeroplanes, *Craigleith Hospital Chronicle*, vol. 5, no. 30, September 1917. The poem is signed 'M.M.'.

Two Pictures, *Oxford and Flanders*.

Searchlights, *The Bombing of Bruges*. Originally published in *Graphic*.

Every Little While, *Airman's Song Book*. A parody sung by RFC pilots at mess parties in 1917–18 to the popular song of the same name. The Sopwith Camel was a scout aeroplane that carried Vickers and Lewis guns.

[Captain Riddell, R.F.C.], *The Gnome*, no. 5, August 1917. The poem is signed 'D.O'D.'.

The Last Lay of the Sopwith Camel Pilot, *Airman's Song Book*. Spads comes from SPAD (Société pour Aviation et ses Dérivés), which was a single-seater biplane.

The Dying Aviator, *Tommy's Tunes*. To be sung to the tune of 'The Dying Lancer'.

Captain Albert Ball, V.C., D.S.O., *The Fledgling*, vol. 1, no. 3, August 1917. The poem is signed 'G.R.S.'. Captain Albert Ball (1896–1917) was one of the legendary figures of the war whose courage and daring as a solo fighter pilot helped to lift spirits at a time when RFC casualties were appallingly high. Awarded the pilot's brevet in January 1916, he was in France the following month. He was credited with 44 victories, and was awarded the MC, the DSO and two bars and, posthumously, the VC. Like his German counterpart, the Red Baron, he was as highly regarded by the enemy as by his own side.

CHAPTER TEN: VERDUN, THE BATTLE OF THE SOMME BEGINS

Verdun, *Punch*, vol. 151, 8 November 1916.

Before Action, *Grapes of Thorns*.

Life and Death, *My Window Sill*. The poem is subscribed 'Ypres, 1917'.

Gommecourt, *Poems*. The poem is subscribed 'B.E.F. 1916'.

German Boy, *Sorrow of War*.

The Bullet, *Ballads of Battle*.

Left Alone, *More Songs by the Fighting Men*.

My Pal and I, *Fragments*, vol. 2, Christmas number, 1918.

R.I.P., *Roads and Ditches*. Le Sars, on the road between Albert and Bapaume, was finally captured on 7 October.

A Soldiers' Cemetery, *The Undying Splendour*.

[Went the day well?], unidentified newspaper cutting in a scrapbook in the RAF Museum (AC97/127/50).

To my Chum, *Wipers Times*, vol. 4, no. 2, 20 March 1916.

Travail, *The Night Sister*.

From the Somme, *More Songs by the Fighting Men*.

CHAPTER ELEVEN: CASUALTIES OF THE SOMME

Walking Wounded, *Fifth Gloucester Gazette*, no. 25, January 1919. The poem is signed 'Woodbine Willie'.

The Messages, *Battle*.

Unloading Ambulance Train, *The Menin Road*. The poem is dated September 1918.

The Casualty Clearing Station, *Rail-Head*. Reprinted in *Soldier Poets: Songs of the Fighting Men*, with a third verse.

Quantum Mutatus, *On Leave*. Translates as 'How greatly changed'.

The Casualty List, *Craigleith Hospital Chronicle*, vol. 3, no. 13, December 1915. The poem is signed 'M.F.'.

[There are tear-dimmed eyes in the town today], *Burnley Express*, 29 July 1916. This stanza appeared in a short article about Lance-Corporal W. Howarth and Lance-Corporal Marshall of the Burnley 'Pals', who were wounded on 1 July 1916. It is part of a longer poem entitled 'The Boys who Fought and Fell' that was published in the *Accrington Observer and Times* on 22 July 1916.

Broken Bodies, *Sorrow of War*.

The Widow, *Punch*, vol. 151, 29 November 1916.

A Little War Tragedy, *Gazette of the 3rd London General Hospital*, vol. 2, no. 8, May 1917. The poem is signed 'H.M.N.'.

To A.M., *The Quest of Truth*.

Lost in France, *The Nation*, vol. 22, no. 2, 13 October 1917. The poem is signed 'E.R.'.

Telling the Bees, *A Treasury of War Poetry*. Originally published in *Saturday Westminster Gazette*.

To a Dog, *ibid.* Originally published in *Vanity Fair*.

The Dead Hero, *To the Living Dead and Other Poems*. The poem is dated February 1916.

CHAPTER TWELVE: THE WOUNDED IN ENGLAND

Ex Umbra, *Gazette of the 3rd London General Hospital*, vol. 4, no. 6, March 1919.

Evening – Kent, *Sorrow of War*.

Charing Cross, *The Lady*, vol. 64, no. 1656, 9 November 1916. The poem is signed 'E.E.W.'.

A Sister in a Military Hospital, *The Spires of Oxford*.

To a V.A.D. from a V.A.D., *Gazette of the 3rd London General Hospital*, vol. 1, no. 8, May 1916. The poem is dated 30 August 1916. Sapolio is a type of soap.

To a V.A.D., *ibid.*, vol. 2, no. 9, June 1917. The poem is signed 'C.D.'.

A Bit of Bunting, *Told in the Huts*.

Wounded, *War Daubs*.

The Band, *A Bunch of Cotswold Grasses*. The poem is no. 5 in a group of poems entitled 'In a Soldiers' Hospital'.

To Melt a Stone, *BEF Times*, vol. 1, no. 3, 5 March 1917. Reprinted in *The Quirk*, December 1917. Cox was the London bank with which many officers had accounts.

In Hospital, *Gazette of the 3rd London General Hospital*, vol. 1, no. 2, November 1915. 'Afton's green braes' comes from Robert Burns's poem 'Flow gently, sweet Afton, among thy green braes'.

The Cripple, *Songs of a Campaign*.

The Road that Brought me to Roehampton, *Roehampton Rhymes*.

My Motor-Bus Conductress, *ibid.*

In a Tramcar, *The Nation*, vol. 23, no. 8, 25 May 1918, War Cartoons I.

After Visiting an Asylum, *Comrades*.

Gold Braid, *Punch*, vol. 152, 21 March 1917.

CHAPTER THIRTEEN: AUTUMN AND WINTER 1916–1917

Before Ginchy, *On Leave*. Originally published in *Fortnightly Review*. The battle for Ginchy took place between 3 and 9 September 1916.

September 25th, 1916, *Front Line Lyrics*.

The German Dug-out, *Dies Heroica*.

Mud, *Evening News*, 4 December 1916.

A Song of Winter Weather, *The Rhymes of a Red-Cross Man*.

An Appeal, *BEF Times*, vol. 1, no. 3, 20 January 1917. The poem is signed 'One & All'.

They Didn't Believe Me!, *ibid.*, vol. 1, no. 5, 10 April 1917.

[The corp'rl and the privit they], *Wipers Times*, vol. 3, no. 2, 6 March 1916.

Cigarettes, *Fifth Gloucester Gazette*, no. 14, September 1916.

Minor Worries, *Wipers Times*, vol. 2, no. 1, 1 May 1916.

To all 'Doubting Thomases', *BEF Times*, vol. 1, no. 5, 10 April 1917.

The Armoured(illo) Train, *The War Men-agerie*.

The Sentrypede, *ibid.*

[The world wasn't made in a day], *Wipers Times*, vol. 1, no. 1, 12 February 1916.

[Little stacks of sandbags], *ibid.*, vol. 1, no. 2, 26 February 1916.

Why Not?, *BEF Times*, 25 December 1917. The Gaby Glide was a dance made famous by the French actress Gaby Deslys (1881–1920). The Turkey Trot and Boston Hop were popular dances which originated in the US.

The Duck Board, *Flanders to Fowey*.

Joseph Arthur Brown, *The Poets in Picardy*.

The Missing Leader, *Punch*, vol. 152, 28 February 1917. RA exhibition is the summer exhibition at the Royal Academy of Arts; '*sæva indignatio*' translates as 'fiercely angry'; Horatio is Horatio Bull, editor of the jingoistic magazine, *John Bull*; a 'Juvenal *renatus*' is a Juvenal reborn; Sir Hedworth Meux (1856–1929) was Admiral of the Fleet between March 1915 and April 1917. He was one of the pall bearers at the burial of the Unknown Warrior. Blenheim Boanerges refers to Blenheim Palace, home of the Dukes of Marlborough, Churchill's family, and to the biblical sons of thunder who called down fire from heaven; Admiral Sir John Fisher (1841–1920) was brought out of retirement by Churchill at the beginning of the war to become First Sea Lord. He resigned in May 1915 over Churchill's use of naval vessels in the Gallipoli campaign.

CHAPTER FOURTEEN: LEAVE

A Song, *Craigleith Hospital Chronicle*, vol. 3, no. 18, July 1916.

The Wire that Failed, *Fragments*, vol. 1, no. 5, June 1917.

Four Words, *Aussie*, no. 8, October 1918.

[If you're waking call me early, call me early, sergeant dear], *'New Church' Times*, vol. 1, no. 2, 1 May 1916.

Of Harold, and his Fatal Taste for Souvenirs, *A Train Errant.* The poem is signed 'J.W.H.'. Printed instructions issued to officers and men going on leave spelt out those articles which it was forbidden for men to take back to England; these included 'Bombs, Shells, Shell cases and fuses. Trophies captured from the enemy (with the exception of German helmets, caps, badges, numerals and buttons.)' Gotha is the generic name for large German aeroplanes that dropped bombs on London, from 'Gotha Wagen Fabrik', where they were made.

Virtue, *BEF Times*, vol. 1, no. 1, 1 December 1916. ABC is the Aerated Bread Company, a chain of popular tea shops.

Mufti Once More, *Punch*, vol. 154, 16 January 1918. The poem is signed 'Evoe'.

A Vision of Blighty, *ibid.*, vol. 152, 11 April 1917.

Ragtime, *A Miscellany of Poetry – 1919.*

At Afternoon Tea, *Gloucestershire Friends.*

On Leave (1), *Depot Review*, no. 5.

On Leave (2), *Magpies in Picardy.*

A Day in Spring, *Love Songs of a Soldier.* The poem is subscribed 'Nottingham, 1917'.

Oxford Revisited, *Punch*, vol. 152, 21 February 1917. The poem is signed 'Algol' and dated 21 February 1917. '*Jeunesse dorée*' is gilded youth; DD is Doctor of Divinity; the VTC is the Volunteer Training Corps, made up of men unfit for the army who were trained in home defence.

On Christmas Leave, *ibid.*, vol. 151, 27 December 1916.

English Leave, *The Splendid Days.* Written during the last leave of Sir Arthur Quiller-Couch's son, Bevil, to whom she was engaged. He survived the war, but died of influenza while serving in the Army of Occupation in Germany in February 1919.

The Train for the Front, *The Lady*, vol. 64, no. 1655, 2 November 1916. The poem is signed 'L.M.O.'.

On Returning to the Front after Leave, *Poems.*

CHAPTER FIFTEEN: SPRING AND EARLY SUMMER 1917

[There was a little Hun, and at war he tried his hand], *BEF Times*, vol. 1, no. 2, 20 January 1917.

More Peace-Talk in Berlin, *Punch*, 24 May 1916.

The Kaiser's Cry for Peace, *War Cartoon Sonnets.* The poem is dated July 1917.

War Aims, *Satire and Sentiment.* Lothringen is the German name for Lorraine, the province in the east of France that became German after the Franco-Prussian war of 1870–1 but was reclaimed by the French after the war.

The Woman who Shrieked against Peace, *Sorrow of War*.

Profit and Loss, *BEF Times*, 22 January 1918.

Arras, *More Songs by the Fighting Men*. The poem was republished in *Roads and Ditches* with substantial changes.

Zero!, *Punch*, vol. 152, 23 May 1917. Reprinted in *The Mudhook*, vol. 1, no. 1, September 1917, and in *The Bomber Gipsy* with some changes. Gavrelle was captured on 23 April 1917 during the Battle of Arras.

Open Warfare, *Punch*, vol. 152, 20 June 1917. Reprinted in *The Bomber Gipsy* with some changes.

Beaucourt Revisited, *The Mudhook*, vol. 1, no. 1, September 1917. Reprinted in *The Bomber Gipsy* with substantial changes. The 63rd (Royal Navy) Division captured Beaucourt, with devastating casualties, on 13 November 1916. Two of Herbert's close friends, James Cook and William Ker, were killed, as was Vere Harmsworth, son of Lord Rothermere.

Meditation in June, 1917, *Collected Poems*.

In the Third Year of the War, *The Nation*, vol. 20, no. 23, 10 March 1917. Reprinted in *A Muse at Sea* with some changes. These are mostly to punctuation: he has used lower case in the opening word of each line within sentences.

Proverbs of the Pessimists, *The Mudhook*, vol. 1, no. 3, January 1918.

CHAPTER SIXTEEN: RED TAPE AND RIVALRY

Urgent or Ordinary, *Wipers Times*, vol. 3, no. 2, 6 March 1916. Omar's Saki refers to the line in *The Rubaiyat of Omar Khayyam*, an immensely popular work of the time: 'And when like her, O Saki, you shall pass.' Ernst Ludwig Kirchner (1880–1938) was a German Expressionist painter and sculptor.

Requisitional, *Punch*, vol. 149, 18 August 1915.

An Ode to Q., *Wipers Times*, vol. 1, no. 2, 26 February 1916.

Our Fighting Men, *Fifth Gloucester Gazette*, no. 10, March 1916. 'A(c) A(c) A(c)' indicates the end of a signaller's message.

Rhymes without Reason, *BEF Times*, vol. 1, no. 3, 20 January 1917.

Professional Jealousy, *Fifth Gloucester Gazette*, no. 15, October 1916. The poem is signed 'Sapper'.

The Infantryman, *Punch*, vol. 152, 31 January 1917.

Ballad of Army Pay, *Gloucestershire Friends*.

To the P.B.I., *BEF Times*, vol. 1, no. 1, 1 December 1916. The poem is signed 'Pioneer'.

Arma Virumque Cano, *ibid.*, vol. 1, no. 5, 10 April 1917. The poem is signed 'C.I.P.'. The title translates: 'Of arms I sing, and the man', which are the opening words of Virgil's *Aeneid*.

To James, *Punch*, vol. 149, 8 September 1915. Reprinted in *The Mudhook*, vol. 1, no. 2, November 1917. 'Asiatic Anne' was a Turkish heavy gun in the Dardanelles.

The Sacred Documents, *The Poets in Picardy*.

Headquarters, *The Guns*. Originally published in *Land & Water*, vol. 66, no. 2800, 6 January 1916, under the heading 'A Song of the Guns'. 'Beer Emma' are the letters BM; 'Esses C' is SC or Staff Captain.

A Staff Captain's Lament, *The Mudhook*, vol. 1, no. 2. Z Day was Zero Day – the day fixed for an important operation. It was preceded by Y Day, X Day, etc.

CHAPTER SEVENTEEN: THIRD BATTLE OF YPRES (PASSCHENDAELE)

The Sound of Flanders Guns, *The Lyceum Book of War Verse.*
The Burning Question, *BEF Times*, 1 November 1917.
Between the Lines, *Battle.*
Missing, *Punch*, vol. 153, 17 October 1917.
Trampled Clay, *Trampled Clay.* 'Samite' was a rich silk fabric worn in the Middle Ages.
Aftermath, *Poems Written during the Great War.* Originally published in *Poetry Today.*
Before Battle, *The Greater Love.*
Comrades, *The Undying Splendour.*
The Soldier. *A Subaltern's Musings.* The poem is inscribed and dated 'Drop Alley Trench, The Somme, 1st October, 1916'. Mann was killed six months later.
Worm, *BEF Times*, vol. 1, no. 4, 5 March 1917. The poem is contained in 'Letters from Edie', and the poem is introduced: 'I've been writing many decadent and Futurist poems while in bed, they needn't rhyme, and are very simple and so effective . . . One was called 'Worm' and went something like this (you probably won't appreciate it, not having read much Futurist poetry, but you may take it from me that it's an excellent specimen of the kind of stuff that is sold in orange paper covered books with black scrolls on the covers).' The poem follows, and then: 'Believe me or believe me not, but I dashed that marvellous thing off in a few moments! Swonderful.'
From the Line, *War Daubs.*
After the Battle, *New Statesman*, vol. 9, no. 221, 30 June 1917. Reprinted in *The Bomber Gypsy.*
Statesmen Debonair, *Sorrow of War.*
The New Trade, *ibid.*
Rain, *War Daubs.*
A Vignette, *ibid.*
The Flanders Rain, *The Mudhook*, vol. 1, no. 3, January 1918.
The Song of the Mud, *The Forbidden Zone.*
Mad, *The Nation*, vol. 17, no. 4, 24 April 1915. Reprinted in *Battle.* The punctuation is taken from *Battle.*
Carrying-Party, *Ballads of Battle.*
The Fatal Wooden Track, *The Dump*, vol. 3, Christmas 1917.
Seen from an Aid-Post, *BEF Times*, vol. 2, no. 2, 8 September 1917.
Gun-Teams, *The Guns.* Originally published in *Land & Water*, vol. 66, no. 2801, 13 January 1916, under the heading 'A Song of the Guns'.
Transport, *Eidola.* Hippolytus was the son of Theseus.
Dumb Heroes, *A Book of Poems for the Blue Cross Fund.*
My Beautiful, *Ballads of Field and Billet.*
Horse-Bathing Parade, *More Ballads of Field and Billet.* Originally published in *Glasgow News.*

The Air Raid, *Beaumont Bull*, no. 1, 11 February 1918.

The Shell, *From Field & Hospital*. The poem is subscribed 'Elverdinghe, April 1915'.

A Flemish Village, *Spectator*, vol. 116, no. 4574, 26 February 1916.

To Belgium, *The Bukshee Ration*.

CHAPTER EIGHTEEN: AMERICA JOINS THE WAR

The Newt-ral, *The War Men-agerie*.

My American Cousins, *Punch*, vol. 152, 23 May 1917.

The American Advance, *Songs from the Trenches*.

Slacker, Think it Over!, *ibid.*

The Crusader, *ibid.* 'Dieu le volt' translates as 'God wills it', reputedly the words with which Pope Urban II called for the first Crusade in 1095.

To the Recruitin' Sergeant, *ibid.*

Somewhere in France (1), *ibid.*

Somewhere, *ibid.*

Passed as Censored, *ibid.*

Der Tag, *Comrades of the Mist*. Originally published in *Arkright*, the weekly newsletter of the US ship *Arkansas* attached to the Sixth Battle Squadron of the Grand Fleet.

CHAPTER NINETEEN: THE FINAL YEAR

[How doth the little busy wife], *War-Time Nursery Rhymes*.

Chairman Rhymes, *Daily Chronicle*, nos 110 and 88, 27 and 1 February 1918.

Food Control, *Gazette of the 3rd London General Hospital*, vol. 4, no. 1, October 1918. The poem is signed 'S.E.R.'. 'Ole Clynes' is John Clynes (1869–1949), who was Parliamentary Secretary for the Ministry of Food in Lloyd George's government.

Economy ad Insaniam, *Punch*, vol. 155, 25 September 1918.

The Soul of a Nation, *ibid.*, vol. 154, 3 April 1918. The poem is dated 28 March 1918.

Watch and Pray!, *Daily Chronicle*, 29 March 1918. The poem is signed 'S.L.'.

[What of our comrades in the forward post?], *Sonnets from a Prison Camp*. Bowman was taken prisoner during the March retreat – this is the 'deeper woe' at the end of the last sonnet. At the end of April and the beginning of May 1918 he wrote, in Rastatt prison camp, the two sequences of sonnets, 'In the Field' (I) and 'The Nadir' (I–IV, VII), from which these are taken.

During the Battle, *Sorrow of War*. The poem is dated March 1918.

The Tide, *Punch*, vol. 154, 8 May 1918. Reprinted in *The Mudhook*, vol. 1, no. 6, July 1918. Bernard Freyburg VC, DSO and three bars (1889–1963) was a hero of A.P. Herbert's Hood Division in the Royal Naval Division. He had led the battalion's attack at Beaucourt during the last days of the Battle of the Somme (see 'Beaucourt Revisited') and earned his VC for refusing to leave his men despite being severely wounded.

The German Graves, *Punch*, vol. 154, 27 March 1918. Ablain St Nazaire is north-west of Vimy.

The Turn of the Tide, *The Poets in Picardy.*

Victory Assured!, postcard in the Rare Book Department of the British Library.

When I Come Home, *From an Outpost.*

To Certain Persons, *Ducks.*

The Call, *Punch*, vol. 155, 21 August 1918. The poem is signed 'C.F.S.'. BC is British Columbia.

Peace Problems, *The Mudhook*, vol. 2, no. 10, Peace Number 1919. The poem is subtitled 'By the "Mudhook" Poet' and signed 'E.E.C.'. 'C.B.' probably has the double meaning of 'Confined to Barracks' and 'Commander of the Bath'.

From a Full Heart, *Punch*, vol. 152, 2 May 1917.

The General, *ibid.*, vol. 152, 18 April 1917.

Herr Hohenzollern, *ibid.*, vol. 155, 18 December 1918. Hohenzollern was the dynastic name of Kaiser Wilhelm.

In Memory of Kaiser Bill (The Butcher), postcard, selling for one penny; l. 3 begins 'Has booked . . .'.

Cousins German, *Satire and Sentiment.* Originally published in part in *Parliamentary Debates.*

CHAPTER TWENTY: ARMISTICE AND THE PRICE OF WAR

The Armistice, *The Splendid Days.*

Bacchanal, *A Miscellany of Poetry – 1919.*

For a Girl, *The Splendid Days.*

Tears, *Wheels, 1916.*

Victory, *The Pageant of War.*

To an Only Son, copied into a scrapbook in the Royal Air Force Museum (AC1997/127/50). The scrapbook was put together by Canon Philpott, whose son, Capt. J.R. Philpott, MC, enlisted into the 7th Suffolk Regiment and later transferred to the RFC. He was shot down near Baghdad, captured and died as a prisoner of war. The poem is signed 'E.L.N.' and dated January 1920.

The Return, *A Miscellany of Poetry – 1919.*

Peace – The Dead Speak, *Ducks.*

The Survivors, *The Survivors.* Originally published in *The Sphere.*

Who Won the War?, *The Bukshee Ration.* Marshall Foch (1851–1925), the French military leader, was created Allied Supreme commander in March 1918, with overall command of all the Allied forces.

The Offside Leader, *Country Life*, vol. 44, no. 1144, 7 December 1918.

To my Mate, *The Nation*, vol. 24, no. 15, 11 January 1919, where the poem was published anonymously. It was reprinted in *Any Soldier to his Son* in 1919, with some changes. 'Pozzy' is jam; the DC Medal is the Distinguished Conduct Medal.

Reconciliation, *The Pageant of War.*

The Reason, *The Poetical Works. 'Dummes Luder!'* translates as 'Stupid creature!'

Peace, *A Miscellany of Poetry – 1919.*

Return, *A Muse at Sea.*

The Victory March, *The Victory March.*

The Unknown Warrior, *The Unknown Warrior.*

Unknown, *The Poetical Works.*

The War Memorial, *New Statesman*, vol. 14, no. 364, 3 April 1920.

Stranraer War Memorial, *Galloway Advertiser and Wigtownshire Free Press*, 7 April 1921. There was a dispute in the town about the location of the war memorial. Councillors wanted it to be within the Town Hall enclosure, but others thought it should be at The Cross, a commanding position at a busy junction of four of the town's busy thoroughfares.

In Flanders, Poppies Red, postcard.

Only an Officer, *The Poetical Works.*

The Unemployed, *The Nation and The Athenæum*, vol. 32, no. 10, 9 December 1922.

In Memoriam, *Galloway Advertiser and Wigtownshire Free Press*, 21 July 1921; *Burnley Express and Advertiser*, 3 July 1920; *Burnley Express and Advertiser*, Saturday 3 July 1920; *Accrington Observer and Times*, 3 July 1920 (the same poem was inserted for Pte Eldred Towler, 1/5th East Lancashire Regiment, who fell in action, 6 November 1918, in the *Accrington Observer and Times*, 6 November 1920); *Accrington Observer and Times*, 13 November 1920; *Galloway Advertiser and Wigstownshire Free Press*, 16 June 1921; *Accrington Observer and Times*, Saturday, 13 November 1920.

The Cenotaph: Armistice Day, *Liverpool Review*, vol. 5, no. 12, December 1930.

CHAPTER TWENTY-ONE: THE RETURN TO FRANCE

The Battle-fields, *The Nation and The Athenæum*, vol. 31, no. 27, 30 September 1922. Reprinted in *Poems of Five Decades* with some changes.

The Menin Road, March 1919, *The Menin Road.*

The Wood, *The Nation and The Athenæum*, vol. 30, no. 22, 25 February 1922.

Behind the Line, *The Nation*, vol. 30, no. 6, 5 November 1921.

Somewhere in France (2), *Spectator*, vol. 115, no. 4552, 25 September 1915. Republished in *The Highway of Hades*. In the original publication lines 23–4 were omitted, '*He*' in line 25 was not in italics, and there was no stanza break following line 26.

At Thiepval, *Grapes of Thorns.*

A Father at the Grave of his Son, *Nineteenth Century*, no. 513, November 1919.

Soldiers' Headstones. Inscriptions on the headstones of Commonwealth War Grave Commission graves in France and Gallipoli.

Perfect Epilogue, *The Tears of War.*

Valete, *Forty Poems.*

CHAPTER TWENTY-TWO: L'ENVOI

The Other Side, *The Poetical Works*, vol. 2. The Gaiety was a popular London theatre. A 'five-nine' (5.9) was a very destructive, much dreaded, German high-explosive shell. Alfred Lester was a music hall and revue artist; Nelson Keys (1886–1939) was a stage and cinema actor.

Glossary

A.D.S.   Advanced Dressing Station

A.E.F.   American Expeditionary Force; some said that it stood for 'After England Failed'

A.I.F.   Australian Imperial Force

A.P.C.   Army Pay Corps

après la guerre   after the war, in army parlance meaning never

Archie   anti-aircraft gun, said to be derived from the music-hall song 'Archibald, certainly not', because of the ineffectiveness of the early anti-aircraft gunnery efforts

A.S.C.   Army Service Corps, otherwise know as Ally Sloper's Cavalry after a children's comic character

Batt. H.Q.   Battalion Headquarters

B.E.F.   British Expeditionary Force, particularly the first Seven Divisions sent to France in August 1914, known as the 'Contemptible little army'

Blighty   slang for England or home; also a wound that was serious enough for the injured soldier to be sent back to England

Bosch, Bosche **or** *Boche*   French name for Germans, adopted by the British

bully   tinned bullied beef

C.A.V.C.   Canadian Army Veterinary Corps

C.B.   Commander of the Bank

C.C.S.   Casualty Clearing Station

chats   lice

C.H.Q.   Company Headquarters

C.O.   Commanding Officer, also known as OC

crump   any heavy shell, named from the sound it made when it burst on impact

C.T.   communication trench

D.A.A.   Director of Army Accounts

D.A.A.G.   Deputy Assistant Adjutant General

Der Tag   'The Day', a pre-war German naval toast that looked forward to the destruction of the British Fleet; it was frequently cited by the British during the war as an example of German arrogance

Div.   Division

D.O.R.A.   Defence of the Realm Act

D.R.O.   Divisional Routine Order

D.S.O.   Distinguished Service Order

duckboard   wooden slats laid along the bottom of the trenches

E.L.C.   Egyptian Labour Corps

firestep   the step built on the rear of the front wall of the trench, from which the men could see across no man's land

F.O.O.   Forward Observation Officer

F.P.   Field Punishment

G.H.Q.   General Headquarters

G.O.C.   General Officer Commanding

G.R.C.   Graves Registration Commission

H.A.C.   Honourable Artillery Company

H.E.   high explosive

H.L.I.   Highland Light Infantry

H.M.   His Majesty the King

Hun   German

Jack Johnson   heavy German shells that gave off a dense black smoke on exploding; named after the celebrated black American boxer

K.C.B.   Knight Commander of the Order of the Bath

M.A.   Master of Arts

Maxims   a type of machine gun

M.C.   Military Cross

Mills   the Mills bomb was a type of grenade

O.C.   Officer Commanding

O.O.   Orderly Officer, or Operational Order

O.T.C.   Officer Training Corps

pavé   shiny, ankle-turning roads of Belgium and northern France made of stone blocks, much disliked by the marching soldiers

P.B.I.   poor bloody infantry

poilu   meaning hairy, it was the universal name for the French soldier

P.O.W.   prisoner of war

Q. or Q.M.G.   Quartermaster General

Q.M.A.A.C.   Queen Mary's Army Auxiliary Corps

Q.M.S.   Quartermaster Sergeant

R.E.   Royal Engineers

R.F.A.   Royal Field Artillery

R.F.C.   Royal Flying Corps

R.M.L.I.   Royal Marine Light Infantry

R.N.V.R.   Royal Naval Volunteer Reserve

R.S.M.   Regimental Sergeant Major

R.T.O.   Railway Transport Officer

S.A.A.   small arms ammunition

sapper   Royal Engineer private

S.R.D.   Service Rum Diluted; initials stamped on rum jars; the soldiers also called these Soon Run Dry and Seldom Reaches Destination

sub.   subaltern; junior officer below the rank of Captain

T.M.B.   trench mortar battery

T.N.T.   tri-nitro toluene – explosive

Tommy   British private soldier, from Tommy Atkins, the hypothetical name of the soldier required to sign the Soldier's Account Book first issued in 1815

V.A.D. Voluntary Aid Detachment

V.C. Victoria Cross

Very light lights fired from special pistols that illuminated no man's land and the enemy positions

Vickers a type of machine gun

whizz-bang a type of German field gun shell, named from the sounds it made as it approached and as it burst

Wilhelm The Kaiser

Wipers Ypres

Y.M.C.A. (Y.M.) Young Men's Christian Association, which organised rest rooms for soldiers behind the lines

Zepp. Zeppelin airship, named after its inventor, Count Zeppelin

List of Authors and Illustrators

Many of the poems, particularly those written by private soldiers for ephemeral publications, were published anonymously.

Albert, E.
In a Tramcar

Alchin, Gordon (?1895–1947)
Worked under the pseudonym 'Observer, RFC'. Commissioned into the Royal Field Artillery, 1914; transferred to the Royal Flying Corps, 1915; awarded the Air Force Cross; achieved rank of Captain. After the war, became a barrister and County Court Judge.
A Song of the Air
Reconnaissance
Two Pictures

Alington, C.A. (1872–1955)
Head Master of Eton, and later Dean of Durham.
The School at War – 1914

Amory, Harold
2nd Lieutenant 101st Machine Gun Bttn, AEF.
Passed as Censored

Anderson, Jessie Annie (b. 1861)
Before the outbreak of war she published ten volumes of poetry; her final volume was published in 1928.
For a Horse Flag Day

Armstrong, Martin (1882–1974)
Poet, novelist and short-story writer, whose first volume of poems was published in 1912. Volunteered in the Artists' Rifles, 1914; commissioned into the 8th Bttn, Middlesex Regt, 1915.
Going up the Line

Asquith, Herbert (1881–1947)
Son of the British Prime Minister Herbert Asquith. Before the war, was a lawyer. Commissioned into the Royal Marine Artillery, 1914; transferred to the Royal Field Artillery; served in France but was invalided home with nervous strain, 1915; returned to the front before he was fully well and suffered the effects long after. After the war he did not return to the law but became a writer and publisher's reader.
A Flemish Village

Ball, Clelland J.
Private in the Quartermaster Corps, AEF.
  The American Advance

Beazley, Mary
  The Sound of Flanders Guns

Bendall, Frederick William Duffield (1882–1953)
A schoolmaster before the war, he was in charge of his school OTC and a Captain in the TA. At the outbreak of war he was promoted temporary Lieutenant-Colonel in charge of the 3rd (Reserve) Bttn, City of London (Royal Fusiliers). He served in the Sudan, where he was OC British Troops, Gallipoli and France; he was wounded during the 3rd Battle of Ypres (Passchendaele), 1917; twice mentioned in dispatches; awarded CMG, 1918; promoted full Colonel, 1920.
  R.A.F.
  September 25th, 1916
  The Blizzard

Bewsher, Paul (1894–1966)
Commissioned into the Royal Naval Air Service, 1915, transferring to the RAF in 1918; awarded the DSC.
  Searchlights

Bigelow, Frank G.
CQM, USS Hinton.
  You Never Can Tell

Bing, Harold F.
A conscientious objector who, in mid-1917, was serving his third sentence of imprisonment with hard labour.
  A Call from Prison

Boden, A.L.
  The Cenotaph: Armistice Day

Borden, Mary (d. 1968)
Worked from 1914 to 1918 in military hospitals attached to the French Army; she stated that the events she described were experienced as part of her war service and that none was invented. In 1918 she married the soldier and military historian Edward (later Sir Edward) Spears.
  The Song of the Mud

Bottomley, Gordon (1874–1948)
Georgian poet and playwright. A friend of Isaac Rosenberg, whose poems he edited for publication in 1922.
  All Souls, 1914

Bourke, J.
In 1918 he held the rank of Lieutenant; he appears to have survived the war.
   Ex Umbra

Bower, John Graham (1886–1985)
Worked under the pseudonym Klaxon. Served in the Royal Navy in the Somali War (1902–4), and throughout the First World War; he rose to the rank of commander; he was awarded the DSO in 1918, and mentioned in dispatches.
   Low Visibility
   To Fritz
   Wet Ships

Bowman, Archibald Allan (1883–1936)
Before the war he was Professor of Logic at Princeton University; commissioned into the 13th Highland Light Infantry, September 1915; was captured during the Battle of Lys in April 1918, and was imprisoned at first at Rastatt then at Hesepe prison camps. In 1926 he became Professor of Moral Philosophy at Glasgow University.
   Rastatt
   Thoughts of Home
   [What of our comrades in the forward post?]

Box, William (1903–87)
Too young to serve in the war, while still very young he volunteered after the war to help clear the battlefields, an experience that had a profound effect on him.
   Valete

Brasher, Paul
Sub-Lieutenant in the Royal Naval Air Service; awarded the DSC. He appears to have survived the war.
   The Dawn Patrol

Bretherton, Cyril H. (1878–1939)
Wrote for Punch under pseudonym 'Algol'.
   Oxford Revisited

Brown, John Lewis Crommelin (1888–1953)
Commissioned into the Royal Garrison Artillery (Special Reserve), December 1915; to France, February 1916; the following month was invalided home suffering from neurasthenia. Between May 1917 and July 1918 was an instructor in the Cadet School at Trowbridge; promoted Lieutenant, July 1917; sent to Salonika, August 1918. He played cricket for Derbyshire.
   Submarines
   The German Dug-out
   The Lusitania

Bryden, Walter M.
In 1916 held the rank of Sergeant. He appears to have survived the war.
The Catechism of the Kit

Burnet, W. Hodgson (b. 1873)
The author of a number of humorous books.
Requisitional

Bynner, Witter (1881–1968)
American poet and man of letters.
The True Pacifist

Cannan, May Wedderburn (1893–1973)
Enrolled in the VAD, 1911; served briefly at Rouen; returned to Oxford as part of the government's War Propaganda Bureau; joined MI5 in Paris, 1918; was engaged to Bevil Quiller-Couch, son of 'Q', who survived the war but died in 1919 from influenza while serving with the Army of Occupation in Germany.
English Leave
For a Girl
Perfect Epilogue
The Armistice

Cappe, Lucas
A Song

Carpenter, Edward (1844–1929)
A writer associated with the arts and crafts movement and social reform. A friend of Siegfried Sassoon, he was part of the pacifist group that gathered round Lady Ottoline Morrell. His book The Intermediate Sex *(1908) was a ground-breaking study of homosexuality.*
Lieutenant Tattoon, M.C.

Carstairs, Carroll (1888–1948)
An American, he claimed to be Canadian and served in the Royal Artillery and Grenadier Guards; Lieutenant; severely wounded in November 1918. The author of A Generation Missing *(1930).*
Life and Death

Chadwick, J.C.
The Wood

Chance, Wade
A Father at the Grave of his Son

Chapman, John Jay (1862–1933)
American-born lawyer and author.
To a Dog

Choyce, A.N.
In December 1918 he was a Lieutenant and being treated for wounds in Heywood Auxiliary Hospital.
    My Pal and I

Churchill, John Strange Spencer, known as Jack (1880–1947)
Younger brother of Winston Churchill. As a Major TA Reserve (later Oxfordshire Yeomenry) he served in the South African War 1899–1900. In the First World War he served in Gallipoli and France; mentioned in dispatches.
    Y Beach

Clarke, E.F.
Contributor to Punch.
    The Infantryman

Clayton, T.
Poet who contributed to the Accrington Observer and Times.
    Leave your Change
    [There are tear-dimmed eyes in the town today]
    Where are the Russians?

Clifford, C.
    In Memory of Kaiser Bill (The Butcher)

Cobb, Walter H.
After the war he became an illustrator of children's books.
    The Armoured(illo) Train
    The German Herr
    The Newt-ral
    The Sentrypede
    The Skunk
    The Sloth

Corbett, N.M.F.
In 1916 held the rank of Lieutenant-Commander, RN.
    The Auxiliary Cruiser
    The Sailing of the Fleet

Coulson, Leslie (1889–1916)
Enlisted in the ranks of 2nd Bttn, London Regt (Royal Fusiliers), September 1914; served in Gallipoli, where he was slightly wounded; in hospital in Egypt; transferred to France; attached to the 12th Bttn, London Regt (The Rangers); promoted Sergeant and took part in the Battle of the Somme; shot, 7 October 1916 and died the following day. He is buried at Grove Town Cemetery, Meaulte.
    From the Somme
    When I Come Home

Cranmer, Elsie Paterson
The Dead Hero

Cutler, Stuart
Lieutenant, 23rd US Infantry, AEF.
Somewhere in France (1)

Dawson, George C.
Sergeant, 19th Railway Engineers, AEF.
To the Recruitin' Sergeant

de Stein, Edward Sinauer (1887–1965)
Enlisted before the war in the Oxford OTC; to France as Captain July 1915; transferred to the Machine Gun Corps, October 1915; promoted Major in the King's Royal Rifle Corps (60th Rifles), 1918. Knighted in 1946.
Joseph Arthur Brown
The Romance of Place-Names
The Sacred Documents
The Turn of the Tide

Dearmer, Geoffrey (1893–1996)
Enlisted at the outbreak of war; commissioned into the 2nd Bttn, London Regt (Royal Fusiliers), September 1914; served in Egypt, Gallipoli and France. Edited BBC radio Children's Hour, *1939–59. The last surviving of the First World War poets.*
Gommecourt
Mudros after the Evacuation

Dennys, Joyce (1893–1991)
Illustrator. Served as a VAD in Cornwall 1915–16.
Concert
[Pansy ran a knitting party]
[The Flag-Day girl is dressed in white]

Dobell, Eva (1867–1963)
Volunteered as a nurse; corresponded with prisoners of war. A published poet before the war, she produced five further volumes of verse afterwards.
The Band

Dowsing, William
Known as William Dowsing of Sheffield, he was the author of books of sonnets, including six volumes inspired by Louis Raemaerker's war cartoons.
The Kaiser's Cry for Peace

Drinkwater, John (1882–1937)
Georgian poet, dramatist and biographer.
England to Belgium

Eastman, Max (1883–1969)
The American socialist writer who in 1913 was appointed editor of The Masses, *a journal whose frequent denunciations of American involvement in the war led to its closure under the Espionage Act in 1918.*
    The Battle-fields

Elton, Godfrey (1892–1973)
Commissioned into 4th Hampshire Regt, 1914; wounded and captured at Kut-al-Amara; prisoner of war in Turkey, 1915–18; promoted Captain, 1918. Fellow and lecturer in Modern History at Queen's College Oxford 1919–39; created 1st Baron Elton, 1934.
    The War Memorial

Ewer, William Norman (1885–1976)
A Fabian Socialist and left-wing journalist, he is alleged to have spied for the Soviet Union in the 1920s, although his later writing took an anti-Soviet line.
    Christmas Truce
    Cousins German
    The Only Way
    To any Diplomatist
    To any Pacifist
    War Aims

ffrench, [first name unknown]
Captain, Royal Air Force.
    [Here in the eye of the sun]

Fish, Wallace Wilfrid Blair (1889–1968)
Contributor to Punch, *1908–17, he was a playwright, poet, journalist and publisher.*
    On Christmas Leave

Fletcher, John Gould (1886–1950)
American-born Imagists poet, resident in London, 1916–33.
    The Last Rally

Fox-Smith, C. (1882–1954)
Poet and children's writer.
    The Call

Foxcroft, Charles T. (1868–1929)
In 1900, during the South African War, he was commissioned into the 1st Somerset Volunteers; came out in 1904 with the rank of Captain. In 1914 he was gazetted Captain in the 2nd/4th Somerset Regt; invalided out in 1916. He was an MP for Bath, October 1918–December 1929.
    A Veteran's View
    Retreat

'Si Monumentum requiris'
Travail

Frankau, Gilbert (1884–1952)

Commissioned into the 9th Bttn, East Surrey Regt, October 1914; transferred to RFA, March 1915; fought at Loos, Ypres and on the Somme; Staff Captain in Italy working on counter-propaganda, October 1916; invalided out with shell-shock, February 1918. Later an author; served in the RAF Volunteer Reserve in the Second World War; Squadron Leader, 1940; invalided out, 1951.

Eyes in the Air
Gun-Teams
Headquarters
Only an Officer
Poison
The Other Side
The Reason
Unknown
Urgent or Ordinary
Wails to the Mail

French, F.H.

Victory Assured!

Freston, Hugh Reginald (Rex) (1891–1916)

Commissioned into the 3rd Royal Berkshire Regt (Special Reserve of Officers) in April 1915; to France, December 1915; killed, 24 January 1916. Buried at Becourt Military Cemetery, Becordel-Becourt.

To A.M.

Fyson, Geoffrey F.

The Survivors
To a Pacifist

Gellert, Leon (1892–1977)

As part of the 10th Bttn, AIF, he took part in the first landings at Gallipoli; he was discharged as medically unfit, June 1916. After the war was a poet and journalist, and Literary Editor and feature writer for the Sydney Morning Herald, *1942–61.*

Anzac Cove
The Cripple

Gibson, Wilfrid Wilson (1878–1962)

Georgian poet; volunteered, 1915; rejected with poor eyesight; accepted in the RASC, 1917 but did not serve abroad.

Bacchanal
Between the Lines
Mad

Ragtime
The Messages

Girling, T.A. (1876–1919)
Captain, Canadian Army Veterinary Corps. He died while still on Active Service on 1 March 1919 and is buried in Belgrade Cemetery, near Namur in Belgium.
Dumb Heroes

Glasgow, Geraldine Robertson
A prolific story writer.
Missing

Goddard, Leslie M.
To a V.A.D. from a V.A.D.

Godfrey-Turner, L.
Cricket Field or Battle Field?

Golding, Louis (1895–1958)
At the outbreak of war attempted to join the OTC but was rejected on medical grounds; served as a hospital orderly in the Fifth Canadian Hospital in Salonika. After the war was a novelist, essayist and travel writer.
Broken Bodies
During the Battle
Evening – Kent
German Boy
Statesmen Debonair
The New Trade
The Woman who Shrieked against Peace

Gordon, Hampden (1885–1960)
Went to work in the War Office in 1908, where he was throughout the war. The author of a number of illustrated and children's books, he remained a career Civil Servant.
Concert
Letters Home
[Patsy ran a Knitting Party]
[The Flag-Day Girl is dressed in white]
[The Women's Volunteer Reserve]

Gorell Barnes, Ronald (1884–1963)
Before the war he was on the editorial staff of The Times. *Captain and Adjutant, 7th Bttn. The Rifle Brigade, 1916, MC 1917, Major, General Staff, 1918, when he was appointed Deputy Director of Staff Duties (Education) at the War Office; founded the Royal Army Education Corps. He succeeded his brother as Lord Gorell, 1917.*
Ypres

Graves, C.L. (1856–1944)
Joined the Staff of Punch *in 1902, assistant editor, 1928–36. With E.V. Lucas translated H.G. Puzzuoli's* The War of the Wenuses *(1898).*
> Beasts and Superbeasts
> The Freedom of the Press
> The Missing Leader
> Winston's Last Phase

Grindlay, I.
3617, QMAAC.
> Khaki
> Route March Sentiments

Guppy, Alfred Leslie (1887–1917)
Company QMS with the 14th AIF in Gallipoli and France; reported missing April 1917; confirmed as German POW June 1917.
> Evacuation of Gallipoli

Hall, Ralph J.
Corporal, Company B, 101st Mounted Police, AEF.
> Slacker, Think it Over!

Hamund, St John (d. 1929)
Before the war, he was an actor with Shakespeare Theatre, Liverpool.
> The Armoured(illo) Train
> The German Herr
> The Newt-ral
> The Sentrypede
> The Skunk
> The Sloth

Hancock, Augusta
Contributor to The Lady.
> The Women
> These Little Ones!

Hannan, Thomas
> A British Boy

Harkins, J.M.
A member of the AIF, he appears to have survived the war.
> The Chats' Parade

Harris, Dudley H.
Cadet, Tank Corps; he appears to have survived the war.
　　Left Alone

Harvey, Frederick William (1888–1957)
Enlisted as Private in the Gloucestershire Regt, 1915; Lance-Corporal, 1915; won DCM during a
reconnaissance raid, August 1915; commissioned, 1915; captured during solo daylight raid on
German lines, August 1916; spent the rest of the war in captivity.
　　A True Tale of the Listening Post
　　At Afternoon Tea
　　Back to the Trenches
　　Ballad of Army Pay
　　Gonnehem
　　Loneliness
　　Peace – The Dead Speak
　　Requiescat
　　The Route March
　　To Certain Persons
　　To the Kaiser – Confidentially

Harwood, Henry Cecil (1893–1964)
Lieutenant in 1916. Was called to the Bar in 1922, and became a journalist.
　　From the Youth of all Nations

Head, Henry (1861–1940)
A distinguished neurologist and Fellow and Vice-President of the Royal Society, he worked with
William Rivers, the psychiatrist, with whom he published Studies in Neurology *in 1922. Virginia*
Woolf was a patient. He was knighted in 1927.
　　Destroyers

Hennesley, Edmund
Sergeant, Honourable Artillery Company; he appears to have survived the war.
　　A Day in Spring

Herbert, Alan Patrick (1890–1971)
Enlisted 1914 as Ordinary Seaman in the Royal Naval Volunteer Reserve; commissioned as Sub-
Lieutenant, March 1915; served in the Royal Naval Division (Hawk Bttn) in Gallipoli and France;
mentioned in dispatches; severely wounded and invalided out, April 1917; promoted Lieutenant,
September 1917 and served on staff of HMS President. *After the war, became an MP and a*
distinguished writer.
　　After the Battle
　　Beaucourt Revisited
　　Eye-wash
　　Open Warfare

The Deserters
The Draft
The German Graves
The Green Estaminet
The Tide
To James
Twitting the Turk
Zero!

Heywood, Raymond
In 1918 held the rank of Lieutenant, Devonshire Regt. He published two volumes of poems.
At Stand Down
Before Battle
On Patrol

Hill, Brian
In 1917 held the rank of 2nd Lieutenant, Durham Light Infantry.
Salonika in November

Hodgkinson, T.
Contributor to Punch.
A Literary War Worker

Hogben, John
Scottish author of several volumes of poetry written before and after the war.
Below
Somewhere in France (2)

Holmes, William Kersley (b. 1882)
In 1915 held the rank of Captain in the Royal Field Artillery. He wrote a number of volumes of poetry, and was a Scottish writer for children, adapting fairy stories.
Horse-Bathing Parade
Letters to Tommy
My Beautiful
Singing 'Tipperary'
The Barrack Room
The Camp in the Sands
The Inspection
The Squadron Takes the Ford

Ingamells, H.
Mine Sweepers

Jenkins, Elinor (1893–1920)
>The House by the Highway
>The Last Evening

Keigwin, Richard Prescott (1883–1972)
Lieutenant in the RNVR; present at the surrender of the German fleet. Before the war he played hockey for England, cricket for the MCC and tennis for Gloucestershire, as well as being a Cambridge blue in cricket, football, hockey and rackets. After the war he became a schoolmaster.
>The Four Sea Lords

Kennedy, Revd Geoffrey Anketell Studdert (1883–1929)
'Woodbine Willie'. Enlisted as army chaplain, December 1915; in the trenches on the Somme, 1916, Messines Ridge, 1917 and final advance, 1918; MC 1917; described his ministry as taking 'a box of fags in your haversack, and a great deal of love in your heart'.
>Walking Wounded
>Waste

Kerr, Roderick Watson (1895–1960)
Before the war was leader writer and reviewer on the staff of The Scotsman. *2nd Lieutenant and later Lieutenant, the Tank Corps, 1916–19; severely wounded and awarded MC during the German attack of March 1918. After the war he returned to journalism.*
>A Vignette
>From the Line
>Music in a Dug-out
>Rain
>Sounds by Night
>Wounded

Knight-Adkin, James H.
Nothing is known about him, but he appears to have survived the war.
>No Man's Land

Knox, Edmund Gregory Valpy (1881–1971)
Worked under the pseudonym 'Evoe'. Commissioned into the Lincolnshire Regt, 1914; wounded at Third Battle of Ypres (Passchendaele, 1917). Editor of Punch, *1932–49.*
>Mufti Once More

Laing, Allan M.
Imprisoned for a year as a conscientious objector in Wormwood Scrubs.
>I Lived a Year in London

Large, D.
Private with the Army Service Corps in Rouen.
>On Leave

Lawson, Henry Archibald Hertzberg (1867–1922)
Australian poet and short-story writer.
Fighting Hard

Lee, Joseph (1876–1949)
Enlisted as Private in the Black Watch, 1914; to France, February 1915; reached rank of Sergeant; commissioned, August 1917 into the King's Royal Rifle Corps (60th Rifles); captured, November 1917 and spent rest of the war in prison in Germany. After the war he returned to being an artist.
Carrying-Party
Macfarlane's Dug-out
Stand-to!
The Billet
The Bullet
The Mouth-Organ
The Penitent
Tommy and Fritz

Leslie, Will
Private, Argyll and Sutherland Highlanders; he appears to have survived the war.
A Letter from Home
Gallipoli – In Memoriam

Letts, Winifred M. (1882–1971)
Served from 1915 as VAD nurse. An Irish playwright and children's author, she contributed to a number of journals, including Punch *and the* Spectator.
A Sister in a Military Hospital
Pro Patria
The Call to Arms

Levey, Sivori (b. 1879)
Lieutenant, 13th West Yorkshire Regt. Before the war he was an established writer of popular songs and verses; his final book, a study of the songs in Shakespeare's plays, was published in 1924.
My Motor-Bus Conductress
The Duck Board
The Road that Brought me to Roehampton

Littlejohn, William Henry (1891–1917)
CSM. A civil servant in the Exchequer and Audit Dept, before the war he was a Sergeant in the Territorial branch of the Middlesex Regt; served in Gallipoli; killed during the Battle of Arras, 10 April 1917. Buried at Wancourt Bristol Cemetery.
The Hospital Ship

Lyon, Walter Scott Stewart (1886–1915)
Lieutenant. Joined the Royal Scots before the war; to Belgium, February 1915; killed near Ypres, 8 May 1915. His body was never found and his name is on the Menin Gate.
Lines Written in a Fire-Trench

Macaulay, Rose (1881–1958)
Novelist, essayist and poet.
    Peace

Macdonald, Nina
    [How doth the little busy wife]

MacGill, Patrick (1890–1963)
Enlisted as Private in the 18th London Regt (London Irish Rifles), 1914; promoted to Sergeant; to France, March 1915; wounded at Loos while serving as stretcher-bearer, October 1915; seconded to military intelligence. After the war became a novelist and playwright.
    After Loos
    [I oft go out at night-time]
    In the Morning
    The Dawn

Mann, Hamish (1896–1917)
Gazetted 2nd Lieutenant in 8th Bttn Black Watch (Royal Highlanders), July 1915; to France, August 1916; wounded, 9 April 1917 in the Battle of Arras, and died the next day. Buried in Aubigny Communal Cemetery Extension, Aubigny-en-Artois.
    The Soldier

Manning, Frederic (1882–1935)
Born in Australia but partly educated in England; enlisted as Private in the King's Shropshire Light Infantry, 1915; failed officer training course; to France, 1916; served on the Somme; promoted Lance-Corporal; commissioned 2nd Lieutenant in the Royal Irish Regt, May 1917; posted to Ireland; resigned his commission because of ill health, February 1918. In 1929 published a highly praised fictionalised account of his war experiences, The Middle Parts of Fortune, *reissued in 1930 as* Her Privates We.
    Epigram, R. B.
    Transport

Marchant, [first name unknown]
Cadet, no. 2 Flying Corps Cadet Wing.
    A Perfect Day

Menzies, George Kenneth (1869–1954)
Contributor to Punch. *Assistant Secretary and then Secretary to the Royal Society of Arts, 1917–35.*
    The General

Meugens, M.G.
    Prisoners of War

Miles, Patrick
    The Victory March

Miller, Alfred
Private, RFA
Mud

Milne, Alan Alexander (1882–1956)
Assistant Editor of Punch 1906–14 and later creator of Winnie-the-Pooh; despite strong pacifist convictions, he volunteered in 1915; was commissioned into the Royal Warwickshire Regt, February 1915; was on the Somme, but was invalided out with trench fever, November 1916, and spent the rest of the war in intelligence.
From a Full Heart
Gold Braid

Mitchell, C.M.
The Widow

Mitchell, Colin (d. 1918)
Volunteered as Rifleman in the 3rd Rifle Bde; to France, early 1915; killed 22 March 1918 during the German spring assault. His body was never found and his name is on the Pozieres Memorial.
Britain's Daughters
Trampled Clay

Nichols, Robert (1893–1944)
Commissioned into the Royal Field Artillery, October 1914; to France, August 1915; invalided out with shell-shock, August 1916. After the war, became a writer and academic.
Noon

Ogilvie, William Henry (1869–1963)
Went to Australia and lived in the outback, 1889–1901. An author and journalist, he published many books of equestrian poetry.
Canadians
The Offside Leader

Oman, Carola (1897–1978)
Served as Red Cross nurse on the Western Front, 1916–19, and in the Second World War. After the war she became a prolific writer.
Night Duty in the Station
The Menin Road, March 1919
Unloading Ambulance Train

Peterson, John
Private, Seaforth Highlanders. Worked under the pseudonym 'Private Pat'; he appears to have survived the war.
Arras
R.I.P.

Phillips, Stephen
>   The Kaiser and Belgium

Physick, Edward Harold (1878–1972)
Worked under the pseudonym 'E.H. Visiak'. In 1916 he registered as a conscientious objector. After the war he was a novelist, poet and literary critic, known particularly for his work on Milton.
>   The Pacifist

Platt, F.W.
Contributor to Punch.
>   Verdun

Plumbe, C. Conway
Contributor to Punch.
>   A Canadian to his Parents
>   My American Cousins

Pope, Jessie (1868–1941)
Contributor to many newspapers and magazines, including Punch, *and the author of numerous children's books. Wilfred Owen's strong dislike of her often thoughtless patriotic verse led him ironically to dedicate his poem 'Dulce et Decorum est' to her.*
>   Deportment for Women

Poulten, W. Clifford
Hood Bttn, RND; he appears to have survived the war.
>   To Belgium
>   Who Won the War?

Preece, H.J.
>   To the Followers of Christ among the Belligerent Nations

Priestley, John Boynton (1894–1984)
Volunteered in the Duke of Wellington's Regt, September 1914; to France, 1915; in the Battle of Loos, September 1915; wounded, 1917 and spent six months in England; commissioned and returned to France; badly gassed and invalided out of active service; transferred to Entertainments Section of the army. After the war, became a prolific novelist and playwright.
>   A Halt on the March

Rees, G.E.
>   Telling the Bees

Rhys, Ernest Percival (1859–1946)
He began his working life as a mining engineer, but from 1886 he worked as a literary editor. In 1890 he was a founder member of the Rhymer's Club, and in 1906, with the publisher J.M. Dent, he

founded the Everyman series, with the aim of publishing 1,000 titles, a total that was achieved ten years after his death.

Lost in France

Reid, Mary

Stranraer War Memorial

Roberts, Richard Ellis (1879–1953)

1st Div. Clerk in Admiralty, 1916–18. Journalist, Literary Editor of the New Statesman *and of* Time and Tide.

The Unemployed

Robertson, Alexander (1882–1916)

Before the war he was lecturer in history at Sheffield University. Corporal. Volunteered as a Private in the 12th (Service) Bttn York and Lancaster Regt. (The Sheffield Pals), September 1914; sailed with the British Mediterranean Expeditionary Force to Egypt, December 1915; to France, March 1916; missing on the Somme, 1 July 1916. His body was never found, and his name is on the Thiepval Memorial.

After Visiting an Asylum

Ryan, J.M.

[Sing us a song of the Northern Seas]

Sackville, Lady Margaret (1881–1963)

Daughter of the 7th Earl de Warr, from 1901 was a prolific writer. She joined the anti-war Union of Democratic Control, 1914; wrote poems denouncing women who supported the war as betrayers of their sons.

Reconciliation
The Return
Victory

Samuels, Louie

Four Words

Sarson, H. Smalley

Private with the Canadian Imperial Force; he appears to have survived the war.

The Armed Liner
The Shell

Saxon, T.A.

Lance-Corporal in the Australian Imperial Force; he appears to have survived the war.

A Dug-out Lament

Scott-Moncrieff, Charles Kenneth (1889–1930)
Commissioned into the King's Own Scottish Borderers, August 1914; Captain, 1915; MC, 1917. After the war became famous as the translator of Proust.
  Back in Billets

Seaman, Owen (1861–1936)
Contributor to Punch *from 1894; editor, 1906–32.*
  Another 'Scrap of Paper'
  Model Dialogues for Air-Raids
  More Peace-Talk in Berlin
  'Punch' in the Enemy's Trenches
  The Soul of a Nation

Seeger, Alan (1888–1916)
Born in New York; went to live in Paris, 1912; enlisted in the French Foreign Legion; killed on the Somme, 4 July 1916.
  On Returning to the Front after Leave

Service, Robert William (1874–1958)
Poet, known as 'The Canadian Kipling'. Born in Scotland, he was a correspondent for the Toronto Star *during the Balkan Wars of 1912–13. Volunteered as an ambulance driver, 1914. After the war he settled in France and was a prolific poet and novelist.*
  A Song of Winter Weather

Shakespeare, William G. (1890–1975)
Trained at the Westminster Hospital before the war; volunteered for the RAMC in 1914; served in France throughout the war, rising to the rank of Major; after the war he stayed in the RAMC, serving in India and China; he was invalided out in 1943 and went into general practice.
  The Refugees
  Ypres Cathedral

Shanks, Edward Richard Buxton (1892–1953)
Enlisted in the Artists' Rifles, 1914; commissioned into the 8th South Lancashire Regt, December 1914; invalided out, April 1915 and served for the rest of the war in the War Office. After the war, returned to being a writer and journalist and was the first winner of the Hawthornden Prize, 1919.
  Meditation in June, 1917
  On Trek
  The Old Soldiers

Shirley, J.
  A Vision of Blighty

Sitwell, Osbert (1892–1969)
Was commissioned into the Sherwood Rangers, 1911, transferring in 1913 to the Grenadier Guards;
part of the original BEF, he finished the war with the rank of Captain and became a man of letters.
    Tears

Sprague, Arthur
SSU 649, Convois Automobiles, AEF.
    The Crusader

Stewart, J.
Private, 2nd Hampshire Regt.
    For the Gallipoli Peninsula

Stewart, John Ebenezer (1889–1918)
Enlisted as Private in the Highland Light Infantry, 1914; commissioned into the Border Regt, 1914;
to France, September 1915; fought in the Battle of the Somme and in the Ypres salient; awarded MC,
1917; wounded during the Battle of Messines, June 1917; promoted Captain; transferred to South
Staffordshire Regt and commanded 4th Bttn; killed near Kemmell, 26 April 1918. His body was
never found and his name is on the Tyne Cot Memorial.
    At Thiepval
    Before Action

Streets, John William (1885–1916)
Before the war was a Derbyshire miner; enlisted in the 12th (Service) Bttn, York and Lancaster
Regt (The Sheffield Pals), 1914; to Egypt, 1915; to France, March 1916; promoted Sergeant;
reported wounded and missing, 1 July 1916; officially notified killed, 1 May 1917. His body was
never found, and his name is recorded on the Special Memorial at Euston Road Cemetery,
Colincamps.
    A Soldiers' Cemetery
    At Dawn in France
    Comrades
    Shelley in the Trenches

Taylor, Ben
Imprisoned as a conscientious objector in Winchester Gaol.
    Compensation

Thorold, R.A.
Contributor to Punch.
    The Traitor

Tostevin, Earle H.
Sergeant, HQ Company, 164th US Infantry, AEF.
    Somewhere

Tripp, D. Howard
Aftermath

Tyrell, Father
From Prison

Walker, F.C.
Contributor to Punch.
To a Bad Correspondent in Camp

Waring, John
The Unknown Warrior

Warren, G.B.
The Battle off Jutland

Waterhouse, Gilbert (d. 1916)
Commissioned into the 2nd Bttn, Essex Regt, May 1915; initially reported missing presumed killed, 1 July 1916, he is buried at Serre Road Cemetery No. 2.
The Casualty Clearing Station

White, Don
Flying Cadet Donald S. White, Aviation Section, AEF.
The Air Raid
To Those Who Wait

Wilkinson, Eric Fitzwalter (1891–1917)
Commissioned 2nd Lieutenant, 8th Bttn, West Yorkshire Regt, October 1914; to France, 1915; awarded MC, July 1915; twice wounded (once gassed); wounded again at Thiepval, 1 July 1916; promoted Captain, February 1917; killed in action, 9 October 1917, during the Third Battle of Ypres (Passchendaele). His body was never found, and his name is on the Tyne Cot Memorial.
To a Choir of Birds

Wilkinson, W.J.
March up to the Colours

Williams, Eliot Crawshay (later Crawshay-Williams) (1879–1962)
Joined the army in 1900 and served in India. Assistant Private Secretary to Winston Churchill in the Colonial Office, 1906–8, and to Lloyd George as Chancellor of the Exchequer, 1910; appointed Lieutenant-Colonel in the Royal Horse Artillery and commanded the 1st Leicestershire RHA in Egypt and Sinai, 1915–17; attached HQ Northern Command, 1918–20. After the war became a novelist and playwright.
A Soldier's Testament
June in Egypt, 1916

Socialist
Sonnet of a Son
To the Nations

Willis, George
To my Mate

Wilson, Eugene Edward (1887–1988)
Lieutenant-Commander US Navy. He retired from the US Navy in 1930 with the rank of Commander, and became eminent in naval aviation.
Der Tag
Stories for Our Sons

Wilson, Theodore Percival Cameron (1889–1918)
Enlisted as a Private in the Grenadier Guards, August 1914; commissioned into the 10th Bttn, Sherwood Foresters (Notts and Derby Regt); to Flanders, February 1916; served as Staff Captain with the 51st Brigade, May 1917–January 1918; mentioned in dispatches, 1917; returned to his bttn and was killed during the German offensive on 23 March 1918. His body was never found, and his name is on the Arras Memorial.
On Leave

Wodehouse, Ernest Armine (1879–1936)
In the Scots Guards. Older brother of P.G. Wodehouse. Won the Newdigate Prize in 1902; before the war he was Professor at Deccan College, Poona; after the war he returned to India.
Before Ginchy
Quantum Mutatus

Wolstencroft, C.
The girlfriend of Private Percy Martin of the Accrington Pals.
[Have you seen the Pals, sir?]

Young, E. Hilton (1879–1960)
Was a Lieutenant in the RNVR at the outbreak of war; served at sea and with the Naval guns in Flanders; awarded DSC; promoted to Lieutenant-Commander; fought in the British force against the Bolsheviks, 1919; awarded DSO. After the war, became a politician.
In the Third Year of the War
Return

Bibliography

TRENCH AND HOSPITAL NEWSPAPERS, MAGAZINES AND JOURNALS

A Train Errant: Being the Experiences of a Voluntary Unit in France and an Anthology from their Magazine, 1915–1919, Hertford, 1919

Accrington Observer and Times

Aussie: The Australian Soldier's Magazine, 1918–19

Beaumont Bull. The Magazine of the Beaumont Detachment of the Flying Cadets, 1918

BEF Times with which are incorporated The Wipers Times, The 'New Church' Times, The Kemmel Times & The Somme-Times, 1 December 1916–26 February 1918

Blighty, A Budget of Humour from Home, issued free to Members of the Royal Navy and the British Expeditionary Force

Burnley Express and Advertiser

Country Life

Craigleith Hospital Chronicle, printed for the Proprietors by Oliver & Boyd, Tweeddale Count, Edinburgh, December 1914–Spring 1919

Daily Chronicle

Daily Herald

Dead Horse Corner Gazette: A Monthly Journal of Breezy Comment, Published, when possible, by the 4th Batt. First Canadian Contingent, BEF, on Active Service. London and Manchester, 1915–16

Depot Review. Base Stationery Depot Rouen, Army Service Corps. Typewritten sheets. Editor Pte D. Large, Circulation Manager Pte H.C. Battcock, Printing Manager Pte C.J. Hough, 1915

Evangelical Christendom

Evening News

Fifth Gloucester Gazette: A Chronicle, Serious and Humorous, of the Battalion while Serving with the British Expeditionary Force, on Active Service, 1915–19

Fragments: The Wounded Soldiers' Magazine. Heywood Auxiliary Hospital, 1917–18

Galloway Advertiser and Wigtownshire Free Press

Gazette of the 3rd London General Hospital, Wandsworth, 1915–18

Glasgow Herald

Glasgow News

Goodwill: A Journal of International Friendship, 1915–18

Honk: The Voice of the Benzine Lancers, Troopship A. 40, France, 1915

Kamp Knews: The Official News-ance of the 3rd West Lancs. Brigade RFA, 1914–18

Kemmel Times, with which are incorporated The Wipers Times & The 'New Church' Times, 3 July 1916

K[ite]. B[alloon]. Tonic, Royal Naval Air Service, Kite Balloon Section, 1915

Land & Water

Liverpool Review: An Illustrated Monthly

'New Church' Times, with which is incorporated The Wipers Times, 17 April 1916–29 May 1916

New Crusader: A Journal of Enquiry into the Foundation of War, published by the Committee for the Promotion of Pacifism, Nelson, Lancashire, 1916–19

New Statesman

News Sheet, issued by the Central New Bureau for Private Circulation Only, HO Camps, published by the No Conscription Fellowship, n.d.

Nineteenth Century

Peeko Journal, the Organ of 'P' Company RAMC, No. 16, Ripon, [1915–16]

Punch

Rising Sun: A Journal of the A[ustralian] I[mperial] F[orce] in France (with which is incorporated 'The Honk'), France, 1916–17

Saturday Westminster Gazette

Somme-Times, with which are incorporated The Wipers Times, The 'New Church' Times & The Kemmel Times, 31 July 1916

Spectator

Summerdown Camp Journal: The Journal of the Summerdown Convalescent Camp, Eastbourne, Sussex, 1916–19

The Dump, the Magazine of the 23rd Div., 1915–17

The Fledgling: Monthly Journal of No. 2 Flying Corps Cadet Wing, Hastings, 1917

The Gnome: The Magazine of the RFC Middle East Brigade, 1917

The Lady: A Journal for Gentlewomen

The Moonraker. The magazine of the 7th Battalion, Wiltshire Regiment, 1917

The Mudhook, with which is incorporated 'Dardanelles Dug-Out Gossip', Journal of the 63rd (RN) Division, Boulogne, 1917–19

The Nation. In 1921 this became *The Nation and The Athenæum*

The Ploughshare: A Quaker Organ of Social Reconstruction, 1912–15

The Quirk, the Magazine of the Royal Naval College, Greenwich, Royal Naval Air Service, 1917

The Swallow: A Monthly Journal Issued by Members of the Friends' Ambulance Unit, Uffculme Hospital, Birmingham, Birmingham, 1917

The Tribunal, published by the No Conscription Fellowship, 1916–20

The Wit, the Organ of the RAMC Training Centre, Ripon, Ripon, 1916

Winchester Whisperer, Fortnightly from His Majesty's Prison, Winchester, MS journal published by the prisoners of Winchester Gaol, n.d.

Wipers Times, or *Salient News*, 12 February 1916–20 March 1916

WORKS BY INDIVIDUAL POETS

Alchin, Gordon ('Observer, RFC'), *Oxford and Flanders*, B.H. Blackwell, Oxford, 1916

Alington, C.A., DD, *Eton Lyrics*, Clement Ingleby, [1925]

Anon., *The Book of William: With Apologies to Edward Lear*, Frederick Warne, [1914]

Asquith, Herbert, *The Volunteer and Other Poems*, Sidgwick & Jackson, 1915

Barnes, Ronald Gorell, *Days of Destiny: War Poems at Home and Abroad*, Longmans, Green, 1917

Bendall, F.W.D., *Front Line Lyrics*, Elkin Mathews, 1918

Bewsher, Paul, *The Bombing of Bruges*, Hodder & Stoughton, 1918

Borden, Mary, *The Forbidden Zone*, William Heinemann, 1929

Bower, John Graham (pseud. Klaxon), *Songs of the Submarine*, McBride, Nast, 1917

Bowman, Archibald Allan, *Sonnets from a Prison Camp*, John Lane, The Bodley Head, 1919

Box, William, *Forty Poems*, Chester & Long, 1944

Brown, J.L. Crommelin, *Dies Heroica. The War Poems: 1914–1918*, Hodder & Stoughton, 1918

Cannan, May Wedderburn, *In War Time: Poems*, B.H. Blackwell, Oxford, 1917

—— *The Splendid Days: Poems*, B.H. Blackwell, Oxford, 1919

—— *The Tears of War: The Love Story of a Young Poet and a War Hero – May Cannan, Bevil Quiller-Couch*, ed. Charlotte Fyfe, Cavalier Books, Upavon, 2000

Carstairs, Carroll, *My Window Sill*, William Heinemann, 1930

Chapman, John Jay, *Songs and Poems*, Charles Scribner's, New York, 1919

Corbett, Lieutenant-Commander N.M.F., *A Naval Motley: Verses Written at Sea during the War and before it*, Methuen, 1916

Coulson, Leslie, *From an Outpost, and Other Poems*, Erskine Macdonald, 1917

Cranmer, Elsie Paterson, *To the Living Dead and Other Poems*, C.W. Daniel, [1920]

de Stein, Sir Edward, *The Poets in Picardy, and Other Poems*, John Murray, 1919

Dearmer, Geoffrey, *Poems*, William Heinemann, 1918

Dobell, Eva, *A Bunch of Cotswold Grasses*, Arthur H. Stockwell, [1919]

Dowsing, William, *War Cartoon Sonnets: Being Sonnets Based on Louis Raemaekers' War Cartoons, in Six Volumes*, volume VI, for the author, J.W. Northend, Printer, Sheffield, 1917–18

Drinkwater, John, *Swords and Ploughshares*, Sidgwick & Jackson, 1922

Eastman, Max, *Poems of Five Decades*, Harper, New York, 1954

Ewer, W.N., *Five Souls and Other Wartime Verses*, The Herald, 1917

—— *Satire and Sentiment*, The Herald, 1918

Foxcroft, Charles T., *The Night Sister and Other Poems*, Methuen, 1918

Frankau, Gilbert, *The Guns*, Chatto & Windus, 1916

—— *The Poetical Works*, volume I, *1901–1916*; volume II, *1916–1920*, Chatto & Windus, 1923

Freston, H. Rex, *The Quest of Truth and Other Poems*, B.H. Blackwell, Oxford, 1916

Fyson, Geoffrey F., *The Survivors, and Other Poems*, Erskine Macdonald, 1919

Gellert, Leon, *Songs of a Campaign*, G. Hassell, Adelaide, [1917]

Gibson, Wilfrid Wilson, *Battle*, Elkin Mathews, 1915

—— *Collected Poems*, 1905–1925, Macmillan, 1926

Golding, Louis, *Sorrow of War: Poems*, Methuen, 1919

Gordon, Hampden, *Our Girls in Wartime*, pictures by Joyce Dennys, John Lane, The Bodley Head, [1917]

—— *Rhymes of the Red Triangle*, pictures by Joyce Dennys, John Lane, The Bodley Head, [1918]

Grindlay, I., *Ripples from the Ranks of the QMAAC* by 3617, I. Grindlay, Erskine Macdonald, 1918

Hamund, St John, *The War Men-agerie*, illus. Walter H. Cobb, Grant Richards, 1915

Harvey, F.W., *A Gloucestershire Lad at Home and Abroad*, Sidgwick & Jackson, 1916

—— *Ducks and Other Verses*, Sidgwick & Jackson, 1919

—— *Gloucestershire Friends: Poems from a German Prison Camp*, Sidgwick & Jackson, 1917

Head, Henry, MD, FRS, *Destroyers, and Other Verses*, Humphrey Milford, 1919

Hennesley, Edmund, *Love Songs of a Soldier*, Nisbet, 1918

Herbert, A.P., *Half-Hours at Helles*, B.H. Blackwell, Oxford, 1916

—— *The Bomber Gipsy and Other Poems*, Methuen, 1918

Heywood, Raymond, *The Greater Love: Poems of Remembrance*, Elkin Mathews, 1919

Hill, Brian, *Youth's Heritage*, Erskine Macdonald, 1917

Hogben, John, *The Highway of Hades: War Verses: With Some Prose*, Oliver & Boyd, Edinburgh, 1919

Holmes, Captain W. Kersley, *Ballads of Field and Billet*, Alexander Gardner, Paisley, 1915

—— *More Ballads of Field and Billet and Other Verses*, Alexander Gardner, Paisley, 1915

Jenkins, Elinor, *Poems*, Sidgwick & Jackson, 1915

Kennedy, Revd G.A. Studdert, *Rough Rhymes of a Padre*, by 'Woodbine Willie', MC, CF, Hodder & Stoughton, [1918]

—— *The Unutterable Beauty: The Collected Poetry of G.A. Studdert Kennedy*, Hodder & Stoughton, 1927

Kerr, R. Watson, *War Daubs: Poems*, John Lane, The Bodley Head, 1919

Laing, Allan M., *Carols of a Convict*, Headley, [1918]

Lawrence, Margery, *Fourteen to Forty-Eight: A Diary in Verse*, Robert Hale, [1949]

Lawson, Henry, *My Army, O, My Army and Other Songs*, Tyrrell's, Sydney, 1915

Lee, Joseph, *Ballads of Battle*, John Murray, 1916

Letts, W.M., *The Spires of Oxford and Other Poems*, E.P. Dutton, New York, 1917

Levey, Sivori, *Flanders to Fowey ('Ypres' and 'Après'): Verses of Active Service, Hospital, and Convalescence by a Wounded Warrior*, The Sivori Levey Publications, 1917

—— *Roehampton Rhymes: Selections from a Dover House Revue, Words Written and Music Composed by Lieutenant Sivori Levey*, The Sivori Levey Publications, [1918]

Lyon, W.S.S., *Easter at Ypres, 1915, and Other Poems*, James Maclehose, Glasgow, 1916

Macaulay, Rose, *Three Days*, Constable, 1919

Macdonald, Nina, *War-Time Nursery Rhymes: Dedicated to DORA*, illustrations by L. Grace Arnold and Irene B. Arnold, George Routledge, [1919]

MacGill, Patrick, *Soldier Songs*, Herbert Jenkins, 1917

Mann, Hamish, *A Subaltern's Musings*, John Long, 1918

Manning, Frederic, *Eidola*, John Murray, 1917

Miles, Patrick, *The Victory March and Other Poems*, Arthur H. Stockwell, [1920]

Mitchell, Colin (Rifle Brigade), *Trampled Clay*, Erskine Macdonald, 1917

Nichols, Robert, *Ardours and Endurances; Also, a Faun's Holiday and Poems and Phantasies*, Chatto & Windus, 1917

Oman, Carola, *The Menin Road and Other Poems*, Hodder & Stoughton, 1919

Peterson, John (pseud. Private Pat), *Roads and Ditches*, T. & J. Manson, Lerwick, 1920

Physick, Edward Harold (pseud. E.H. Visiak), *The Battle Fiends, and Other Poems*, Elkin Mathews, 1916

Poulten, W. Clifford (A.B. Poulten, Hood Battalion, RND), *The Bukshee Ration and Other War-time Sketches*, The Souvenir Book of the Royal Naval Division, Morland Press, [1919]

Priestley, J.B., *The Chapman of Rhymes*, Alexander Moring, 1918

Rhys, Ernest, *The Leaf Burners and Other Poems*, J.M. Dent, 1918

Robertson, Alexander, *Comrades*, Elkin Mathews, 1916

Sackville, Lady Margaret, *The Pageant of War and Other Poems*, Simpkin, Marshall, [1916]

Sarson, H. Smalley, *From Field & Hospital*, Erskine Macdonald, 1916

Scott, Frederick George, *In the Battle Silences: Poems Written at the Front*, Constable, 1916

Seaman, Owen, *From the Home Front*, Constable, 1918

Seeger, Alan, *Poems*, Constable, 1917

Service, Robert, *The Rhymes of a Red-Cross Man*, Fisher Unwin, 1916

Shakespeare, William G., *Ypres and Other Poems*, Sidgwick & Jackson, 1916

Shanks, Edward, *Poems*, Sidgwick & Jackson, 1916

—— *Collected Poems, 1909–1925: Arranged in Six Books*, W. Collins, 1926

Stewart, J.E., *Grapes of Thorns*, Erskine Macdonald, 1917

Streets, J.W., *The Undying Splendour*, Erskine Macdonald, [1917]

Titterton, W.R., *Guns and Guitars*, Cecil Palmer & Hayward, 1918

Vickridge, Alberta, *The Sea Gazer*, Erskine Macdonald, 1919

Waring, John, *The Unknown Warrior*, Arthur H. Stockwell, [1922]

Warren, G.B., *For the Sceptre of the Sea*, John Long, 1916

Waterhouse, Gilbert, *Rail-Head and Other Poems*, Erskine Macdonald, 1916

Williams, Eliot Crawshay, *Clouds and the Sun*, George Allen & Unwin, 1919

—— *The Gutter and the Stars*, Erskine Macdonald, 1918

Willis, George, *Any Soldier to his Son*, George Allen & Unwin, 1919

Wilson, Eugene E., *Comrades of the Mist and other Rhymes of the Grand Fleet*, George Sulley, New York, 1919

Wilson, T.P. Cameron, *Magpies in Picardy*, The Poetry Bookshop, 1919

Wodehouse, E. Armine, *On Leave: Poems and Sonnets*, Elkin Mathews, 1917

Young, E. Hilton, *A Muse at Sea: Verses*, Sidgwick & Jackson, 1919

ANTHOLOGIES PUBLISHED DURING THE WAR

A Book of Poems for The Blue Cross Fund (To Help Horses in War Time), President Lady Smith-Dorrien, Jarrolds, 1917

An Annual of New Poetry: 1917, Constable, [1917]

Georgian Poetry 1916–1917, Poetry Bookshop, 1918

More Songs by the Fighting Men: Soldier Poets: Second Series, Erskine Macdonald, 1917

One Hundred of the Best Poems on the European War: By Poets of the Empire, vol. 1, ed. Charles F. Forshaw, Ll.D., Elliot Stock, 1915

Oxford Poetry 1914–1916, B.H. Blackwell, Oxford, 1916

Poems Written during the Great War 1914–1918: An Anthology, ed. Bertram Lloyd, George Allen & Unwin, 1918

Soldier Poets: Songs by the Fighting Men, Erskine Macdonald, 1916

Songs & Sonnets for England in War Time: Being a Collection of Lyrics by Various Authors Inspired by the Great War, John Lane, The Bodley Head, 1914

Songs from the Trenches: The Soul of the AEF: A Collection of Verses by American Soldiers in France, brought together by Herbert Adams Gibbons from Poems submitted in the Prize Competition of the New York Herald, Harper and Bros, New York and London, 1918

The Anzac Book: Written and Illustrated in Gallipoli by the Men of Anzac, ed. C.E.W. Bean, Cassell, 1916

The 'Country Life' Anthology of Verse, ed. P. Anderson Graham, Offices of Country Life, 1915

The Lyceum Book of War Verse, ed. Alys Eyre Macklin, Erskine Macdonald, 1918.

The Muse in Arms: A Collection of War Poems, for the Most Part Written in the Field of Action, by Seamen, Soldiers, and Flying Men who are Serving, or have Served, in the Great War, ed. E.B. Osborn, John Murray, 1917

Told in the Huts. The YMCA Gift Book. Contributed by Soldiers & War Workers. With Introduction by Arthur K. Yapp. Illustrated by the late Cyrus Canoe, Being the Last Work of this Famous Artist. Published for the Benefit of the YMCA Active Service Campaign amongst our Soldiers, Sailors & Munition Workers, in all parts of the World, Jarrold, [1916]

Tommy's Tunes: A Comprehensive Collection of Soldiers' Songs, Marching Melodies, Rude Rhymes, and Popular Parodies, Composed, Collected, and Arranged on Active Service with the BEF, by F.T. Nettleingham, 2nd Lt R.F.C., Erskine Macdonald, 1917

Wheels: A Third Cycle, an Anthology of Verse, B.H. Blackwell, Oxford, 1917

LATER ANTHOLOGIES

A Miscellany of Poetry – 1919, ed. W. Kean Seymour, Cecil Palmer & Hayward, 1919

A Treasury of War Poetry: British and American Poems of the World War, 1914–1919, ed. George Herbert Clarke, Professor of English in the University of Tennessee, Hodder & Stoughton, [1919]

Airman's Song Book: Being an Anthology of Squadron, Concert Party, Training and Camp Songs and Song Parodies, the Whole Set out in Chronological Order to Present a Historical Picture of the RAF through its own Songs, ed. C. H. Ward-Jackson, Sylvan Press, 1945

Anthology of War Poetry 1914–1918, assembled by Robert Nichols, Nicholson & Watson, 1943

Cambridge Poets 1914–1920: An Anthology, ed. Edward Davison, W. Heffer, Cambridge, 1920

From Gallipoli to Gaza, ed. Jill Hamilton, Simon & Schuster, East Roseville, NSW, 2003

Poems from Punch 1909–1920, Macmillan, 1922

GENERAL

Brown, Malcolm, *The Imperial War Museum Book of the Western Front*, Sidgwick & Jackson, 1993
—— *Tommy Goes to War*, Dent, 1978
Gregory, Adrian, *The Silence of Memory: Armistice Day 1919–1946*, Berg, Oxford, 1994
Moorehead, Alan, *Gallipoli*, Hamish Hamilton, 1956
Reilly, Catherine W., *English Poetry of the First World War: A Bibliography*, George Prior, 1978
Wilson, Trevor, *The Myriad Faces of War*, Polity Press, Cambridge, 1986

Index of Titles and First Lines